T0243453

DUTCH
MASTERS

DUTCH
MASTERS

When Ajax's Totaalvoetbal Conquered Europe

Gary Thacker

First published by Pitch Publishing, 2023

Pitch Publishing
9 Donnington Park,
85 Birdham Road,
Chichester,
West Sussex,
PO20 7AJ
www.pitchpublishing.co.uk
info@pitchpublishing.co.uk

ISBN 978 1 80150 441 6

Typesetting and origination by Pitch Publishing
Printed and bound in India by Replika Press Pvt. Ltd.

Contents

This book is dedicated to my wife Sue, to Megan and Luke, Lydia and Gregory, and to my precious granddaughters Eve and Polly.

It is also dedicated to those who always supported and believed in me. You are my strength.

And to those who only ever doubted me. You are my inspiration.

Acknowledgements

MANY PEOPLE have assisted in the production of this book. The following have generously agreed to be interviewed directly, by email, telephone or similar, and allowed me to use their wise words:

- Jan-Willem Bult – former professional player and KNVB-qualified coach. He's now an international film and TV maker, football expert, initiator of Twitter account @ Netherlands1974.
- John Georgopoulos – international football journalist and interviewer from Greece.
- Massimiliano Graziani – journalist of the Italian radio and television broadcaster Rai. He is a coordinator and radio commentator of the long-running broadcast *Tutto il Calcio Minuto per Minuto*.
- Qasim Hakim – football journalist who works for *Dagblad de Limburger*, and a student of football history. He has previously worked for the *De Telegraaf*, *De VoetbalTrainer* (the biggest coaching magazine in the Netherlands) and Voetbalzone.nl.
- Rafa Honigstein – author, journalist, broadcaster and presenter.
- Ronald Jager – accounts manager in the Netherlands who has written four football books dating back to 2008, and also coaches at amateur level.

- Auke Kok – Dutch author and journalist and two-time winner of the Nico Scheepmaker Award. As well as his work appearing in newspapers and magazines, and featuring on television and radio, he wrote the famous *1974. Wij waren de besten* book, a reflection on the 1974 World Cup. He has also written another 13 books, including a biography of Johan Cruyff, published in 2019.

- Ruud Krol – played more than 500 games for Ajax across a 12-year career with the club, winning two European Cups, two European Super Cups, an Intercontinental Cup, six Eredivisie titles and four KNVB Cups. He also captained the side from 1974 until he left in 1980, and later returned as coach.

- Rob McDonald – former professional player and coach with several Eredivisie clubs after moving to Dutch football from Hull City in 1979. He is now a professional mediator, seeking to match up investors with clubs in Europe. He still lives in the Netherlands.

- Roberto Pennino – Dutch lawyer of Italian descent living in the Netherlands. He's also an author and freelance journalist focusing on Dutch football.

- Menno Pot – Amsterdam-based music journalist and football writer. He is an Ajax columnist for newspaper *Het Parool* and author of several books about the club. He also hosts a weekly Ajax podcast for the *Het Parool* newspaper, called *Branie* ('*Swagger*').

- Steven Scragg – an award-nominated author and member of the senior management team at *These Football Times*.

- Sonny Silooy – played almost 300 games for Ajax in two spells totalling 14 years. He is a former assistant coach to the national team and former coach of the under-18 and under-19 sides. He's a senior consultant and ambassador at the Ajax Coaching Academy, currently attached to Sharjah FC.

- George Tsitsonis – Greek-American freelance writer and author of the book *Achieving the Impossible: The Remarkable Story of Greece's Euro 2004 Victory.*
- Pierre Vermeulen – former professional and Dutch international.
- Piet Wildschut – former professional and Dutch international.
- David Winner – author of *Brilliant Orange.*
- My thanks also go to all at *These Football Times*, particularly Stuart Horsfield, Aidan Williamson, Paul MacParlan and Omar Saleem for their unstinting support and encouragement.

Grateful acknowledgement to these websites for their help on statistical information:
- www.voetbal.com
- www.afc-ajax.info
- www.rssf.com
- https://english.ajax.nl/
- www.knvb.com
- https://www.footballcritic.com/

Unless otherwise stated and sources cited, quotes used within the book are taken from my own interviews.

Finally, as ever, my thanks go out to the wonderfully professional team at Pitch Publishing, without whom this book would still merely be an idea floating around inside my head.

Introduction

THE DUTCH are 'the envy of some, the fear of others, and the wonder of all their neighbours', so wrote Sir William Temple, English ambassador to the new Dutch Republic in 1673.[1]

Temple penned this description 25 years after the Dutch Republic had been born in the wake of victory over the forces of Phillip II of Spain in the Eighty Years' War (1568–1648). With Spain defeated and England engulfed in civil war, there was an opportunity for a new European power to take centre stage. The Dutch Republic filled that vacuum and emerged as the most prosperous nation in Europe. The continent had a new power, one that would take the lead in commerce, arts and the development of new sciences.

The birth of the Dutch Republic also ushered in a period of cultural, religious and social freedom, that manifested itself in the arts and, in particular, painting. It was the time of Rembrandt and Vermeer, of Steen and Hals, as Dutch artists discarded the traditional subjects of religion and social hierarchy, creating a new paradigm guided by some of the greatest painters ever to have lived. It was a time that

---

1 Prak, Maarten, *The Dutch Republic in the Seventeenth Century: The Golden Age* (London, Cambridge University Press, 2005).

historians refer to as the Dutch Golden Age. It was the age of the Dutch Masters.

Rembrandt Harmenszoon van Rijn, perhaps the greatest of all portrait painters flourished in this time. By the middle of the 17th century his work had become characterised by innovation, the use of bright colours and elaborate brushstrokes.

Although largely ignored in his lifetime, Johannes Vermeer worked in the same era. His use of colour and the interaction between light and dark epitomised his work and led to him later becoming recognised as a worthy member of the pantheon of great masters.

Jan Steen projected humour and a measure of disorder into his painting. His work emphasised a sense of human untidiness above more sanitised depictions of everyday life. It also inspired the Dutch phrase of something being described as a 'Jan Steen House', being both full of untidiness and vigorous life.

Frans Hals had a more fluid style to his painting. The brushwork was looser and freer, giving his paintings a sense of energetic movement, devoid of more staid tradition, with layers of one colour, set on the other. His *Laughing Cavalier* is not really laughing at all; instead he has an enigmatic but contented smile, suggesting he has already accomplished things that others are yet to fully comprehend.

Fast forward 300 years from the time of Temple's observations about the Dutch and there's a ringing echo of those words in football, with a new Golden Age. Once more, the staid traditions of southern European orthodoxy were to be expelled, and a liberation of new ideas and approaches flourished. A new, even more modern Prometheus would set light to the established stifling doctrines, and scorch the continent's football pitches, by stealing a magic formula from the gods and laying it before us mere mortals to enthral and enrapture, bemuse and bewilder, bewitch and beguile. In Amsterdam, a football club had risen to unprecedented heights. Their play invoked colours more vivid than the pigments of Vermeer, with more innovation and scope than Rembrandt and his brushstrokes, livelier and with greater layers than Hals.

Their canvases were football pitches. Their passing and fluent movement on those verdant surfaces were the elegant strokes of a brush that painted beautifully entrancing pictures and their palette was the myriad colours of their ability. White shirts with a broad red stripe down the centre were as iconic as any style. They stood for flair and flamboyance, for talent and technique, for elan and elegance, allowing observers to enthuse joyously, marvelling at the dazzling beauty of the new.

The team would upset the tidiness of football's established dogma with a rebelliousness of self-belief, wantonly overturning tables of the *ancien régime*, transforming football into a 'Jan Steen House' of their very own freeform design. Born in the mists of times past, they assumed identity in the mid-1960s. From there, they prospered and grew. By the early years of the following decade, they had established a Dutch Golden Age of their very own. As with Hals's *Cavalier*, they had accomplished things that others were yet to fully understand. Their Golden Age would endure relatively briefly, and yet it provided a legacy that lives on to this day. It was an age of the new Dutch Masters. It was the age of Ajax Amsterdam and they would conquer Europe with their *totaalvoetbal*.

Part 1: In the beginning

What is *totaalvoetbal*?

Some things simply refuse to be found. The secret of perpetual motion has remained hidden from the greatest scientific minds across the ages. The location of Atlantis is firmly anchored in the realms of myths, legends and the imagination of blockbuster film makers. Dark matter accounts for around 85 per cent of all things in the universe. It is the very glue that holds everything together. It's all around but impossible to see, touch or even define. And then, there's 'Total Football' or, in Dutch, *totaalvoetbal*.

Even the name itself has a whiff of the unknown about it and, when Ajax were scorching the football pitches of Europe with their revolutionary play, no one at the Amsterdam club would have defined their philosophy as being *totaalvoetbal* – not least because the phrase had yet to be coined. The story runs that it was the British journalist Brian Glanville who gifted the description 'Total Football' to the world, using it to describe the patterns of play deployed by the magical *Oranje* team at the 1974 World Cup. At least that's the belief held by some.

Auke Kok is a Dutch author and journalist, and two-time winner of the prestigious Nico Scheepmaker Award for sports books. As well as his work appearing in newspapers and magazines, and featuring on television and radio, he wrote the famous *1974. Wij waren de besten* book, a reflection on the 1974 World Cup, among 13 other titles, including his latest work, a biography of Johan Cruyff published in 2019. As such, his theories on such matters demand respect. He considers, 'The term is older than 1974; Michels already used it halfway through the '60s and some Dutch journalists used it at the beginning of the '70s to describe the game of Ajax. There also are some references to the Hungarians in the '50s but, as a general phrase, it was the English, like Brian Glanville and David Winner, who mentioned it again and again and after that the Dutch and others also did. Michels and the players in 1974 hardly use the term, because they saw their game as something that occurred rather spontaneously on the pitch.'

Credence is added to Kok's assertion by the long-serving Ajax player Sjaak Swart who – as is mentioned in the pages that follow – recalls Michels using it to him after the new coach arrived at the De Meer Stadion. It's probably safe to say, however, that at the very least there are still doubts about the origination of the term.

Not too far into the future, first-hand memories of the Ajax teams of the early 1970s will be gone and, like the great club teams of the past, Honvéd and Real Madrid in the 1950s, Benfica and *Il Grande Inter* of the 1960s, the legend will drift into the realms of mythology, where only misty-eyed reflections of images, available through grainy video offerings, can lift the veil of history and offer glances into the past. The football world will be left to wonder how a club from a country consisting of a mere 13 million people became trendsetters for the global game. How they managed to tear up the old established ways and, iconoclasts through and through, eased the existing footballing hierarchy to one side, taking the crown as champions of Europe for themselves.

A new paradigm was established and the *totaalvoetbal* played by the Ajax teams of first Rinus Michels and then Ştefan Kovács achieved Continental hegemony. They did it with their version of *totaalvoetbal*. So what is it?

Ask any football fan old enough to remember, or studious enough to have discovered the Ajax teams of the early 1970s or the magnificently vulnerable ones wearing *Oranje*, bequeathed by the Netherlands sides who lost successive World Cup finals in 1974 and 1978, and they'll nod their heads sagely at the very mention of that magic incantation of *totaalvoetbal*. To know *totaalvoetbal*, to appreciate it, to rejoice in its grandeur, is more a question of faith than one of scientific definition. Like the proverbial Scotch mist, reach out to try and touch it and its essence may simply melt away before your very eyes.

Not convinced? Well, if you think you're in the know, try this little exercise. It was offered to your author on a podcast a while ago. 'So, tell me. What is *totaalvoetbal*?' After the first hesitant seconds, when brimming confidence begins to melt into hapless, blubbering impotence, you realise that perpetual motion, Atlantis and dark matter have another member of their club. You start reaching out for a few well-heeled phrases: it's about players being able to interchange positions and roles; It's about use of space, expanding when in possession, and compacting when the other team have the ball; it's about attacking football; it's about keeping possession and making the ball do the work.

Of course, there are elements of each of those things in *totaalvoetbal*, but could an oblique series of hastily formed concepts reeled rapidly off the tongue capture the real essence of this football credo? Hardly. It's like trying to condense Communism into workers having control of the means of production, or Christianity into the importance of going to church on a Sunday. Having struggled to find a few sentences that would provide a concise and yet comprehensive description of *totaalvoetbal* – and palpably failed to do so – perhaps canvassing the opinion of others, who have viewed Ajax's play from various degrees of distance and time, may be more instructive. Maybe they can access *totaalvoetbal*'s very own Rosetta Stone and decipher its encrypted essence. Do they possess the contented understanding of Hals's *Laughing Cavalier* compared to the naive ignorance of others?

David Winner, author of *Brilliant Orange,* the seminal book on Dutch football, offered his ideas: 'Total Football was, among other things, a conceptual revolution based on the idea that the size of any football field was flexible and could be altered by a team playing on it.'[2] He went on to explain that this means when your team is in possession, players should seek to exploit all areas of the field to the maximum extent possible. Conversely, when possession is lost, the team should limit space as much as possible, by compressing the play, hunting the ball aggressively in the other half of the field, and looking to play an offside trap. With Ajax, Cruyff was the high priest of the doctrine, but it was not merely a matter of him alone, as Winner explained: 'An acute sense of the fluid structure and dimensions of the pitch was shared by everyone.'

The importance of pressing the ball immediately when possession is lost is echoed in the thoughts of Dutch journalist, commentator and former owner and chief editor of the magazine *ELF Voetbal,* Jan-Herman de Bruijn, when he pondered the question. He considered that one of the key elements of *totaalvoetbal* is that 'ball possession has to be regained within six seconds because the opposition is not organised by then'. He also added that, more importantly, a key element in driving Ajax's *totaalvoetbal* was: 'Cruyff's lack

---

2 Winner, David, *Brilliant Orange* (London: Bloomsbury, 2000).

of physique. He understood that he could never function as a central striker in the old-fashioned way. He always wanted to get out of the heat. So, when he was all over the place his team-mates had to do the same. He had the unique talent to organise during the game.' Necessity as the mother of invention?

Auke Kok's thoughts have echoes in those offered by De Bruijn in relation to Cruyff: 'Total football developed from the '60s: wing defenders running up front to surprise opponents, centre-forwards seeking space in midfield and escaped there from man-markers. Coaches demanding from their attackers to do more defensive things. This happened with Cruyff: also by walking in midfield he had his opponents in front of him, instead of behind his back, which gave him more safety. When he was gone [from the] front line, midfielders would run into the open space and surprise [opposing] defenders. Others then had to take their places, and so on: the carrousel. Therefore, players had to be intelligent and "*totaal*", had to be able to do the right thing on various places in the field. Much of this happened spontaneously, not by explicit instructions of the coach.' Kok's final sentence hints that, once an understanding of *totaalvoetbal* was firmly established in the players' mindset, the philosophy of it set other things free and allowed the team to dance to the mood music in synchronised movement.

Roberto Pennino is a Dutch lawyer of Italian descent living in the Netherlands. He's also an author and freelance journalist focusing on Dutch football. He believes that the advent of Ajax's *totaalvoetbal* was perhaps the final development of the game; a move that took football to a higher level: '*Totaalvoetbal* ... to me is a way of footballing that was maybe the last great change of the game. A high level of pressure on the opponent, players who were required to be able to play in all field positions if necessary ... So, there was no specialisation or holding your position. If a defender decided to go in attack, immediately a midfielder had to take his place. In the heyday that all worked as in an organism: smooth and without the necessity to have to think about it. There was also a maybe underestimated (and unprecedented) side to *totaalvoetbal*: to play on offside. In my humble view those three elements together (pressure, the constantly changing of positions and playing on offside) made it such a success. Not to forget that Michels (and after him Kovács) had the best players in the world to play *totaalvoetbal*.'

It's an important point to consider. Could *totaalvoetbal* have conquered Europe with lesser players? As Pennino contends, both Michels and Kovács were blessed with an exceptional squad of players. They possessed both the ability and footballing intelligence to embrace the concept. Pennino continues, 'Apart from Johan Cruyff, a player as Johan Neeskens (the dynamo of the team), John Rep (flamboyant and versatile), Piet Keizer (underestimated but very important on the left wing) and of course Ruud Krol (superb defender and later *libero* with great flair) are all well remembered. But to be fair, naming a handful doesn't do enough justice to the rest of the team, especially someone as Gerrie Mühren, who rivalled Cruyff in technical skills, Arie Haan, etc. They all had their part in one of the finest teams of all time. Especially in [*totaalvoetbal*] terms, all 11 players were equal, although some were more equal than others.'

Journalists, authors and writers of a similar ilk are required to possess an analytical eye as part of the tools of their trade when writing about a particular subject. This is especially so when engaged in the loftier task of writing books, rather than the punchier and necessarily more concise reports and articles in newspapers and magazines. What they gain in perspective observing from a distance, however, they may lose in the detail truly revealed only to those on the inside. Looking in from the outside may not be the best position from which to fully understand the essence of the *totaalvoetbal* of the 1970s Ajax teams. Players who lived it, breathed it and especially those who prospered because of their understanding and embracing of it, may offer a clearer insight. If that is the case, where better to start than with the thoughts of Johan Cruyff?

In his autobiography, he offered a brief description that chimes with much of the thoughts already proposed: 'Total Football is, aside from the quality of the players, mostly a question of distance and positioning. That's the basis of all the tactical thinking. When you've got the right distances and the formation right, everything falls into place. It also needs to be very disciplined. You can't have someone striking out on their own. Then it doesn't work. Someone will start to pressurise an opposition player and then the whole team has to switch gear.'[3]

Each player responding to a prompt from another is a theme repeated by other Ajax players of the era, Barry Hulshoff among them. The bearded *libero* played in each of Ajax's European Cup successes of the early 1970s, and would later coach the club. For Hulshoff, *totaalvoetbal* meant that each player must be able to both defend and attack, even though his prime role must always be his first priority, and after changing, he should seek to return to his position as quickly as possible, because that way the team is stronger.

Sjaak Swart holds the record for the number of appearances for Ajax, playing almost 600 games for the club, scoring 207 goals. He won seven Eredivisie titles, five KNVB Cups, three European Cups, one Intertoto Cup, two European Super Cups, plus an Intercontinental Cup. Although he only

---

3 Cruyff, Johan, *My Turn* (London: Macmillan, 2016).

played the opening half of the first of those European Cup Final triumphs, and remained on the bench for the other two, few players have spent more time playing under Michels and drinking in the coach's *totaalvoetbal* philosophy. His thoughts have clear echoes with those of Cruyff and Hulshoff, emphasising the coordination and team play necessary to make *totaalvoetbal* function. When right-back Wim Suurbier went forward, as the wide right forward player, Swart knew that he was required to drop back and cover. Soon it became purely instinctive for all the players as the *totaalvoetbal* philosophy was absorbed.

Ruud Krol played more than 500 games for Ajax across a 12-year career with the club, winning two European Cups, two European Super Cups, an Intercontinental Cup, six Eredivisie titles and four KNVB Cups. He also captained the side from 1974 until he left in 1980, later returning as a coach. For him, under Michels, an ability to interchange positions was a key factor: 'Michels made us run less and take over each other's positions, which was revolutionary. It was the first time there was a totally different vision of football. Total Football spread all over the world. It was the only real change in football for almost 40 years. He stunned the world.'[4]

Arie Haan was the half-time replacement for Swart in that first European Cup Final success in 1971, and played a full part in the next two finals. His view was that, as with Cruyff's assertion that to make *totaalvoetbal* work, all 11 players needed to be involved. For him, the philosophy wasn't about formations. It couldn't be compared to 4-4-2, or 4-3-3. It went beyond that, demanding full application by all of the players – and exceptionally talented players at that.

---

4 https://www.uefa.com/uefachampionsleague/news/0253-0d7ff54908f6-5927d0a16600-1000--the-greatest-teams-of-all-time-ajax-1971-73/

Everyone was always involved, whether 5 or 60 metres away from the ball.

It wasn't, of course, necessary to be an Ajax player to have experienced *totaalvoetbal* at first hand. While Cruyff, Hulshoff, Swart and Haan were intricate elements in its majestic sorcery, some were compelled to face its glory on the field as opposition players, while others arrived at Ajax after the extraordinary years of the early 1970s but were still blessed by its enduring legacy.

Pierre Vermeulen played for Roda JC, Feyenoord and MVV Maastricht during more than a decade in the Eredivisie, before moving on to continue his career in France. He also played for the *Oranje*. Making his professional debut in 1974, Vermeulen had grown up inspired by Ajax: 'When Feyenoord and later on Ajax dominated in the [European Cup] I was a teenager with only one thing in mind: football. I was, you could say, in that time an Ajax supporter, although later in my career I would play for Feyenoord. But that's another matter. In 1970 Feyenoord won the cup, but when Ajax won it in 1971 it had a greater impact on me, as in the years 1972 and 1973. I loved the way Ajax played: Total Football. It was revolutionary.'

Training with Roda as an aspiring young player, Vermeulen would have a ringside seat of Ajax's triumphs and saw the full flowering of their *totaalvoetbal*, but what did it mean to him? 'The [*totaalvoetbal*] of Ajax was a totally different class, compared to other top clubs in Europe and even in the world. I can't remember that other teams really tried to copy the Ajax way of playing because no other team had the players to play [*totaalvoetbal*] as they could. Rep, Neeskens, Cruyff, all world-class players of course. Individually I was able to copy Keizer ... but no team could copy Ajax as a whole.

'In 1974 Ajax's reign was over, but I was able to attend two matches of [the] *Oranje* during the World Cup of 1974: against Argentina and against Brazil. It was fascinating to see the combination of Feyenoord and Ajax players that managed to take [*totaalvoetbal*] to another level. I especially remember Cruyff's second goal against Argentina in Gelsenkirchen in the pouring rain. A stroke of brilliance. I will never forget that moment. Later on, I was in Dortmund for the Brazil match. A real fight between the reigning champions and – as we thought – the future world champion. It wasn't to be, but the way [the] *Oranje* played is something that will never be forgotten.'

Jan-Herman de Bruijn agreed: 'The result was seen during World Cup '74 when players schooled by Happel [at Feyenoord] and the Ajax group worked together. Total Football was never played better than during that tournament. Just watch the action of some of those games.'

Playing for Feyenoord would have afforded Vermeulen an opponent's perspective, but Sonny Silooy's experience of appearing in almost 300 games for Ajax in two spells, totalling almost 14 years, put him inside the club, albeit six years after their third European Cup triumph. As well as being a former assistant coach to the Dutch national team and former coach of under-18 and under-19 sides, at the time of writing he is a senior consultant and ambassador at the Ajax Coaching Academy, currently attached to Sharjah FC. He also played under Rinus Michels for the *Oranje*, and offered a concise explanation when asked to explain *totaalvoetbal*. He emphasised the importance of the whole over the individual: 'Organised, individual technique and working together like a team. Michels [was] all about the total thing, the team has to work together. It is still one of the five "core values" of Ajax. Cruyff was more of the individual player. You can play with 11 good individual players, but Michels made them into a team.'

* * *

Who invented *totaalvoetbal*?

Einstein unveiled the intricate workings of relativity. Livingstone discovered the source of the Nile and Galahad found the Holy Grail. It surely shouldn't therefore be too difficult to trace the beginnings of *totaalvoetbal*. The creator of a system of play that delivered a new paradigm to the game is surely recognised and lauded. Well, you'd think so, wouldn't you? The problem is, that just isn't the case.

Very much like the theories surrounding the origins of Homo sapiens, there seem to be multiple roots reaching back into the history of the game and various locations. In Europe, however, there's a lineage of coaches working in the Netherlands, and particularly with Ajax, that seems to be influential in the very genesis of *totaalvoetbal* in that country.

While the English football establishment polished its perceived glory and preened its feathers as the self-proclaimed leading power of the game, in the earlier and middle years of the 20th century, several coaches, dissenters from the hegemony of long ball, strength and power tactics, sought refuge and open minds among the more liberated attitudes of Continental European clubs. In Britain, they were condemned as traitors and purveyors of an outlandish snake-oil medicine form of football. Not for them the endless weights, exercises and running up and down terracing to heighten fitness, toughness and strength. They championed finesse over fitness, technique over toughness and skill over strength. Had the English game been more open to new ideas, the history of *totaalvoetbal* may well have been very different. Britain is widely regarded as the birthplace of football, and there's a coherent argument to be made that it also provided the midwives of *totaalvoetbal*. That birth was delivered, and blossomed, in Continental Europe rather than Britain, however, and particularly in the Netherlands

Jimmy Hogan, although shunned by the entrenched attitude of the English FA, is widely considered on the Continent as one of the pioneers of modern coaching. His groundbreaking ideas on tactics and systems of play influenced the development of the game in Austria, Hungary and, among other countries, the Netherlands. The term Total Football would have meant nothing to Hogan, but if the label had yet to be applied, the essence of the system was already in his mind. His coaching ethos was based on what was popularly, at the time, termed as the 'Scottish School' of play. It emphasised the importance of controlling the ball in possession and short accurate passing, rather than driving long balls forward and relying on fitness and strength to triumph over technique.

After a fairly ordinary playing career, beginning in the early years of the 20th century, Hogan took up his first coaching position with FC Dordrecht in the South Holland region of the Netherlands in 1910. He was just 28 years old, but with a firmly established belief in how the game should be played, as Norman Fox explained in his biography of Hogan, 'Versatility was a fundamental part of what he taught. Simply, he expected all of his players except the goalkeeper to change places and, in the modern phrase, be "comfortable on the ball".[5] It's surely of little surprise that this ethos was preached in the country of Ajax, Cruyff and Michels. Fox went on to summarise, 'In later years, the philosophy would be called

---

5 Fox, Norman, *Prophet or Traitor?: The Jimmy Hogan Story* (Manchester: The Parrs Wood Press, 2003).

"Total Football". He was teaching it more than 20 years before … Johan Cruyff was born.'

From the Netherlands, Hogan would travel around Europe, preaching his coaching gospel and taking in periods in Hungary, Switzerland, Austria and France. In Austria, he worked alongside Hugo Meisl and contributed to the development the famous *Wunderteam* of Josef Bican, Anton Schall and the 'Papery Man', Matthias Sindelar. The 'Austrian Whirl' system of play, wherein players would interchange positions dependent on where they found themselves during various scenarios within a game, was a clear forerunner of the system so effectively developed in Amsterdam. The Austrians would dominate European international football in the early years of the 1930s, and were probably the first national team to play a form of *totaalvoetbal*.

Ernst Happel missed the golden generation of Austrian international talent. His professional career didn't begin until 1942 and, by the time he wore his first Austria national jersey five years later, the *Wunderteam* were more a golden memory than the golden generation. The way they had played, however, had left a legacy and, when Happel later coached at Feyenoord, taking them to the European Cup in 1970, they played his own variation of *totaalvoetbal*. Happel even inadvertently assisted in the development of Ajax's system and convinced Michels to evolve his tactics after a crucial Eredivisie game shortly before the Austrian took his team to the San Siro in Milan to defeat Celtic and become the first Dutch team to be crowned European champions. That game between Ajax and Feyenoord features later in the story.

During the following decade it was the 'Magical Magyars' of Nándor Hidegkuti, Sándor Kocsis, Zoltán Czibor and Ferenc Puskás profiting from the teachings of Hogan. When they travelled to Wembley in 1953, tearing asunder the isolationist arrogance of English football, they were astonished to discover that Hogan was not an honoured guest at the event. Hogan was in fact at the game, but not as a guest of the FA. By this time he had returned to England and was a relatively unheralded coach working with a youth team from Aston Villa. As *The Guardian* later detailed, 'Sitting in the stands was a 71-year-old, white-haired little Lancastrian surrounded by athletic-looking young men. His name was Jimmy Hogan and the youths were Aston Villa juniors he was still coaching. If ever there was a prophet without honour in his own country it was Hogan and, poignantly, shortly after the game ended, the president of the Hungarian Football Association, Sándor Barcs, said, "Jimmy Hogan taught us everything we know about football."'[6]

Very much in the same vein, Gusztáv Sebes, the Hungary coach who had been much influenced by Hogan's methods, made clear the debt his country's football owed to the peripatetic visionary Englishman, as he reflected on his team's destruction of Hogan's home country: 'When our football history is told, his name should be written in gold letters.'[7]

The seeds of *totaalvoetbal* planted in the Netherlands, the development of the Austrian *Wunderteam*, and the Magical Magyars all have links to Hogan, but there were other teams that developed similar systems in Continental Europe and, indeed, South America. For example, in Italy, the *Grande Torino* team transformed their fortunes by adopting the more attacking *sistema* form of play, discarding the stifling tactics of *metodo* that relied heavily on defence and striking from counter-attacks, before their burgeoning glory was destroyed

---

6 'How total football inventor was lost to Hungary', *The Guardian*, 22 November 2003.

7 Fox, Norman, *Prophet or Traitor?: The Jimmy Hogan Story* (Manchester: The Parrs Wood Press, 2003).

when their aeroplane crashed against the retaining wall of the Basilica of Superga in 1949.

In South America, the River Plate team of coach José María Minella, with a forward line christened as *La Maquina* – so well synchronised were their movements – were playing their own brand of *totaalvoetbal*. Between 1941 and 1947, they won four Primera Division titles. '[By] playing a prototype "Total Football" 30 years ahead of their time. Perhaps the greatest praise for *La Maquina* came from one of its biggest arch-rivals. Ernesto Lazatti, the Boca Juniors star from the 1940s, had this to say, "I play against *La Maquina* with the full intention of beating them, but as a fan of football, I would prefer to sit on the stands and watch them play."'[8]

Their five forwards, most famously made up of Juan Carlos Muñoz, José Manuel Moreno, Adolfo Pedernera, Ángel Labruna and Félix Loustau, would play without assigned positions, merely going where the pattern of the game took them. Pedernera would often start in a centre-forward slot but then drift back into midfield, pulling the defender marking him out of position and creating openings for his fellow cogs in the machine. In the Magical Magyars team, Hidegkuti would adopt a similar role, although there's little to reference that this was developed from Pedernera. Despite popular contemporary acclaim to the contrary, the 'false nine' concept was not invented in the early years of the 21st century in the Camp Nou with Lionel Messi playing under the guidance of Pep Guardiola, although the latter is truly part of the *totaalvoetbal* legacy.

While football in other countries flirted with their own versions of *totaalvoetbal*, back in the Netherlands, those seeds planted by Hogan took root and were tended by other coaches

---

8 https://footballsgreatest.weebly.com/river-plate-1941-47.html

following in his footsteps, until they blossomed. In the same year as Hogan joined FC Dordrecht, Jack Reynolds, another English coach, was taking his first steps into coaching on the Continent, joining Swiss club St Gallen. He would stay in Switzerland for two years, before moving to the Netherlands to take over at Ajax, for what was the first of his stints in charge of the club totalling almost a quarter of a century. During that period, Ajax won eight league titles and Reynolds became one of the most influential coaches in the history of the club. Reflecting on his contribution, Cruyff later described him as 'the visionary Englishman who had been first team coach in the 1940s and helped lay the foundations that Total Football would later be built on'.[9]

Years later, another innovative British coach, Jesse Carver, would launch his career in the Netherlands at the Rotterdam club, Xerxes. As with Hogan, Carver would later work across several European countries, taking in some of the greatest clubs on the Continent as well as the *Oranje*, but he plied his trade only briefly in his native country. While in Rotterdam, building on the work of Hogan, the legendary Dutch player Faas Wilkes came under Carver's control. The talented young forward would benefit greatly from the Englishman's emphasis on training with a ball rather than merely working on fitness. He would go on to play at some of the top clubs in Italy and Spain before returning to the Netherlands.

In an interview with *De Telegraaf*, Tonny Bruins Slot, who worked as a coach under Cruyff at both Barcelona and Ajax, related, 'Cruyff loved that style: the perception, the vision of play and going past two or three players dribbling. Cruyff's favourite players, like Faas Wilkes, his idol when he

---

9 Cruyff, Johan, *My Turn* (London: Macmillan, 2016).

was younger, had those qualities.'[10] The young boy who would later become the high priest of *totaalvoetbal* was already falling under its persuasive enchantment.

In the Netherlands, land of tulips, the green shoots of Hogan's initial work were beginning to sprout forth and, if the initial spadework had been completed by the pioneering coach, evolution and development would follow as others assured its growth. So, who was it that truly invented *totaalvoetbal* in the Netherlands? Was it Hogan or the men who followed him and worked to make the system blossom into full-flowering beauty of the early 1970s? It's a question that only has opinions masquerading as answers. Surprisingly, those who followed Hogan weren't Dutch. In the main, they were British.

* * *

The British are coming!

Between 1910 when they appointed their first coach, and 1965 when Rinus Michels took control of the club's fortunes, Ajax had made 12 appointments to the post and, in 43 of those 55 years, the man leading the club was British. It was hardly a unique situation across the Continent. Widely acknowledged, and self-promoted, as the premier footballing country in the world, there was a natural tendency for clubs to appoint coaches from England, seeking to adopt the successful ways of English football. As with Hogan, however, many of the young British coaches who sought to ply their trade on the Continent were dissenters from the dominant orthodoxy, renegades and outliers – or at least perceived to be so by the English football establishment.

---

10 https://m.allfootballapp.com/news/La-Liga/Cruyff-would-have-enjoyed-De-Jongs-game-enormously/1197788

The reputation of British football made coaches from those islands attractive in other countries, but the belligerent addiction to orthodoxy meant that its coaching exports were often those who eschewed the values prized in the British game, and found employment at home difficult to secure. Some of the coaches appointed by Ajax stayed in post for only a season or two and are largely forgotten, but the club were fortunate that, across those 43 years when British coaches were in post, for more than half of them the men at the helm were two of those dissenters, Jack Reynolds and Vic Buckingham.

Amsterdamsche Football Club Ajax were formed in 1900 as a reincarnation of Football Club Ajax, who had been founded six years earlier, but perished not long afterwards. In 1910, the club appointed their first coach, former Irish player Jack Kirwan. Early success followed under Kirwan as Ajax gained promotion to the top tier the following year. Their stay would be brief – relegation followed in 1914 and led to Kirwan's departure. That promotion, however, would cause a significant change in the club's identity.

For their first few years, Ajax had played in red-and-white-striped shirts and black shorts. Existing top-tier club Sparta Rotterdam wore a similar ensemble and, upon promotion, Ajax were compelled to change their strip if they were to take up their allotted place in the division. Reluctant to totally abandon their red and white stripes, they opted instead to have a single broad stripe down the centre of an otherwise white shirt, with white shorts completing the change. The following year, the Dutch national team also changed their preferred playing kit. Previously they had played in a white shirt with a red, white and blue sash cut from the shoulder to represent the national flag of the Netherlands. Facing England – who also wore white shirts –

in 1912, the Dutch changed to an orange shirt, symbolic of the royal House of Orange. They lost the game 12-2 – still the national team's record international defeat – but the choice of shirt was established. The iconic shirts of both Ajax and the Netherlands were not only established in the early years of the 20th century, but also within a year of each other.

As the relegation in 1914 saw the end of Kirwan, in his stead Ajax appointed Jack Reynolds. The coach had left his Swiss club and was set to take control of the German national team, but the conflagration of World War One made that move impossible. Instead he moved to Amsterdam. German football's loss would be Ajax's gain. The consequences of such moments would dramatically affect how football developed in Europe.

Reynolds had retired from playing in 1911 after a less-than-wholly-impressive nine-year career. After joining Manchester City, but finding a first-team place beyond him, he began a nomadic journey with moves to Burton United, Grimsby Town, The Wednesday, the then non-league club Watford, and Gillingham before hanging up his boots following a brief stay with Rochdale. His achievements as a coach could hardly be more in contrast to his journeyman playing days. Over the years it has been shown to be the case that having an ordinary playing career does not preclude someone from becoming an outstanding coach. Reynolds would bear witness to the theory, as would Rinus Michels 50 years later, but that's not the only link between the coaches regarded with such reverence by Ajax and their fans.

On the outside, Reynolds looked every inch the Englishman of contemporary popular culture. He often wore a bowler hat or flat cap; the former portraying the image of a London businessman, the latter of a workman from his native Lancashire. He was known as 'Good Old Jack' or, as the

Dutch would pronounce his name, *Sjek Rijnols*. His coaching methods were anything but typically English though. When Reynolds arrived, the club based in east Amsterdam were hardly successful even within the city itself, let alone the Netherlands. Relegation had dropped Ajax back into the second tier of Dutch football and they had never won a trophy. All that would change after Reynolds' arrival, and the club would never be the same again.

Very much in the manner of the time, Dutch football was amateur in both definition and attitude. A quote from Hogan when he had briefly taken control of the national team for a game against Germany in 1910 serves to illustrate the point. He recalled that his team 'drank like fishes and smoked like factory chimneys but were a jolly lot of fellows'.[11] Unsurprisingly, a similar attitude permeated Dutch clubs as well. Menno Pot is an Amsterdam-based music journalist and football writer, an Ajax columnist for *Het Parool* and host of a weekly Ajax podcast for the newspaper, called *Branie* (*'Swagger'*). He has also written six books about the club, and had little doubt about the beneficial effects of Reynolds, as he explained in an interview with the BBC in 2011: 'He was all over the place and really reshaped the club into something "professional" even though the players weren't paid at the time. Football was an amateur game, but he introduced professional training methods, and professional facilities that really allowed Ajax to make a huge leap forward.'[12]

That professionalism was a doctrine that Reynolds lived by, as well as preached. He learned Dutch, hardly an easy task, especially in those days, and worked from eight in the morning to late in the evening taking care to develop a system

---

11 Fox, Norman, *Prophet or Traitor?: The Jimmy Hogan Story* (Manchester: The Parrs Wood Press, 2003).

12 https://www.bbc.com/news/uk-england-manchester-12464632

of play for Ajax that extended across all teams at the club, from the first team through to the junior levels, as Menno Pot explained in the same BBC article: 'He was the man who came up with the idea that every team at Ajax should play the same system and the same formation. He wanted them to play offensively, and to play with skill rather than physical power.' At Reynolds' Ajax, that system was recognisable as a form of *totaalvoetbal*. It was the genesis of the club's now fabled youth development system

How important was that innovation? Pot considered to the BBC, 'While the great manager's winning record was worthy of praise – winning the Dutch Cup in 1917 and winning eight league titles – his masterstroke was the invention of a system that changed Ajax forever.'

One of the young players who became schooled in that system after joining the club towards the end of Reynolds' time, would go on to coach the club and take up the baton of *totaalvoetbal* some 20 years later. As with Reynolds, he was a dedicated, often driven professional and a disciplinarian. He would take Ajax and his development of *totaalvoetbal* to the zenith of Continental footballing success. His name was Marinus Jacobus Hendricus Michels, universally known as Rinus Michels.

In his first season with the club, Reynolds guided Ajax to what should have been promotion back to the top tier. The war had prevented him taking up the post with Germany, however, and also meant that any attempts for a rapid reversal of the club's relegation would have to be put on hold. Ajax wouldn't be able to re-establish their higher status until 1917. By this time Reynolds had delivered their first trophy, lifting the Dutch Cup in the 1916/17 season. It was the start of a glorious run of silverware for a club whose trophy cabinet had previously served little purpose.

While Reynolds' coaching was key to the club's advancement – Menno Pot detailed how he 'introduced professional training methods, professional facilities, that really allowed Ajax to make a huge leap forward'[13] – they also had some talented players. The new coach was astute enough to build his team around them. One such player was Jan de Natris. Hugely temperamental, but with a talent to match, De Natris carried echoes of several players who would wear the Ajax shirt six decades later. In their initial season back in the top division, Ajax secured their first title, winning the national championship for the first time by finishing the play-off league three points from Deventer-based club Go Ahead – who would later become a troublesome thorn in their side – after qualifying through the regionalised system.

In the deciding game, Ajax travelled to face Willem II. They would win it but no thanks to De Natris. For some unspecified reason, he had missed the train to Tilburg and stayed in Amsterdam. The title went to Ajax regardless and the club fined De Natris. In the following season, with the player serving a six-month ban, Ajax retained their championship without losing a single game. They were on the way. That unbeaten record remained unique for three-quarters of a century and, ultimately, it was replicated by the same club.

Wim Schooevaart, a former Ajax archivist, was 93 when the BBC interviewed him about Reynolds in 2011. His father and uncle had played under Reynolds and, as a boy visiting the club, he had seen Reynolds in action, and his dad had regaled him with tales of the English coach's methods. He recalled how Reynolds had revolutionised Ajax by introducing wingers, something that had never previously been seen in

---

13 https://youtu.be/PIrtPQ_nHiQ

the Dutch club game. Under Reynolds, Schooevaart said, 'Ajax played football always in the same way ... always with an outside-left and an outside-right and always open play. He made links from left-half to outside-right and right-half to outside-left, with the long balls.'[14]

In the 1920s, Reynolds guided Ajax to three regional titles and several minor cup successes. By the 1930s they were the country's dominant footballing power, taking the league title in 1930/31, 1931/32, 1933/34, 1936/37 and 1938/39. With players such as Dolf van Kol, Jan van Diepenbeek and prolific forward Piet van Reenen, Ajax were enjoying a Golden Age of their very own. Their possession-based attacking play and rapid inter-passing style with wingers stretching the play saw them sweep opponents aside. The *Volkskrant* newspaper lauded Reynolds' team and their system of play: 'Ajax comes close to the English professional game and lacks only the spirit that English teams have.'[15] It's unclear whether Reynolds would have considered if addressing the final part of that sentence would be something beneficial to his team or not. The 1930s also saw Ajax move to a new home stadium. Officially dubbed Het Ajax-Stadion, it quickly became popularly referred to as the De Meer, named after the area of the city where it was located.

As well as global armed conflict leading to Reynolds joining Ajax, war had blighted the coach's early years within the Netherlands, and the same would happen in World War Two. He was still in Amsterdam when the German army swept into the country in 1940 and spent years in an internment camp until liberation. He returned to take up his coaching role afterwards and delivered his eighth and final

---

14 https://youtu.be/PIrtPQ-nHiQ
15 Winner, David, *Brilliant Orange* (London: Bloomsbury, 2000).

league title to the club in the 1946/47 season, before retiring and opening a tobacconist's shop in the city. In his 24 years in charge at Ajax, he coached the club to many triumphs and developed some outstanding talents. Much more important, though, was the legacy he left behind. Reynolds would pass away in 1962 aged 81.

Few, if any, other coaches of that era had the profound effect on a club that Jack Reynolds delivered for Ajax, not just in terms of raising their profile from the doldrums of second-tier football to being the dominant power in the Dutch domestic game, delivering trophies and building successful teams, he also laid down a philosophy and system of play that led to such triumphs, one that would be followed as others built on his work. The debt Ajax owed to the Englishman is openly recognised by the club. Ajax named a stand at the De Meer after him and later transferred that honour when they moved to the Amsterdam ArenA – now known as the Johan Cruijff ArenA. The new stadium greets VIP visitors as they enter via the Jack Reynolds Lobby, where they pass a plaque that the club produced to honour the English coach and his achievements with Ajax. As well as Cruyff's ringing endorsement mentioned above, Jany van der Veen, the youth coach who discovered Cruyff, considered Reynolds to be Ajax's greatest ever trainer. Menno Pot put it in simple terms: 'Ajax would never have become the force they are without Jack Reynolds. There's no way. Basically, everything that this club is about, and everything that this club is known for, was invented and introduced by Jack Reynolds.'[16] Given the later success and celebrated status of the club in football's history, that is some bequest gifted by the Englishman.

---

16 https://youtu.be/PIrtPQ-nHiQ

Pot has little doubt about the significance of Reynolds' contribution to Ajax, as was clear when the author asked him about the former coach: 'His importance cannot be exaggerated. He was Ajax's godfather, the man who turned Ajax into Ajax. He invented the whole thing. He was, in many ways, the Rinus Michels of his time, but even more important as he started with nothing. He arrived in 1915 and retired as a coach in 1947. During those years he coached Ajax for 25 seasons in total. That's still more than 20 per cent of the club's existence, which is amazing!

'When he arrived at the club during World War One (in which Holland remained neutral) Dutch football was still in its infancy. It was an amateur game played by students, mostly. Most clubs didn't even have a coach, they basically coached themselves and played football without a plan. Football in Britain was at a totally different level. Reynolds started taking things seriously. He focused on fitness (which was a totally new thing in Dutch football at the time; some opponents even felt it was unfair). He introduced the club's first tactical plan, with specific instructions for each position. Many clubs played a pretty physical game in those days. To Reynolds it was all about speed and skill: quick, short passing in little triangles, keeping the ball low … with the occasional cross-pass from full-back to winger.

'At first the Ajax players had no clue what Reynolds was trying to teach them. They had to do exercises during training which they had never heard of before. But they soon started getting the point – and they became a team that was almost unbelievably good by Dutch standards. By the end of World War One, Ajax played football that looked totally futuristic. They became a national sensation. This process took place during World War One, in which Dutch football made a huge leap forward. When the war ended in 1918, Ajax – more than anyone else – was the epitome of the progress Dutch football had made. They were the future.

'Jack Reynolds was the first real "boss" in Dutch football. He basically ran the whole club. He coached the first team and the second – and in later years he coached the youth teams too. Everybody loved him. He lived in Amsterdam until his death in 1962. He was at the club every day. During World War Two he was interned in a concentration camp, but after the war he returned for one final season. During that season he had a big, chunky striker in his squad named Rinus Michels. Michels always said that he was totally indebted to Reynolds: he copied Reynolds' coaching style and his basic ideas about how football should be played. Reynolds deserves the credit for inventing the "Ajax style".'

Given Pot's comments about Michels' confessed indebtedness to Reynolds, it's worth noting that in *Brilliant Orange*, David Winner related that while Michels conceded that he 'learned much from [Reynolds] … he later dismissed his training regime as old-fashioned'.[17] Despite initial appearances, the two points may not be contradictory. Given that Michels would have been talking around half a century after Reynolds had taken over at Ajax and two decades after his retirement, an updating of the training regime is entirely understandable if the overall ethos was to be secured, and under Michels it was. Reynolds would surely have approved.

Tactics weren't the only thing that Michels was indebted to Reynolds for, as Pot explains:

'Reynolds was known as a very warm personality, a father figure for his players. There is no doubt that Rinus Michels had Reynolds in mind when he, himself, became a bit of a father figure to Johan Cruyff (Johan's father died when he was

---

17 Winner, David, *Brilliant Orange* (London: Bloomsbury, 2000).

12). Cruyff's mother was unable to take her son to the club every day, so Michels would pick him up for training. Johan would also have dinner at Michels' home once a week (steak, most of the time, as he was way too skinny).'

As often is the case, when a successful coach leaves a club – especially after a prolonged period in charge – there's a downturn in fortunes as an identity, now lost, is sought again. Inevitably a rebuilding of the team and refocusing of the club was required if the success and momentum built by Reynolds weren't to be squandered. As successful as Ajax were in replacing Michels almost a quarter of a century later, they would struggle after Reynolds retired. They first turned to another Englishman, Robert Smith. Although Smith was a Lancastrian, as was Reynolds, that's where the similarity ended and he was swiftly moved on and replaced by Walter Crook. It was Crook's first coaching position and he would remain at the club until the end of the decade before a brief stay with Sparta Rotterdam resulted in a move back to England and Accrington Stanley. Crook would return to Ajax three years later, but this time the stay would be even shorter, as he left the following year to join Wigan Athletic.

Although the odd regional championship was secured, the fall from grace under Reynolds was clear. In November 1950 Ajax looked north of Hadrian's Wall, offering the coach's position to Scotsman Robert Thomson. It was his first and only job as a coach in the professional game and he was dismissed in December 1952. Perhaps it was time to look away from British shores.

Karel Kaufman had taken over as coach of the *Oranje* after the end of World War Two, becoming the first Dutch coach of the national team since Cees van Hasselt had left the job in 1908. 'Going Dutch' was hardly a roaring success either and, after Crook's brief return in 1954, the idea was ditched when Austrian Karl Humenberger was given the task of returning the club to its former glories. Ajax hadn't been crowned Dutch champions since Reynolds had retired, but developments outside of the capital were driving major changes in Dutch football.

Much as with the FA, the KNVB had fought long and hard against the perceived pernicious effects of professionalism that was forcing its way across European football. By 1955 there were simply not enough KNVB fingers to plug the growing holes in the dyke of resistance to the move and football in the Netherlands became professional, in name at least. In the 1956/57 season, a decade after Reynolds had delivered their last title, Humenberger took Ajax to the top of the newly formed Eredivisie, securing the championship in the first year that the national league had existed. Winning 22 of their matches in the 34-game programme, they finished four points clear of Fortuna '54. There were promises of a new era of success opening up, but the Austrian failed to build on the success and, ahead of the 1959/60 season, the brief dalliance with central Europe was abandoned, as was Ajax's first journey into the European Cup, the tournament that just over a decade later would be their vehicle to dominance. After easing past East German club SC Wismut Karl Marx Stadt, the Hungarians of Vasa were far too powerful. A 2-2 draw in Amsterdam being followed by a four-goal trouncing in Budapest's Népstadion. Humenberger left and Ajax eyes were cast once more to England, landing on Vic Buckingham, then coach at West Bromwich Albion.

Similar to Hogan and Reynolds, Buckingham's playing days had hardly suggested an outstanding coaching career awaited him. Playing in the Second Division, he spent his entire career with Tottenham Hotspur and accumulated more than 200 games for the north London club before retiring and turning to coaching in 1949. After cutting his teeth with Pegasus, a club made up of students from Oxford University, he spent two seasons with Bradford Park Avenue before moving to The Hawthorns in 1953, to replace Jesse Carver who, after his time in the Netherlands with Xerxes, was continuing his tour of Europe with a move to Lazio.

As with Reynolds and Carver, Buckingham was a progressive coach, and one of the very few who had managed to relatively prosper in the English game without sacrificing his ideas of how football should be played. In 1954 he took the Baggies so close to the first English league and FA Cup double of the 20th century. Despite lifting the FA Cup by defeating the Preston North End team of Tom Finney, they came up just short in the First Division, finishing four points behind Black Country rivals Wolverhampton Wanderers. The appointment with Ajax would only last for two seasons. In that time, however, the ethos of *totaalvoetbal* enjoyed a revival and success followed.

In his first season Buckingham guided Ajax to the 1959/60 Eredivisie title. His team scored 109 goals, averaging more than 3.23 per game. It still took a play-off against Feyenoord, though, to secure the championship after both clubs finished on 50 points. A 5-1 victory conclusively decided the issue in a game that featured the burgeoning talents of Sjaak Swart and Piet Keizer, both who would go on to be important elements of Michels' teams.

After battling against the entrenched ways of English domestic football, Buckingham had found a natural home for his way of playing the game. During his later years at White Hart Lane, Buckingham had gained first-hand knowledge of Spurs manager Arthur Rowe's revolutionary push-and-run style of football. It wasn't *totaalvoetbal*, but it was heading in that general direction. In the two years after Buckingham retired, Spurs would go on to win back-to-back Second Division and then First Division titles. He may have missed out on the glory of those years, but Rowe's coaching methods had left their mark on Buckingham.

The ground had been well prepared by Reynolds and, despite the lapses in the intervening years, the pioneering work of the English coach remained evident in the ability of the players Buckingham inherited when he moved to Amsterdam. 'Their skills were different,' Buckingham mused, talking of the players at Ajax – a young Johan Cruyff, who was making his way through the ranks at the club, very much included. 'Their intellect was different and they played proper football ... I influenced them but they went on and did things above that which delighted me.'[18]

Cruyff had been discovered and taken to Ajax by Jany van der Veen, a former player at the club – and briefly a team-mate of Michels – who had returned as a coach. He took the young prodigy under his wing and later Cruyff attested to the debt he owed to Van der Veen. Of all his early influences, he asserted that Van der Veen had been the 'most important'.[19] The coach had a specific training format that focused on the basics of a football education for young players at the club. Cruyff later called it the 'five basic fundamentals of football: shooting, heading, dribbling, passing and controlling the ball'.[20] He believed that the lessons from Van der Veen taught him an understanding of the game that allowed his skills to flourish.

Buckingham was probably the first genuine kindred spirit of Reynolds, among those who followed him, and he could

18 Winner, David, *Brilliant Orange*, (London: Bloomsbury, 2000).
19 Cruyff, Johan, *My Turn* (London: Macmillan, 2016).
20 Cruyff, Johan, *My Turn* (London: Macmillan, 2016).

see tremendous potential at Ajax, despite the newly adopted professionalism in Dutch football having more to do with definition than reality. 'I thought they were the best team in Europe even then,'[21] he declared. Maybe so, but official recognition of that status was still more than a decade away.

That distance was emphasised in the 1960/61 European Cup, when Ajax were eliminated in the first round by the Norwegian amateur side Fredrikstad. Despite leading 1-0 and 2-1 in the away leg, it took a late goal by Bennie Muller to keep Ajax in the tie at 4-3. Only 7,500 fans were able to cram into the compact Fredrikstad Stadion for the first leg. As was often the case for bigger games, back in Amsterdam Ajax took their home leg away from the De Meer to the larger capacity Olympisch Stadion, and 35,000 fans turned up expecting to see the sole-goal deficit easily overcome. A goalless draw, however, offered up a hearty denial of Buckingham's assertive claim for his team. Buckingham was often described as a coach ahead of his time. On this occasion, his words certainly suggested that to be very much the case.

Despite his success, Buckingham's initial stay in Amsterdam would be brief. In May 1961, just a few weeks before the end of a season in which Ajax would finish second in the Eredivisie to Feyenoord but lift the Dutch Cup, the coach left for reasons still clouded in mystery. Buckingham had left before the cup final, but three goals in a late ten-minute spell by Henk Groot were enough to defeat NAC and deliver the second piece of silverware of Buckingham's curtailed reign.

By this time, that trend of Englishmen appointed to lead Ajax, having less-than-impressive playing careers behind them before turning to coaching, set by Hogan and then followed

---

21 Winner, David, *Brilliant Orange* (London: Bloomsbury, 2000).

by Reynolds and Buckingham, was established. The man who replaced Buckingham would take that trend to a whole new level, although his time with Ajax lacked somewhat as well. Keith Spurgeon's playing career had traversed the less-celebrated clubs of Margate, Leytonstone, Folkestone Town, Herne Bay, Snowdown Colliery Welfare and Clapton. In 1961, when Buckingham left, he became coach of Ajax – if only for one season.

Spurgeon continued much of Buckingham's style, but without garnering the major trophies of his predecessor. A fourth-placed finish in the Eredivisie was a backwards step. They lost 11 games but finished the same number of points behind champions Feyenoord. An early Dutch Cup exit offered little consolation with a similar disappointment in Europe as the Cup Winners' Cup run fell at the first hurdle with a 4-3 aggregate loss to Újpesti Dózsa. Victory in an early incarnation of the Intertoto Cup was hardly enough to convince the club that Spurgeon would improve matters. His exit at the end of the season brought a brief hiatus to the run of English coaches. Despite their short period in office, though, Cruyff would later relate that Ajax benefitted from the coaching of Buckingham and Spurgeon: 'Football in Holland then was good but it was not really professional. They gave us some professionalism because they were much further down the road.'[22]

Vienna-born Joseph Gruber was installed to replace Spurgeon with Ajax perhaps hoping that the new man could replicate the initial success of Karl Humenberger, who was also a native of the Austrian capital. With no European distractions, Gruber could concentrate on domestic matters,

---

22 'Everyone can play football but those values are being lost. We have to bring them back', *The Guardian*, 12 September 2014.

but to no great avail; Ajax finished second in the Eredivisie to PSV. A 5-2 defeat to the champions in the penultimate game of the season had decided matters and a fourth-round extra-time defeat to Willem II in the cup meant the end of Gruber as the fortunes of Ajax continued to wane.

Jack Rowley was a step away from the blueprint of English coaches whose light had hardly shone as a player. Rowley had spent 17 seasons at Manchester United, notching 182 goals in 380 league games. At the time of writing only three other players in the history of the Old Trafford club have scored more than 200 league goals: Bobby Charlton, Denis Law and Wayne Rooney. It's exalted company. He had also collected a First Division title and won the FA Cup with the Red Devils, and appeared six times for England, scoring the same number of goals. If coaches with average playing careers could succeed, perhaps a former star player could do better.

Rowley had just taken Oldham Athletic to promotion into the Third Division when Ajax appointed him. The experiment was hardly a roaring success. At the end of the season, Ajax had slipped to fifth place and, without any compensation of success in the cup, Rowley exited. He would later return to coach in Britain, first at Wrexham and then Bradford Park Avenue before returning to Oldham. Unknown at the time though, the squad that would later flourish was slowly gathering. With Swart and Keizer already present, the season under Rowley saw a young Wim Suurbier play the first two games of his Ajax career. There would be many more to follow and glory aplenty.

When Buckingham left he moved to Sheffield Wednesday, replacing Harry Catterick, who had been lured to Everton. The Owls had finished as runners-up in the First Division when Buckingham was appointed, so there was clearly potential, and an opportunity to reprise the success of his time with West Bromwich Albion. Buckingham kept the Yorkshire club near the top of the English game, finishing in sixth place for three successive seasons, and when he was sacked it was hardly for footballing reasons. In 1964, three Sheffield Wednesday players were convicted of betting on their own team to lose a game against Ipswich Town in December 1962. Although there was no evidence, indication or even suggestion that Buckingham had been involved, the club decided that his liberal approach to control and lax discipline of his players may have contributed to the problem, and he was dismissed.

With Rowley out, and the club in decline, Ajax were in need of a new coach and Buckingham was offered the chance to return and revive their flagging fortunes. Overall, it's difficult to see the single season of his return as anything but a failure. It did, however, have one redeeming incandescently bright spot as a skinny 17-year-old, once described by Buckingham as 'a useful kid'[23] made his debut for the club in November 1964 in a 3-1 defeat away to GVAV, who would be renamed as Groningen FC in 1971. In the next game, Cruyff would score in a 5-0 home win over PSV Eindhoven. It was a false dawn, however, and when Ajax visited the De Kuip for their next fixture, they suffered a humiliating 9-4 hammering at the hands of Feyenoord. Each time they took one step forward, they seemed compelled to take two more in the opposite direction. Buckingham's fate was sealed from that day. Ironically, across the next six Eredivisie games, Ajax were only beaten once – to Go Ahead Eagles, in what was a forerunner of what would become their regular role to come as Ajax's trickiest domestic opponents – winning four times and drawing the other game. It may have been a tentative sign of renaissance, but it came far too late.

---

23 Winner, David, *Brilliant Orange* (London: Bloomsbury, 2000).

Cruyff would feature in ten games across the remainder of that season, but Buckingham would miss many of them. On 21 January 1965, just two months after Cruyff first wore the Ajax shirt, Buckingham was dismissed. When he had returned to the De Meer, Ajax had finished in fifth position in the Eredivisie, and the club were expecting an improvement. By the time of his dismissal they were hovering dangerously close to the foot of the table. Time had run out. Rinus Michels was lined up as his replacement.

It wasn't quite the end of all links between Ajax and Buckingham. He returned to England to coach Fulham, before a brief time spent in Greece with Ethnikos Piraeus. In 1969, however, he was appointed as coach of Barcelona and, with memories of that 'useful kid' still fresh in his mind, he sought to bring Cruyff to the Catalan club, but the Spanish league's restrictions on foreign players ruled out the plan. Much as he had been frustrated at Ajax and succeeded by Michels, the same happened in Catalonia. When Michels replaced him once more, taking over at the Camp Nou in 1971, his move to secure the transfer of Cruyff was successful.

Michels had retired from playing in the 1957/58 season after a persistently troublesome back injury had brought his career to a halt. Never really a star of the team under Reynolds, he was a hard-working and dedicated forward who relied on power and heading ability, rather than an exuberantly talented ability, for his goals. The pattern of an ordinary playing career that could lead to an outstanding one in coaching was dropping into place again, although at the time no one knew it. His playing debut for Ajax had promised much. Opening his career with a game against ADO Den Haag in the 1945/46 season, Michels scored five goals in an 8-3 victory. By the time he hung up his boots, though, he would had featured in 264 league games for the club, scoring 122 goals, his goals to game ratio much diminished. He did enjoy success and was part of the team that won Reynolds' final title in 1946/47, then collected his second championship when Humenberger's team won the first Eredivisie in 1956/57. He also played five games for the national team. Not only did he fail to score in any of them, however, the *Oranje* would also lose each one.

After retiring, Michels studied at the Amsterdam Sports Academy, taught gymnastics at a local school and began coaching amateur teams in the city. It was hardly a compelling CV but, with the club in trouble, when the call to take over at Ajax arrived, Michels had little doubt in his ability to deliver the required transition. He arrived at the De Meer in an old Skoda, with the club floundering, despite the brief recovery before Buckingham's departure. The state of Ajax reflected that of Michels' car. All that would change, however, as, across the next half a dozen years, he would transform Ajax into a finely tuned Ferrari.

Hitting the floor running was vital and, much as with his playing career, Michels enjoyed a goal glut victory in his first game as coach. On 24 January 1965, MVV Maastrict arrived at the De Meer and for the first 25 minutes Ajax struggled to break down the visitors' defence but, when Cruyff played in a free kick, Swart was on hand to open the scoring. By the end of the game Swart had added a further four goals. Cruyff chipped in with a brace, and Klaas Nuninga, who had signed from GVAV-Rapiditas the previous season under Buckingham had also netted twice. A 9-3 win was the ideal start for the new coach, and yet, as with Buckingham's record, one win hardly set off a run of success. Ajax avoided relegation but they only won two of the remaining 11 games of the Eredivisie season. They finished in 13th position, three points away from relegation.

It's unknown whether there were doubts among the club hierarchy as to whether Michels should be retained for the following season, but perhaps the warm glow from that resounding victory was enough to melt away any doubts. Few of the players had much doubt, as Sjaak Swart recalled: 'At the start, Michels said, "We are going to make Ajax more professional. If anyone is not with me in wanting more discipline and training, say so now, then you can leave." His training sessions were always perfectly prepared. And he put the right players in the right positions. That seems simple, but it isn't. If I had become a coach, I would have done it just like him. I never had a better coach then Rinus Michels.'[24] From the next season, a legend would be born, and then grow as Michels' Ajax team and their *totaalvoetbal* initially dominated Dutch domestic football and then moved on to conquer Europe.

If Reynolds' legacy to the club was as important as previously described, what should be said of Michels' importance? It's a question Robert Pennino has pondered: 'When he left the club in 1971 and was succeeded by Ștefan Kovács, he left behind both a great team and a revolutionary football concept. Was he the inventor of *totaalvoetbal*? That's not undisputed. Under Ernst Happel Feyenoord played a similar way of football, albeit with quite a few different accents. And let's not forget that Kovács gave the Ajax stars more freedom, which especially in the season 1971/72 had as a result the peak of beautiful football with great results. So yes, Michels has of course been a revolutionary coach with his way of [professionalising] and football vision. Without Michels the giant leap of Dutch football may never have happened.

---

24 https://www.uefa.com/uefachampionsleague/news/0253-0d7ff54908f6-
   5927d0a16600-1000--the-greatest-teams-of-all-time-ajax-1971-73/

But was he the inventor of total football? I'd rather say that he perfected the idea of *totaalvoetbal* that was already entering in the DNA of Dutch football in those days.'

Undoubtedly Reynolds and – to some extent – Buckingham were important figures in the Ajax story, but it was Michels who not only restored the club's position at the top of the domestic game as he developed their *totaalvoetbal* in his own image, but also led them to Continental glory as well. That journey began in his first full season at the De Meer.

Part 2: Milestones on the journey

Michels arrives

If the previous season had seen Ajax limp over the line to safety, the new term was an entirely different story as the Rinus Michels regime began in earnest. Four wins and a draw in a series of friendly games set the tone for the season, with Ajax notching 15 goals and conceding just six. Their first Eredivisie game on 22 August saw DOS visit the De Meer and it took a late goal from Sjaak Swart to secure the points after a Co Prins opener had been negated before half-time. It was an unsteady start, but Ajax prospered from there.

With the points in the bag from their opening fixture, Ajax would win their next seven games before a 1-1 draw away to Heracles Almelo on 3 October, and then a 1-0 home defeat to Sparta Rotterdam the following week put a stumble into their march towards the title. That reverse against Sparta would be a rare occurrence as they would only suffer defeat in one more Eredivisie fixture before the season ended. Ajax galloped away towards the Eredivisie title, finishing seven points clear of Feyenoord. Other championships had been secured across the recent years, in 1946/47 and then a decade later in 1956/57, but they failed to herald a new era of success as, disappointingly, the club fell back into mediocrity the following season. At the time it was widely perceived that this Ajax success, with their new and unproven coach, would be something similar, merely another brief flaring that would quickly fade away again. That would prove to be so very far from being the case on this occasion.

There was little doubt now that Johan Cruyff was becoming a key member of the squad, as he flourished under Michels' development of *totaalvoetbal*. He was just 18 at the time and the youngest member of the team, but Michels quickly recognised the talent he possessed. His basic football education was about to move from school to university, and he had an insatiable hunger to learn. Michels would often take the teenager to one side to involve him in his plans and discuss tactics. It was a tutorial granted to no other player.

Swart, Piet Keizer and Wim Suurbier were also now established as first-team players, each playing more than 30 Eredivisie games that term, and a young Barry Hulshoff made three appearances. Inevitably it was Cruyff who benefitted most under the new regime, as Arie Haan would later recall: 'So much has been said and written. Michels taught us the discipline and structure of the game, something that was missing until then in the team, where the talent and the joy of the game overflowed. He instilled in us the mentality of a winner; as he said, good play is the means to success and not an end in itself. In this part he was closer to the then dominant German mentality. In conclusion, I would say that the two of them, Cruyff and Michels, complemented each other perfectly, something that was also [later] reflected in the Dutch national team.'[25]

In Michels, Cruyff had found someone who held similar views to his own. The youngster hardly rejoiced in

---

25 Interview by Dimitris Dimoulas with Arie Haan 30-05-2021 in *Proto Thema*. (Translated)

the increased training, especially the cross-country runs designed to increase stamina, but on the field things were very different. The *totaalvoetbal* approach of Michels, with a 4-2-4 formation and emphasis on attacking football, drew the very best from the emerging talent. Cruyff had been as an empty page awaiting a story. Michels knew the plot and had the pen.

As well as innovation, discipline was a key weapon in the new coach's arsenal. Ironically, this was in sharp contrast to his time as a player. Although hardly a renegade, Michels was still regarded as an outgoing personality by his Ajax team-mates. Bobby Haarms played alongside Michels and described the forward as 'easy-going ... on the pitch, with a taste for practical jokes off it'.[26] Many years later, in 1967, Haarms reconnected with his old team-mate and became a coach at the club. The difference between Michels' personality as a player and his new incarnation as a coach was obvious to Haarms, who also added in *Brilliant Orange*, 'He was completely different from when he was a player. The main thing with him now was discipline. Fantastic discipline.'

When asked to describe Michels, the discipline highlighted by Haarms was a characteristic that Menno Pot emphasised: 'Michels was a revolutionary coach if ever there was one in the Netherlands. When it comes to coaching there's a bit of an Ajax bloodline, running from Jack Reynolds to Rinus Michels to Louis van Gaal. Both Michels and Van Gaal were originally gymnastics teachers. They were "teacher types" demanding full attention and commitment from their pupils at all times. When he became manager in 1964 Ajax could hardly be called a "professional" football club. Players got paid a little bit, but it wasn't [anywhere] near enough to

---

26 Winner, David, *Brilliant Orange* (London: Bloomsbury, 2000).

make a living. They trained a few times a week. Ajax were a nonentity on the European stage.'

Initially, only Cruyff and Keizer were paid as professionals. When Cruyff got into the first team and was awarded a contract Keizer befriended him, as the future icon would later relate: 'When I started to play for the first team, Piet Keizer took me under his wing. He was almost four years older than me and had been playing in the first team for three seasons when I was picked. Ajax were only just starting to offer professional contracts, and Piet was the first to receive one. I was the second.'[27]

The two players would become key to Ajax's success and although, undoubtedly, Cruyff would always be named as the most important player of that era with Ajax, invariably, Keizer would be named second.

Ronald Jager is an accounts manager in the Netherlands and has written four football books dating back to 2008, and also coaches at amateur level. He certainly sees it that way and also illustrated the relationship between the two. 'I consider Piet Keizer … as the other key player,' he explained. 'When Cruyff was young and he was in the city too late, Piet Keizer took him home and he listened in his early years to Keizer's advices. He met his future wife Danny at Keizer's wedding.'

That relationship would become strained over time and, when Keizer was elected to captain the team for the 1973/74 season, Cruyff cited it as the reason that made him leave Ajax. Even with the advent of contracts at the club, as Menno Pot suggested, such payments were small, and certainly insufficient to live on. Cruyff filled out his earnings with odd jobs at the printing works of *Sports World* magazine and

---

27 Cruyff, Johan, *My Turn* (London: Macmillan, 2016).

would also take his turn standing outside tobacconists or in the high street selling the magazine to passersby. Keizer could have been inside of one of those tobacconists, as he ran one to compensate for his meagre earnings as a professional footballer with Ajax.

Pot explains that the situation was far from satisfactory from Michels' perspective, even as more players were paid. He required improvement and progress.

'When Michels arrived, everything changed. He dumped the old guard and went for a new crop of youngsters … In the meantime, he urged the Ajax board to think more commercially. The club needed money, Michels wanted players to be paid better so he could demand more from them. He wanted to be able to buy players and pay them wages that would make them stay for a while. This was a revolution in Dutch football.

'Ajax grew up under Michels: he was very demanding, doubled the number of training hours and was constantly drilling the team. It was all about discipline and focus. The way Ajax played looked very adventurous and "free", but they probably had a stricter plan than many others clubs from the era. Michels is also a legend as a character. He was nicknamed "The General" or "The Sphinx". Creaky voice. Stiff Amsterdam accent. Very short sentences. And often grumpy in a very funny way.'

The new coach's methods certainly left a mark with his players. The end of Michels' playing career and the beginning of Swart's had overlapped slightly. Swart revealed, 'I'd played with Michels during his last season as a player for Ajax and he was a very good centre-forward. When he arrived [as coach] he came to sit with the players and said, "Boys, we're going to play total football." And then he said everyone had to train seven times a week, eat and sleep well to become more professional. If there were boys who couldn't do that, they could go home.'[28]

The regime was undoubtedly hard and some players resented it at first, but Michels was adamant that increased fitness and discipline was key to what he was building. He had little concern about whether he was liked or not, he wanted respect. Affection was something he could live without.

The first sentence in that quotation from Swart is interesting. Perhaps Michels did use those words, although Swart may be have intended it to be taken as an implied declaration rather than some verbatim revolutionary statement of intent. After all, Ajax had been playing a version of *totaalvoetbal* since the days of Jack Reynolds and did so under Vic Buckingham as well, Michels' direct predecessor, albeit perhaps not in the total grace that would follow around the turn of the decade.

Arie Haan, who joined Ajax later, had similar recollections, but the progress for the players, club and Dutch football as a whole, followed. He explained in the same article as Swart, 'Michels was very hard. We were numbers for him. It was the beginning for Dutch football to be professional. Before that, Holland was a good football-playing country but not with the mentality of a professional. He changed all that, he changed the whole mentality of Dutch football.'

As with several other players, Barry Hulshoff, for example, Piet Keizer would later experience a strained relationship with Michels but, in those early days, the respect that the new coach established was clear. Michels improved players' conditions of employment and he demanded things in return. For anyone unwilling to accept the new regime, the consequences were clear. Keizer would later reflect, 'When Michels took over,

---

28 https://www.champions-journal.com/1000/ajax-71

he changed the playing staff considerably, and he changed the training even more. His was the hardest physical preparation I ever had. We sometimes had four sessions a day. He also introduced the Italian system of taking the players away for a period of concentrated training before a big match. We would start work in the morning and carry on until the evening. He was by no means a miserable man, but he was very strict with the players and there were lots of arguments about discipline. The message was pretty clear; those who did not like it would have to leave.'[29]

Michels was an innovative coach but those new ideas did not replace the time-honoured practice of rigorous fitness, they were built on top of it, and were successful partly because of it.

The improvements on the field were the most noticeable, but there were important changes taking place in other spheres of the club. There needed to be, as Cruyff explained: 'When Michels arrived ... he shielded the team from the rest of the club's management, which [at the time] was completely amateur.'[30] This was the other side of the coin to Michels' work on the pitch and, had those changes not have happened, the new coach's efforts may have all been in vain. Together they delivered the 'revolution' that Menno Pot referred to, and Ajax prospered.

Jaap van Praag became president of the club in 1964. A lifelong fan, he had begun his working life in his father's music business before later branching out on his own after identifying the potential growth in gramophone records. It was the forerunner of various similar successful businesses and enterprises including a televised talent show. Upon

---

29 https://www.theguardian.com/news/2005/mar/04/guardianobituaries. football

30 Cruyff, Johan, *My Turn* (London: Macmillan, 2016).

becoming president, Van Praag sought to professionalise Ajax with the support of two fellow successful businessmen, real estate developer Maup Carensa and textile manufacturer Leo Horn. Both had been long-term investors, and Horn had offered several of the club's players paid work in the days before professionalism.

Van Praag's major financial support came from a different source; he was backed by the controversial brothers Freek and Wim van der Meijden. During the wartime German occupation, the Van der Meijdens' building contractor business had worked widely for the German forces and government they imposed on the country. Their company constructed barracks to house the occupying forces and, reportedly, even gun emplacements. From the distance of many years, it's inappropriate to state with any certainty the enthusiasm with which the work was undertaken, but such activity was hardly likely to generate sympathy among a Dutch population suffering the yoke of occupation, or even afterwards with such dark memories still deeply scarred into their memories.

Understandably, especially following the liberation, businesses such as the Van der Meijdens, and more specifically their owners, who had grown wealthy by such means, were viewed with suspicion and often shunned. It was an inevitable reaction, whether fully justified or not.

The brothers were both Ajax fans though, and sought to reinforce their rehabilitation, and increase influence, by bankrolling the club. They financially supported Van Praag's drive to win the presidency, and then reportedly provided the funds to bring in Michels and deliver on his aspirations of signing better players, and paying them increased wages.

Before Van Praag's presidency, very much reflecting Dutch football as whole, Ajax had been run on a largely amateurish ad hoc basis, somewhat akin to a weekend hobby, by people with more important things on their mind during weekdays. Finance came in from wealthy benefactors who were asked, or at times offered, to underwrite specific fees paid to bring players in and then sometimes to provide them with part-time employment in the days before professionalism, or when wages were too low to sustain anything like a reasonable lifestyle. It meant that players were compelled to work during the day, often in strenuous jobs, train in the evening and then play at the weekend. It was hardly a recipe for success – and it showed. Van Praag, supported by his new backers, revolutionised the club, instituting a much more organised and professional regime that could support Michels and his aspirations.

* * *

1966/67 – Domestic double, Liverpool glory and Dukla Prague despair

Since the end of World War Two, Ajax had been Dutch champions on two occasions. Each time they had failed to build on the success, but the first domestic triumph achieved under Michels would be very different. On 22 September 1966 they played the seventh friendly game of the season with the list interspersed among five Eredivisie matches. Quite why the traditional round of pre-season games extended into the Eredivisie fixture list isn't clear, but they certainly brought an avalanche of goals. Among the lesser lights such as AGOVV, Noordwijk, Spartaan '20, JOS and Roodenburg, Michels also pitched his team against Aston Villa and CSKA Sofia. Across those seven games Ajax scored 59 goals and conceded just four. It could be suggested that a few of those games hardly comprised a contest at all, of course. For example, Spartaan conceded no fewer than 21 goals. In those five league fixtures, mixed up among the plethora of friendlies, however, Ajax fared no worse.

On 14 August they visited Elinkwijk in Utrecht. Five goals clear at half-time, they eased down in the second period and finished with a 7-0 win. At home to NAC the following week, they put a further four goals past the visitors, conceding just one in reply. The next fixture took them to Enschede to face FC Twente. Another win, albeit by a reduced margin, looked on the cards when Klaas Nuninga put Ajax ahead, but a late goal by Pahlplatz spoilt the 100 per cent record. The old warning about tweaking a tiger's tail was probably apposite after that game as a 5-0 win at home over DWS, a 4-2 victory against MVV in Maastricht and a 5-0 home win against Sparta Rotterdam followed.

The scene was set for the sort of domestic season that would eclipse even the glory days of Jack Reynolds. At the end of the 34-game league programme Ajax had bucked the trend of the club's previous postwar title-winning teams and retained the championship, finishing five points clear of Feyenoord. The astonishing statistic of the season, though, was that Ajax scored 122 goals in those 34 matches. The next highest was Feyenoord's 81. Ajax's tally averages out at 3.59 goals per game and puts the seemingly unbeatable record of Buckingham's team in 1959/60 of 109, averaging more than 3.23, comfortably into the shade. With such dominance of domestic football, it's hardly surprising that Ajax also won the KNVB Cup, thanks to another Nuninga goal in extra time seeing off NAC Breda in the final. Cruyff had scored an impressive 34 goals in just 33 league games and 41 in 42 appearances across all competitions. Henk Groot, who Michels had brought back to Ajax from Feyenoord the previous year, scored 25 league goals, as did Nuninga. Suurbier was now clearly a regular starter in the team, and Hulshoff featured in a third of the league fixtures.

Michels was casting his eye further afield, however. Dominating domestic Dutch football would not sate his hunger for success. Ajax's title win of 1965/66 had granted them a return to the European Cup. It was their first foray into the continent's premier club competition since Buckingham's team were unceremoniously eliminated by the Norwegian amateur side Fredrikstad. On 12 July 1966, Ajax played the home leg of their first-round tie at the Olympisch Stadion in front of more than 50,000 fans against the Turkish champions, Beşiktaş.

Goalkeeper Gerrit 'Gert' Bals was another of Michels' recruits in his first season at the De Meer, signing him from PSV where he had won the Dutch league in 1962/63, and he was in goal for the match against Beşiktaş. Deployed in Michels' 4-2-4 formation favoured at the time, the defence comprised of Suurbier, Anton Pronk, skipper Frits Soetekouw and Theo van Duivenbode. For Soetekouw, this would be his last season with Ajax. When Ajax were eliminated Michels was so furious at his erstwhile captain that he would never play for the club again, and was swiftly transferred to PSV. Van Duivenbode would suffer a not too dissimilar fate a couple years later when considered surplus to requirements by Michels, but would enjoy a delicious slice of revenge soon afterwards. The two midfield players were Groot and Bennie Muller, who had joined the club's youth team in 1956 and stayed with Ajax until 1970, before moving to Holland Sport. Swart started on the right of the four-man forward line with Cruyff and Nuninga inside and Keizer on the left. Due to an apparent colour clash, Ajax changed to all-red shirts for the game.

The game got off to an encouraging start for Michels' team after quarter of an hour. Awarded a free kick around 20 metres from goal, Keizer took advantage of Beşiktaş's decision not to erect a defensive wall and fired in a shot, striking the ball with the outside of his left foot. In goal, Necmi Mutlu was halfway through a 12-year career that would see him play more than 250 games for Beşiktaş. Such an experienced custodian should surely have had little problem dealing with the shot, which was hit firmly, but perhaps heading only a metre or so to his left. By striking with the outside of his foot, however, Keizer had departed spin on the ball and, as Mutlu fell to his left, the shot arced back and passed through his legs into the net.

A one-goal lead would have been a fragile advantage to take back to Istanbul, but with the last minutes of the second period draining away it appeared likely that it it would be what Ajax would take with them seven days later. With four minutes to play, however, Keizer hit a long cross from the left across to Bennie Muller closing in from the right. The midfielder hit a rising shot past Mutlu to double the advantage.

Three days later, Ajax visited HV Sittardia with a team featuring just one change as Co Prins replaced Groot. Whether it was to do with the aftereffects of the Beşiktaş game, thoughts being on the journey to Istanbul for the return leg three days later, or just one of those matches, Ajax were held to a draw after taking a first-half lead through Cruyff. Either unperturbed by the result, or keen to give the team an opportunity to redeem themselves, Michels then selected an unchanged team for the game in the intimidating atmosphere of the Mithat Pasa Stadyumu.

An early goal for the home team could have made the tie difficult but, despite pressure from Beşiktaş, urged on by 34,000 fans, the game was still scoreless at the break, Bals dealing comfortably with a couple of efforts from long range. Ajax had returned to their normal shirts and looked comfortable as the home fans became frustrated with their team as they failed to eat into the deficit. Eight minutes after the restart, however, that changed. Faruk Karadogan fought for a long pass with the Ajax central defence, nodded the ball forward into the penalty area, and fired low into Bals's right-hand corner. The goalkeeper was well beaten. Both the tie – and the stadium – were suddenly alive again.

The tension lasted for around eight minutes as Beşiktaş pressed, but Cruyff would deflate Turkish hopes. Cleverly gaining possession, he drifted forward, swaying past a defender before crossing for Swart to fire home the equaliser. It was a key moment, and not long afterwards a chance fell to the home team but was played wide of the post. It was their last opportunity. Breaking forward in the final minute with the home defence spreadeagled, Keizer cut in, swayed left, then right, before firing the concluding goal home. Ajax had advanced to the quarter-finals and would face Liverpool, the champions of England, who had beaten the Romanian team Petrolul Ploieşti 2-0 in a play-off after their aggregate scores had been tied. There would be no need for such a deciding issue in the game between Rinus Michels' team and that of Bill Shankly. The aggregate margin was decisive.

Before facing the Merseysiders a couple of months later though, there were Eredivisie issues to take care of. Ajax would complete eight fixtures in that time, seven of them in the league, with a friendly against FC Köln thrown in for good measure. The game against the German club would see Barry Hulshoff claim his first Ajax goal, although some references state it as an own goal by Köln's Rumors. Young *libero* Hulshoff would play 14 games that season as he began to establish himself in the XI alongside Suurbier, Keizer and Cruyff. The nucleus of the team that would dominate Europe a few years later was taking shape.

The game against Köln ended in a 1-1 draw, but it was the only one that Ajax failed to win during the gap between the triumph over Beşiktaş and the tie against Liverpool. Across those matches Ajax scored 30 goals, conceding just nine. A five-goal demolition of arch-rivals Feyenoord and an 8-3 goal glut against GVOV in the game before Liverpool visited the Netherlands were of particular mention. Approaching the meeting with the Reds, confidence would not have been an issue for Michels' team.

That confidence was hardly reflected in the press, however, especially in England, where Dutch football was still largely seen as amateurish in both format and style. Sjaak Swart recalled, 'Everyone in England asked, "Who is Ajax?"'[31] In contrast, Liverpool were competing in their third season of European competition having reached the semi-final of the European Cup and the final of the Cup Winners' Cup in the two previous campaigns. It was a pedigree enhanced by the presence of Roger Hunt and Ian Callaghan, who had been part of Alf Ramsey's World Cup-winning England squad a few months earlier. The previous season, Liverpool had also secured their seventh league title, the second in three seasons. It was probably Shankly's first great team, and was widely accepted to be the best that English football had to offer. A place in the last eight of the competition seemed destined for Merseyside – at least that was the story in England.

The seventh day of December 1966 saw Amsterdam clouded in a thick blanket of fog, with conditions at the Olympisch Stadion hardly ideal for watching, let alone playing, a game of football. A 24-hour postponement appeared likely but, with Liverpool due to face Manchester United in a crucial league match three days later, Shankly was concerned about

---

31 https://www.champions-journal.com/1000/ajax-71

the consequences for the weekend had there been a delay. In the end the decision was left with Italian referee Antonio Sbardella, who decided that the game should go ahead. More than 55,000 fans crowded into the stadium, but many were denied the opportunity of seeing the entire game as visibility at any distance greater than 50 metres or so was obscured by a haze of fog. It feels malignly obtuse that fate deigned to cloak the match in this blanket of haze. It denied both those in attendance, and many others watching on television, a full view of the events, leaving just grainy, grey video clips, as Ajax's football shone like a beacon and dazzled the best team in English football.

Michels selected Blas in goal behind a back four of Suubier, Pronk, Soetekouw and Van Duivenbode. Groot and Muller were the midfield pairing and Swart, Cruyff, Nuninga and Cees de Wolf, stepping in for Keizer, formed the four-man attack. Although some references suggest a different formation, the majority say Liverpool also lined up in 4-2-4. Shankly had Tommy Lawrence in goal with Chris Lawler, Ron Yeats, Tommy Smith and Bobby Graham comprising a formidable defence. Willie Stevens and Geoff Strong were in midfield. Callaghan and Peter Thompson had the flanks with Hunt and Ian St John as the spearhead. That illustrious forward line would see little of the ball across the 90 minutes, but that had very little to do with the prevailing meteorological conditions.

Liverpool wore an all-red strip for the first time in their existence. Ajax were completely in white, bereft of their normal red stripe. Their achromatic appearance was perhaps fitting, though, as from the first whistle to the last they played like wraiths, unencumbered by earthly restrictions, flitting in and out of the gloom and appearing as if from nowhere, often leaving their visitors to forlornly chase shadows.

The first goal arrived inside three minutes. It was a herald of what was to follow. Swart wriggled down the right flank and past two defenders, but Yeats came across to put the ball out of play for a throw-in. The wideman took the throw himself towards the near post where it was clipped across Lawrence's goal. Cees de Wolf is widely accredited as being on the end of the cross to convert, but some references offer Groot as opening the scoring. If Liverpool fans thought it was a freak goal and their team would quickly recover, their hopes would be dashed on 17 minutes when Cruyff scored after another scything run by Swart and an effort by Nuninga had been blocked by Lawrence.

Despite the fog, the difference between the teams was clear enough for all to see. Even having Suurbier limping as a passenger at right-back hardly seemed to put a stumble into Ajax's stride and they scored again on 38 minutes when Nuninga fired home after a period of goalmouth bagatelle following a free kick. 'This is absolute disaster for Liverpool,' opined Gerry Loftus commentating for the BBC. Three goals down, and looking stunned by the shock and awe of the football being played against them, getting into half-time with no further damage looked an appealing option for Liverpool, but with three minutes to play they conceded again. 'Oh no, not another one!' was all Loftus could offer as Nuninga bundled the ball over the line for the fourth goal. At the break, Loftus considered the 4-0 scoreline to be 'incredible', but such an assessment was surely based on preconceptions of hubris held before the game rather than after watching the 45 minutes of action on the field. The lead was fully justified, and its extent hardly flattered Ajax.

In the second period the play was more even but, when Groot fired in a fierce free kick on 75 minutes, any lingering hopes of a Liverpool revival were surely extinguished, and

Lawler's injury-time goal was only of interest to statisticians. At the end of the game Loftus offered up hope of Liverpool turning around the tie at Anfield in what he suggested would be an 'exciting' second leg, but it sounded unconvincing, whistling in the dark as the fog thickened, as did the gloom among Liverpool fans. For many, the convincing victory in Amsterdam was Ajax's announcement that they were entering the big time in European football. Looking back on that game, Ronald Jager considers it to be hugely significant in the development of Michels' team and their *totaalvoetbal*: 'The 5-1 win over Liverpool in 1966 was in my opinion the first time Ajax showed their potential, and Piet Keizer wasn't even available.' It was true; without one of their key players, Ajax had torn the English champions asunder.

In typically belligerent fashion, Shankly sought to keep Merseyside hopes alive with confident defiance, claiming the result was 'ridiculous' and that Ajax had played 'defensive football'. The return, he promised, would be very different. 'We never play well against defensive teams. Ajax got lucky. Next week, in Liverpool, we'll beat them 7-0,' he told the press. Motivation is very fine of course, but to call Ajax's display 'defensive' was stretching things way beyond the breaking point of credulity. Cruyff's assessment – 'Everything Michels was putting in place was working. In a technical sense, the English champions were blown away'[32] – seemed much more reflective of the way the game had played out.

A week later, Shankly's confidence would be put to the test in front of 53,000 fanatical Liverpool supporters at a seething Anfield. This time it was Liverpool changing strip to yellow shirts and black shorts with Ajax adding that now-

---

32 Cruyff, Johan, *My Turn* (London: Macmillan, 2016).

familiar broad red stripe to the plain white shirts of the first leg. Shankly was able to bring Gordon Milne back into his midfield and Michels returned a fit-again Keizer to Ajax's left flank, in place of De Wolf.

Needing to score four times, unsurprisingly Liverpool attacked with intensity early on, but Ajax were poised to counter-attack with Swart and, of course, Cruyff looking particularly dangerous. Inevitably Ajax were compelled to ride their luck for periods of the first half as Liverpool stormed forward, trying to validate their manager's bold prediction of a seven-goal win. Thompson struck the bar for the home side in the third minute, after a slicing through pass by Yeats, but the ball flew up and away. Geoff Strong headed wide from close range after a Stevenson free kick found him lamentably unmarked. At the break, though, the scoreline was still blank. Liverpool were struggling to find a way past Michels' defence, and any goal, let alone seven, remained frustratingly elusive.

Five minutes after the restart, the killer blow arrived as Liverpool squandered possession around halfway and Keizer swept forward down the left flank before passing to Nuninga, who controlled and laid the ball square to an unmarked Cruyff. The young forward confidently drove past Lawrence, and even Loftus was forced to concede it was all up now for the Merseysiders. 'I think that must be the end of the Liverpool hopes,' he accepted with undisguised reluctance.

It was, despite Hunt tapping home from a few yards after St John had set up the simple opportunity ten minutes later. 'It brought a bare glimmer of hope to Liverpool,' Loftus suggested, qualifying it by adding that the Reds were now '6-2 down on aggregate'. There were brief half-chances for a second Liverpool goal, but with less than 20 minutes to play that glimmer was extinguished as Cruyff slid in to score his and Ajax's second. Once more he benefitted from enterprising work by Keizer, supported by Nuninga. Hunt would equalise on the night inside the final ten minutes but it was a goal more for pride than anything else. Liverpool, the English champions, had been well beaten by the little-known Dutch club with the prodigiously talented teenage Johan Cruyff leading the way. Anfield had witnessed Ajax's coming-out party, and the birth of a legend.

It was an occasion not lost on Swart as he later reflected on the tie, Shankly's comments and his sporting attitude at the end of the Anfield game:

'Liverpool's coach, Bill Shankly, said after losing 5-1 that his team would win 7-0 at home. But it was 2-2 and afterwards he came to the dressing room to say well done. I'll never forget that. They had a great team with the likes of Tommy Smith, Peter Thompson, Ian Callaghan and Ron Yeats and we beat them 5-1. From that moment, everything changed. Everyone talked about Ajax.'[33] Michels knew there was still a way to go before his team was ready to conquer Europe, but they were on the way, adding in the same interview, 'Those two games [against Liverpool] signified the birth of Ajax at international level.'

It was a significant marker on the club's progress and established their pedigree on the European stage, but there would be trouble waiting further down the road. The quarter-final draw paired Ajax with Czechoslovakia's Dukla Prague, but it would be the first day of March 1967 before European football would return following the winter break. In the interim, Ajax turned their attention to domestic matters. There were ten Eredivisie games to be completed before the home leg against the Czechs. Ajax would win seven of them, draw one and suffer just two defeats. In between, there

---

33 https://www.champions-journal.com/1000/ajax-71

was a friendly played against the Belgian club Anderlecht on 1 February. Up until that point, Michels' team had been unbeaten across half a dozen league encounters, winning five times, and drawing 1-1 against DWS in the other game.

One of those wins came on Boxing Day 1966 when Ajax entertained Elinkwijk at the De Meer. Despite the victory's proximity to the season of goodwill, there was little sentiment about their performance as they rattled in eight goals without reply. An own goal by Van der Merkt in the first period had given Ajax a narrow lead at the break, but the team from Utrecht were submerged under a cascade of goals after the restart with Nuninga netting a hat-trick and both Cruyff and Swart bagging a brace. The game was perhaps more significant for the debut of a new player.

Velibor Vasović had officially joined Ajax on 19 October 1966, moving to Amsterdam from Partizan Belgrade after the Yugoslavian club had lost the 1966 European Cup Final to Real Madrid. Playing as a *libero* in the final, Vasović had put his team ahead ten minutes after the break but quickfire replies, first by Amancio, and then Fernando Serena, had seen the Spaniards over the line. Vasović would stay in Amsterdam for five seasons and become the club's first non-Dutch captain. The move cost Ajax some 25,000 guilders but Van Praag would later describe the fee as 'a bargain'.[34] Ronald Jager wouldn't dissent from that opinion. He described Vasović as one of the 'key players' due to his experience and someone who 'taught the team discipline'.

Despite Vasović's experience of playing at the heart of the defence, Michels initially placed him into Ajax's midfield, leaving the central pariing of Pronk and Soetekouw in tandem. It was a move he would repeat when introducing defenders

---

34 https://www.afc-ajax.info/en/soccer-player/Velibor-Vasović#matches

to the team across the years. *Totaalvoetbal* demanded that defenders understood the role of midfield players if they were to be fully attuned to the discipline. Giving Vasović his debut there in such a comfortable game offered the Yugoslav a gentle opportunity to integrate himself into the style of the team, but his move to a more familiar position would not be long delayed.

Following his debut, Vasović had a further five starts in his midfield role before he was dropped to the bench for three games. In each of those he entered as substitute. He wasn't involved in the games against Dukla Prague but the events in the second leg would lead to his elevation into the team on a regular basis. Vasović knew he had been signed to be the older, experienced head of a young team, and once Michels deemed him to be ready, there was a big role for him to play: 'Michels made this plan to play very offensive football. We discussed it. I was the architect, together with Michels, of the aggressive way of defending.'[35] It may read like self-promoting hubris from Vasović, but Cruyff also recognised the significance of his arrival, describing it as taking Ajax 'one step closer to total football'.[36]

Ironically, despite their table-topping form, Ajax went into the game against the Czech champions following a rare defeat. Visiting the Philips Stadion on 26 February, Michels' team faced PSV Eindhoven in an Eredivisie fixture. The 11 that played Liverpool at Anfield, and would face the Czechs a few days later, should have gone ahead just past the half-hour mark, but Swart failed to convert from the penalty spot. That profligacy proved costly as goals from Verdonk and then Schrijvers put the home team on the road to victory. A late

---

35 Winner, David, *Brilliant Orange* (London: Bloomsbury, 2000).
36 Cruyff, Johan, *My Turn* (London: Macmillan, 2016).

Pronk goal reduced the arrears but failed to recover the game. In comparison, the Czechs were on a run of five straight victories. If Liverpool had been punished for underestimating Ajax, anyone from Amsterdam doing so with regard to Dukla Prague would have been making a similar error.

The game at the Olympisch Stadion was a frustrating time for the Ajax fans. Although their team dominated much of the possession, Dukla Prague, with goalkeeper Ivo Victor – who would star for the national team in Mexico three years later – and a disciplined defence rebuffed the early home attacks. The break was reached with the scoreline still blank. Ajax did have the ball in the net ahead of half-time but the goal was ruled out by Azerbaijani referee Tofiq Bahramov, who had gained fame – or infamy, depending on your perspective – as the 'Russian linesman' who decided Geoff Hurst's second goal had crossed the line in the World Cup Final six months earlier.

Swart eventually breached the Czech lines five minutes after the restart, powerfully firing Ajax ahead at the far post and offering little chance to Victor, as the goalkeeper hesitated to collect a back-pass from a defender. As the home fans celebrated in song, it was expected that their team would go on to establish a healthy lead to take to central Europe the following week. It wasn't to be. Dukla had offered hints of danger on the break but on the hour, when Ivan Mráz crashed the ball past Bals, it was a surprise from which Ajax failed to recover and the game ended in a 1-1 draw. Unlike with the Liverpool tie, there was no domestic fixture between the two European legs for Ajax to negotiate and, seven days later, Michels sent the same 11 out to try and turn things around.

Compared to the 55,765 fans who had watched the first leg in Amsterdam, the compact Stadion Juliska in Prague housed only a third of that number, and a significant portion of those had travelled from the Netherlands in boisterous mood, confident of seeing their team get the conclusive result that had been denied them back in Amsterdam. A few even invaded the pitch flaunting banners and Ajax flags ahead of the game, elaborately displaying their undoubted optimism. At the final whistle, though, the scene would be very different, with the Prague fans celebrating and rushing on to the pitch to acclaim their heroes.

The game followed a strangely mirrored course to the first leg, with one vital difference. The first half was competitive, with the Czechs having much more of an even share of the play than in Amsterdam, but at the break the game remained scoreless. Once more it was Swart giving Ajax the lead shortly after the restart, scoring from close range after Nuninga had worked the opening and supplied the pass. Once more though, the advantage would be short-lived. Seven minutes later, a robust challenge by Pronk on Mráz, the man who had equalised in Amsterdam, was adjudged to be a penalty and Stanislav Štrunc fired high into the left of Bals's goal for the equaliser, with the goalkeeper comprehensively beaten.

Ajax had been on top for most of the play across the two games but, when the decisive moment came, it would go against them. An attack from the left saw the ball played into the Ajax box. Amid missed opportunities to clear, and panic, it was skipper Frits Soetekouw who headed the ball past Bals and into his own net with three minutes left. Michels was furious at having seen his team dominate their opponents across two games and still be eliminated. Much as the Liverpool game had been a milestone on Ajax's journey, so too was this night, but for a different reason.

Michels determined to reshape his team and the central defensive partnership of Soetekouw and Pronk – both of whom the coach deemed responsible for each of the Prague goals – was discarded. Soetekouw would never kick a ball for the club again and was sold to PSV Eindhoven later that year. Pronk survived but, as time moved on, he was often moved into a midfield position as well as still making occasional appearances in defence.

Despite Michels being convinced that his team let him down against the Czechs, others have a different theory. In *Brilliant Orange*, David Winner related how many of the Ajax players were superstitious, and how that may have conspired in the defeat. Their physiotherapist had forgotten to pack his lucky hat and his wife couldn't send the usual ossenworst sausage as the butcher's shop was closed. Much more pragmatic, Michels declined to blame the missing hat or absent sausage, and focused on the performance of the players.

For the next game, in the Eredivisie against DOS, the centre of Ajax's defence comprised Vasović and the emerging Barry Hulshoff. For the following four years or so the pair would be the bedrock of the back line. Vasović was the elder statesman and Hulshoff his young apprentice, adding valuable experience to his burgeoning talent. The team was still far from the finished product as Vasović later acknowledged, but another piece of the jigsaw had been slotted into place. Ajax and Michels would have to be content with the domestic double for the season, but the European Cup remained an itch – which the Eredivisie title would offer another opportunity to scratch in the following season.

* * *

1967/68 – *Another league title and a Real European roadblock*

Arie Haan joined Ajax in the early period of the new season. As with Nuninga, he made the move from amateur club WVV. At the time the KNVB had mandated a fixed fee for any player joining a professional club from an amateur organisation and, in October 1967, Ajax paid the sum of 3,000 guilders to WVV and officially signed Haan. The midfielder had just turned 19 and would have to wait for a real opportunity to establish himself in the team. That wouldn't happen until the 1970/71 season when he played 15 games, but the early friendlies of the new season, plus the semi-final and final of the KNVB Cup, offered a chance for the teenager to display his potential.

Before the Eredivisie got under way, Ajax played three friendlies. They travelled to Cambur and won 2-1 on 3 August, then three days later Anderlecht visited the De Meer and were beaten 3-1. Finally, on 9 August, Everton travelled to Amsterdam and were beaten 3-0. Michels used these games to experiment with players; Pronk returned to defence and Hulshoff was moved into midfield with Groot also advanced from his midfield role to the forward line. Haan even had the chance for an appearance from the bench against Cambur.

The real business started on 13 August and Ajax began the campaign to retain their title in fine style, easing past Go Ahead Eagles 2-0 at the De Meer. They then added a further three victories and, by the time they visited the De Kuip to face Feyenoord on 3 September, they not only had a 100 per cent record but hadn't conceded a single league goal. Ben Peeters had been promoted to take over from Austrian Wilhelm Kment at the De Kuip and, the following year, the young coach would take the Rotterdam club to a domestic double, denying Michels a fourth consecutive title. Before that, though, Feyenoord were already establishing themselves as Ajax's main domestic rivals and a header from Ruud Geels, who would later move to Amsterdam, from an indirect free kick inflicted their first defeat of the season.

Stung by the reverse, Ajax then went on a three-game goal spree. An 1-11 away win in a friendly against VV Egmondia was followed by a 7-1 Eredivisie home victory over RKSV Volendam, before another friendly brought nine goals without reply against GSV. During these games, Michels had shifted his players around. Hulshoff had played in midfield and defence, while Pronk was stationed next to Vasović when the towering young defender was deployed further forward. Three days after the rout of GSV, the new European campaign kicked off and Ajax were given the unenviable task of facing the Spanish aristocracy of Real Madrid. Four days earlier, the team that had dominated the early years of the European Cup had defeated Real Sociedad 9-1 in a La Liga encounter. The first-round draw had hardly done Ajax any favours.

On 20 September, the reigning champions of Spain, who had won their sixth European Cup in 1965/66, arrived at the Olympisch Stadion. Having lost their crown to eventual winners Internazionale in the quarter-finals the previous season, Miguel Muñoz was intent on taking his team back to the summit of European football. He had assembled a star-studded and experienced squad to help him achieve the aim.

In comparison, the Ajax team was still light on European experience and, despite the loss to Dukla Prague, this game would see Michels' players pitted against the strongest team they were yet to encounter in European competition. The coach was easing Hulshoff into a regular starting position and, after a few games playing in midfield, against the Spaniards he was posted on the left of the back four. Suurbier was on the right, with Vasović and Pronk in the centre. Groot and Muller were paired in the middle of the field. Swart and Keizer had the wing positions in attack with Cruyff and Nuninga inside. A crowd of almost 56,000 watched Michels' European apprentices take on the masters of the game.

The early encounters were busy as both teams probed for an opening, and when the first goal arrived on 17 minutes it owed more to a defensive blunder than enterprising attack. The ball was swept out to the wing and Keizer floated a cross into the area. Cruyff and Nuninga were outnumbered by four white-shirted defenders, but a glancing header by the former caused panic in the visitors' defence as it dropped towards the latter. An attempted clearance only served to play the ball back to Cruyff who hooked in a shot that bounced twice on its journey towards goal. Since 1958, the Spanish newspaper *Marca* has awarded the Zamora Trophy to the goalkeeper with the lowest ratio of goals conceded to games played in La Liga. In 1967/68 the award would go to Real Madrid's Andrés Junquera. His attempt to keep Cruyff's mishit shot, however, suggests that he must have performed so much better in other games. It's only a slight exaggeration to say the ball merely bobbled towards the net but Junquera conspired to let it slip under his body and, despite a desperate flailing attempt to prevent it crossing the line, Ajax had the lead. The nature of the goal mattered little to the jubilant Ajax fans who celebrated wildly.

The lead lasted for 20 minutes or so but *Los Blancos* were hardly likely to let the home team have things their own way and, with the break ten minutes away, José Pirri played a neat one-two on the edge of the Ajax area before firing high past Bals to equalise. The second half saw both teams have chances to score again but they all came to nought. A plunging save from Bals facing a one-on-one, as time ticked away, was probably the closest to a deciding moment in the game. At full time it was the Spaniards in the box seat with the home leg in Madrid's Estadio Santiago Bernabéu to come on 20 October.

Before travelling to Spain, Ajax played four games – two friendlies and two in the league, scoring 22 times without conceding a goal. If there was a need for a confidence boost ahead of taking on Real Madrid again, sitting top of the table and in sparkling goalscoring form meant Ajax had it, and they began with the same 11 as in the home leg. In comparison, Real Madrid's recent form had been far less impressive. Since the draw in Amsterdam, a goalless draw away to Real Zaragoza and a disappointing 2-2 result at home to Espanyol meant that the Spanish champions hadn't won in three games. Of the 120,000 fans in the stadium though, all but the 3,000 who had travelled from Amsterdam expected that run to end against Ajax.

The first half was tight and close, with the evergreen Francisco Gento, just ten days short of his 34th birthday, a thorn in Ajax's side – the Dutch team's left side mainly. Cruyff was similarly threatening at the other end, and one run past three Madrid players looked to have opened up a chance as he scampered into the box but an experienced defensive block and Junquera diving on the loose ball killed Dutch hopes. The deadlock hadn't been broken by the break.

Thirteen minutes after the restart that changed after a dazzling run by Sanchis created space on the edge of the area for Gento. Receiving the ball, the veteran coolly controlled before sweeping inside Bals's far post with his left foot. Now ahead in the tie for the first time, the celebrating fans expected the home team to complete the job. It would not have been surprising if the Dutch had wilted under the pressure, but they kept a foothold in the game and ten minutes later a free kick played into the area by Swart was nodded home by Groot from around the penalty spot. The header was well-directed towards Junquera's top-right corner, but the stumbling half-dive by the goalkeeper looked a mere token gesture. Positioned in one corner of the stadium, it was now the turn of the isolated pocket of Ajax fans to celebrate – and they did.

Having fought their way back into the game it was Ajax who threatened most to avoid extra time. A scything run by Swart and pass created a chance for Nuninga, but a challenge as he unleashed his shot meant the effort was screwed wide. With time ebbing away the best chance fell to Cruyff. Keizer cut in from the left and drew two defenders towards him before squaring to a waiting Cruyff standing by the penalty shot. His effort was tired, though, and Junquera redeemed his earlier misdemeanour by diving to his right to save. The tie was eventually settled as a tiring Ajax back line were undone when a Veloso run and shot from outside the area beat Bals ten minutes into the first period of extra time.

The loss against Dukla Prague had annoyed Michels as Ajax had been eliminated despite being the better team. Against Real Madrid that was far less the case, with perhaps the main difference being the experience of top European competition possessed by the Spanish club's players. It was still part of the learning process for Ajax though. Michels' team would benefit from the experience, as the following season's European Cup would show, but there was still plenty of developing to do. Vasović later commented that this side, '[Was] two steps behind the real Ajax. It was half the team that would go to the top.'[37]

Ajax ensured that they would have another chance at the European Cup by retaining the Eredivisie title, three points clear of Feyenoord. The key game came in March 1968 when Ruud Suurendonk scored to secure a 1-0 win over the Rotterdam club, 20 minutes after arriving from the bench to replace Keizer. Success in the KNVB Cup would have meant another domestic double and, when they were paired in the semi-final with mid-table FC Twente at the De Meer, things

---

37 Winner, David, *Brilliant Orange* (London: Bloomsbury, 2000).

were looking promising. It would, however, be a game with plenty of drama and, what to modern eyes seems, a strange conclusion.

As well as missing Cruyff, Michels had to cope without Suurbier who was ill and Bennie Muller who was on compassionate leave due to family circumstances. Bals was in goal behind a back four of Suurendonk, Pronk, Vasović and Van Duivenbode. Making his competitive debut, Haan was partnered in midfield by Hulshoff, with Swart, Swedish forward Inge Danielsson, who had joined from Helsingborgs in December 1967, Nuninga and Keizer as the front four.

Things didn't start well for Ajax. Just a dozen minutes in substitute Groot was introduced into the action to replace the injured Nuninga, but there were no goals until the 63rd minute when Jeuring put the visitors ahead. It looked like being enough to send Twente into the final but Keizer drove home directly from a free kick in the 89th minute to force extra time. With four minutes of the additional half an hour remaining, Pronk popped up in the opposition box to surely put Ajax into the final. This time, however, it was the visitors enjoying a last-minute reprieve when De Vries levelled in the dying seconds, and the game would now be decided by a penalty shoot-out. Unlike today, however, the format was that one team would take all five of their penalties, one after the other. Then the opposition would take their five, or as many up to that number as was required to settle the issue.

Efficiently, Keizer, Groot. Pronk, Van Duivenbode and Vasović converted to give Ajax five out of five and pile maximum pressure on to the Twente players, now compelled to match them or be eliminated. Drost converted first but, when De Vries stepped up to reprise his last-minute equaliser, he came up short and Ajax were in the final where they would face ADO Den Haag at the Zuiderpark Stadion in June 1968.

Ajax had one more league fixture to play to secure the Eredivisie title. Ironically, that game would also be against ADO but, whereas the final would be an away game for Ajax, this fixture was at the De Meer. Cruyff returned to replace the injured Nuninga who joined Suurbier and Muller on the unavailable list, and Groot replaced Haan. An early goal after three minutes looked to have opened the door for Feyenoord to catch Ajax, but Danielsson equalised within 60 seconds and, when Keizer put the home team ahead after 37 minutes after neat work by Swart, they saw out the game to confirm their status as champions once again.

Suurbier was back for the final, replacing Suurendonk in an otherwise unchanged back line from the league game a week earlier. Muller also returned, replacing Haan alongside Hulshoff. The teenager dropped to the bench but would see action as the game progressed. Groot moved forward to partner Danielsson in the centre of the forward line with Swart and Keizer on the flanks.

As at the De Meer, Den Haag struck first through Schoenmaker after 23 minutes. This time, however, instead of conceding immediately, they quickly added a second through Aarts just three minutes later. At the break the lead was still intact. Haan replaced Groot for the second period, but Keizer's goal, ten minutes after the restart wasn't enough to rescue the game. For fans of Den Haag the victory felt long overdue. It was their fifth final in the last ten years, and they had lost all of the previous four. A young Austrian coach had arrived in 1962 and taken the club to three of those four losing finals before this victory over Ajax. He would later become very well known to Ajax, Michels, the club's players and indeed all of Dutch football as his career progressed. His name was Ernst Happel. A year later, he would take over as manager of Feyenoord and soon guide them to European Cup glory.

Before then Ajax would have a chance to reach that summit first, as Michels continued to chase his European Cup dream.

Domestically, teams facing the three-time Eredivisie champions were regularly lining up against Ajax with what Michels described as a 'wall' of defenders, looking to, at best steal a point, at worst, avoid a severe defeat. The development of *totaalvoetbal* offered a way to demolish those walls. Encouraging players to rotate positions as the game dictated was fairly easy in one respect. Most players would be keen to join the attack but perhaps the reverse doesn't always apply. The approach would only work if all players were committed to it. Having the system is one thing but it only works when you have the players to deliver on it. Some were already at the club and, over the coming seasons, the other players who would help to make *totaalvoetbal* the dominant force in European football would be added.

A young Ruud Krol was contracted to the B team for this season, but wouldn't enter the first-team reckoning until 1968/69 when he played in a single Eredivisie game against DWS in December 1968, making his bow on 74 minutes as a substitute for Keizer. His first start came the following March in a friendly against Schalke, playing at left-back. In the same game the teenage Haan also saw action, replacing Keizer from the bench. Only 5,000 fans at the De Meer watched as Krol, who would become an Ajax legend as they conquered Europe, and captained the team for many years, first started for the club, and Haan continued his development.

Heinz Stuy was also contracted to Ajax. He wouldn't play a first-team game in 1967/68 and appeared in seven minor fixtures the following term before making his Eredivisie debut in April 1969, and adding his second appearance in June of the same year. The unassuming and often unheralded goalkeeper would be the man to gradually replace Bals, and had been established as first choice by the time the 33-year-old was transferred to Vitesse Arnhem in June 1970.

Opinions of Stuy vary among people who studied this era of Ajax. Ronald Jager, for example, suggests, 'In my opinion Bals was the best goalkeeper ever in the Netherlands who didn't play one single cap for the Dutch national team. Cruyff liked Bals very much as a goalie, much more than Stuy. But with a central defending duo of Hulshoff and Vasović – and as from the 71/72 season Horst Blankenburg in the place of Vasović – there wasn't much need for a goalie who was very good in playing soccer himself. Stuy [would play] in three EC finals in a row. A 2-0 win, 2-0 win and 1-0 win. So, no goals in the three finals against him. You could say [Ajax] were by far the best team those three seasons, but [Stuy] deserves the credit.'

In fact, Stuy became, and at the time of writing remains, the only goalkeeper to play in three successive European Cup finals without conceding a goal. And yet Jager suggests that Stuy may not have been Michels' first choice as the replacement for Bals: 'Ajax tried to get Jan van Beveren in 1970 from Sparta, but [he] didn't come back to Amsterdam, his place of birth.' Van Beveren would later join PSV instead.

Stuy would also achieve another record that, according to Jager, still stands at the time of writing, and yet it's maintenance also seems to be tinged with less than the fullest of graces: 'After his career Stuy became a bit of a tragic man. He is – until today – the goalie who holds a clean sheet for the longest time in the Dutch Eredivisie (I believe it is 1,082 minutes). Impressive, but when [any goalkeeper is going] a long time without [conceding] a goal against him in the Eredivisie, [Stuy] gives flowers to the one who scores against that goalie. In the 1995/96 season Edwin van der Sar [kept clean sheets] for many matches from the beginning of the season. When Feyenoord's Clemens Zwijnenberg scored against Van der Sar, Stuy gave Zwijnenberg flowers. Van der Sar said in his biography [to] author Jaap Visser that he was disappointed in Stuy. Van der Sar, "He was like me an Ajax goalie and then being pleased and giving someone flowers who scores against his own club just to keep your own record, didn't make me happy. Since then, I am not a fan from Stuy anymore."'

So much of football, and indeed footballers, is about opinions and, although giving full credit for Stuy's success, it's clear that Jager has reservations about him. Conversely, Menno Pot speaks highly of the goalkeeper, be it on or off the pitch: 'And then there's the man who never gets a mention, the one who's always overlooked (an ironic choice of words, 'cos he's a massive man): Heinz Stuy, the goalkeeper. Three European Cup finals, three wins, three clean sheets. In the early years he used to play without gloves and catch the ball with one hand (he has absolutely enormous hands). He's still alive. A very sweet man.'

* * *

1968/69 – So near, yet so far; Benfica renaissance and Milan reality check

Despite the loss in the KNVB Cup Final, the previous term had still been largely successful. The league title had been retained, offering another chance for Ajax to compete in the continent's most prestigious club tournament.

The new season began on 7 June with the start of a series of friendly games, a dip into an early version of the Intertoto Cup and a brief pre-season tournament in Czechoslovakia. A week after that first game, a 3-1 Intertoto victory over Serie A club Torino, Ajax announced the signing of midfielder Gerrie Mühren from FC Volendam. Mühren had joined *Het Andere*

Oranje ('The Other Oranje'; labelled as such in deference to the Dutch national team) as a teenager in 1963 and, 22 by the time he moved to Amsterdam, had played well over 50 games for his hometown club. He would make his debut in the Slovan Bratislava 40 tournament, playing 45 minutes in each of Ajax's two games. From there, his integration into the team across the coming season would be significant, especially towards the end of the term as he became an increasingly important member of Michels' squad, predominantly in domestic fixtures. Later, he would also be instrumental in Cruyff becoming synonymous with the number 14 shirt.

The serious stuff began on 18 August as Ajax travelled to Deventer to play Go Ahead Eagles in their first Eredivisie game of the season. If Michels had been looking for a good start to his team's defence of the crown, he would have been disappointed. Cruyff was unavailable through injury, so Nuninga partnered Danielsson in the centre of the front four, with Swart and Keizer on the flanks. In defence, Suurbier, Vasović, Pronk and Van Duivenbode, lined up in front of Bals with Muller and Groot the midfield pairing. Things started well when Nuninga put the champions ahead ten minutes before half-time, but the second period would see a turnaround in fortunes. Twenty minutes after the restart Gerrit van Tilburg equalised for the home team and, after Hulshoff had replaced Keizer with 15 minutes to play, Hoekema hit the winner for Go Ahead inside the final five minutes.

The next game saw NAC visit the De Meer. Someone was always going to catch the backlash from Ajax's opening-day defeat, and the club from Breda were front and centre. Suurbier was unavailable so Suurendonk filled in at right-back, and Cruyff returned to replace Danielsson. At the break Ajax were comfortably ahead after goals by Cruyff and Keizer, and in the second half they really cut loose by scoring another six goals. The only blot on the day was when Visschers brought the score back to 5-1 on 70 minutes. A clean sheet would have been the perfect way for Bals to celebrate a century of appearances for the club.

Suurbier returned for the 1-0 win away to Sparta Rotterdam and Gerrie Mühren took his Eredivisie bow in the next game as Ajax eased to a 2-0 win over Fortuna SC. A 1-1 Intertoto Cup draw and then a 4-0 KNVB Cup win sent Ajax into their European Cup first round tie, against Bundesliga champions 1. FC Nürnberg. Not for the last time, the competition had been affected by political action in Europe. Following the Soviet Union's invasion of Czechoslovakia, UEFA decided to pair all of the eastern European entrants against each other, causing many to withdraw from the first two rounds. Ironically, one of the clubs that didn't follow this path were Spartak Trnava, champions of Czechoslovakia, and they would meet Ajax in the semi-finals.

Vasović and Muller had both been rested for the KNVB Cup game, with Hulshoff partnering Pronk in the centre of defence and Suurendonk in midfield, while Danielsson returned to the forward line. The European tie would see more changes – both in personnel and formation. In what would become the first-choice pairing, Hulshoff partnered the returning Vasović, with Suurbier and Van Duivenbode on the flanks of defence. Some resources suggest that Michels had a front four of Swart, Cruyff, Nuninga and Keizer, with Groot and Muller in midfield. The majority, however, differ and list the Ajax starting 11 as a foretaste of things to come. They quote Michels selecting a midfield trio for the opening away leg, comprising Groot, Muller and the retained Suurendonk. The front three, according to these accounts, were Swart, Cruyff and Keizer.

Whichever was the case, the game started badly as Volkert gave the Germans an early lead after six minutes. It took until the final ten minutes for Ajax to equalise when Cruyff headed home from Keizer's cross. While a single-goal defeat would not have been disastrous, the draw seemed to offer an open door for Ajax to progress. There were two Eredivisie games before the return leg. The first saw a scrappy 2-1 home win over NEC Nijmegen and the second was an even less satisfactory 1-1 draw away to DOS. Ajax's grip on the Eredivisie title was looking less than secure and, when Feyenoord later knocked them out of the KNVB Cup, the European competition became their main focus for the season.

There's less contention about the team selected by Michels for the second leg on 2 October. In a return to 4-2-4, Nuninga started alongside Cruyff, and Suurendonk was on the bench in an otherwise unchanged starting line-up. The German team had clearly arrived in Amsterdam with the intent to keep things tight and look for a break to conjure up an unlikely away goal. For the first 20 minutes or so they succeeded in frustrating the hosts, and particularly the crowd who were introduced to the sort of away team performance that would become very familiar at the De Meer, and indeed the Olympisch Stadion, across the next five years or so.

Midway through the first period, Ajax got the breakthrough that, to all intents and purpose, decided the tie. A left-wing corner was lofted in by Keizer and the diminutive Swart rose at the near post to guide the ball past Jürgen Rynio and inside the far post. At half-time, the lead was still statistically slender but, with the German club offering little going forward, it also seemed secure.

Soon after the restart, any lingering doubts about the outcome would be dismissed. On 51 minutes an attack prompted by Muller and continued by Nuninga invited

Cruyff to skip past his marker before crossing low towards the advancing Nuninga at the near post. A tangle of legs between the forward, two defenders and goalkeeper prevented Nuninga from finding the net, but he managed to flick the ball on towards the far post where Swart closed in and managed to bundle the ball into the net after his first effort struck the post, for his second goal of the game. Immediately swallowed up by a posse of photographers, keen to get a close-up of the goalscorer, the winger was quickly joined by his team-mates, now surely confident of victory.

With the game now won entering the final quarter of an hour, Michels removed the two-goal hero, sending on Suurendonk to replace him and reverting back to the 4-3-3 of the first leg. It seemed to have little effect on dousing Ajax's desire for more goals. Ten minutes later Keizer strode past a couple of challenges, driving down the right flank before being upended in the box as he deceived the third German. Northern Ireland referee John Adair pointed to the spot and Groot drove firmly home.

With the match now considerably past the point of being a contest of any real description, one Ajax fan decided to offer up a little comic relief. He invaded the pitch and led a dozen or so Dutch policeman, some with dogs, a merry dance around the ground, dashing in and out of the bemused players much as Cruyff did to opponents. It took a full three minutes before the culprit was apprehended in what was more of a bored and fatigued surrender than capture. He was then escorted from the field by at least half a dozen policeman, surely fearing if they released him from their armlock grasp they may never see him again. Three minutes later, perhaps inspired by the interloper, Cruyff performed his own tantalising and defiant dance before firing home the fourth goal. A controlled away performance followed by a dominating one at home was the ideal template for European success.

The second round would pitch Ajax up against Fenerbahçe, the champions of Turkey, with the first leg taking place on 13 November. In the interim, playing four Eredivisie games and the next round of the KNVB Cup saw Ajax rattle 24 goals, conceding just three, with Michels continuing to select the occasional 4-3-3 formation before resorting back to the more familiar 4-2-4. When the Turks arrived at the Olympisch Stadion, the team selected to face them looked like a traditional 4-2-4 but for much of the game played more like a 4-3-3, with Nuninga often dropping into the midfield. It was Nuninga who scored the first goal in a match dominated by the muddy condition of the pitch with a little under quarter of an hour played after Swart had created the chance. Five minutes later, a chance to go two clear was squandered when, unusually, Groot failed to convert from 12 yards. The home fans would have to wait until the 74th minute for the second goal to arrive, when Muller netted; the 2-0 victory looked both comfortable and satisfactory.

European success was hardly being matched in domestic competition. Before the second leg in Turkey, Ajax suffered a 1-0 reverse at home to Feyenoord in a result crucial for the destination of the league title, and then followed up with a tame 2-2 draw in Maastricht, conceding a late equaliser to MVV's Willy Brokamp. Perhaps Europe was proving to be an unwelcome diversion.

For the second leg, conditions in Turkey were hardly conducive to open football as a muddy pitch condemned the match to be played to suit the wet and deteriorating circumstances. Suurendonk and Suurbier were both unavailable through injury, requiring a reshuffle of the Ajax back line. Pronk was brought in at right-back alongside

Vasović, Hulshoff and Van Duivenbode, behind Muller and Groot, with Swart, Cruyff, Nuninga and Keizer further forward. The playing surface prevented Ajax playing their normal way, and for much of the 90 minutes they settled for containment, seeking to keep the eager home attacks at bay. At the break, with the scoreline goalless, the task was halfway to being completed.

Ten minutes after the restart Turkish hearts were anything but delighted when Keizer opened the scoring. Latching on to a pass from Nuninga, he drove forward as the ball bobbled then stalled in the mud. Heading towards the penalty area, the winger looked to have overhit the ball, with it surely destined for the welcoming arms of home goalkeeper Yavuz Şimşek. Instead, as it reached the penalty arc, the cloying surface refused to release the ball and Keizer ran on to crash it home. The second came in almost identical fashion with 16 minutes to play. A through ball from Cruyff was again held up by the mud on the edge of the penalty area and this time it was Nuninga advancing to hit home. Ajax were into the quarter-finals, but all thoughts of Europe now had to be put away until mid-February. Their domestic title was under serious threat at home and there was work to be done.

From the start of December, until that February date with Portuguese champions Benfica, Ajax played ten Eredivisie fixtures – and won nine of them. The only reverse came against DWS when a brace from Geurtsen was more than enough to see the small Amsterdam club to victory despite a late headed goal by Groot. The system of playing Nuninga in a deeper role also became more prevalent. It was hardly ideal for the player, who was much more comfortable in an orthodox forward position, and it was hardly a commitment to change but, for the time being, it seemed to be delivering results.

Disposing of Nürnberg and Fenerbahçe in the earlier rounds had been worthy enough, but Benfica were a club of an entirely different stripe. Runners-up in the previous year's tournament after losing to Manchester United in the final held at Wembley, *As Águias* ('The Eagles') had a formidable array of talent at their disposal. As well as the prolific Eusébio and the power of Torres in attack, the wily creative genius of Mário Coluna and António Simões prompted from midfield in a team full of international stars. Ajax would need to be at their best to advance to the last four, and the contest would be another milestone in the club's development.

Piet Wildschut would have a 15-year career in Eredivisie football, achieving international status and featuring for the *Oranje* in the 1978 World Cup. As a football-mad ten-year-old growing up in the Netherlands, he recalls Ajax's European Cup adventures, and particularly the games they played against Benfica in the 1968/69 tournament: 'Yes, I clearly remember the Wednesday evening soccer games of Ajax, getting better and better. Not sure what I would consider the highest point but I remember and I loved Ajax v Benfica in 1969.'

In an Eredivisie game four days before the Lisbon club visited Amsterdam, Ajax thumped DOS 7-0. With Bals in goal, the now settled first-choice back four of Suurbier, Vasović, Hulshoff and Van Duivenbode, were in place, but they were hardly troubled with most of the action at the other end of the pitch. Nuninga was again played in a deeper position with Muller and Gronk completing the midfield. Swart, Cruyff and Danielsson formed the forward line with Keizer rested on the bench. With Ajax already four goals clear at the break, however, Keizer was brought on to replace Cruyff as he too was permitted only 45 minutes of action with the Benfica visit just a few days away and the league match already won. Ajax would therefore be in confident mood for the last-eight European Cup tie. Michels selected almost the same team from four days earlier, with the exception of Keizer returning in place of Danielsson, but the outcome would be much different to that of the Eredivisie romp that they had enjoyed against DOS.

February in Amsterdam is more akin to the bitingly icy cold of January, when many of the canals often freeze over, than to the nascent spring of March, and on 12 February 1969 that situation definitively applied. Heavy snow in the city had put the game in doubt but, after many hours of effort to clear the pitch, Scottish referee – somewhat suitably named Robert Holley Davidson given the Christmas feel to the weather – decreed that, despite the pitch having a white coating, the lines were cleared so that the match could take place.

With the Dutch club more accustomed to the prevailing inclement weather of northern Europe, and the Portuguese usually playing in much warmer conditions, the state of the Olympisch Stadion pitch may have been considered to favour Ajax. With the treacherous conditions as players slipped and slid wearing studs that offered as little traction as ice skates, the home team's intricate passing and patterns of play were struggling against the power of Benfica, with the muscular José Torres particularly effective.

The overwhelmingly white strip of the Dutch champions may well have offered a camouflage against the snowy backdrop of the pitch but that wasn't the reason they played in different colours, turning out in an all-blue ensemble, with white socks. As the away club, Benfica played in their famous red shirts, requiring Ajax to switch. Ajax in blue looked strange and, as the game got under way, their play was decidedly off-colour as well as the visitors dominated the opening phases, and two goals in a six-minute spell just past the half-hour looked to have decided not only the first leg but the tie as well, dooming Ajax's European aspirations once more.

First Jacinto Santos comfortably beat Bals from the penalty spot, sending the tracksuit-bottomed goalkeeper sprawling to his right as the ball flew high into the opposite side of goal. Even before they had cleared their heads from that setback, the lead was doubled. Suurbier gained control of the ball midway into the Ajax half and played a pass back to Vasović. Attempting to clear long downfield, the defender slipped, causing the ball to cannon into Eusébio who quickly controlled and fed Torres. From the edge of the area, the forward brushed aside a challenge and powered home.

The conditions had unquestionably been a major factor, not only in both goals, but also how the game had developed. At the break, however, Michels appeared to reason that his 4-3-3 formation was also contributing to the problem. He removed Nuninga and sent on Danielsson to partner Cruyff in what was now a more rigid 4-2-4. It was the beginning of the end for Nuninga's Ajax career and he would miss out on the subsequent game against Benfica then make just a dozen more appearances, including nine in the Eredivisie and a second-half promotion from the substitutes' bench in the final against Milan. His last appearance, ironically, would be in midfield in the final Eredivisie game of the season, a 2-1 win over GVAV in Groningen.

Nuninga had played a key role in the three successive Eredivisie titles of 1965/66, 1966/67 and 1967/68, and the KNVB Cup triumph of 1966/67. At the end of the season he was transferred to DWS. Five years earlier, he had been brought to Ajax from GVAV as a 23-year-old by Buckingham for a fee later reported by *De Telegraaf* for 250,000 guilders,[38]

---

38 *De Telegraaf*, 1 September 1978.

then a club record transfer fee, although other reports suggested a different figure. In his 150 Eredivisie games he scored 23 goals but now, still only 28, Michels was ready to move him on. His flexibility to offer a deeper-lying option may well have doomed him.

Michels' decision to remove Nuninga and play the Swede alongside Cruyff brought immediate dividends. A pass reached Cruyff some 20 metres from goal. He played the ball inside to Danielsson, who survived a lunging challenge to drive past an exposed José Henrique and reduce the arrears. Inspired by the goal, Ajax pressed forward but the surface was alien to their play and they struggled to deliver any meaningful threat.

When the next goal came it was at the other end of the field. A corner from the left unforgivably cleared Bals and all of his defenders, leaving José Augusto to nod home at the far post. Celebrating, the substitute who had replaced a struggling Simoes on 40 minutes, jumped into one of the banks of snow piled around the pitch, raising a lump of it into the air before realising there was little to do with it from there, and dropped it back on to the floor. From Ajax's point of view it was 'snow joke' and at the end of the game, trailing by two goals, with the away leg to come, elimination was beckoning.

Unusually compared to previous European Cup encounters, there was no domestic fixture for Ajax to play before the return leg in Lisbon seven days later, with the adverse weather in the Netherlands meaning only one domestic fixture was played between 8 February and 9 March. It at least offered Michels' team an opportunity to recover physically and for the coach to consider his options.

The weather in Lisbon was much warmer than Amsterdam, and provided Ajax with a far more accommodating surface for their game. Michels selected ten of the team that had ended the first leg, with the only change being Pronk introduced into a solid-looking midfield pairing with Groot. Muller dropped to the bench. This time it was Benfica compelled to change strip as Ajax returned to their normal colours. The challenge of winning by two clear goals against the Portuguese champions in an Estádio da Luz, packed with 60,000 fans expecting to see their team complete the task already largely accomplished in Amsterdam, was daunting. At such times clubs need their stars to step up and, in this game, Cruyff did just that.

Already looking more comfortable with grass rather than snow under his feet, Ajax's totemic star had already taken a grip on the game when, out on the left, he scuffed an attempted cross. Quickly regaining possession at the byline, he clipped in a cross that perfectly met up with Danielsson's run towards the near post and the Swede's glancing header deceived Henrique, finding the far corner of the net. Just nine minutes had been played and Ajax were back in contention. Three minutes later, the arrears had been totally dismissed as Cruyff turned from provider to scorer, and with 30 minutes on the clock he added the third goal. The deficit from the frosty encounter in Amsterdam had melted away in the warm Lisbon evening and, remarkably, Ajax were ahead in the tie. It's little wonder that these games left a mark on the young Piet Wildschut.

At the break, seeking greater security in midfield, Michels removed Danielsson, replacing him with Muller in a reinforced midfield three alongside Pronk and Groot. Ajax would now seek to frustrate Benfica's expected attacks and look to lock out the tie on the break. There was still drama to come though, and a headed strike by Torres with 20 minutes to play meant mirrored scores in both legs, requiring a play-off to decide who would progress to the semi-finals.

The play-off would take place on 5 March at the Stade Olympique Yves-du-Manoir in Paris and, with their European Cup prospects still on hold, there was the isolated Eredivisie fixture to play, when Holland Sport visited the De Meer on the first day of the month. The club based in the Scheveningen district of The Hague had been Dutch champions in 1955 and were invited to compete in the first European Cup tournament. They declined, however, and PSV Eindhoven took their place. By the 1968/69 season, their fortunes had declined dramatically and they would end this term in mid-table, before merging with ADO Den Haag to become FC Den Haag two years later. If Michels was looking for a comfortable victory, however, the visitors – still in their own colours at this stage – weren't about to make things easy.

Resisting the temptation to rest players with the play-off imminent, Michels instead opted to field a strong team in search of valuable Eredivisie points to help sustain Ajax's defence of the title. The goalkeeper and back four were retained and he returned to a three-man midfield, this time dropping Cruyff back to join Pronk and Groot. Nuninga was in his preferred forward position alongside Danielsson and Keizer. The 4-3-3 formation seemed fated to disappoint, however, and inside the first ten minutes Ajax fell behind as Teske opened the scoring for the visitors. By the break a header from Pronk, and a Cruyff strike following Keizer's free kick had the champions in front. The points were not secured, however, and ten minutes after the restart Valkenhoff scored to earn the visitors a draw and further weaken Ajax's grip on the title.

More than 63,000 packed the compact Stade Olympique Yves-du-Manoir four days later to see the denouement of the Ajax v Benfica trilogy, and that figure didn't include the hundreds who scaled the trees surrounding the stadium to ensure they got a glimpse of the action. Ajax didn't lack for vocal support as tens of thousands Dutch supporters travelled the 450km to the game. Their journey would be rewarded, although a good measure of patience would be required. It was back to 4-2-4 for Michels. The regular defence was in place with Pronk and Groot in midfield and Swart joining Cruyff, Danielsson and Keizer in attack.

With both clubs having conceded heavily at home, it was of little surprise that the game was tight with few chances at either end. They looked for opportunities to attack but with the emphasis on not falling behind as the prime consideration. After 90 minutes the scoreline remained goalless but minutes into extra time the deadlock was finally broken as Cruyff scored with a left-footed shot. The flight of the ball seemed to deceive Henrique, with the hint of a deflection the probable cause.

Somewhat appropriately for a Dutch team, the goal seemed to breach the dyke and, after 92 minutes of goalless sparring the Benfica defence was beaten twice more. A dozen minutes after the first goal, with the Dutch section of the crowd still in uproarious celebration, Danielsson pounced on the loose ball after Henrique had blocked at the feet of Swart and unerringly struck home to double the lead. The Benfica players' downcast demeanours, as the Ajax team and fans celebrated, suggested that they knew the game was up, and any lingering doubts were dismissed three minutes later when the Swede struck again. Sprinting into the box, he clipped the ball over Henrique as he plunged to try and block. Even at three goals clear Michels was taking no chances, removing Swart to send on Muller and strengthen the midfield. It was understandable caution but Benfica were already a beaten side. At the end it was Danielsson being chaired from the pitch by the Dutch fans.

The remaining clubs alongside Ajax in the semi-finals were reigning champions Manchester United, Italian Serie A winners AC Milan and the little-known Czechoslovakian club Spartak Trnava. With the play-off shortening the period between quarter-final success and semi-finals, Michels would have been delighted to avoid the two big clubs and instead be drawn to face Trnava for a place in the final. Conversely, with the trauma of elimination against Dukla Prague still a recent memory, the prospect of facing another Czechoslovakian club would have compromised any satisfaction gleaned from avoiding Manchester United and AC Milan.

Four days after the game in Paris, Ajax's interest in the KNVB Cup was ended as Ben Peeters' Feyenoord visited the De Meer and a brace from Kindvall outweighed Pronk's first-half header from a corner to eliminate Michels' team, as he again resorted to 4-2-4. The De Kuip club were looking increasingly likely to be on the way to a domestic double of their own. A home game against Ajax – between their two legs against Trnava – would be the ideal opportunity to cement things in their favour. After successes in a couple of friendlies against Bundesliga teams, Ajax strung three consecutive Eredivisie wins together ahead of the home leg of the semi-final. A 2-0 victory at RKSV Volendam got things moving in the right direction, but was compromised by an injury to Vasović who had to be withdrawn at half-time and would miss the next two league games, the first leg of the semi-final, plus the vital Eredivisie match away to Feyenoord. Pronk was slotted in alongside Hulshoff.

The replacement was a solid, if unspectacular defender, but lacked both the ability and leadership qualities of Vasović. As with Nuninga, he would be released by the club at the end of the season. Somewhat fittingly for a player who had spent six years at the De Meer, winning league and cup honours, his final appearance was the European Cup Final against Milan at the Estadio Santiago Bernabéu. At 28 years of age, there should still have been plenty of playing time ahead of Pronk at the top level, albeit not with Ajax. Instead he opted for retirement, but just 12 months later he had a change of heart and joined FC Utrecht, requiring his new employers to pay a reported sum of 50,000 guilders to Ajax for his registration. He would stay with Utrecht for four seasons before permanently retiring in 1974, later rejoining Ajax as a scout and then serving as chief scout under Louis van Gaal. Pronk is credited with bringing the outstanding talents of both Jari Litmanen and Zlatan Ibrahimović to Ajax. His contribution to the club's ongoing success significantly outlived his playing days.

The loss of Vasović did little to upset Ajax's attacking verve and a six-goal thrashing of GVAV followed with Gerrie Mühren starting and scoring the fourth goal. Finally, a 4-1 triumph over Telstar in the small port city of IJmuiden, North Holland, rounded out the domestic fixtures. It was a game that carried extra significance beyond the scoreline and points, as it marked the Eredivisie debut of goalkeeper Heinz Stuy. His second league start would come in the final game of the season, the 2-1 win over GVAV. The same fixture also marked Nuninga's final bow in Ajax colours. Just 12 months later, Stuy had supplanted Bals as Ajax's goalkeeper and the then 33-year-old former number one was sold to Vitesse Arnhem for a reported 45,378 guilders,[39] but that was for the future. In each of these three Eredivisie games Michels had sent his team out in a 4-2-4 formation, but what would he do when the Czechoslovakian champions visited the Olympisch Stadion on 13 April?

---

39 *Limburgs Dagblad*, 13 June 1970.

Confidently rolling over smaller teams in the Dutch league was one thing, but the semi-final of the premier club tournament in European football was a task of entirely different proportions. The Czechoslovakians may have been widely deemed to be the weakest of Ajax's possible opponents in the semi-final draw, but any team reaching the final four of the European Cup was worthy of respect, and Spartak were no different. UEFA's pairing of east European clubs had pitted them against Steaua București in the first round of the competition. With Spartak trailing by three goals with 15 minutes to play in the away leg, the return in Czechoslovakia was beginning to look likely to be a mere statistical formality. A late strike by Ladislav Kuna, however, offered up a glimmer of hope and a crushing 4-0 victory at the Spartak Stadium completed the unlikely recovery.

In the next round, a 16-2 aggregate romp against the Finns of Reipas Lahti confirmed that Spartak had plenty of goal power in their team, and they would use it against Ajax after AEK Athens were beaten 3-2 on aggregate in the quarter-final. In their three home legs to this stage Spartak had scored 13 goals – seven of them had been against the hapless Finns – and Ajax would need a comfortable home victory in order to travel to the second leg with confidence. They would achieve that aim, but their progress to the final would fall under pressure until the final whistle in the second leg.

With Vasović still out injured, Michels was compelled to go into the game without his key defender and Pronk retained his place alongside Hulshoff. The chosen formation was 4-2-4, as the coach opted to go with a two-man midfield of Groot and Muller. Swart and Keizer had the flanks of the front line, with Cruyff and Danielsson inside of them.

With the last lingering traces of the Dutch winter now past, the Olympisch Stadion's playing surface was back to its verdant green from the snowy white of the Benfica home leg. Whereas the Ajax precision passing and pressing game of *totaalvoetbal* had been compromised against the Portuguese champions, now Michels' team could revert to their normal game, unhindered by metrological inconveniences. A crowd of 55,450 had assembled for the game, expecting Ajax to build an unassailable lead to take to the second leg and, by the end of the night, that seemed to have been achieved.

Ajax pressed from the start and visiting goalkeeper Frantisek Kozinka's goal was twice threatened by headers before the first goal arrived. First a cross by Keizer found Cruyff unmarked by the penalty spot, but the poorly directed header fell comfortably into the Kozinka's arms. Then, from a right-wing corner, Hulshoff arrived at a gallop to powerfully head past Kozinka, but a defender blocked the ball on the line. On the bench, Michels was becoming visibly anxious as chances came and went. The spectre of Dukla Prague would have been persistently nagging away at the back of his mind. An astute pass put Danielsson into a dangerous position, but his pull-back across goal rolled harmlessly away with no Ajax player on hand for the tap-in.

Around 25 minutes into the game, a bizarre incident broke up play as a large hare found its way on to the field of play. Had it been brought in by someone in the crowd? It seems implausible that a wild animal of that size would be randomly wandering around a packed stadium in the capital of the Netherlands. The hare was eventually caught and removed by an Ajax official, its eventual fate unknown. Perhaps the hare had served as a surrogate lucky rabbit's foot, however, as, soon after, Hulshoff duplicated his run and header from another right-wing corner. This time the ball was arrowed down to the side of Kozinka. The goalkeeper plunged to block, but Cruyff was on hand to force the rebound home from around one metre and Ajax had the lead. At the break it remained the only goal of the game as Spartak defended with calm and assured resolution, while Ajax probed, looking for the intricate move that would pick the lock for a second time.

Seven minutes after the restart, Swart found the key with a blistering finish to double the advantage and on the hour the first leg, if not the tie, was settled when Swart crossed for a scandalously unmarked Keizer to nod home the third goal. A place in the final now looked assured. Michels seemed to consider that three goals would be sufficient, and removed Swart inside the last ten minutes, sending on Suurendonk in his place. Surely Ajax wouldn't let such a lead slip in the return.

Four days after the 1-1 draw with Feyenoord in Rotterdam, Ajax travelled to Bratislava for the return leg. Vasović was welcomed back into the defence, but instead of losing his place, Pronk was pushed forward into midfield alongside Groot and Muller, with Swart, Cruyff and Keizer making up the front line. It looked like a 4-3-3 selection, but for much of the game Pronk dropped into a five-man defence, with Swart assisting Groot and Muller and leaving just Cruyff and Keizer to pose a threat to the home defence. Whether that adaptation was by design, or imposed by the pressure Spartak applied, is unclear, but for much of the game Ajax were unarguably on the back foot and compelled to defend.

Ajax had a few opportunities to break on counter-attacks, but most of the first 20 minutes was taken up with Spartak attacks on Bals's goal. With Vasović organising, Pronk reinforcing, and Bals in outstanding form though, the home attack was kept at bay. The Ajax cause wasn't helped on 23 minutes when an injury to Cruyff brought Danielsson from the bench to replace him. Four minutes later, they conceded.

Bals collected an intended back-pass and looked to clear long upfield. His contact on the ball was poor, however, and it fell to Kuna a mere 25 metres from goal. Without hesitation, the midfielder fired the ball straight back, and it cleared Bals with the goalkeeper helplessly stranded out of position. The home team now had just over an hour to find the other two goals required to wipe out Ajax's advantage from the first leg, and they set to the task with vigour and renewed belief.

Despite enhanced pressure, roared on by the crowd of 23,000 packed into the compact Spartak Stadium, Ajax survived until the break. Four minutes after the restart, though, their advantage had been reduced to a single goal after a free kick from the right was crossed into the box and Kuna headed past Bals. The three-goal lead, which had looked so commanding in Amsterdam, was now revealed to be perilously insufficient. Ajax's hopes of reaching the European Cup Final were hanging by a thread. Dukla Prague all over again? It looked to be heading that way. For Ronald Jager, the situation represented the most difficult of games for Ajax, and they relied heavily on their goalkeeper to escape. 'They had won 3-0 at home but were down 2-0 … in the second game. Goalkeeper Gert Bals saved the day and played a perfect game.' After his error for the opening goal, Bals redeemed himself to get his team over the line.

For the remainder of the second period, a now increasingly confident Spartak side swarmed forward time and again in search of the all-important third goal. Inside the last 30 minutes Michels sent on Suurendonk to replace Keizer. Any thoughts of attacking were very much put on to the back burner with all hands required at the other end of the pitch. Bals stood up against a one-on-one, forcing the Spartak player to guide the ball wide of the post, and then he threw himself to the left to palm a close-range header wide. From the resulting corner a goalmouth scramble ended with another effort flying narrowly wide. At the final whistle though, Ajax had prevailed and they celebrated as much in relief as joy. The resolution that had allowed them to come back against Benfica when seemingly apparently heading for the exit door had come through again. On 28 May 1968, Ajax would play AC Milan in their first European Cup Final.

There were six Eredivisie fixtures to play before that date, though, five of them at home. With Cruyff still injured and Suurbier unavailable, Hulshoff dropped in at right-back with Pronk partnering Vasović in central defence and Nuninga replacing Cruyff in attack for the 2-1 win over MVV three days after the Spartak game. Twente then visited Amsterdam as a more familiar side, although still lacking Cruyff, won 2-0 thanks to a late brace from Swart.

When DWS visited the De Meer on 11 May and left with 3-2 defeat there were just 17 days remaining until the big game in Madrid, but Michels still had the Eredivisie title to defend. Given Feyenoord's advantage, to do so successfully was a steep uphill task, especially as he was also walking a tightrope of selecting first-choice players with fingers crossed, hoping injury wouldn't rob him of key men for the final. Walking uphill on a tightrope is a challenging task, but Ajax were clinging to any hopes that their rivals from Rotterdam would slip up if they could keep taking maximum points from their own games. On 15 May, those title dreams were all but extinguished when a virtually full-strength Ajax lost at the De Meer to PSV Eindhoven. They would win each of their remaining league fixtures to the end of the season but couldn't catch Feyenoord, and Peeters' team won the title by three points, qualifying them for the European Cup the following season. All that remained now for Ajax was the little matter of their final. Losing to Milan would now carry an additional sting as only by being defending champions could Ajax qualify for the following season's competition.

Under venerable coach Nereo Rocco, Milan had already scaled the mountain that Michels and Ajax sought to conquer. In 1962/63 a brace by Brazilian forward José Altafini had taken the *Rossoneri* to the summit of European club football as they defeated Benfica in the Wembley final to lift their first European Cup, guided by the golden boy of Italian football, Gianni Rivera.

Rocco then moved to Torino for a short period seeking to recreate the era of *Grande Torino*, before returning to the San Siro in 1967. Success had been immediate. In his first season back in charge Milan coasted to the Serie A title, finishing a full nine points clear of runners-up Napoli. For good measure they added the Cup Winners' Cup, defeating Hamburg 2-0. They were comfortably the best team in Serie A and were many pundits' favourites to extend their realm across the continent. If Ajax were to achieve their first European Cup triumph, they would need to do so as overwhelming underdogs against an experienced and confident Milan.

After defeating Malmö in the first round 5-3 on aggregate, Milan's run to the final had hardly been full of goals. A bye in the second round sent them to face Celtic in the quarter-finals, where a 1-0 victory in Glasgow after a goalless draw in the San Siro was enough to vanquish the 1966/67 champions, after which they faced the holders of the trophy, Manchester United. A two-goal victory in Italy proved too high a hurdle for Matt Busby's team to clear at Old Trafford and Rocco's studied defence only conceded once to reach the final. It all meant that the Italian champions had scored more goals in a single game against the minnows of Malmö than in all the subsequent games on route to the final combined. For Rocco, however, the ends always justified the means and victory wasn't the most important thing: it was the only thing. His steely, focused approach was neatly captured in an interview with Vittorio Zucconi of *La Republica*. Rocco remarked that whenever, ahead of a game, an opposing coach would say to him, 'May the best team win.' his consistent and frank reply was always, 'Let's hope not.'

The acidly honest reply may well have been more for effect than expectation, but it neatly summed up the difference between the two teams who would contest the final. On one hand there was the case-hardened, hard-nosed serial winners of AC Milan, filled with experience and dogged determination. On the other, a young but innovative and ambitious Ajax team who had just lost the domestic league title. The difference wasn't lost on *The Times* in its preview of the final. The game, it suggested, would be 'a fascinating duel between aggressive youth and one of the tightest defences in world soccer'.[40]

The newspaper went on to predict in the same article that Ajax, 'playing in their first European Cup Final, are expected to gamble everything on flat-out attack during the 90 minutes … against the tough ruthless Italian defence'. Rocco, however, was confident that his team could deal with the ebullient attacking approach of the Dutch team, and 'was not worried that many of his veterans' may struggle. 'He prefers experience, coolness and cunning ability to the risks of fielding quicker but less reliable younger players,' the newspaper wrote. The analysis paints a picture of a team of apprentices pitted against worldly wise old practitioners, and that was very much how the contest turned out.

In the biggest game of his time with Ajax so far, Michels elected to play in a 4-2-4 formation. The regular back four

---

40 *The Times*, 27 May 1969.

of Suurbier, Vasović, Hulshoff and Van Duivenbode were ranged in front of Bals. In midfield the defensive proficiency of Pronk was preferred over Muller to partner Groot. It was perhaps Michels' sole concession to caution. The front line comprised Swart, Cruyff, Danielsson and Keizer. It was a selection purely based on choice with no player unavailable to the coach.

The crowd of 31,782 in Madrid's cavernous Bernabéu left huge tracts of empty spaces, but thousands of Ajax fans had made the trip from north to southern Europe and, if anything, outnumbered those supporting the *Rossoneri*. Flares launched from the sparse crowd lit up the Madrid evening as the teams entered the pitch accompanied by a phalanx of photographers and assorted officials from the competing clubs and hosts. Not long after the start of the game, Milan lit the blue touchpaper on some fireworks of their own when they opened the scoring with just seven minutes played.

Inside the first couple of minutes, Ajax had already experienced a fortunate escape. The Italians had pressed from the start, dominating possession and position, when Angelo Anquilletti slipped a pass to Pierino Prati just inside the box. His shot beat Bals but rebounded to safety after striking the far post. They wouldn't be so fortunate the next time a chance dropped to the Italian forward just minutes later.

After the initial rush of Milan pressure, Ajax had begun to establish a foothold in the game, threading passes with intricate runs, when they fell behind. With Suurbier forward, Hulshoff was drawn out of the middle to close down on Angelo Sormani but the Brazilian-born forward easily skipped past an ineffective tackle and crossed into the box towards Prati, whose looping header deceived Bals. Milan were ahead and few could dispute that it was a warranted lead. On the respective benches there would have been contrasting emotions and thoughts about their team's prospects. Rocco's experience of seeing his team score the first goal in a game and then locking out the opposition would have had him purring in satisfaction as Milan had struck early. On the Ajax bench, the height and steepness of the mountain that Michels was seeking to scale had just been added to.

For the next 30 minutes or so, Ajax probably shaded possession, but without having anything tangible to show for that marginal advantage. This was Milan's game. A one-goal lead, defending in depth with studied concentration, and always prepared to strike on the counter-attack. It was straight out of Rocco's playbook. Ajax strived but, as previous European champions Celtic and Manchester United had found out in the earlier rounds, breaking down their defence was anything but a simple task. Cruyff twisting in the area to create a half-chance, from an acute angle, that Fabio Cudicini diverted into the side-netting was as close as they came in the first dozen minutes after falling behind, and even that was hardly close at all.

Milan's *catenaccio* approach had their back door securely bolted, and the nearest to another goal came at the other end of the pitch. Just past the halfway mark of the first half, Hulshoff was felled upfield as he drove forward to support an attack. Sensing a potential opening, with the defender limping back, Swedish forward Kurt Hamrin found Prati inside the box. A neat turn created a precious half a yard of space away from Vasović and Suurbier, but the forward's shot just evaded Bals's right-hand post with the goalkeeper a mere spectator.

With each passing minute, Ajax's concerns were growing. The more they pushed forward the greater potential there was for Milan to strike on the break. Just past the half-hour an interception in the Milan defence set Rivera running free through the middle of the field. Drawing the last line of defenders towards him, he fed a perfect pass out to Prati who fired just wide of the post. The Milan forward looked the most dangerous player on the field, and the most likely to score. Ajax were playing with fire, and at such times there's a propensity to get burnt. Four minutes later their fingers were nearly scorched as a scything run from Lodetti against a hastily covering Ajax back line left space for Prati on the edge of the box. A simple pass would have put him clear with just Bals to beat, but Lodetti ignored the pleas of his team-mate and drove on before shooting high, wide and, in no way, handsome.

Since going ahead on seven minutes, Milan had kept Ajax's eager attacks at arm's length from their goal, suffocating their forward play with a blanket defence organised by the 'coolness and cunning ability' of Rocco's 'veterans'. It had been a masterclass in choking off an opposing attack and the icing on the cake came on 38 minutes when Prati struck again. Suurbier was lying injured near to the Milan corner flag as Rivera charged forward. Exchanging passes, he regathered possession, trotting towards the Ajax penalty area, before a neat back-heel left the ball for Prati to run on to, and fire high past Bals. Two goals clear and Rocco would have been smiling to himself – at least on the inside, as he maintained his gruff exterior. So far, it had been a *catenaccio* performance *par excellence*. Perhaps the only thing disturbing the Milan coach was that the best team *was* winning! Firecrackers echoed around the stadium as the fallen Suurbier was still receiving treatment when Ajax sought to restart the game. As far as the Milan *tifosi* were concerned, one goal was usually sufficient to win a game and two was bordering on the excessive; the game was over. As Spanish referee José María Ortiz de Mendíbil blew for half-time, few would have disagreed.

The first 45 minutes had been like a schoolday for the younger, more inexperienced Ajax players. Many still had much to learn, and their naivety in the game at the highest level had been ruthlessly exposed by a Milan team hardened by the finishing school of Italy's Serie A. Some had received lessons that needed to be absorbed. Others, however, had shown that were simply not up to the required level. Roberto Pennino recalled that the game had shown Michels 'there were players outclassed by an opponent like Milan. So, they had to leave. He was a real general in those things. You had to keep up otherwise you were out.'

Suurbier had hobbled through the final few minutes of the first period but was in no condition to continue. Michels sent Muller on instead, dropping Pronk into the back line. He also brought on Nuninga for Groot. At the time, Ruud Krol was still a member of Ajax's youth team, but he well remembered the game against Milan – and its significance. 'Milan played better on that day. They countered Ajax's attacking and attacked well, and some players in positions for Ajax were not of the highest quality. Michels saw that – in fact he knew it before and he had already wanted to try different answers,' he recalled.

Unfortunately Michels only had two cards in his hand at the time. Ideally, he'd have played aces but, as Krol alludes to, instead he only had the two and three of clubs. He played them anyway. More comprehensive changes would have to wait. Krol continued, 'After '69 he rebuilt the team – like he did every year. Every year he took his weakest point out of the team and tried to find a stronger point.' That process would blossom wonderfully in the long run, but was of little help to Ajax in this game.

The early minutes of the second half suggested little change to the established pattern. Ajax had a comfortable amount of possession but offered little threat on goal, while Prati remained a constant danger for Milan. Three minutes in, a diving header from Prati nearly brought the *Rossoneri* a third goal, but the ball drifted wide of the far post. Sormani also came close to getting on to the scoresheet. On 55 minutes a brief scramble in front of Bals ended with the ball dropping to the feet of the Italian forward, some seven metres or so from goal. Leaning back, however, he lofted the ball comfortably clear of the crossbar. It seemed a matter of trifling importance with Ajax struggling to make any kind of impact at the other end of the pitch where, other than collecting back-passes and teeing the ball up for goal kicks, Cudicini was largely a spectator.

On the hour, however, the Milan goalkeeper was brought into the action. Initially there was little danger when Keizer sought to run on to a pass from Cruyff near the edge of the Milan area. Facing three defenders and Lodetti closing from behind, the Dutch wideman managed stretch out a foot and flick the ball around the first defender but, with it running away from goal, the danger was slight. Perhaps losing composure for the briefest of seconds, Lodetti slid into an impetuous challenge, upending Keizer and leaving the referee little option than to award the spot-kick. Italian protests were driven more by habit than conviction.

In the final three years earlier, Vasović had scored from the penalty spot for Partizan when his former club had lost 2-1 to Real Madrid, and his nerve held as he made a long run to convert this time. As Vasović approached the ball, Cudicini advanced from his line so that, when the Yugoslav defender stopped before striking, the goalkeeper had almost breached the six-yard line of his goal area. Both players appealed to the referee, pointing accusing fingers at the other for the perceived misdemeanour. The official, however, merely sent each player back to their starting positions and, when Vasović ran forward for the second time, his shot went low to Cudicini's right as the goalkeeper threw himself in the opposite direction. Ajax had hardly looked like scoring from open play, and perhaps a penalty was the only way that the Milan back line was going to be breached. Statistically Ajax were back in the game, but it had taken the rarest of defensive blunders to gift them a goal, and they still needed another one, at the very least.

The celebrations of Ajax fans in the crowd were hardly matched by the players on the pitch. Perhaps the size of the task still confronting them subdued the moment of joy. It's often said that a team is particularly vulnerable soon after scoring, and Milan appeared keen to prove that old chestnut to be true. They nearly struck back immediately when Rivera was freed in the Ajax area to shoot across Bals, but the ball slid past the far post with the goalkeeper beaten. Then, two minutes later, Bals was called on to block a drive from Hamrin as the Sweden international broke into the area, and he also ensured that Sormani didn't profit from the rebound.

The goal had offered Ajax a brief glimpse of a distant light at the end of a very long tunnel though, and they picked up the pace of their game. Cruyff swayed away from Trapattoni, accelerating towards the penalty area. Ensuring he was outside of the area as he positioned himself to bring the run to a halt, Anquilletti had little interest in the ball when Cruyff flicked it past him. The sole intent was to send the forward tumbling to the turf. It was a task he accomplished with practiced aplomb. Keizer's free kick thudded into the wall and on the bench Rocco would have nodded approvingly.

If Ajax fans had been encouraged by Cruyff's sally, they would be disheartened just minutes later. Receiving a pass inside his own half, Sormani advanced towards the Ajax area as defenders chose to back away rather than close him down. Reaching the edge of the area, still without facing any kind of challenge, that passive defence was shown to be fatal. Sormani calmly shifted the ball slightly to his left and drove it past Bals and into the corner of the net to restore Milan's two-goal advantage. Ajax heads dropped. There's an old saying that it's difficult to fully appreciate how dark the night is unless you've experienced the brightness of daylight. Vasović's penalty was a brief glimpse of light, but now for Ajax the night was dark indeed.

Michels' team pressed forward but without real conviction, and belief looked to be draining away as sand running through fingers. The following day, *The Times* reported that the game was now 'too one sided'.[41] It was an apt description of the play and, with 15 minutes left, the *coup de grâce* was delivered. A perfect wall pass allowed Rivera to run clear of the Ajax back line. He rounded Bals but was forced wide. Looking up, the captain, who would later in the year be awarded the Ballon d'Or, saw that two defenders had recovered to reach the goal line. It meant that any direct shot on goal may well have been blocked. Instead of chancing his arm with a surely wasted effort on goal, Rivera coolly waited as support arrived before clipping in a cross for Prati to run in and head home, completing his hat-trick. It was goal of rare quality with *The Times* lauding it as 'a display of arrogance bordering on impertinence'. The time remaining on the clock was irrelevant. The game was over, and Ajax had been swotted away by Milan with disconcerting ease. The headline in *The Times* read 'Milan overwhelm Dutch defence'. A more apposite header could have said 'Milan defence overwhelm Ajax' but the message was clear enough.

---

41 'Milan overwhelm Dutch defence', *The Times*, 29 May 1969.

Ajax had come a long way from struggling near the foot of the Eredivisie table when Michels arrived, to reaching the final of the European Cup, just a few years later. As Menno Pot remarked, 'Ajax had become a great football team, but they were still naive in many ways.' They remained a mixture of the 'not quite yet' and the 'never will be'. Michels would work to further develop the former and replace the latter.

That naivety highlighted by Pot was something that several of the players were painfully aware of. Sjaak Swart recognised that clear lessons needed to be learned if Ajax were to improve: 'In the 1969 final against AC Milan, they played their *catenaccio* style and their forward Pierino Prati scored three goals on the counter-attack. We lost 4-1. We learned that you couldn't only rely on your attacking ability.'[42] Later, Barry Hulshoff would reflect not only on the pain of losing in such an important game, but also the lessons that had to be learned if the team was to progress: 'They sometimes say you have to lose a final to win a final, and it's true.'[43] Lessons delivered, Ajax went away to absorb and improve.

Hulshoff would initially feel the cold steel of Michels' axe of dissatisfaction, albeit only temporarily. In the new season he would be dropped for five early games. The coach demanded more from the man who would later become the cornerstone of the Ajax defence. Hulshoff was an intimidating figure. He was tall, muscular and physically equipped to deal with any type of aggression from an opponent, but he was also blessed with outstanding talent, and often relied on that to subdue opponents, rather than resorting to a physicality beyond the laws of the game, as the Milan defenders had demonstrated

42 https://www.champions-journal.com/1000/ajax-71
43 Winner, David, *Brilliant Orange* (London: Bloomsbury, 2000).

could work so effectively. Michels considered the attitude as lacking something. Hulshoff could give more if he adapted his play. Michels wanted more. He wanted that talent on top of physicality, not instead of it. The coach would return Hulshoff to the team after what he considered an appropriate time for self-reflection and adjustment. Ever the rebel, however, and the master of his own direction, Hulshoff wouldn't turn into the mean man the coach wanted, but his talent allowed him to dominate opponents even more effectively, without resorting to unsavoury tactics.

When asked how much losing the 1969 final would have changed Michels' thinking, David Winner's response was hardly surprising. 'Quite a bit,' he replied. 'Mainly [Michels] decided he needed the team to be tougher and more ruthless. So, it was pretty much the end for gentlemanly old-school nice guys like Van Duivenbode, Nuninga and Pronk. Rijnders and Mühren were tougher/quicker more dynamic in midfield … Winners basically.'

The season had been a chastening experience for Ajax and their coach. Not only did they fail to win the Eredivisie title for the first time since Michels' first full season in charge, they also missed out on the KNVB Cup. It meant they ended empty-handed, with only qualification for the Inter-Cities Fairs Cup as some minor consolation. It was time for another of Michels' 'rebuilds' as Ruud Krol described them. As well as Pronk retiring – at least temporarily – and Nuninga leaving for DWS, Inge Danielsson returned to Sweden and joined Helsingborgs, and Van Duivenbode moved to arch-rivals and new champions Feyenoord. As things transpired, the discarded defender profited greatly from the transfer. In the following season, he collected the European Cup winners' medal that had been denied him in the Milan final, and had the added satisfaction of netting a late winner at the De Kuip as his new club defeated his old one in his first *Klassieker* wearing Feyenoord colours in November 1969.

A young Ruud Krol would step into Van Duivenbode's left-back role. Initially, at just 20 years of age, Krol had doubts about the promotion coming too early for him, but Michels dispelled any such concerns, telling the young defender, who at that stage had only played at left-back once – and that was in a friendly – not to be concerned. He was keen to convince Krol of his trust, insisting to him that he shouldn't worry about the established Van Duivenbode, and that he was a better player.

Gerrie Mühren was already at the club and building a growing reputation as the sort of competitor Michels was seeking. That would continue and the club also secured the signing of Nico Rijnders from Go Ahead Eagles, Dick van Dijk from Twente, and little-known Danish forward Tom Søndergaard from Rapid Vienna, who would leave for Metz 18 months later having appeared in just 20 official games. Auke Kok reflected: 'After the defeat against Milan, Michels concluded he needed more "modern" players who could be rational and tough on the pitch, more professional, like soldiers, as he called it, and more dynamic.' With the maturing youth players, new signings and a more concentrated Hulshoff, Michels had what he wanted in place for the new term.

Van Dijk and Rijnders would be the most influential of the newcomers. Both would play in the 1971 European Cup Final, with the latter scoring the opening goal. Rijnders would be sold to Club Brugge during the summer following the Wembley triumph, while Van Dijk would stay with Ajax for a further year after that. Ronald Jager suggested that Van Dijk's arrival from Twente had carried a measure of controversy with it, suggesting perhaps, if fate had played out differently, the history of Dutch, and indeed European football may well have looked very different. Consulting a biography of the then FC Twente coach Kees Rijvers, Jager explained, 'Dick van Dijk was a good player at FC Twente under Kees Rijvers. But, in the German [town of] Ruhpolding, halfway through the 68/69 season (FC Twente was training there to avoid Carnaval in Enschede) he and three other FC Twente players [went] out (there was a carnival there too) and FC Twente coach Kees Rijvers was furious. When they came back … they had a serious argument and the coach slammed his attacker, but he let him play as normal after that. Very quick after that Ajax bought Van Dijk for the next [season] and Van Dijk asked Rijvers to let him out of the team for the rest of the season. Rijvers refused but in his biography *Prof* in 2016, written by his granddaughter Antje Veld, Rijvers admitted Van Dijk wasn't playing at 100 per cent. Rijvers [said] in 2016, "If Van Dijk would have given all perhaps FC Twente could have been the Dutch champions of '69." If they had, Feyenoord would never have won the European Cup for champions in 1970, because FC Twente would have played in that competition.'

It's an interesting scenario to ponder. Did Ajax signing Van Dijk and perhaps unsettling him at Twente help Feyenoord to the Eredivisie title and the European glory that followed? Twente finished in third place, ten points adrift of the Rotterdam club at the end of the season, which suggests perhaps a little overreach by Rijvers. A closer analysis of the matter, however, may add weight to the coach's assertion. With 22 of the season's 34 fixtures completed, Twente had won 19, drawn two, and been beaten on only one occasion. The draws had come in a goalless game away to NAC on 6 October – before which Van Dijk had scored in every league match since the opening of the season – and then away to Holland Sport by the same scoreline on the first day of

December. The sole defeat had, unsurprisingly been at the De Meer, three days before Christmas. On that day, Feyenoord took over at the top of the table from the Enschede club, and would only briefly cede it back to them – for one game – before the end of the league schedule.

Following that defeat, Twente played a further seven games, winning five and drawing two until their second defeat, a 4-0 loss against Ajax's bogey team Go Ahead Eagles. By this time, Van Dijk had added a further eight strikes to bring his goal haul to 22 in 24 matches. From this point, however, Twente's fortunes would fall away. They would win only three more times, drawing one and losing the other half a dozen, including their final four.

Conversely, Van Dijk's goal contributions appeared broadly unaffected. As his team's performances and results declined over their last nine games the forward netted another seven times in his remaining seven appearances, missing the other two due to suspension. So, did a less-than-fully committed Van Dijk lead to the title hopes of Twente falling away after the deal with Ajax was agreed, and open the door for Feyenoord? There may be a case to be made, but at best perhaps the scenario suggested by Rijvers remains unproven. The story has a sad ending after Van Dijk retired, although it also illustrates the esteem with which he was held by Ajax, as Ronald Jager related: 'He died far too young at the age of only 51 in 1997. His former Ajax colleagues played a special match soon after that in his birth place Gouda and the money they made with that game was for the family of Van Dijk.'

In Rotterdam, Feyenoord's Eredivisie success had been particularly welcome, in that it broke the stranglehold that Michels' team had established on the Eredivisie title. Adding the KNVB Cup, while Ajax finished the season empty-handed, merely underscored that De Kuip was now the home of the top club in Dutch football. As with Ajax, Feyenoord were also looking beyond the borders of their own country, seeking success further afield. Ajax's feat in reaching the final of the European Cup, albeit before being comprehensively beaten by Milan, had fired their aspirations. They had even officially changed their name from the original Dutch Feijenoord to the more anglicised version of Feyenoord to make it more recognisable, and easier to pronounce outside of the Netherlands and the Dutch language.

If Ajax could reach the final then, logically, the club that had bested them in direct competition – in three unbeaten games, Feyenoord had won in Amsterdam in the Eredivisie, drawn the home league game, and then also knocked Ajax out of the KNVB Cup – could surely realistically aspire to go one better. To achieve such progress would require a giant step up in European performances over this term's endeavours. Despite the domestic triumphs achieved under Peeters, Feyenoord's campaign in the Inter-Cities Fairs Cup had been stymied before it had even begun.

Drawn to face Newcastle United in the first round, Feyenoord were soundly defeated at St James' Park, conceding four goals without reply to Joe Harvey's team. A side including the likes of Rinus Israël, Wim van Hanegem, Wim Jansen, Coen Moulijn and Ove Kindvall should surely have fared better. Back at the De Kuip, a 2-0 win thanks to goals from Kindvall and Frans van der Heide restored a little respectability but, despite the Geordies going on to win the competition, it was thought that perhaps the sobering experience had exposed a gap in the experience and ability of Peeters to deliver outside the boundaries of the domestic game. Feyenoord decided that, if there was to be a sustained attempt to bring the European Cup to Rotterdam in the new term, a change would be necessary. Their focus alighted on an ambitious Austrian.

In the same season's Cup Winners' Cup, following their triumph over Michels' team in the KNVB Cup Final of the previous season, ADO Den Haag and Ernst Happel had beaten the Austrians of Grazer AK before being eliminated by Bundesliga club 1. FC Köln in the second round. It was hardly a ringing endorsement of his success in European competition but, despite both Peeters and Happel being of similar ages, there was no doubting the latter's greater experience – and pedigree of success. With the memory of ADO's success over Ajax in the KNVB Cup fresh in the mind of the Feyenoord hierarchy, Happel reportedly sealed his appointment by sending a brief but productive, note to the club. It simply read, 'Future: Feyenoord?' and was signed at the bottom, 'Yours, Ernst Happel.' He was appointed soon afterwards, and the affable Peeters returned to his post with the club's youth team. 'It's part of our profession,' he explained. 'You just have to see it as a business issue.'[44]

As with Ajax's appointment of Michels, installing Happel at the De Kuip would prove to be the most astute of decisions. Happel was an inspirational leader who had improved his previous club impressively with his advocacy of a 4-3-3 system and a well-drilled, pressing tactical approach, emphasising the importance of fitness and commitment. Similar would apply at the De Kuip, as Van Hanegem later related: 'We didn't change the way we played too much, but we did get stronger, and stronger mentally as well.'[45] The new coach's approach would not only bring European glory to Feyenoord but, in a late-season Eredivisie game, would also

44 https://www.champions-journal.com/1000/feyenoord-forever-first
45 https://www.champions-journal.com/1000/feyenoord-forever-first

contribute towards Michels' development of *totaalvoetbal* in Amsterdam.

* * *

1969/70 – Another double, the numbers game and envious eyes cast towards Rotterdam

Ajax opened the new season with a friendly away to junior club Bergeijk. The final 15-0 scoreline was of far less significance than the new names included in the squad for the visit to North Brabant. Rijnders, Van Dijk, Mühren, Krol and Stuy all made the journey. Each would play at least 45 minutes of the game. Another half a dozen friendlies would take place before the first Eredivisie encounter on 10 August and the visit to GVAV. Michels had plenty of opportunity to assess his options.

Vasović was suspended and missed the journey to Groningen. Aside from him, however, Michels put out what was now his first-choice 11. Bals was still in goal, but this would be his final season with Ajax, before Stuy stepped up to take over. Suurbier, Hulshoff and Krol were joined in the back line by the versatile Suurendonk, who replaced Vasović. Had the Yugoslav been present, the four would have later been Michels' preferred defence for the European Cup Final in 1971, but an unfortunate injury to Krol would prevent that. Rijnders, Groot and Mühren made up a three-man midfield, with Van Dijk, Cruyff and Keizer in attack. A 3-1 victory set Ajax off on a run of five wins up to 17 September and the first round of the Inter-Cities Fairs Cup where they had been paired with West Germany's Hannover.

Intermixed with those league wins were two friendlies. The first saw Ajax travel to Turin on 27 August to face Juventus, where Groot would score in the 2-1 defeat, after coming from the bench following the break to replace Mühren.

123

On 7 September, Groot was called up to the Netherlands squad for a World Cup qualifying game away to Poland, and played the 90 minutes despite suffering a knee injury during the game. It would keep him out of the Ajax team for six weeks and, after an abortive attempt to return to action, a longer period on the sidelines followed. Eventually, in March 1970, Ajax announced that Groot would never play at the top level again due to the knee injury. He retired having scored 196 goals in 279 Eredivisie games, and stayed with Ajax as a scout until 1971.

Both Keizer and Cruyff were absent for the short trip across the border to Hannover. It promised to be a difficult encounter, and Michels was glad to have Vasović back with Suurbier, Hulshoff and Krol in front of Bals. The midfield reflected the coach's concerns and, alongside Rijnders, Mühren and Muller, Suurendonk was drafted in, with just Swart and Van Dijk to offer an attacking threat.

The German club had finished in an undistinguished 11th place in the Bundesliga the previous season, with only the quaint intricacies of Inter-Cities Fairs Cup qualification criteria allowing them entry into the competition ahead of five teams who finished above them. Even more strange was that Hertha Berlin also qualified, despite finishing just three points away from the relegation zone. Under Yugoslavian coach Zlatko Čajkovski, Hannover had been difficult to beat, losing just 11 games across the Bundesliga season, a record only bettered by the champions Bayern Munich and two other clubs. The tie looked to be anything but easy, as was borne out by Ajax's away leg, when they suffered a 2-1 defeat. Other than the friendly 2-1 loss to Juventus in Turin, it was their first reverse of the season.

There was one domestic fixture to complete before the return leg and, with Cruyff and Keizer back in the team, and

4-2-4 the order of the day again, Ajax thumped HFC Haarlem 4-0 at the De Meer to repair any dents in confidence. Three days later the Germans visited Amsterdam and faced a largely different team to the one they had overcome a week earlier.

Staying faithful to the 4-2-4 system, the back line from the Haarlem game remained in place with a combative midfield pairing of Mühren and Rijnders supporting Swart, Van Dijk, Cruyff and Keizer. The Germans had profited from the absence of Cruyff and Keizer in the first leg, but their return was quickly shown to be decisive when a solo run and goal by the former wiped out the narrow aggregate deficit midway through the first period. Just after the restart, Swart added the second after neat work by Krol, and Mühren put things beyond doubt, adding the third with 17 minutes to play. It was a comprehensive victory and Michels even had the luxury of giving Keizer a rest with ten minutes to play, sending on Muller to see out time and the win.

The victory propelled Ajax into a run of four Eredivisie games where they scored 11 times, conceding just once, in a 4-1 away victory over Holland Sport, from a late penalty when the home team were already trailing by four goals. Moving into the late-autumn period, the unbeaten league record would then face its sternest test with a visit to the De Kuip on 2 November. More than 65,000 people were jammed into the stadium as Michels' team faced the club who had usurped them as national champions. In the opposite dugout sat Ernst Happel. Now a few months into his reign in Rotterdam he had already drilled his squad into his required pattern of play and, as Van Hanegem mentioned above, they were both physically and mentally stronger than they had been when winning the Eredivisie title the previous season.

The game was tight and often overly physical as both teams battled for ascendancy, with experienced referee Jef

Dorpmans hard-pressed to keep the temperature below boiling point. Chances occurred at each end but, with time running out, a goalless draw seemed to be inevitable. It was then that the discarded Van Duivenbode had his moment of glory. Striding forward on the left flank, he hit a rising shot from 25 metres that gave Bals little chance and won the game for Feyenoord. The modern-day principle of not celebrating goals against a previous club was still some way off into the future and, although there was little evidence of the player seeking to mock the visitors' bench, his joy was justifiably effusive.

The defeat was a setback for Ajax, but there was little time for licking wounds and self-sympathy. Two more Eredivisie victories quickly followed before the second round of the Inter-Cities Fairs Cup came around on 19 November and a visit from the Polish club Ruch Chorzów. The same 11 and formation that had overwhelmed Hannover at the De Meer took the field for the first leg and left 90 minutes later with the game and tie settled. Even though it had taken 42 minutes to break the deadlock, seven goals without reply were more than enough to make the second leg largely redundant. A 2-1 win in Poland completed the job with plenty to spare.

In Europe, despite losing in Hannover with a depleted team, 4-2-4 was working well for Michels and, understandably he persisted with it as his players continued to dominate domestic games. Two more Eredivisie victories were secured before the next European task. This one promised to be far more testing, however, as Ajax were paired with Napoli. Just six months after enduring the defeat to Milan, the level of development of Michels' new team would be tested against another Serie A club.

The Stadio San Paolo – now renamed as the Stadio Diego Armando Maradona – is an intimidating place for any visiting team and, for the first leg played in Naples, as with the trip to Hannover, Michels was unable to select Cruyff or Keizer for his squad, with the former suspended and the latter injured. The now-default defence was in place in front of Bals and, to strengthen his team's presence in the middle of the field, Michels added Muller to the Rijnders and Mühren regular pairing. The attack comprised Swart, Van Dijk and Denmark's Tom Søndergaard.

The Italians had been characteristically efficient in the earlier stages. In the first round, a 1-1 draw in France against Metz set them up to complete the task, winning 2-1 at home in the return. In the next round, a goalless draw in Stuttgart was again the perfect start, and a late goal in Naples by Canzi saw them progress. Having not been behind in either tie, and with a young Dino Zoff in goal, if Napoli could achieve any kind of lead in the home leg then Ajax would have a difficult task overcoming it. Despite Michels' caution, however, his team did concede, with Pier Paolo Manservisi putting Napoli ahead after 37 minutes, and they took that lead into the return game. Unusually, the tie was scheduled to have straddled the Christmas and New Year festivities. The game in Naples took place on 10 December, with the return in the calendar for 7 January. As with the tie against Liverpool four years earlier, the winter fog in Amsterdam intervened, and the second leg was delayed for two weeks.

Four days after the first leg, Ajax beat the Haarlem-based amateur club EDO 4-0 in the KNVB Cup, but didn't play again until the 0-0 draw at NEC on 18 January, more than a month since their last outing. A further three days later they would face the return leg against Napoli. The huge gap in fixtures posed a problem for Michels. Should he play his best team in Nijmegen to ensure they had a game before the Italians visited, or would that risk an injury after such a long absence from serious competition? He opted for the first-choice 11. On any normal occasion the coach would have been confident of a win against the team who finished below halfway in the league, but the result probably justified his thinking that shaking off the rust of inaction was less of a risk against domestic opponents. In a scrappy game, without an injured Keizer, and goalless at half-time, Ajax eventually prevailed 2-1 after falling behind on 65 minutes to a goal from Bouwmeester. Immediately after conceding, Michels sent on Suurendonk to replace Søndergaard, and a late brace by Swart swung the game in Ajax's favour.

In the big game, Michels went with his 4-2-4 formation now having a fit Keizer back to face the Italians. The fog had gone but the January Amsterdam evening was still bitingly cold and frost carpeted much of the pitch, with gloves and hats de rigueur on the benches and slips and slides unavoidable on the treacherous playing surface. Scoring against such a resolute and experienced defence would not be easily achieved, as had been proven against Milan. Just as dangerous, however, was the threat of an away goal from the visitors, which could have snuffed out all hope.

Unsurprisingly, with the Italians keen to protect their slender advantage, there was little room for much of Ajax's attacking play as the visitors' organised defensive line snuffed out the early home attacks. The breakthrough came on 35 minutes. A short corner was played back to Keizer and, when his cross came in, it was bundled home by the diminutive Swart from a couple of metres. The aggregate was now level but the goal did little to change Napoli's approach to the game.

Studied defence was still their watchword, while looking to strike on the break. It largely served its purpose. Throughout the remainder of the night, neither side could force an opening and, at the final whistle, extra time was required to settle the issue.

Whether driven by caution or necessitated by an injury to the removed player, before the 30 minutes began, Suurendonk was called on to replace Van Dijk. Cometh the hour – well, the half-hour in this case – cometh the man, as they say. Whatever the cause, Michels and Ajax would reap a rich dividend from the change. Other than in friendlies the midfielder would only score ten goals for Ajax across a six-year career in Amsterdam. Remarkably, three of them would come in a nine-minute spell in this game.

The first 15-minute period came and went without any goals but, shortly after the teams had changed ends, Suurendonk began his glut. The first came when a pass from Cruyff found him in space on the edge of the Napoli box; a swift left-footed shot ripped into Zoff's net and Ajax had the lead. On the Ajax bench and in the crowd behind it, the clouds of hot breath exhaled and rapidly condensing in the cold with celebrations almost created a new blanket of fog.

Suurendonk's previous goal had been in October 1968 against Sport Holland, some 16 months earlier, but after putting Ajax ahead he wouldn't have to wait that long for his next one. Only four more minutes had passed when Zoff parried a shot from Mühren and the ball fell invitingly for Suurendonk to fire home unchallenged. The substitute had entered the field wearing number 14. That shirt would later become synonymous with another Ajax player but, it's doubtful if even the great man himself had ever had such an impact on a game in so short a time.

The game now looked won and Michels took Swart off, strengthening the midfield by replacing him with Muller soon after the goal. Suurendonk wasn't done with the Napoli defence just yet though. Five minutes later he met Muller's cross from the right to flick the ball home at the near post. The celebration of the hat-trick goal was, not unreasonably, a mixture of joy and disbelief. He had never scored more than one in a match, and would never in the rest of his time with Ajax do it again. Three in nine minutes of such an important game was the very stuff of dreams. For the next Eredivisie fixture, however, the hero of the hour was back on the bench as reality and the cold steel of the coach's axe shook the midfielder from the seductive embrace of a golden memory.

Throughout the remainder of January, through February and into March, Ajax continued to garner Eredivisie points. The only team to deny them a win were MVV who earned a 1-1 draw in Maastricht, thanks to a late equaliser by Quaedackers after Keizer had put Ajax ahead in the first half. The last eight of the Inter-Cities Fairs Cup paired Ajax with the East Germans of Carl Zeiss Jena, with the first leg away. A confident squad travelled to the city on the banks of the Saale river on 4 March in search of a result that would make the return in Amsterdam a relatively comfortable task. Michels' established first 11 were deployed and the briefly prolific Suurendonk was even on the bench in case of emergencies. They were in for a rude awakening. After a hectic ten-minute spell, by the 32nd minute the home team had established a three-goal lead with Ducke netting a brace and Stein scoring in between. Instead of anticipating a comfortable game in the return, Ajax were staring at the exit door. A late goal by Vasović offered a glimmer of hope but the East Germans still held a substantial lead.

With the second leg due the following week, there was just time for Ajax to secure another Eredivisie win, before the Germans arrived in Amsterdam. There were no changes to Michels' selected first 11 as they sought a rescue act. It was another bitter night with the visiting players wearing tights inside their shorts, but it was Ajax forced to feel the ice-cold grip of impending doom when a long clearance from the visiting goalkeeper was helped on towards Ducke, who compounded his hero status from the first leg and gave his side the lead after 16 minutes. The players celebrated with the coaches on the bench as if the tie was now beyond Ajax, and it took the intervention of referee Norman Burtenshaw to break up the party.

The slippery surface was hardly conducive to Ajax's slick passing game, with turning in any kind of short distance fraught with the danger of falling to the ground. Regardless, however, they now needed a minimum of four goals to progress. The first came just four minutes after they had fallen behind as Vasović, up in support of the attack for a set piece, collected a ball headed clear from a corner and drove low through a crowd and into the net. It was a start but more goals were needed. The strike had reignited the Dutch belief and, shortly afterwards, a Cruyff header was turned over the bar by a diving save after some extravagant play by Keizer. The resulting corner was driven in low by Keizer, and, after a brief scramble, the ball popped up into the air for Swart to score with a diving header. Ajax were ahead on the day and back in the tie.

The visitors were now becoming prisoners in their own half as Ajax poured forward in waves of attacks. Each time the Germans regained possession, the ball was merely pumped long downfield to relieve the pressure, albeit briefly before the next attack came. With the break beckoning, another long clearance was hit into the Ajax half but a towering header from Hulshoff returned it with interest, and a flicked header on found Keizer in the box. A drilled low shot squared the aggregate scores.

The home team were now clearly in the ascendancy with the Germans struggling to contain the increasingly ebullient Ajax attacks. The half-time break brought little respite and the established pattern of play quickly reappeared after the restart. It took a further eight minutes for Ajax to go ahead when Swart scored again after work from Van Dijk, and Cruyff added the fifth. There was still 20 minutes to play but Jena were, by now, a beaten team and Ajax coasted to a victory that had looked hugely unlikely 50 minutes earlier. They were into the last four of the competition and would face the English club, Arsenal.

Returning to domestic matters, a further four Eredivisie games followed with successive victories as Ajax consolidated their position at the top of the table before the first leg of the Fairs Cup semi-final away to Arsenal. The Gunners had finished 11 points behind champions Leeds United the previous season but, as the highest-ranked London club, they took the 'one club per city' allocation in the competition. A scrappy 3-1 aggregate win over Glentoran and an impressive 3-0 home victory against Sporting Lisbon, after a goalless away draw, had taken Bertie Mee's team to a last-16 encounter against Rouen of France. A single-goal win and another goalless draw were sufficient for progress and in the quarter-final they hammered Dinamo Bacău of Romania to reach the last four. Since disposing of Liverpool five years earlier, the tie would be Ajax's first encounter with an English club. It would be a sobering experience.

On 8 April, Michels selected his established first team for the visit to Highbury. In front of Bals, the regular four of Suurbier, Vasović, Hulshoff and Krol lined up behind the midfield pairing of Mühren and Rijnders with Swart, Cruyff, Van Dijk and Keizer as the front four. In the biggest games, despite the occasional reversion to 4-3-3, Michels still placed his faith in 4-2-4. The next couple of months, however, would bring that faith into serious question, illustrate the need for the missing piece of Michels' Ajax jigsaw, and complete the *totaalvoetbal* revolution.

Mee's mixture of English and Scottish players, who would complete the double of First Division championship and FA Cup triumph the following season, matched up with the visitors by deploying a 4-4-2 formation and, on a muddy, cloying Highbury pitch, they dominated much of the game. Wearing their change strip of yellow shirts and blue shorts, the more muscular Arsenal players ploughed through a pitch that prevented Ajax playing their natural game, and it was of little surprise when they went ahead on 16 minutes through Charlie George.

Bals's goal had already come under strong pressure when a headed clearance fell to George some 20 metres from goal, and he fired low past the Dutch goalkeeper to open the scoring. For a while Ajax were forced back as the Gunners pressed for the second strike. A couple of half-chances fell to Ajax but, in the home goal, there was little of much concern to Bob Wilson. At the break, Michels sought to solidify his team's play and sent the more solid Suurendonk on to replace Keizer. The move seemed to have the desired effect and Ajax gained more of a foothold in the game with the substitute often dropping deeper into midfield to reinforce Rijnders and Mühren, effectively converting Ajax into a 4-3-3 formation. There were even more concerted forays forwards and one occasion saw Swart fire into the side-netting from a dangerous position.

Inside the final 15 minutes, a broadly acceptable single-goal defeat looked achievable for Ajax, but tired minds and limbs aching from the exertions demanded by the playing surface would work against such aspirations. With 13 minutes to play a shot from the right beat Bals but was blocked on the line. The rebound was hammered back in by Sammels, and this time there was no last-ditch clearance. Arsenal had doubled their lead. Finally, with just five minutes to play, the tie was surely put beyond redemption when George converted from a penalty, hitting low to Bals's right and into the net, when the goalkeeper many well have done better.

Back in the Netherlands, while Ajax fans were compelled to contemplate elimination from European competition, around 50 miles away in Rotterdam the supporters of Feyenoord had opposing emotions. A goalless draw away to Legia Warsaw on the first day of April had left Happel's team just any kind of home win away from reaching the European Cup Final. Two weeks later, on the same evening that Ajax were facing a seemingly insurmountable task against Arsenal, Feyenoord would complete the task with goals from Van Hanegem and Vasil to take their place in European club football's biggest game in Milan's San Siro against Celtic. Where Ajax had foundered 12 months earlier, Happel and Feyenoord would triumph. Before that occasion, though, a key Eredivisie game between the pair would do so much to shape the fortunes and future of both clubs.

Arsenal arrived in Amsterdam in a confident and relaxed frame of mind to face the same starting 11 that had lost at Highbury, but wearing a changed strip of all blue, as the Gunners reverted to their traditional colours. Arsenal's domestic season had petered out into a mid-table position, with just one league fixture to complete after returning from the Netherlands. With early exits from both English cups the Inter-Cities Fairs Cup now had their full focus, while for Ajax their attention was also on the Eredivisie title and KNVB Cup. If Michels' team were to offer a realistic challenge to break down the three-goal deficit, an early strike was surely required.

The opening phases of the game had been fairly even, although Arsenal were more content to sit deep and defend, awaiting opportunities to strike on the break, while defence was their first priority. Neither goalkeeper had been seriously tested when the first goal came. On 16 minutes, a pass to Keizer saw him into the Arsenal box, and his cross-shot was parried by Wilson. Following in, Mühren just got to the ball first and forced it over the line. Ajax had their foot on the first rung of the ladder they needed to climb.

For the next five minutes, perhaps stung by the goal, Arsenal pressed forward with more purpose. The change delivered a little more threat on Bals's goal, but also opened up space for the Ajax forwards that had been largely denied to them before the goal. It wasn't long, however, before wiser counsel – and insistent promptings from the bench – returned the visitors to their initial formation, with John Radford occasionally supported by George as their sole attacking threat. A two-goal advantage was still a fairly comfortable cushion and, aside from the goal, Wilson had hardly been troubled.

As the rain began to fall on the crowd, their enthusiasm was slowing being dampened. Arsenal were raining on the Ajax parade. After the excitement of the goal, the crowd of almost 40,000 at the Olympisch Stadion felt their hopes were being washed away as the English club played out the remainder of the first 45 minutes without any further major scares. Other than a clearance from the line by Frank McLintock in the dying minutes of the half, Arsenal had kept Ajax's forwards at bay with a measure of comfort.

The job was now half completed, and Arsenal opened the second half in resolute fashion. For the first ten minutes they hardly looked to push forward at all, content to rebuff the eager but so often ineffective attacks of Ajax. With

George Graham and George Armstrong both dropping off to reinforce the midfield and overwhelming Rijnders and Mühren, any considered build-up play by Michels' team was being strangled before it reached the Arsenal area. It meant that Ajax were often compelled to hit long balls that hardly suited their players. It was, however, meat and drink to an Arsenal back line very much accustomed to this type of play in the English game, and they mopped up at the back with some comfort. There were even threats at the other end occurring as well. Towards the hour mark, a cross from Graham required an acrobatic tip away from Bals, with Radford waiting to pounce.

As the half ticked on, the mood of disenchantment growing in the crowd was beginning to be mirrored on the field as a string of niggling fouls and impossible passes, which squandered possession and frittered away time, illustrated the frustration of the Ajax players as they struggled to deliver any meaningful threat on the Arsenal goal. Approaching the final 15 minutes, the tie was nearly put beyond the diminishing hopes of Ajax and their fans. A shot from the edge of the box by Eddie Kelly was blocked by Bals, but the ball ran out to Graham. His shot passed the still fallen Bals but also slipped beyond the far post. With time ebbing away, it probably mattered little, but just emphasised the growing confidence among the visitors that the job was now almost done.

At the final whistle, the defeat had not been as comprehensive as the one suffered against Milan, but the opposition was not as strong either, although Arsenal would go on to win the Fairs Cup. Even throwing Hulshoff forward as a last throw of the dice had failed. For Michels' team it was another lesson on their journey, harshly delivered. Progress was undeniably being made but there was still a distance to travel. What had proven largely sufficient to sweep aside the lesser lights of Dutch domestic football had been shown to still be lacking on the continental stage. Bertie Mee certainly thought that to be the case. 'Ajax were very effective and played particularly well with very talented individuals, but somehow they didn't quite look the part physically,' he said, before adding, 'They looked very amateurish.'[46] The end of the season would see more changes.

A 7-1 victory away to DOS and then a quarter-final success in the KNVB Cup against DWS would have done little to ease the coach's minds, but those victories would lead up to what would later be regarded as the key game of the season. Back in November, that late strike by former Ajax player Van Duivenbode had sent Michels' team to defeat at the De Kuip. Despite that, when the reverse fixture came along on 26 April, Ajax were topping the table and, for Feyenoord just ten days ahead of their date with Celtic in Milan, if they were to retain their league title, a win would be required.

Michels sent out his first-choice 11, the players who had started both games against Arsenal. If they could avoid defeat in the fixture, with just half a dozen league games to follow, it would be broadly akin to being crowned champions and securing another run in the European Cup. With 20 minutes remaining, however, that looked to be a distant dream as Feyenoord were dominating and leading 3-1. Kindvall had put the visitors ahead after 11 minutes and, despite a Swart header levelling things up 15 minutes later, the lead had been restored by Hasil before the break. And when a header by Wery made it 3-1, it looked like the title chase would be thrown open. Happel's fluid 4-3-3 formation had seen them control much of the game. Feyenoord's superiority in the midfield, as they outnumbered Rijnders and Mühren, had made Michels'

---

46 Winner, David, *Brilliant Orange* (London: Bloomsbury, 2000).

4-2-4 look staid and rigid. It was the very opposite of what was required to operate a *totaalvoetbal* system.

There's a Dutch phrase, *Meten is weten* (Measuring things brings knowledge). Michels took the necessary knowledge from the game. Seeing his team outplayed, and himself outthought, by Happel convinced Michels that his adherence to 4-2-4 must be ended, with 4-3-3 adopted instead. The decision would lead to another major signing in the summer and set Ajax on to a course of European domination. The defeat to Arsenal had been a cautionary tale and the game against Feyenoord had been another milestone on Ajax's journey. This one, however, not only stated that the end was in sight, it also pointed the way forward.

The game itself would also prove to be significant for Feyenoord and Happel, but not in the way the Austrian would have expected after Wery's goal put his dominant team two goals clear with just 20 minutes to play. When he had taken the job, Happel had decided to relegate the established goalkeeper and sometime captain of the club, 35-year-old Eddy Pieters Graafland, to the backup spot and bought in 23-year-old Eddy Treytel from Xerxes as the new number one.

Treytel had retained the position as Feyenoord's first choice ever since, and was still between the posts in this game. His performance against Ajax would, however, be costly both for his team and himself. Just 60 seconds after Wery's strike evaded Bals and ended up in the back of the Ajax net, a Treytel error gifted Ajax a way back as Cruyff profited both from Keizer's pass and the goalkeeping error. Then, to compound things, inside the last ten minutes, another poor piece of goalkeeping by Treytel allowed Suurbier to equalise. The game, and Feyenoord's realistic chance of retaining their league title, had slipped through the goalkeeper's gloves. The mistakes would cost Treytel as, when the big day came in

Milan, Happel selected the veteran Graafland, with Treytel relegated to the substitutes' bench.

The draw was sufficient to blunt Feyenoord's title challenge and, in the remaining games, Ajax garnered sufficient points to win the league. They had won 27 of their 34 matches, scoring precisely 100 goals and finishing five points clear of their Rotterdam rivals, with PSV a further nine points adrift in third place. Both clubs had only lost once, Ajax at the De Kuip and Feyenoord a significant 3-0 defeat away to PSV. Ajax also went on to win the KNVB Cup, defeating Vitesse 4-0 in the semi-final and then PSV 2-0 in the final. Another domestic double restored a little of Ajax's pride as top club in the Netherlands, but that was dented significantly by Feyenoord's win in Milan to become the first Dutch club to be crowned as champions of Europe.

When asked how Feyenoord's triumph was received at the De Meer, Ruud Krol was clearly still feeling the raw emotions of the day: 'Ajax were the first to reach a final, but Feyenoord were the first to win the cup. Of course, there was big rivalry between Ajax and Feyenoord. We were happy that a Dutch club had won the European Cup but, of course, we were disappointed that it wasn't us.' At the time, Arie Haan was still awaiting his major breakthrough at Ajax and would play just one first-team game that season. It was 18 days after Feyenoord's European triumph, in the final Eredivisie game – away to ADO Den Haag – when the title had already been secured. He played the full 90 minutes and scored Ajax's 80th-minute equaliser. The young midfielder concurred with Krol's assessment, but also recalled seeing the triumph of Ajax's arch-rivals as an incentive for the future.

Jaap de Groot, who would later become the celebrated *De Telegraaf* journalist, remembered how many Dutch football fans took a much less partisan view. Having a Dutch club win the European Cup wasn't only a triumph for Happel, Feyenoord and Rotterdam, he suggested, it was also a reason for the whole country to celebrate, especially after Ajax had been beaten by Milan in the previous year's final. A Dutch club were champions of Europe, and 'it didn't matter if it was Rotterdam or Amsterdam, everybody was for Feyenoord'.[47] A fine sentiment, but it may well have found many dissenting voices around the De Meer.

The following season, for the first time, the European Cup would have two Dutch clubs competing for the title: Ajax as Eredivisie champions, and Feyenoord as the holders. When the time came for Feyenoord to hand over the trophy to the new champions, it would only need to travel around 50 miles to find its new home, where it would live for the following three years. Before then, though, with the lessons of the season measured and learned, Michels would have another of his rebuilds.

Bals left for Vitesse Arnhem with Stuy promoted as number-one goalkeeper for the new season. Groot had retired earlier in the season and was joined by Pronk, albeit temporarily. Muller moved to Holland Sport and Søndergaard would join French club Metz in December. Rebuilds are primarily about who comes in rather than who leaves, though, and, among eight new recruits were three names who would become legends at the club.

Johann Neeskens joined from Racing Club Heemstede for a sum reported as 136,134 guilders, although some 'newspapers mention an amount that is higher than 300,000 guilders'.[48] Whatever the true figure, the value of Neeskens to Michels' plans was clear. It was the dynamic midfielder's

---

47 https://www.champions-journal.com/1000/ajax-71
48 https://www.afc-ajax.info/

play that allowed the 'pressing' element of *totaalvoetbal* to be fully deployed. It was the final piece in the jigsaw. The picture now looked complete.

The electrifying effect of Neeskens' introduction would be immediate. The other two recruits destined for fame would have to wait a little longer before being invited to the big party. Johnny Rep joined from his local club, ZFC Zaandam, that summer, but wouldn't be involved in first-team action until the 1971/72 season. The other player was German defender Horst Blankenburg, who moved to Ajax from 1860 Munchen. He was destined to take over from Vasović as Hulshoff's defensive partner when the Yugoslav retired in the summer of 1971, but also came close to starting the 1971 European Cup Final after injury had denied Ruud Krol a place at Wembley. He would eventually see action as a half-time substitute.

As well as the players Michels had added in 1970 and across the previous seasons, many of the established first-team squad who had risen through the ranks were also becoming more experienced. Players such as Suurbier, Hulshoff, Krol, Keizer, Swart and, of course, Cruyff were now increasingly experienced and maturing into the finished article.

It was a situation that the coach would later describe in his book: 'Football coaches have often been compared to conductors. Every musician plays his own role and instrument in an orchestra. It is not only the task of the conductor to ensure that every one of the individual musicians is able to contribute, he must also ensure that the result is harmonic. It is the important prerequisite to achieve a unique performance, which is greater than the sum of the individual achievements of all musicians together.'[49]

---

49 Michels, Rinus, *Teambuilding: The Road to Success* (Spring City: Reedswain Incorporated, 2013).

Michels' orchestra was ready to play, but the loss of their lead violin would strike an early season note of discord before the sweetest of music could be performed.

Part 3: 1970/71 – The beginning of an era! The end of an era?

THE NEW season opened with the traditional string of friendlies as Rinus Michels tested and tried out his squad. The first game saw the team travel to Assen. With Gert Bals now departed, Ajax required a replacement goalkeeper as cover for Heinz Stuy and signed Sies Wever from AS Assen, offering the new arrival his first game in goal against his old club on 22 July. Wever would stay with Ajax for four seasons, stepping into the breach when required, as and when Stuy was unavailable. His career in Amsterdam would only comprise 30 games but he would achieve a distinction that Stuy did not, and nor did most other goalkeepers at any club.

During a friendly in 1972 against VV Drachten, Wever was covering for the injured Stuy. Despite the stand-in custodian conceding a goal on five minutes to the amateur club, Ajax were leading 9-2 when they were awarded a penalty as time drifted away. Wever was invited to come forward and take the score into double figures from the spot. He duly obliged. Stuy would later have a chance to level things up in the final league game of the season. With the title already lost to Feyenoord – the Rotterdam club needed a single point in their final game at home to bottom-of-the table Haarlem – and the European Cup secured in the Wembley final four days earlier, allegedly for a bet some suggest, while for others it was following a request from the goalkeeper to the coach, Stuy was selected to play as a forward against Go Ahead Eagles. Wever returned in goal to facilitate the change but neither player covered themselves in glory. Stuy failed to find the back of the net, and Wever conceded four goals as Ajax lost 4-1. As was expected to be the case, it mattered little; Ersnt Happel's team beat Haarlem 2-1 to secure the title. Ajax's same game was also significant for Velibor Vasović who came off the bench to replace Wim Suurbier with 15 minutes to play. It was his final game for the club before retirement.

Wever's success from 12 yards in a friendly was hardly likely to enhance his status a number-two goalkeeper, and Stuy quickly returned to claim the gloves on a regular basis as the more serious games of the season drew near. Before the first Eredivisie fixture, Michels had flirted between 4-2-4 and 4-3-3, still apparently to be totally won over by the need to change. When the league programme got under way with a visit to Nijmegen on 23 August, however, the latter was the preferred option, even though the selected players and result were hardly what the coach would have chosen. Johan Cruyff had suffered an injury 20 minutes from the end of a friendly against Club Brugge in Belgium earlier in the month and was unavailable with problems to ankle and groin ruling him out. It boded ill for the club as a laboured performance only resulted in a goalless draw. Cruyff wouldn't return to full fitness until the end of October, and Ajax were far less effective without him.

For Ajax's first home league game of the season MVV visited the De Meer. The draw in their opener against a club that had finished mid-table in the previous term was far from satisfactory, despite it being played away from home. Anything other than victory against the club from Maastricht was unthinkable. Against NEC, Michels had played Barry Hulshoff as part of a midfield three alongside Johan Neeskens and Nico Rijnders, with Ruud Suurendonk slotting in next to Vasović in the back line, alongside Suurbier and Ruud Krol. The front three of Sjaak Swart, Dick van Dijk and Piet Keizer had failed to find the net, but the same 11 started against MVV.

Another 40 minutes passed without Ajax scoring and Michels decided on a change at the break. The gamble of using Hulshoff's dominating presence in midfield and Suurendonk's forward thinking at the back had failed to ignite his team. A goal by Krol, set up by Hulshoff, may have put some doubt into the coach's mind but, when the players emerged for the second period, Suurendonk was missing. Hulshoff was back alongside Vasović, and substitute Gerrie Mühren slotted into the gap in midfield. Any team reliant on the skills of Cruyff would look poorer without him but, with a more settled look to the team, Ajax's performance improved after the restart and Van Dijk added a second goal on 65 minutes. It hadn't been overly convincing but Ajax had that all-important win.

Michels was still looking for the magic formula that would compensate for the missing totemic influence of Cruyff as Ajax travelled to the Hague to face ADO a week later. The newly acquired dynamism of Neeskens had immediately impressed the coach and, with the experiment of playing Suurendonk next to Vasović now discarded, Neeskens was given the role, and tasked with increasing the vibrancy of his team that 4-3-3, and *totaalvoetbal* allowed. Hulshoff returned to the midfield, offering the flexibility of dropping back to cover any forward enterprises from Neeskens or Vasović.

The club that Happel had left in order to take control at Feyenoord was now playing under Czechoslovakian coach

Václav Ježek, who had moved to the Eredivisie after leading Sparta Prague to two league titles in his country of birth. Picking up the team that Happel built, Ježek would lead ADO to the top of the Eredivisie table in 1970/71, and they remained there until Feyenoord and Ajax both reeled his team in during the spring. ADO would finish in a highly creditable third place. Ježek proved to be an accomplished coach and would later lead the Czechoslovakia national team to European Championship success in 1976. His team would defeat the *Oranje* in the semi-final, before Antonín Panenka completed a penalty shoot-out victory against West Germany in the final with a spot-kick that would bear his name for evermore. The coach would return to Dutch domestic football in 1978, taking over at Feyenoord and delivering the KNVB Cup in 1979/80.

His ADO team were playing confident football and Ajax struggled to get back on even terms once Schoenmaker had given the hosts a first-half lead. With 25 minutes to play, Michels sent on Arie Haan to replace Hulshoff and Suurendonk instead of Keizer, but it made little difference. Three league games into the new season and Ajax had a single win to their name. Cruyff was still absent and it seemed that, without him, 4-3-3, and *totaalvoetbal*, was proving ineffective.

On 12 September, Cruyff was rushed back into the team for the visit of DWS and yet, somewhat perversely, Michels reverted to 4-2-4. Hulshoff was back alongside Vasović with Suurbier and Krol guarding the flanks. Rijnders and Neeskens were in midfield, with Cruyff joining the forward line. The returnee lasted for just 17 minutes though, before having to be replaced by Suurendonk. Ajax would run out as 4-0 winners, but the gamble on Cruyff's fitness had catastrophically failed. There would be a price to be pay for gambling on his fitness;

Cruyff's next competitive game wouldn't come until 30 October, ten games later.

As both Krol and Haan mentioned in the previous chapter, the success of Feyenoord in winning the European Cup had filled Ajax with added determination to also reach the summit of European club football. The same desire burned within Michels and, with the first round of the European Cup scheduled for just four days after the game against DWS, the desire to get Cruyff back into his team may well have seduced the coach into his failed gamble. Ajax were pitched against 17 Nëntori. On 16 September they visited the Qemal Stafa Stadium in Tirana and if, after reaching the final a couple of seasons previously, opponents from Albania looked to offer a fairly comfortable passage to the second round, such assumptions were to be summarily dismissed.

Michels had, at least temporarily, abandoned the notion of slotting a midfielder into his back line to increase the team's dynamism and Hulshoff was back next to Vasović. It would be a move destined to bring dividends, with Hulshoff a complete enough footballer to give the forward momentum to his team when playing out from the back anyway, without sacrificing any defensive solidarity. Rijnders, Neeskens and Mühren were in midfield with Swart, Van Dijk and Keizer as the forward line as Michels returned to 4-3-3. When Ajax passed the hour with a two-goal lead none of those three forwards had found the net, but perhaps *totaalvoetbal* had. Rampaging down the right, with the freedom of having others to cover his sallies forward, Suurbier had scored both goals.

Seven minutes after Suurbier's second strike, a header from Kazanxhi halved the deficit, and Michels would have been disappointed for his team to have conceded a late equaliser with five minutes to play. A draw, with the home leg to come, is always a useful result, but the coach would have been expecting more, especially after being two goals clear. His team were still settling into their new mode of play though, and Cruyff's absence remained a major roadblock on the road to achieving that end.

Perhaps things were at least beginning to gel though. A comfortable 3-0 victory against RKSV Volendam and then a 3-1 win over Telstar brightened up Ajax's Eredivisie standing ahead of the return leg against Nëntori, who visited Amsterdam on the last day of September. Suurendonk had been introduced into the starting line-up after the trip to Tirana and his willingness and ability to shuttle between midfield and forward line as the game required had proved to be a key element in the improvement. He was retained for the second leg and Michels was rewarded with another two-goal lead, thanks to an early goal from Keizer and a late one from Swart. This time the Ajax defence held firm to earn a second-round tie against Basel, with the first leg in Amsterdam on 21 October.

On the same day as Ajax eased past 17 Nëntori, Feyenoord's brief reign as European champions was unexpectedly brought to an abrupt end. Drawn to face the little-known Romanian club Arad in the first round of their defence of the title, a disappointing 1-1 draw at the De Kuip meant that a goal in the away leg was the minimum required in order to progress. Despite fielding many of the players who had won the title in Milan just over four months earlier, a drab goalless draw in Arad's compact Stadionul Francisc von Neuman meant elimination on away goals for Happel's team. Few had expected the Romanians to offer serious opposition to the reigning champions let alone knock them out, and Arad returned to more expected form in the following round when shipping six goals against Red Star Belgrade on their way through the exit door. Feyenoord's elimination left Ajax to fly the flag for Dutch football in the competition.

Four days after the victory over the Albanians, Ajax's next Eredivisie game was an away fixture against Excelsior in Rotterdam. Maintaining the momentum achieved by recent results was important but Michels was compelled to make a change to his starting 11, replacing the unavailable Keizer with Mühren. The switch hardly helped. Despite Van Dijk putting the visitors ahead early in the second half, an equaliser by Kwakkernaat with 15 minutes left meant the points would be shared. After Ajax's defeat against ADO, Michels had gambled – and lost – by bringing Cruyff back into the team. On 11 October he did so again, for a friendly against Blauw-Wit, deploying the returning forward in a deeper midfield role. The result, a 3-2 victory for Ajax was far less important than the fact that, once again, it looked to have been a mistake to play him and he would miss the next three games, including the home leg against Basel.

There was one more Eredivisie fixture before the Swiss champions arrived in Amsterdam, as Sparta Rotterdam visited the De Meer in the middle of October. Mühren replaced Suurendonk in his midfield/forward role for the game. The latter dropped to the bench, but the demotion would only be temporary as, at half-time, with Ajax trailing to an Heijerman penalty, Suurendonk was brought into action to replace Swart. The change delivered immediate dividends as the substitute equalised three minutes after the restart. Vasović added a penalty to put Ajax ahead and, when Michels sent the young and energetic Haan on to replace Keizer with 20 minutes to play, it was a ploy aimed at preserving the win rather than adding to the lead. Ajax were undone, though, when Heijerman reprised his success from the first period and beat Stuy from 12 yards for the second time in the closing minutes of the game, and another valuable two points turned into just one.

Flexibility was becoming the watchword of Michels' selections and the 11 named for the game against Basel at the Olympisch Stadion suggested something akin to a 3-2-5 formation. Suurbier, Vasocvic and Hulshoff were at the back, behind Neeskens and Rijnders, with Suurendonk, Swart, Mühren, Van Dijk and Keizer in attack. The play would show that both Mühren and Suurendonk would support the midfield, however, in what was designed to be a fluid system, very much in the form of *totaalvoetbal*. The ploy would bring an early reward with 17 minutes played. Keizer charged forwards, played a wall pass with Suurendonk on the edge of the area, and then drove low past Kunz to give Ajax the lead.

The fluidity of the system continued to give the Basel midfield and defenders more than enough problems. They were compelled to chase elusive shadows as the Ajax players rotated roles, drawing markers out of position, and Van Dijk doubled the lead eight minutes after the first goal following a move underscoring the fluidity of the Ajax players. Discarding his left flank, Keizer took possession on the opposite side of the field. Dribbling forward, he laid the ball inside to Suurbier as the full-back appeared in the centre-forward position. A return pass inside the Basel left-back put Keizer into space inside the penalty area. Hitting the byline, he cut the ball back to Van Dijk outside the far post. The forward controlled and drilled home. Even without Cruyff, Ajax were beginning to look like a team comfortable with *totaalvoetbal*, and reaping the dividends of it.

The break came and went with Ajax in total control of the game and, 15 minutes after the restart, the third goal arrived. Keizer crossed a corner in from the left as Hulshoff made a dart into the area from a deep position. His run and powerful leap dismissed any and all arguments as he claimed the ball with a bullet header that crashed on to the bottom of the crossbar and dropped into the net with Kunz a helpless bystander. Two minutes later, sated with the three-goal lead, Michels removed Swart and sent on Krol to set up a more traditional back four and Ajax cruised to a comfortable win. It had bordered on being the perfect performance.

Cruyff was now nearing full fitness but, encouraged by his team's performance against Basel, Michels decided to leave him out for what looked like a straightforward Eredivisie game away to FC Twente in Enschede. Bringing back Krol and leaving Van Dijk on the bench, the defence was back to a four-man line, with Neeskens, Rijnders and Mühren comprising the midfield. Keizer and Swart were forward with Suurendonk also slotted into the front line to provide the link-up play.

Against Basel, an early goal had opened up the game for Ajax, allowing them to play with freedom. This game was different. They struggled to make the breakthrough and, despite the rotation of positions, without Van Dijk the attack lacked a cutting edge. After an hour of goalless play, Michels removed Suurendonk and sent Van Dijk on to the field. Ajax looked more incisive but, as is so often the way, just as their game improved, the late winning goal went to the home team; René van de Kerkhof scored it on 86 minutes.

Despite the encouraging success, and result, against Basel, Ajax had played 14 games without Cruyff and won only half of them, drawing five and suffering two defeats. The importance to the team of the talismanic forward, who was still only 23 at the time, was clear to see, and would be underscored a few years later when he left to follow Michels and joined Barcelona. For now, a fit Cruyff would return to a team that would suffer only two more losses across the remainder of the season – one of which would be wiped out on aggregate. The early months of the season had seen Michels' orchestra tune up and deliver its prelude. Their magnum opus would follow. As if to herald that, a legendary moment in the history of Ajax would be acted out as Cruyff prepared to return to the starting 11 for the Eredivisie fixture at home to PSV, and a part of his iconic identity would be created.

Until this stage of his career with the club, Cruyff had worn the number ten shirt or, more often, number nine. In the recent matches, with Cruyff absent, that shirt had been given to Mühren. Ahead of the PSV game, though, with Cruyff's return imminent, Mühren passed the shirt to Cruyff, considering it was the appropriate thing to do. As Auke Kok confirmed when asked about the incident, 'Cruyff was never really interested in numbers. They mattered very little.' Perhaps the exception to that would be when negotiating contracts, but those on the back of a shirt were hardly significant to him. As Mühren was retaining his place, Cruyff declined the offer and said his team-mate should stay with the shirt he had been wearing. At the side of the players, a pile of unused shirts lay on a table. Cruyff dipped his hand into the pile and pulled one out, declaring that he'd wear that shirt instead. The number on the back was 14. It's the sort of story that you read about and can only hope is true. In November 2019, Kok's latest book *Johan Cruijff: de biografie* was published. Who better then to ask about the validity of the story? He confirmed that it was true. In the game against PSV, Mühren wore nine and scored the only goal. Cruyff wore 14 for that day – and the rest of his career.

Following the success against Basel, Michels went for a similar plan for the visit of PSV. Krol was back on the bench as the nominal three-man back line was returned. Suurbier, Vasović and Hushoff lined up in front of Stuy. Neeskens,

Rijnders and Mühren patrolled the middle of the field, with a four-pronged attack comprising Swart, Van Dijk, Keizer and the returning Cruyff. It took until 69 minutes for Mühren to secure the breakthrough goal but, as against Basel, once he considered the game won, Michels reverted to a back four with Krol replacing Van Dijk three minutes later, and Suurendonk coming on in place of Swart as the clock ran down. It was the last day before Halloween and, in the remaining ten matches of the year, Ajax would remain unbeaten, winning all but one of them.

With Cruyff back to full fitness, and a three-goal lead from the home leg, Ajax approached the visit to Switzerland for the return against Basel in confident mood. Michels set his team up in a 4-3-3 formation that suited the returning Cruyff perfectly. Krol was back as part of the regular defence in front of Stuy. Rijnders, Mühren and Neeskens were the midfield triumvirate, with Cruyff added to the front line alongside Swart and Keizer. Perhaps aside from a debate about Van Dijk, it was probably Michels' preferred starting 11, and they duly completed the job of progressing to the quarter-finals.

Switzerland international midfielder Karl Odermatt offered a measure of hope to the home fans in the St Jakob Stadium when he converted from 12 yards after Irish referee Dermot Barrett had awarded Basel a penalty. Up to that point, and even after the goal, Ajax largely had control of the game, looking the more dangerous and likelier to score. The equaliser came on 69 minutes, conjured up by a piece of impudent magic from Cruyff. A lofted pass into the Basel penalty area by Vasović found the forward but forced him wide and tight to the goal line, facing the corner flag, where he was boxed in by two defenders. Untroubled, Cruyff flicked the ball up and then lofted it over his head, and those of the defenders marking him, to match up perfectly with a run by

Rijnders who beat Kunz in the air to head home. The goal went to the midfielder but the kudos was all Cruyff's.

With 20 minutes to play and Basel now a beaten side, Neeskens delivered the final blow three minutes later. Again, Cruyff was the architect. Hulshoff shuttled the ball forward to Neeskens who turned it inside first time to Cruyff. Another first touch saw it diverted down the left flank to Mühren, who crossed deep beyond Kunz. Cruyff had continued his run after delivering the pass and met up with the cross, flicking the ball back towards the left-hand post, where Neeskens arrived to finish off the move. Ajax were into the last eight of the European Cup.

Success in Europe had hardly been matched by results in the league. Three defeats by mid-October, given that they had suffered only one Eredivisie reverse across the entire previous season, meant that Ajax had plenty of ground to make up on Feyenoord, especially as the Rotterdam club had no European distractions for the remainder of the season, allowing them an unrestricted concentration on domestic matters. Until the European Cup started up again in March, Ajax were in a similar position, and needed to capitalise on it.

Discounting a friendly 7-0 stroll against Veerse Boys – who had invited the reigning Dutch champions to play a game to mark the commissioning of the new floodlights at their stadium – Ajax had six domestic fixtures until the end of the year, four of them away from home. A run of victories would do much to restore their position in the league, especially as the last of those six games was an away Eredivisie fixture at Feyenoord on 20 December.

The first order of business was a KNVB Cup encounter with Heracles, and Michels retained the same starting 11 that had won in Basel. An early goal from Neeskens started the game well, and second-half strikes by Cruyff and then

Van Dijk, on as a substitute for Keizer, eased Ajax into the next round. Rijnders had been injured in the first half against Heracles but both he and Keizer were back in that same unchanged starting 11 to face NAC in Breda in the Eredivisie. Again, Ajax triumphed without conceding a goal as Cruyff and Keizer found the back of the net to keep their winning streak on track.

On 22 November, Ajax returned to play in Amsterdam for the first time since the win over PSV on 30 October. Holland Sport visited the De Meer, with former Ajax player Bennie Muller appearing for the visitors. Van Dijk had been unfortunate to miss out on previous games but, with Michels playing 4-3-3 and Cruyff a shoo-in for the nominal centre-forward position, the former FC Twente man had been largely relegated to the bench after Cruyff's return. For this game, however, Michels returned the forward to the starting 11 as part of a four-man front line. Krol dropped to the bench with just Suurbier, Hulshoff and Vasović guarding Stuy.

The displaced young defender wouldn't be on the bench for long. On 27 minutes he was back into the action, when Hulshoff was injured and had to be replaced, and he slotted seamlessly into the back line. It was hardly a testing time for the defensive trio. Holland Sport would finish just above the relegation zone of the Eredivisie, winning only five games all season and averaging just a single goal per league fixture. At the other end of the pitch things were very different, and Ajax should have been two goals clear at the break.

Swart had opened the scoring on 40 minutes and, when referee Frans Derks awarded the home team a penalty shortly afterwards, Van Dijk stepped up to convert. His shot was saved, however, and despite keeping his place for the romp to mark the advent of the junior club's floodlights, he would be out of the team for the next Eredivisie game. An effort by

Roggeveen kept the visitors' goal per game ratio going and briefly threatened to spoil Ajax's homecoming after almost four weeks away, but another strike by Swart midway through the second period secured the points.

Following the injury sustained against Holland Sport, Hulshoff missed the friendly against Veerse Boys, but he returned for the home Eredivisie game against AZ '67 on 29 November. With Van Dijk dropped back to the bench, Michels could field his first-choice 11 in the 4-3-3 formation that suited them – and their *totaalvoetbal* – best. The team, and especially Cruyff, responded splendidly. The reinstated Hulshoff opened the scoring on 15 minutes, thundering in a direct free kick. Two minutes later, Mühren added a second. From there, however, the game very much became the Johan Cruyff show and by half-time he had notched a hat-trick. Each goal, as was the case with Mühren's, was created from the left by Keizer. Five minutes after the restart De Jager put a temporary halt to the carnage, nibbling away at the deficit for the Alkmaar club. It was only a brief respite as by the end of the game Cruyff had doubled his first-half haul, securing a double hat-trick. The final goal of his 'six of the best' came with 15 minutes to play after a mesmerising, coruscating solo run through the visitors' bemused defence, culminating in a sublime finish.

After such a pulsating victory no one would have been keen to face Michels' rampant team next, but the fixtures decreed that the dubious honour would fall to HFC Haarlem, and a buoyant Ajax travelled the 17km to face the club who would finish bottom of the Eredivsie at the end of the season having won just one game. Despite the goal rush against AZ, Michels made changes to his team with Krol again dropped to the bench to accommodate a three-man defence and an extra forward as Van Dijk returned. After his six-goal haul,

Cruyff struck out in Haarlem, with Van Dijk seizing on his return to net a brace. On the hour, with the game clearly won, Cruyff was removed and Krol sent on. Ajax were already four goals clear and Van Dijk's second strike would make it five by the end.

A week later, and just seven days ahead of the vital encounter with Feyenoord, Ajax welcomed Utrecht to the De Meer. Their last two Eredivisie fixtures had produced 13 goals and, throwing in the friendly against Veerse Boys, their total was 20 in three games. Any hopes the visitors may have held that Ajax had fully sated their hunger for goals were to be rudely dismissed. Starting with the same team that rattled in five at Haarlem, they were 5-1 up at the break. A lone goal by Groenendijk was overwhelmed by braces for Swart and Cruyff, plus another goal for Van Dijk. At the end of the game the total had reached seven with Swart and Cruyff both completing their hat-tricks against a dejected Utrecht defence.

Despite his team racking up the goals against lesser opposition, Michels was keenly aware that the game against Happel's Feyenoord would be an altogether different task. Ajax's run of wins had helped to fuel their bid for the title as they sought to recover from the early season points dropped when Cruyff was absent. At the same time, Feyenoord had hardly been struggling either and had little deficit to make up. With 15 Eredivisie fixtures played, ADO were the early pace-setters with 25 points. Feyenoord were in second place, trailing by a single point, but ahead of city rivals Sparta on goal difference. Ajax were back in fourth place with 23 points. The big two wouldn't head the table until spring of the following year.

Understandably, Michels temporarily abandoned his three-man back line, reverting to a 4-3-3 formation for the visit to the De Kuip. There was, however, a surprise selection.

Michels dropped Swart back from the forward line to police the right flank of defence, to cover for the absense of Suurbier. Hulshoff, Vasović and Krol completed the defence in front of Stuy. The midfield trio was the usual Neeskens, Rijnders and Mühren. Up front, the decision to reposition Swart allowed Michels to square the circle and include Van Dijk alongside Cruyff and Keizer.

At half-time things were going well for Ajax with Rijnders profiting from Neeskens' assist to open the scoring ten minutes before the break. Seeking more security for the second period, Michels removed Swart and sent on the young German defender Horst Blankenburg. While adding a defender in place of Swart was entirely logical with a one-goal lead to protect, it was Blankenburg's debut and the cauldron-like atmosphere of the De Kuip packed with almost 65,000 fans would be a test of the young defender's nerve as much as his ability. Ajax held out until just before the hour but, when Hasil equalised, it was difficult to suggest that it hadn't been deserved. At the end of the game, in terms of league positions, Happel would have been more satisfied than Michels with the draw. Both still had the task of hauling in ADO, but that would have to wait until the new year.

Between Christmas and New Year, Ajax entertained Eintracht Frankfurt in a fairly low-key friendly. Michels used the game to give Blankenburg a little more experience of first-team football, playing the defender in midfield. Underscoring his ability, the German duly scored as Ajax ran out 6-2 winners. The more serious stuff wouldn't restart until 10 January with Ajax facing NEC in the Eredivisie. If they were to both catch ADO, and overtake Feyenoord and Sparta, a run of domestic victories before the European competition resumed in mid-March, when Celtic visited Amsterdam, was essential. Including friendlies, Ajax would play ten fixtures before facing Jock Stein's team. They would win nine of them and, by the time the European Cup returned, the Eredivisie title looked likely to be a two-horse race with ADO no longer involved.

Resuming domestic action, Ajax welcomed NEC to a chilly De Meer. Michels was still looking for a way to include Van Dijk in a three-man attack that already had an established trio of Swart, Cruyff and Keizer in place. His solution for this game was to again position the forward in a midfield role in place of Rijnders. It seemed a good solution as Van Dijk had scored from there previously. Just five minutes into this encounter he did so again and, for good measure, added his second on 25 minutes. In between, Suurbier had also scored and, with Ajax 3-0 up at the break, the game was clearly won. NEC cut the deficit on 73 minutes through Jendrossek but it was all they could manage. Inside the final ten minutes Blankenburg was given more playing time as he replaced Neeskens and there was even time for Vasović to miss a late penalty. It mattered little; the result had been decided well before then.

Travelling to Maastricht the following weekend, Michels eased Van Dijk into the forward line by playing the 3-3-4 formation that the team had profited from in some earlier games. Once again it was Krol demoted to the bench to facilitate the change. Despite previous successes, this time the system failed to gel and, in an uninspiring performance, Ajax conceded a late goal to Dijkstra on 83 minutes and returned to Amsterdam empty-handed with the prospect of a visit from league leaders ADO for the following weekend.

After beginning the year with a 3-0 win away to NAC, while Ajax were losing in Masstricht, ADO had stumbled to a goalless home draw with Holland Sport. Neither team were bringing scintillating form into the game at the De Meer.

After the disappointment of losing to MVV, Michels ditched the 3-4-4 and reverted back to the more regular 4-3-3, with Van Dijk missing out. Krol was back in the usual back four, with Neeskens, Rijnders and Mühren as the midfield trio and Swart, Cruyff and Keizer in the attack. It was a return to the tried and tested formation and it brought the required response. By half-time Ajax were three up following a brace from Keizer, and a goal by Cruyff just two minutes before the break. In the third league outing of the season it had been ADO leading after the first 45 minutes, with Ajax unable to get back into the game. This time the situation was reversed and Ajax coasted to victory.

The defeat, following that goalless draw with struggling Holland Sport, marked the beginning of ADO's decline from their top spot. They would lose three of their next four Eredivisie games, the only exception being a 6-0 triumph over hapless HFC Haarlem. As the club from the Hague fell away, Ajax and Feyenoord would move forward to contest the title with Ježek's players compelled to settle for what was still a hugely commendable third place.

Starting with the same 11 players and formation, Ajax strung another two victories together. On a day of double joy they beat DWS 1-0 away, while Feyenoord were falling to defeat against NEC in Nijmegen, following that up by bringing Go Ahead Eagles crashing down to earth with a 5-1 home win on 7 February. It would be Ajax's last Eredivisie fixture for two weeks, during which time they played and won three friendlies, before RKSV Volendam visited the De Meer.

Swart had been injured in the middle one of those three friendlies, against Noordwijk, and was substituted at the break. He wouldn't be available against Volendam, and Van Dijk replaced him in the only change to the starting 11 from the previous Eredivisie game. In what was a fairly comfortable victory Ajax scored twice in each half, cantering to a 4-0 win. Keizer scored the first just ahead of the half-hour mark and a Mühren header from Krol's cross sent Ajax into half-time two ahead. Cruyff added the third three minutes after the restart, and Van Dijk emphasised his value with the fourth inside the final ten minutes, after which Michels sent Blankenburg on to replace Neeskens with the game secure.

There was now just a single domestic match before the visit to Glasgow. Ajax travelled to the small port city of IJmuiden on the last day of February knowing that the value of a win could be enhanced by the outcome of another game the same day, with Feyenoord away to ADO. Swart returned at the expense of the unfortunate Van Dijk as Michels dropped back into his preferred 11 on what was now firmly established as the favoured formation, 4-3-3.

Cruyff put Ajax ahead on 20 minutes following work by Neeskens, but there was great concern for the coach ten minutes later when the dynamic midfielder was injured and had to be substituted. Blankenburg again slotted in as required. Just ten days ahead of the first leg against Celtic, losing Neeskens would have been a major blow, but there was sufficient time for him to recover and take his place against the Scots. There was also relief in the game, as well. A penalty awarded against Ajax with ten minutes to play threatened to derail the win but Stuy denied Bond from the spot, and it stayed 1-0. The bonus was received after the final whistle with news that ADO had recovered some of their early season form and beaten Feyenoord 2-0. The title race could go down to the wire from this point. Feyenoord's visit to Amsterdam in the penultimate round of fixtures had always looked likely to be the key game in deciding who would be champions. Now that seemed to be almost inevitable.

The previous year, Celtic had been beaten in the final as Feyenoord claimed the crown of European champions, three years after the Scottish club had worn that mantle themselves. Jock Stein's team were eager to reclaim the title and, so far, had benefitted from favourable draws in reaching the last eight of the competition. A 14-0 aggregate win over KPV of Finland had been more akin to a training session for the Hoops and, in the second round, things hardly changed with a 10-2 stroll against Irish club Waterford. The game in Amsterdam would be a much sterner test.

For such an important game, there was little chance of Michels playing anything other than his preferred starting 11 in a 4-3-3 formation and that was how Ajax lined up in front of 63,000 at the Olympisch Stadion. Turning out in yellow shirts and green shorts, Celtic had several survivors from their 1967 final win over Internazionale in Lisbon and the loss to Feyenoord in Milan three years later. Chief among them was the flame-haired Jimmy Johnstone who, when granted the freedom to wander and cause mayhem by Stein, had made Inter's *catenaccio* defence look more like an open barn door than one secured by a 'bolt' in 1967, but he had been largely subdued by Happel's astute tactics in Milan.

The ease of the road Celtic had travelled to reach this stage shouldn't disguise the quality of the players at Stein's disposal for the game. They had qualified as champions of Scotland, finishing eight points clear of perennial rivals Rangers, scoring an impressive 96 goals in just 34 league outings. They would retain the title in 1970/71, adding the Scottish Cup to complete the domestic double. Much as Celtic faced a difficult task, the one confronting Ajax would also be their most severe test in the competition so far.

The first quarter of an hour was as tight and competitive as expected, with Ajax having the edge in possession and advanced positions on the field but failing to create any meaningful chances. Cruyff dropped deeper, allowing Suurbier, Krol and mostly Vasović to move forward into the spaces created. Rijnders also served his time in the back line as Michels' players sought to create gaps through their rotation of positions. The first real chance fell to Cruyff after 15 minutes. A corner from the left dropped to him, a dozen metres or so from goal, but his shot flew high over the bar. Breaking down the well-drilled Scottish defence would take time and patience.

Five minutes later, Ajax were reminded of the threat that Celtic carried. Initially there looked to be little danger as Wallace apparently aimlessly hooked the ball into Ajax's half of the field. Bursting from midfield though, George Connolly seized on the chance and raced clear, with Hulshoff and Krol in hot pursuit. As the defenders closed on him, Connolly chose to shoot from outside of the area, and Stuy scrambled the ball wide of the post. A quick bit of thinking from the restart saw a corner find Lennox in space in the area, but he headed wide.

It was only in the dying seconds of the half that Evan Williams, in the visitors' goal, was called into serious action. First, he dived at the feet of Keizer as the winger played, and received, a neat wall pass to penetrate into the Celtic area, before being foiled by Williams. Then, seconds later, a header by David Hay – intended to cut out a cross – flew dangerously close to the Celtic line, requiring a diving save from Williams to prevent the defender putting through his own goal. The nervous smile on the face of Hay, who had spent a busy 45 minutes chasing the shadow of Cruyff on a man-marking mission, betrayed both his relief and gratitude to the goalkeeper.

Other than the shovelled save by Stuy from Connolly, they were the only moments of real menace in the first period.

Ajax were committed to creating a goal with their enterprising interplay and rotation. Celtic would take any kind of goal. Neither team looked like profiting from their intentions as the break approached. Reporting in *The Times* the following day, Geoffrey Green wrote that Ajax had been 'uninhibited in all their approach work, but inhibited as soon as they reached the edges of a crowded Celtic penalty area ... While Celtic were playing soft pedal in defence, Ajax were hard at attack.'[50]

The penetrating cold and damp of a wet March Amsterdam evening was settling over the Olympisch Stadion as Portuguese referee Antonio Saldanha brought the first half to a close. Walking from the pitch, the players' breath condensed in the air like steam from a kettle. As with the chances created in the first half, it was merely a case of hot air on a cold night. The second 45 minutes would be very different.

In the dressing rooms, Stein would have been asking his players for more of the same as the enticing prospect of a goalless draw, with the return leg in Scotland to come, looked eminently achievable. Michels would have been pleased to some measure as well. His team had controlled large portions of the game so far and he had confidence that, if they continued to play and press as they had done, the breakthrough would arrive. It did and, as Green stated in *The Times,* Ajax would deliver 'a brilliant second half exhibition [as they] at last burst into life like a flame to turn what looked like a dreary night into one of diamonds'.

Celtic's determination to hang on to what they had was illustrated in the first few minutes following the restart as Cruyff and Mühren were sent crashing to the turf by robust challenges. As a declaration of intent, Stein would have been

---

50 'Cruyff the master as Celtic collapse', *The Times,* 10 March 1971.

well pleased. Michels' players were also keen to make their mark on the second period as quickly as possible and, as Rijnders retreated to cover, Hulshoff drove forward to create an attack that Celtic were happy to see end in just a corner.

The next sally forward came from a deep-lying position by Cruyff. Gliding past defenders in his inimitable style, only a poor cross blighted the moment. The danger hadn't passed though. Cruyff quickly regained possession, crossed into the box and sprinted forward for the return. Reading the run, Mühren headed the ball into Cruyff's path and a toe-poke past Williams looked certain to produce the opening goal. The collision with the goalkeeper sent Cruyff tumbling though, and the ball was cleared for a throw-in. A penalty? Unsurprisingly, the Ajax players thought so and remonstrated with Saldanha, but the diminutive official was having none of it. From the throw-in the ball was swept towards the far post as Neeskens arrived, but it was smuggled behind for a corner.

The pressure was building and Ajax were beginning to pick holes in the Celtic back line as they pressed forward, pulling the defenders out of position with clever runs that were, increasingly, only halted by fouls. For the first ten minutes following the break, Williams was the only Celtic player to enjoy anything but the most ephemeral relationship with the ball.

Wallace was becoming an increasingly isolated figure, ploughing a lone furrow as Celtic's front man, with his team-mates committed to closing off gaps at the other end of the pitch, as with the Dutch boy plugging holes in the dyke with his fingers. The problem was that, even with ten sets of hands, there was still insufficient fingers to plug all of the holes being created by Ajax's intricate play. And yet, when the first goal came on 63 minutes, it was more akin to British route one than Dutch *totaalvoetbal*. Stuy thumped a long ball from his hands deep into the Celtic half towards Neeskens whose impudent flick found Cruyff galloping into the area 'like a sudden thought', Green suggested poetically in *The Times*, and his low shot beat Williams.

Even a single-goal defeat would have been acceptable to Celtic, but unless the Scots could find a way to still the dominating pattern of Ajax's play then one goal was never likely to be the only price to pay. Were there more than 11 Dutch players on the pitch? It seemed that way as every loose ball, every 50-50 challenge and every tackle fell in their favour. They were quicker in thought and deed, and Celtic resembled Canute seeking to hold back the tide, and yet being just as convinced as the fabled Danish king that a greater power than theirs would likely confound their endeavours.

Seven minutes after the first goal, a clumsy challenge by McNeill into Cruyff's back was penalised resulting in a free kick on the edge of the penalty area. As Cruyff climbed to his feet, the Celtic skipper clapped sarcastically into his face suggesting that he had made far more of the challenge than was warranted. The defensive wall was reluctant to retreat and Cruyff offered to help the referee by pacing out the ten yards for him. The proffered aid was swiftly rejected by the official with a dismissive wave, but the point was made and the Portuguese took his own ten-yard walk, requiring the Celtic players to join him. He cemented the decision with a robust push or two before accepting that seven or eight yards was all he was going to achieve.

Keizer stood patiently over the ball as the referee stepped clear of the yellow-and-green barrier and blew the whistle. The Ajax winger faked to take the free kick, causing a restart in the defence as Hulshoff advanced from deep and drove the ball through one of the holes that a Celtic finger had been unable to plug, and past Williams to double the lead. After celebrating with his team-mates, Hulshoff trotted back to his defensive post in his distinctive loping gait, socks around his ankles, as always, looking anything but the complete *totaalvoetbal libero* he was developing into.

The only question remaining seemed to be whether the Scottish champions could avoid conceding again and maintain, at least, a fingerhold on the tie. Despite being comprehensively outplayed since half-time, Celtic were rarely second best to any opponent when it came down to grit and determination and a tug of the shirt by Callaghan as Cruyff threatened to break free suggested that Stein's team were nowhere near throwing in the towel.

Michels had designs on making such resistance forlorn. With 15 minutes to play, Van Dijk was sent on to replace Swart, who had hardly enjoyed his best game. Unusually the substitute entered the field wearing number ten, that being the shirt relegated from first 11 use by Cruyff's adherence to number 14. A third goal would surely seal the deal, despite the impending visit to Glasgow, and confirm Ajax's progress.

As time drifted away and Celtic saw the finishing line honing into view, their energies revived and Ajax seemed to be sated with the two-goal lead, but the *coup de grâce* would be delivered. Although neither of the first two goals had been directly created by *totaalvoetbal*, both were results of the pressure that Ajax's play had inflicted on the Celtic defence. The third goal would be different, as Geoffrey Green's narrative in *The Times* exquisitely captured: 'In the last minute, Ajax drove in the last nail and did so brilliantly. Cruyff beat two men in a mazy dribble and made a short pass to Keizer, who turned on a guilder and fired high into the net.'[51]

---

51 'Cruyff the master as Celtic collapse,' *The Times*, 10 March 1971

As the teams lined up for the restart, two flares thrown on to the pitch briefly belched smoke into the damp night air, but nothing could hide the brilliance of Ajax's second-half performance. Seconds after the resumption the full-time whistle signalled the end of the match, and effectively of the tie as well. There was still the return leg in Glasgow to play two weeks later, but surely only the most unlikely of major turnarounds could deny Ajax a place in the semi-finals of the European Cup now.

Four days after the triumph, Ajax hosted FC Den Bosch in a KNVB Cup third round encounter. Michels rested Neeskens and Swart, the former allowing another game in midfield for Blankenburg. Much as Michels had done with Vasović and Hulshoff at the beginning of their careers with the club, the German defender's football education would be completed by playing in a midfield role. It was all part of the *totaalvoetbal* philosophy. Defenders were expected to be comfortable seamlessly switching into midfield during a game as and when required. A grounding in the requirements of that role was, therefore, an essential part of the *totaalvoetbal* finishing school under Michels. Four goals clear at the break, Ajax coasted through the second period and into a quarter-final against Feyenoord, offering the coach the opportunity to also give Cruyff and Keizer an early end to the game as well.

Ajax were now in contention for three trophies. With ADO falling away, so long as Ajax and Feyenoord kept their winning streaks going, the penultimate week of the league season would decide the title, and the draw for the last eight of the KNVB Cup had also paired the rivals together, meaning whichever triumphed would surely be favourites to lift the trophy. And then there was the European Cup as well. It was only 21 March, with still more than a dozen weeks until the end of the season, when Ajax travelled to Rotterdam to face

Sparta, but every game now was like a cup final, each carrying massive significance.

German coach Georg Keßler had led the *Oranje* for four years, introducing many of the key players at Ajax, and indeed Feyenoord, to international football before taking over at Sparta for the 1970/71 season. He would stay in Rotterdam for just a single season before departing for Anderlecht. In that year, however, he would add a steel to the team that always struggled in the shadow of Rotterdam's biggest club, and they would lose just five league games all season, a record that would equal that of Ajax.

The second leg against Celtic was just three days away but, having rested players in the cup game, Michels was wary of doing so again and risking dropped points. He selected the 11 players who had started the home leg against Celtic but to no avail. The home defence coped without any great disasters and, when the game ended in a goalless draw, Sparta's neighbours from across the city had good reason to thank Keßler's team for their efforts.

On the same day, Feyenoord triumphed 1-0 at Volendam, and the damage done to their cause by the loss to ADO while Ajax were beating Telstar in the previous round of league matches was largely repaired. Happel's players could now sit back and watch as Ajax travelled to Scotland to hopefully complete the job against Celtic. A three-goal cushion afforded a substantial amount of security for Michels' team, but regardless of the scoreline, a game against Celtic at Hampden Park, in front of more than 78,000 belligerent Scots, outnumbering the 5,000 or so who had travelled from Amsterdam, was always going to a difficult test and eat a little more into the energy reserves of the Ajax players.

With an understandable eye to caution, Michels brought Blankenburg back into midfield deploying his defensive nous in front of the regular back four. He maintained the 4-3-3 formation though, by easing Mühren into, at least nominally, a more forward role alongside Cruyff and Keizer. There was little doubt that the coach understood that, in such an environment, progress would be secured as much by tenacity as talent. It seemed to be the mentality that Michels had left ringing in his players' ears as he sent them out for the game. Perhaps pleading a case of 'when in Rome', the players were in no mood to be bullied out of the tie.

Menno Pot described how the Ajax team of this time were seen as pure footballing artists, but there was a steel inside that velvet glove: 'At the same time, more and more people [now] realise that the Ajax team of the early 1970s wasn't just about beauty. They could be absolutely merciless as well. People like Neeskens, Suurbier and Hulshoff were troopers, hard as nails. They must have been quite intimidating in their day. So, the "Beautiful Ajax" was also a bit of a street gang.' That street gang in Glasgow were prepared to do what was necessary to reach the semi-finals.

They conceded on 27 minutes after a free kick was floated into the area by Bertie Auld. The cross was half cleared by a Dutch head, but dropped to a Celtic player, who hooked it back into the danger area. This time a Celtic head won the aerial duel, flicking the ball forward, and allowing Johnstone to nip in ahead of a plunging Stuy and prod it over the line. The extent of Celtic's task still to come was illustrated by the fact that Johnstone's goal was the first that Ajax had conceded in a competitive game going back to the 5-1 win over Go Ahead Eagles back on 7 February – and the Hoops still needed to score twice more, just to get level.

It wouldn't happen and as Ajax recovered solidly from the blow of conceding they largely choked off the game. It wasn't until the 78th minute that Scottish hopes were raised again as McNeil flicked on another Celtic free kick and Hughes nodded past Stuy. The celebrations were quickly curtailed by the referee awarding a free kick against McNeil for handball; the lack of protest from the Celtic players underscored the validity of the decision. In the end, despite the Scottish team's hearty endeavours, they had produced little of any real danger, and certainly not enough to turn a tide that was flowing so strongly against them.

Reporting on the game for *The Times* the following day, David Downie pulled no punches about the Ajax approach to the game as Celtic had sought a way back into a tie that had surely already been lost to them in Amsterdam: 'Whenever Celtic attacked, Cruyff was the only Dutchman outside the Ajax penalty area, and shots from perfect crosses by Johnstone and Hay simply rebounded from the barrier of blue-shirted defenders. If a Scotsman became too dangerous, he was simply tripped and the goalmouth filled to meet the free kick. Mr Lo Bello [Italian referee Concetto Lo Bello who had also officiated in Celtic's defeat to Feyenoord in the previous season's final], handed out four informal warnings in the first 19 minutes, but didn't take any names.'[52] So much of Downie's description of the game may have been flavoured by the fact that it was largely for domestic consumption but, even taking that into account, there's a need for some measure of balance that may have escaped his notice.

That said, it was a broadly accurate summation of Ajax's approach but, compromised more than a little as, somewhat grudgingly, Downie also accepted, 'One wondered if [Ajax] might not again have won but for a brilliant display by Brogan who five times dispossessed the dangerous Cruyff after he had broken clear.' In the end he summed up the night and Ajax's

---

52 'Packed defence makes task even harder', *The Times*, 25 March 1971.

approach: 'Ajax did what they had come to do.' They had indeed and were through to the last four of the European Cup.

There was little time for reflection and self-congratulation for a job well done in Glasgow as three days later Ajax were back in Eredivisie action, entertaining FC Twente. Kees Rijvers, who would later go on to enjoy great success with PSV, was coaching in Enschede, and had turned them into a difficult team to beat. Across the 34-game Eredivisie season they would concede just 18 goals, posting the best defensive record in the league. Back in October Ajax had lost the away fixture, thanks to a late goal by René van de Kerkhof, who would also enjoy success with Rijvers at PSV. Feyenoord had an entirely winnable home game against Telstar on the same day as Ajax took on Twente, with two points for Happel's team looking inevitable. Ajax simply couldn't afford dropped points with just eight league games to play before Feyenoord visited Amsterdam.

Despite the importance of the fixture, Michels omitted Cruyff from the starting 11, reinstating Van Dijk into the forward line and dropping Mühren back into midfield. Swart also returned and Blankenburg dropped to the bench. An early goal is always a boon against teams with a strong defence, and a gift came Ajax's way three minutes in when Droost put through his own goal to put the home team ahead.

It was the only strike of the first period, but three minutes after the restart a towering header by Hulshoff from a Swart free kick doubled the lead, and surely secured the win. Michels took Keizer off two minutes later, adding Blankenburg into the midfield mix, and a third goal on 58, by Swart, closed out the result. Feyenoord had scored four times without reply against Telstar, so Ajax's victory had been vital to keep pace with the Rotterdam club, especially as their next fixture would see them visit the De Kuip for a KNVB Cup quarter-final.

In a massive show of confidence for his two young players, Michels drafted both Blankenburg and Haan into the midfield three alongside Rijnders, relegating both Mühren and Neeskens to the bench for the clash with Ajax's arch-rivals. The established back four was in front of Stuy and Cruyff returned alongside Swart and Van Dijk in attack.

Without Mühren and Neeskens, inevitably the Ajax midfield lost a measure of its normal coherence and the first period of the game was dominated by Feyenoord. It was no surprise when Wim Jansen put Happel's team ahead on 19 minutes and, for the remainder of the first half, little looked like changing. Michels gambled at the break. Krol, who had been struggling with an impact injury, was removed, with Blankenburg dropping back into defence and Mühren taking over in midfield. After the restart the match became more even and a Swart header, from a Cruyff cross with 20 minutes to play, brought the scores level.

With his team now in the ascendancy, Michels, in search of the win, rolled the dice again with 15 minutes to play, taking off his other full-back Suurbier for Neeskens in what was now a 3-4-3 formation. The gamble was rewarded with two minutes left when Van Dijk capitalised on work by Swart to notch the winner. Whether progress into the last four of the KNVB Cup was outweighed by the psychological advantage of winning on Feyenoord's own turf after being a goal down is a debatable point, but in the next Eredivisie fixture, four days before travelling to the Estadio Vicente Calderón and facing Atlético Madrid for the first leg of the European Cup semi-final, Ajax rattled in seven goals without reply against Excelsior with a team set up in a 3-4-3 formation. No such risks would be taken against the Spanish champions.

Coached by the club's former goalkeeper, Frenchman Marcel Domingo, Atlético had secured the La Liga title by a single point from Bilbao's Athletic Club and could boast the firepower of José Eulogio Gárate and Luis Aragonés. The two Atléti forwards had tied for the Trofeo Pichichi as La Liga's top scorer, each netting 16 goals alongside Real Madrid's Amancio during the previous season. Somewhat characteristic of a club coached by a goalkeeper, they also had an enviable defensive record at home, conceding a miserly seven goals in La Liga as they headed for the title. Atlético were the pick of the four semi-finalists and favoured by many to lift the trophy.

Taking the pitch on 14 April, Michels' team represented what was still his tried and trusted first-choice 11 for the biggest games. Established first choice they may have been, but they were still a young and developing team with an average age of a little over 25. Vasović and Swart were the only players over 30. Remove those two and the average tumbled to just 22.70. Stuy was in goal, behind Suurbier, Hulshoff, Vasović and Krol. Neeskens, Rijnders and Mühren formed the midfield with the attacking triumvirate of Swart, Cruyff and Keizer. It had been five years since any Spanish club had won the European Cup, when Real Madrid defeated Partizan Belgrade – and a certain Velibor Vasović – back in 1966, and 44,000 fans crowded into the stadium on the banks of the Manzanares river, expecting Atlético to vanquish the Dutch team and go on to bring the trophy back to the Spanish capital.

At the coin toss, Vasović called incorrectly and home skipper Isacio Calleja chose to change ends from how the teams had warmed up. The posse of photographers quickly scampering across the pitch to positions behind Stuy's goal was an indication of where they thought most of the action would be focused. Anything positive that Ajax could achieve in Madrid would be both hard-won and highly prized.

The early minutes confirmed the sagacity of the snappers' decision as the home team dominated both possession and position. Yet the first attempt on goal came from a rare Ajax sortie upfield when Mühren fired in a shot from some 30 yards that goalkeeper Rodri handled with comfort. It was a rare event for Ajax to move forward as the home team's pressure forced Mühren, Neeskens and Rijnders deep to supplement the defence, leaving Ajax's front players largely isolated.

After rebuffing the early thrusts of Atlético, Ajax came into the game a little more, establishing occasional periods of possession. The hosts still largely controlled the game but, with the Ajax defence solid, it wasn't until midway through the first half that Stuy was called on to make a save. A cross from the left found the head of Irureta, but the goalkeeper tumbled to his left to save without too much trouble. Minutes later, an indirect free kick in the Ajax area led to a frantic scramble but the final shot flew wide of the post. Neeskens also took a blow to the mouth blocking one effort on goal.

On the half-hour mark German referee Gerhard Schulenburg caused a moment of panic among the Ajax ranks after a home attack broke down. Marching into the penalty area, he pointed towards the spot. Ajax players crowded around him, incensed at the apparent injustice of the random decision. Calmness resumed when it became clear the decision was against, rather than for, the home team. The best chance of the game then fell to Rijnders. Keizer cut in from the left and his pass found the midfielder with Rodri struggling to regain position, but Rijnders screwed his shot painfully wide, then Cruyff's volley flew perilously close to Rodri's crossbar.

As the break approached Michels would have been largely satisfied with the performance, and definitively so with the scoreline. The job was nearly half done – but not quite. José Ufarte cut in from the right and fed the ball into the feet of Gárate on the edge of the penalty area. A clever turn exposed both Vasović and Hulshoff, creating a rare glimpse of space and an unerring pass found the run of Irueta, who fired past Stuy to give Atlético the lead. Ajax had spent 43 minutes subduing the opposition on the pitch and defusing the enthusiasm of the fans in the stadium. Two minutes from the sanctuary of half-time, all that work had been undone.

Understandably, Atlético started the second period with the wind in their sails, and Ajax were forced to defend deep before re-establishing a foothold in the game. Yet, even with the momentum against them, Keizer and then Mühren twice, in just a couple of seconds, should have profited from a defensive mix-up, but two blocks and a shot fired high and wide saw the chances slip away. The second half was now adopting a similar pattern to that of the first period. The home team comfortably dominated possession, but found the Ajax back line difficult to break down with any meaningful strike. A header by Aragonés, from a scandalously free position, was an example, as the ball dropped conveniently into Stuy's arms.

With ten minutes to play, Michels signalled his intentions to settle for a single-goal defeat by sending on Blankenburg to replace Cruyff as the Spanish team knocked, with increasing urgency, on the Ajax door, without being granted entry. Another five minutes passed and Van Dijk replaced Swart. A second goal would give Ajax a mountain to climb in Amsterdam. They had conceded late in the first half and to do so again, with the final whistle in sight, could have been devastating to their aspirations, but they held on. It was far from being the perfect result for either team, but both would consider themselves to have a decent chance of progressing to the final. In the other semi, Red Star Belgrade looked to have booked their place in the final with a 4-1 first-leg victory over Panathinaikos. That was certainly *The Times*'s take on the events of the first leg as it declared, 'Red Star Belgrade are virtually through to the final of the European Cup.'[53] Football, on so many occasions, makes such claims appear overly presumptive, and reality would paint this particular one in that embarrassing hue as well.

Four days after the game in Madrid, Ajax returned to Eredivisie action for an away match in Eindhoven against PSV. The fixtures were now piling up ahead of Ajax as they continued their pursuit of three trophies. Across the next six weeks they would play 13 games, with the increasing danger of so many fixtures leading to a defeat and elimination. Michels rested Krol against PSV, and had the luxury of withdrawing Cruyff a dozen minutes into the second half with his team two goals clear, before Van Dijk added a third to seal the win.

Three days later, they played NEC in the semi-final of the KNVB Cup at the De Meer. Michels went with a 4-2-4 against the team from Nijmegen. Pairing Neeskens and Mühren in midfield allowed the coach to play four forwards with Van Dijk joining Swart, Cruyff and Keizer in attack. The formation also allowed Cruyff the freedom to drift deeper without diminishing Ajax's threat up front. It was a game that would have serious repercussions for the returning Krol, and his memories of the events of the day understandably remain vivid.

'In the game where I broke my leg, the pitch was not good,' he recalled. 'It was cold and they even had to change the posts before the game. The game was hectic. [The challenge that] broke my leg [happened] in the first half, but I still played 15 minutes until half-time. And then they took my boots off, because I was hurting. Then the swelling became very, very big in one moment and the doctor said you can't play anymore.'

---

53 'Red Star over Wembley', *The Times*, 15 April 1971.

The scoreline had been goalless at the break, and Michels sent on Rijnders to replace Swart as the team returned to the regular 4-3-3. Blankenburg would replace Krol and Ajax won through a penalty from Mühren and a last-minute strike by Cruyff to take their place in the domestic cup final. For Krol, though, there were only the dawning realisations of what the injury may have cost him. 'Then, in the evening, after we won the game,' he related sadly, 'I went to hospital and they put me in plaster. Then I realised, of course, that we may get to the final [of the European Cup] and I will miss that.' For a young player in his first regular season with the club, it was a devastating blow and, for the final 11 games of the term, with three trophies to compete for, Michels would be denied a key component of his first-choice defensive quartet.

Krol's broken fibula meant surgery to both the injury and the Ajax defence. Blankenburg had proved his ability as a midfield player but now he would be required to step into the absent Krol's boots and guard the left flank of the Ajax defence, starting with the return game against Atlético Madrid. Some newspapers had already decided that Ajax against Red Star would be the perfect final. 'These Dutchmen and Yugoslavs could provide a fitting climax to the most sought prize in European club football,'[54] *The Times* predicted rashly. One club would reach that final. The other, however, would be on the wrong end of a stirring comeback.

With Blankenburg the only change to the team that started in Madrid, 4-3-3 was definitely the order of the day for Michels against Atlético, who had problems of their own, with Gárate unavailable. More than 65,000 fans were in the Olympisch Stadion to watch the game and they received an

---

54 'Absence of Hollins could tip scales against Chelsea', *The Times*, 28 April 1971.

early boost. It had taken Atlético almost all of the first period to score in Madrid but in the second leg there were a mere six minute on the clock when the first goal came.

Attempting to build an attack, Ufarte was mobbed by half a dozen Ajax players as they swarmed around him in typical *totaalvoetbal* mode. Stealing away possession, Cruyff accelerated around the first defender before being crudely sent tumbling to the turf by the second challenge, some 30 metres from goal. Striding forward from a short run, Keizer struck the free kick with such venom that it was still on the rise as it whistled past Rodri, with the Spanish goalkeeper helpless to intervene.

The home fans celebrated wildly and looked forward to their team adding more goals to ease their way into the final. After they had taken the lead in Spain, Atlético had pressed Ajax back as they searched for the second goal. Now it was the Spanish club's turn to defend in numbers as the eager Ajax forwards pushed for a second goal. As well as conceding just those seven goals at their own stadium, however, Atlético's back line were almost as mean on their travels, allowing a mere 20 goals to breach their defence in the entire La Liga season of 30 games. Ajax attacked, but Atlético defended with determined vigour and an experience and assuredness born of success. Chances were created without any tangible reward. Perhaps the best fell to Swart, but his shot flew high into the night.

Half-time came and went. Rodri saved from Hulshoff and then from Mühren but, with just a dozen minutes to play, it looked like the goalkeeper and his defence would be rewarded for their redoubtable endeavours with a period of extra time. They would be denied. Out on the right, Suurbier fired in a speculative long shot. The ball bounced in front of Rodri who somehow fumbled it over the line to give Ajax the lead in both the game and tie overall. Surely there was only one team going to win now.

Atlético were forced to gamble, pushing more players forward in search of the goal that would stand the tie on its head. Inevitably it left spaces at the back, and another error by the goalkeeper sealed the Spanish club's fate. Stretching to cut out a Mühren cross heading towards Swart on the far post, Rodri flapped at the ball, causing it to drop towards Neeskens by the penalty spot. The young midfielder joyously drove home to send Ajax into the final. Watching the game from the stand, his leg in plaster, Ruud Krol would later admit to considering the victory to be one of Ajax's most memorable performances across those early years of success in the European Cup.

Earlier in the competition, Panathinaikos had scrambled past a hugely unfortunate Everton team to reach the last four on away goals. The 1-1 draw at Goodison Park was key to the outcome. John Georgopoulos is an international football journalist and interviewer from Greece and noted a strange group of circumstances around the Greek team's away goal, 'Antoniadis opened the score nine minutes before the end of the game, the date was 9 March, the time of scoring the goal nine o'clock and the number of his shirt was also nine.' Panathinaikos would also reach the Wembley final on away goals. Trailing Red Star Belgrade 4-1 going into the semi-final home leg, the team coached by the legendary Ferenc Puskás had wiped out the deficit just past the hour mark and went on to eliminate the highly favoured Yugoslavs.

Ajax returned to domestic matters level on points with Feyenoord and five league games to play before Happel's team visited the Olympisch Stadion on Thursday, 27 May. The Eredivisie had agreed to bring the game forward from the weekend in order to give Michels' team more time to prepare for the game against the Greek champions at Wembley on 2 June.

Ajax would win all five of those intervening league games, scoring 16 times without conceding a goal. They would also secure the KNVB Cup, beating Sparta Rotterdam 2-1 in a replayed final on 20 May after a 2-2 draw a couple of weeks earlier. Netting maximum points was all that Ajax could hope for but unfortunately Feyenoord mirrored their success and the clubs were still locked together, both on 53 points, as they ran out for the fixture that had, for so long, looked likely to decide who would be Eredivisie champions. Aside from Blankenburg filling in for Krol, Michels selected his first-choice team set out in a 4-3-3 formation. More than 65,000 fans were in the stadium to watch the action on a rain-soaked playing surface, and millions of others tuned in to watch the first Eredivisie game to be broadcast live on television.

Wearing their change strip of all blue, Ajax struck first. With 11 minutes played Mühren swept the ball out to Cruyff on the left flank. Keizer had moved into the middle leaving space for Cruyff to exploit on the flank as the wideman drew his marker out of position. Lifting the ball into the area, Cruyff found Keizer on the six-yard line and his header from close range left goalkeeper Eddy Treijtel with little chance. Frustrated to have seen his team-mates caught out by Keizer's run, Rinus Israël first crashed into the back of the Ajax man as he headed on goal, causing him to collide with the goalkeeper, then turned and berated his right-back, Dick Schneider, for leaving the space for Cruyff. Schneider was far from being the first defender to fall foul of Ajax's positional switching, but he would gain redemption later in the game. Unfortunately for Ajax the collision with Treijtel had left Keizer limping and he was replaced by Van Dijk. The concerned look on the winger's face as he left the pitch suggested that being fit enough for the European Cup Final was a worry.

The danger of sustaining an injury and missing the following week's big game had already settled like a dark cloud over the minds of several Ajax players, and Keizer leaving the field only added to the anxiety. Alive to the situation, Feyenoord were happy to be as robust as referee Ad Boogaerts would allow, and their aggressive play allowed them to take control of the game. With the Ajax forwards wary of entering the Feyenoord penalty area – territory of Israël and centre-back partner Theo Laseroms – and Wim van Hanegem subduing the thrusts of Neeskens, after the use of an elbow, the game swung in the visitors' favour.

The pitch was hardly conducive to constructive football anyway; heavy rain had pummelled it, with standing water beginning to appear in a few areas. Ajax had a big match pending. Feyenoord did not. A physical approach by the Rotterdam club was therefore likely to benefit them as the Ajax players were reluctant to get involved and risk potential injury. On such a surface, where the official was inclined to offer a measure of leniency, it was a scenario always likely to affect the outcome of the game.

Ajax got to the break with the lead intact, but eight minutes after the restart their advantage had been eliminated. A header put Van Hanegem into possession on the right of the Ajax box, and a clever feint deceived Suurbier, allowing the midfielder to hit the byline before cutting the ball back for Ove Kindvall to equalise from a metre out. A further eight minutes had passed when Feyenoord took the lead. A shot from Kindvall was beaten out by Stuy but, following up, Schneider was on hand to crash home the rebound, with the goalkeeper still prone on the floor. As the Feyenoord players celebrated, on the Ajax bench, Michels bowed his head slightly. Whether he felt that the proximity of the European Cup Final had clouded his players' concentration wasn't clear, but he seemed to appreciate that, for this game, the die had been cast. With six minutes to play, that thought was confirmed as Schneider scored his second of the night with a ferocious drive from outside the area that Stuy could only push on to the bar and then into the net.

The win put Feyenoord two points clear of Ajax with one game each to play, and Happel's team entertaining the league's bottom club HFC Haarlem, needing just a point to confirm the title. They would win that and qualify for the following season's European Cup. Ajax could still join them in pursuit of European glory, but would need to beat Panathinaikos at Wembley and become European champions to do so.

Ahead of the final, Michels took his players away to a training camp. With Krol's injury rendering him unavailable for the final it would have been easy and, to some extent, understandable, had the young defender been left at home, and his situation drifted to the back of the coach's mind. As Krol recalled, however, that wasn't the case, Michels was keen to ensure that he remained part of the squad and, more importantly, was made to feel that way too, amid the preparations for the game: 'Michels did very well. He took me with the team to the training camp before the final, so I made all the preparations with them before the final, even though I was walking with a stick. He told me that I belonged with the team. I was also there in the celebrations [after the game] and that was a very satisfying moment for me. I was at training. I was in the dressing room. I was everywhere where the players were.'

As had been suggested in *The Times*, the Greek champions were hardly any pundits' favourites to reach the big game and yet no club reaches a European Cup Final without deserving to be there, and Panathinaikos were no exception. George Tsitsonis is a Greek-American freelance writer and author of the book *Achieving the Impossible – The Remarkable Story of Greece's Euro 2004 Victory*. He related how the success of the club is perceived in Greece: 'To this day, the feats of that Panathinaikos side are still lauded in Greece. Tribute is paid every year by the Greek press to what has become known as "The epic (or saga) of Wembley". The achievement in reaching the European Cup Final places this side above all others when talk turns to the greatest Greek club of all time. The Greek victory at Euro 2004 has somewhat overshadowed this success on some level. However, as the Champions League has become one of the most celebrated tournaments in world football, and as Greece's clubs seem further away than ever in competing at the latter stages of European competitions, the Panathinaikos run is considered a fairytale and has taken on mythic status. The downing of Everton and the miraculous comeback against Red Star are massive sources of pride for the club's fans. However, Greek football supporters, in general, remember the team's journey and subsequent performance in the final against that Ajax side with a real sense of honour.'

The Greeks certainly had a potent attacking threat. Centre-forward Antonis Antoniadis, who notched the all-important goal against Everton, would finish as the tournament's top scorer, recording ten goals in the eight games ahead of the final. Panathinaikos were far from being a one-man team though, as Tsitsonis explained: 'Antoniadis finished as the tournament's top scorer in that season with ten goals and was clearly the main man in attack for Panathinaikos, [but] Mimis Domazos, known as "The General", was the maestro in the Greens' midfield. The diminutive playmaker was the heart of the Panathinaikos attack with his fine dribbling ability and penetrative passing. He starred in the final as the French newspaper *L'Équipe* noted by saying, "Domazos will live with the assuredness that he pleased all present in the home of football." He is considered one of the best Greek players of all-time. Kostas Elefterakis was a midfielder, nicknamed "The Deer", who provided an x-factor for this team. He was able to marry his galloping runs with timely goals, and was a constant threat with his direct approach. The other major goal threat besides Antoniadis was Aristidis Kamaras. He played as a right-back and centre-back for the club as well as a holding midfielder. He was the man who scored the key away goal against Red Star Belgrade and then followed it up with the final goal in the 3-0 victory over the same side in the return leg, the historic strike that sent Panathinaikos through to the final.'

Arie Haan would start on the bench for the final, although he was introduced into the action at half-time and scored the decisive late second goal. As Panathinaikos were one of the lesser-known teams to reach a European Cup Final, the information on their players available to Ajax was less than comprehensive. In an interview in May 2021, Haan recalled the situation: 'At that time, as you can imagine, gathering information was not as easy and fast as it is today, in the age of the internet. We knew that Panathinaikos had a well-tuned team with Domazo, Antoniadis and Kamara under the guidance of the great Ferenc Puskás and that in the semi-final they had eliminated Red Star in an imposing way!'[55]

Puskás had played on Wembley's hallowed turf as part of the Magical Magyars team that tore England asunder in 1953 and destroyed the myth of British invincibility on the football field. Now, as a coach, he was bringing his team back to the

---

55 Interview by Dimitris Dimoulas with Arie Haan 30-05-2021 in *Proto Thema*. (Translated)

scene of his triumph. Despite being relatively inexperienced in the role, Puskás's aura had served him well him in Greece, as George Tsitsonis explained: 'Puskás's stature as one of the game's greats undoubtedly gave him an air of authority when he came to Panathinaikos. He instantly garnered respect. And that was the case despite the fact he came to Greece without much of a coaching resumé. He had only had brief and relatively unsuccessful short stints at clubs such as Hércules, San Francisco Golden Gate Gales, Vancouver Royals, and Alavés. The Panathinaikos job was the first in which he was able to manage a side for more than one season.

'Puskás's name was enough as he came to Greek football … It was the experience of Puskás and confidence he gave to the team as a result that was the greatest benefit to Panathinaikos during his spell in charge. His knowledge of the European game and the fact that he had done it all was of massive importance to a group of players who were very talented but lacked any sort of pedigree in the latter stages of continental competitions. Puskás famously said "11 of them, 11 of us" as he attempted to show his players that these European giants [that] they encountered were men just like them. It worked. This combined with a more professional approach to training and game preparation was key in bringing a group of essentially semi-professional players to brink of European glory.'

Tsitsonis makes perfectly valid points but, as Geoffrey Green pointed out, Ajax were most people's favourites to lift the trophy. In *The Times*, he suggested, 'If the man in the street was asked to nominate the winners of the European Cup Final at Wembley, his answer, probably overwhelmingly, would be Ajax,'[56] before concluding, 'The Dutchmen start

---

56 'Grit could be the Greek for success', *The Times*, 2 June 1971.

as firm favourites.' Green did, however, hold out some hope for the team he described as 'the dark horses Panathinaikos, wearing a Shamrock emblem ... Ajax no doubt have the refined skill, but there is more to football than that, and the Greeks may well reach the happy isles through sheer grit'.

The final would mark the end of Kenneth Wolstenholme's tenure as BBC's football commentator. The doyen of the hackneyed phrase would have perhaps wanted to mark the occasion of hanging up his microphone by saying, 'They think it's all over. It is now!' But he resisted the temptation. It would also be a near swansong occasion for another personality at the game. Going into the final, no one at Wembley other than the coach himself was aware of the situation, but it would be Rinus Michels' penultimate match in charge of Ajax.

When the big day came, Michels sprang a surprise with his selection. Blankenburg had been a steady and largely successful stand-in for the injured Krol, but the young German would be on the bench at Wembley. When faced with the loss of a key player Michels' *totaalvoetbal* philosophy would often require a less than obvious solution. In 1974 when Hulshoff's injury ruled him out of the *Oranje*'s World Cup squad, Michels chose to deploy midfielder Haan in his place rather than another defender. His solution to the problem of Krol's absence at Wembley was right on trend.

Pulling Neeskens into the back four on the right flank, and switching Suurbier to the other side, allowed the coach to include Van Dijk in his front line alongside Swart and Keizer, with Cruyff dropping deeper to join Mühren and Rijnders in midfield. It was a decision that brought early dividends. There were just five minutes on the clock when Rijnders slipped the ball inside to Hulshoff, advancing into the centre circle. The big *libero* glanced upfield, and then pinged a pinpoint 50-metre pass to Keizer out on the left flank of the Panathinaikos penalty area. Two touches and a skip past Kamaras allowed the winger to cross into the box. Anticipating the move, Van Dijk escaped his marker with a run to the near post. The cross met up with the forward's instinctive dart. A flicked header inside the far post wrong-footed Ekonomopoulos in the Panathinaikos goal and gave Ajax an early lead.

Despite being signed for big money back in 1969, the former FC Twente forward had struggled to establish himself in Michels' first-choice 11. With the preferred 4-3-3 formation in place for *totaalvoetbal*, there was only space for one forward to play in the centre with two others either side of him. Inevitably that place went to Cruyff, despite Van Dijk's record of 105 goals in 152 games, often coming from the bench. It's interesting to contemplate whether, had Krol not missed out on the final and Neeskens had played in his normal midfield berth, Van Dijk would have been on the bench rather than opening the scoring. It seems the most likely outcome of such a hypothetical scenario.

From there Ajax largely assumed control of the first 45 minutes, but it was hardly their best performance, as Menno Pot recalled: 'Most finals are shit games. Ajax weren't particularly great … They were better than Panathinaikos, but it wasn't their best game. They were nervous, too. Cruyff was not at his best.' Playing in a deeper role kept Cruyff away from the 'sharp end' of the final more than if he had been deployed in his normal position. His wanderlust was impossible to contain, however, and he remained a key factor in Ajax's attacks. Even when 'not at his best', Cruyff still offered a threat and as well as creating chances for others – particularly a cross for Mühren that the midfielder headed wastefully wide – his ability made him a constant threat with Ekonomopoulos thwarting Cruyff three times when through on goal. In a tribute to a former hero, the goalkeeper played wearing the black jersey of the legendary José Ángel Iribar, goalkeeper of Bilbao's Athletic Club and the Spain national team.

Michels was aware of the threat that Antoniadis posed and sought to cut off the supply to the big centre-forward, often from by the Greek left-back Giorgos Vlachos, who would hoist diagonal balls into the box, or overlap to cross, for his striker to exploit using his height and power. Hulshoff was more than capable of combating such threats, but Michels took the view that a problem avoided is better than one solved, and instructed Swart to close Vlachos down when he was in possession and limit the danger at source. After the early goal, however, the winger's application to the task appeared to wane. That indiscipline would cost Swart his place on the field at the break. Fortunately for Ajax there was little cost, as Hulshoff largely subdued Antoniadis. His only chance ahead of the break came when an attempted clearance by Vasović was sliced, sending the ball spiralling into the Ajax penalty area. Despite the rare luxury of space from the suffocating attentions of Hulshoff, Antoniadis headed tamely wide with Stuy in no-man's land.

At the break, Ajax were largely in control but only led by a single goal. With Kamaras prompting with darting runs seeking out opportunities to feed his striker, Domazus looking to deliver killer passes and Antoniadis waiting for another chance, the game was far from over. In the Ajax dressing room, Michels was intent on changes. Blankenburg came on for Rijnders and Swart lost out to Haan. It would have been easy to drop the German into the back line, promoting Neeskens back into his usual midfield position alongside Haan with Cruyff going forward to replace Swart. But this was *totaalvoetbal* and Michels trusted his players to perform in unconventional roles.

Understandably Swart was upset at the decision, but later rationalised Michels' motive as being driven by his determination to win the game, enhance his reputation and – although no one knew at the time that the move was imminent – to go to Barcelona as a European champion. Unlike the tactical decision to remove Swart, the rationale for substituting Rijnders was entirely different. The club doctor advised Michels that the midfielder had heart problems and couldn't continue. It was a dread portent of the fate that would later befall the tragic Rijnders.

The changes looked like a ploy to solidify the lead, but Panathinaikos were not yet beaten. These players clearly weren't Greeks bearing gifts but Ajax still needed to be aware of them. Ruud Krol recalled that the second period was more of a battle: 'Ajax played good in the first half, but the second was more equal but we scored the second goal to win the game.' That goal would have to wait, although it so nearly came with just five minutes of the second period played. Clever work by Blankenburg set up Haan with a clear shot. Perhaps it came too early for the substitute who later admitted that his knees had been hugely nervous when Michels sent him on. Those nerves betrayed him as, leaning back, he hoisted the shot high over the bar.

There was little for Panathinaikos to gain by sitting back and they came much more into the game, as tension seemed to increase in the Ajax team, with time ticking by and winning the trophy edging nearer. Roberto Pennino said that the players looked unsettled and off colour, but offered a reason why: 'Ajax played a bit nervous after a brilliant campaign that brought them to Wembley. Surely the 4-1 defeat of two years earlier in the final against AC Milan was still at the back of the heads of the players who had survived after that.' In that final, the average of the Ajax team was 27.35. At Wembley it was 26.25 but, armed with an established philosophy of *totaalvoetbal*, the players were much more accomplished and accustomed to this level of competition, and coped as the Greeks sought to fight back after half-time.

Panathinaikos had chances as journalist John Georgopoulos suggests: '[Ajax] gave space to Panathinaikos to attack. The Greek side had some opportunities to score as well. For example, there was a nice header from Antoniadis, or a big error of goalkeeper Stuy [but] Kamaras couldn't exploit it. Overall Panathinaikos played according to their plan, possessing the ball although they failed to score from the goal situations they created.'

A cacophony of trumpets and horns from the Dutch fans had provided a consistent backdrop to the game. It wasn't quite the same as the infamous wailing of the vuvuzelas during the 2010 World Cup in South Africa but it was getting there. And, as the minutes ticked away, doubtless fuelled by pre-celebratory alcohol consumed ahead of kick-off, the volume only increased.

Most of the fight had drained away from the Greek players as the final entered the last few minutes, but the Ajax victory would be crowned with a moment of exquisite *totaalvoetbal*, only slightly compromised by a deflection on the scoring shot. Driving forwards from his defensive position, Neeskens accelerated between two tiring Greek players and fed the ball into Van Dijk, who swiftly moved it on to Cruyff, cutting in from the right and casually advancing before flicking a deliciously disguised pass into the run of Haan. The substitute swept a shot on goal that clipped off Kapsis as he threw himself to the ground to intercept. The ball ballooned into the air, over Ekonomopoulos, and dropped into net. It was all over, as Wolstenholme might have said. The Ajax players piled on top of the goalscorer to celebrate a triumph that was now surely confirmed. Understandably, Haan later described the moment as 'a beautiful feeling'.[57]

Minutes later, at the final whistle, hundreds of Ajax fans flooded on to the pitch to chair their heroes towards the Royal Box, where their trophy awaited. The prearranged marching band looked like a surrounded infantry square defiantly blaring out their tunes as the Ajax players, some wearing exchanged shirts, mounted the stairs. After his penultimate game for the club, Vasović hoisted the European Cup high into the air, maintaining the Netherlands' grip on the trophy. It was high time for the Low Countries, and Amsterdam in particular. This time it was Rotterdam's turn to be encouraged to look at the bigger picture.

Author George Tsitsonis offered an accurate summary: 'The early goal played a huge role in the way the match unfolded. It was a big blow to Panathinaikos, who would have undoubtedly preferred to keep matters close and be able to concentrate on nullifying Ajax. As it was, they were forced to play a bit more open than they would have liked. The gulf in class watching that final was evident. Ajax were the superior side and never looked like losing. That said, Panathinaikos were superb in playing to their potential. The brave goalkeeping of Ekonomopoulos was complemented by some incredibly resilient defending. In attack, the team opted for a direct approach with numerous balls played into the heart of the area and this provided some uncomfortable moments in defence for Ajax with the likes of Antoniadis, Kamaras, Elefterakis, and Grammos all managing decent chances.

'The Greeks felt like they were in it up until Haan's late goal. Still, Ajax had spurned many big chances throughout.

---

57 https://www.champions-journal.com/1000/ajax-71

It was a good showing by Panathinaikos, but the speed of the Dutch attack along with the pressing of Ajax was just a different level to anything Puskás's team had experienced. In the end, Ajax were comfortable winners.'

Haan recalled that, years later, the tables were turned in a charity game: 'Panathinaikos got its rematch many years later, when it had prevailed in a veterans' match with 1-0.'[58] Sadly for the Greek players, it would surely have been of little compensation.

Back in 1971, for John Georgopoulos, 'That final was the beginning of Ajax's empire.' It was but, for the emperor, it was also the beginning of the end. Ajax returned to Amsterdam and a ticker-tape parade. They played their final game of the Eredivisie and then Michels was gone, seduced by the siren calls of Barcelona. Ajax had won the European Cup but were far from being one of the economic powerhouses of continental football. Ruud Krol remembered the day that Michels informed the players that he was leaving: 'When Michels told us that he was going to leave Ajax – I grew up in the club with Michels, he was my mentor, taught me a lot about positions, tactics and made me a professional – it was disappointing. But we know in football that the world goes round and does not stop. Of course, we did not know anything about the new coach at that time. That came later.'

The club who had just reached the pinnacle of European club football had suddenly been plunged into an uncertain future.

---

58 Interview by Dimitris Dimoulas with Arie Haan 30-05-2021 in *Proto Thema*. (Translated)

Part 4: 1971/72 – The King is dead. Long live the King!

IT WAS a strange set of circumstances. Ajax had just won the European Cup and, by that measure, were surely the best team in Europe. Yet their coach had deserted them. What was their future? At one moment it seemed like the footballing world was at their feet. Now everything was cast into doubt.

Despite the disappointment and concern of some players, such as Ruud Krol expressed in the previous chapter, others were less upset. Barry Hulshoff's relationship with Rinus Michels, for example, had always been professional rather than cordial. 'Sometimes you hated him,'[59] the defender revealed, adding that the man you spoke with socially was very different in work situations. Legend also has it that, upon hearing the news of Michels' imminent departure, Piet Keizer jumped on to a nearby table and danced with joy.

Whatever the players' opinion of Michels, his achievements were hugely impressive, as Roberto Pennino confirmed: 'Michels changed Ajax from a semi-amateur club into the professional world team that conquered Europe at Wembley Stadium in 1971 against Panathinaikos. From 1965 onwards he assembled players that could perform the

---

59 Winner, David, *Brilliant Orange* (London: Bloomsbury, 2000).

way he liked to play, first nationally and after that also internationally.' As well as the loss of Michels, the other concern was who would, indeed who could, replace him? Ajax needed someone to pick up the baton and ensure that the stunning progress of the club across the past seasons wouldn't drift off into mediocrity.

Taking over the European champions was an enticing task, and many of the top coaches around the continent, and beyond, would surely have welcomed the opportunity. When the appointment was made, however, the new man in charge was a little-known Romanian with a broadly impressive but far from outstanding CV. The man to assume control of Ajax after Michels was Ștefan Kovács.

The Guardian revealed the barely believable tale of how the appointment came about: 'Ajax drew up a list of 15 names to replace [Michels]. They ended up with the cheapest. Kovács had led Steaua Bucharest to a league title and three Romanian Cups in the previous four years and as a player had had a brief spell with the Belgian side Charleroi, but he was far from well-known in the Netherlands and his arrival was greeted with a mixture of bewilderment and scepticism. Even he could not quite believe his luck and, it is said, bought a return ticket from Bucharest to Amsterdam because he didn't think his stay would be a long one.'[60]

The return portion of that ticket would remain unused for a while. Kovács's stay in Amsterdam would last for two seasons, and they were glorious ones.

The decision to employ Kovács was apparently driven by financial considerations. The Ajax hierarchy believed that the ethos of the club was now set and, almost regardless of

---

who was coaching the team, their continuing success was assured. Kovács was appointed with that naive logic guiding their hand, but was it possible that Ajax really could continue to prosper without the man who had arrived with the club struggling near the foot of the Eredivisie, and left half a dozen years later, with them acknowledged as the best team in Europe? How much of the success had been solely down to the coach, and how much down to an outstanding group of players, or was it merely a case of the stars aligning as the celestial spheres bestowed copious blessings on Amsterdam, and a fortuitous combination of both? As with so many things concerning the success or failure of football clubs, especially when looking back through the eddying clouds of history, there are more theories than answers.

Qasim Hakim is a football journalist who currently works for *Dagblad de Limburger*. He was previously at *De Telegraaf*, *De Voetbal Trainer* and Voetbalzone.nl and is a student of football history. He was born ten years after Michels left Ajax for Barcelona, and reflects on the issue from a modern-day viewpoint: 'Michels is, in my perspective, remembered as a coach who won a lot, but he had always good players. A lot of people say that Johan Cruyff was the real boss in the Dutch squad and Ajax in the '70s.'

That idea of Cruyff being the power behind the throne, and on many occasions also in front of it, has support from Ronald Jager. He told your author, 'When coach Rinus Michels was – before a game – saying how they should play, Cruyff often changed the tactics. Keizer and Cruyff had an interview for a *Voetbal International Special* in 1992 with Jan Donkers and Johan Derksen. Keizer, who as you know was very negative about Michels, said, "We just let him talk and then Johan changed it. Michels didn't see that during the games and was very proud when we won another game. But if we would have played like Michels said, we never won any prize." Cruyff didn't deny it, but said that Michels was – with Vasović – very worthy for a better discipline at the team.' Perhaps the widely held belief of Michels being the controlling disciplinarian, and Kovács more placid libertarian, may not be completely accurate.

As so often is the case when considering personalities, and reflecting back across several decades, there are many different perspectives. Auke Kok says, 'Kovács was considered to be friendly but weak.' Many of the players who had been schooled under Michels' more rigorous and disciplined regime had similar thoughts; Gerrie Mühren for example, felt that the Romanian may have been an easier coach to like, but was perhaps more difficult to respect. Other players took a different view, perhaps influenced by their age and status with the club at that time. Johnny Rep looked upon Kovács as being much easier to work under, and thought that some of the players had become tired of the discipline demanded by Michels.

Rep was still an up-and-coming youngster looking to make his mark when Michels left, while Mühren was an established first-team player. It's interesting that Mühren, who had played his career under Michels, saw the change to Kovács's less-strict approach to the players as a downside. Rep, a younger member of the squad who made the significant breakthrough to the first team under the Romanian, perhaps understandably saw things differently, while still carrying respect for Michels: 'Kovács was a nice coach [and you could] have fun with him … I will never forget a great time with Kovács, [but] Michels, my trainer in the world championship in 1974, was also a top coach.'

If Mühren was a member of the 'old school', and Rep a newcomer, Arie Haan was a little of both, and his views seemed to reflect that. He appreciated the contribution to the club's success of both coaches. Michels' discipline had laid down the basic tenets for success, but there was a fantasy element, a freedom about their play that was missing. It was something that Kovács recognised and released, allowing his players to indulge themselves and give their talents free and full rein.

Looking back, Sonny Silooy believed, 'the success of the team wasn't only because of Michels, not only because of a brilliant set of players. It was the combination of both of those things. Michels could only have succeeded with Cruyff at Ajax. They also succeeded at Barcelona together. Cruyff and Michels together was a good couple. They make Dutch football what it is right now.' Despite that, he was aware of the development under Kovács, and how that may well have been necessary if Ajax were to climb to even greater heights. He added, 'Sometimes it's good when you change the coach, because the guys need new words.'

Perhaps the change from Michels to Kovács may not have been such a seismic shift anyway, at least when the new regime had settled into a regular pattern. Although the head man had changed, many of the backroom staff and coaching team remained in place. So there was a sense of continuity, as Ruud Krol recalled: 'Things were a little bit more relaxed [under Kovács]. It was different training, not so disciplined and, of course, after that we became a little less physically prepared. But then Bobby Haarms took over the physical training, and Kovács was only controlling the tactical training. From that moment, he had no part in the physical training. The heavy training was all with Bobby. But Kovács had a very strong link with us in the relation between trainer and players.'

For many, and perhaps this was the way the Ajax hierarchy saw things developing, Kovács changed nothing, merely following the template that Michels had bequeathed him. There is some validity in that assessment, but it fails to deliver the full story. The Romanian was certainly wise enough to recognise the things that were working well and leave them in place, but also sufficiently astute to make amendments where he saw the need. Auke Kok summed the situation up well: 'Michels was far more influential than Kovács. Michels was a pioneer. Kovács kept everything as it was, only giving Cruyff more freedom and his ways. Therefore, under Kovács the [*voetbal*] became more *totaal*, more "Cruyffian", no more adapting to opponents, as Michels often did. No more 4-2-4, or 5-3-2 on occasions, but always 4-3-3.'

One of those changes under Kovács was the decision to sell Nico Rijnders. Arie Haan's development had created an overload in demand for the three midfield places that, as Kok suggests, was de rigueur under the new coach. A move to Club Brugge in Belgium was completed on 17 June. The European Cup Final was Rijnders' last game for Ajax. There was also a tragic after-story for the midfielder. On 12 November, playing for Brugge against RFC Liège in a Belgian league game, he collapsed and, despite feverish on-field medical attention, was clinically dead when removed from the pitch. Miraculously, the medical team resuscitated him moments afterwards. The incident inevitably ended his footballing career and he never fully recovered. Three years later, aged just 28, Nico Rijnders died.

Velibor Vasović had already decided to retire at the end of the 1970/71 season. As well as appearing in the Wembley final as a substitute, Horst Blankenburg had appeared in more than two dozen games for Ajax across the previous season, latterly stepping in to cover for the absent Krol, and with Hulshoff ready to assume the role as the senior member of the central defensive pairing, the German would now slot in alongside him. That was the plan anyway, but injuries to other players meant Blankenburg would often be used to plug other holes in the team until the end of October 1971, when he was finally able to settle into what would become his established role alongside Hulshoff.

Six players were brought into the club. Some would have small roles to play in the coming season, others more so. Two especially would go on to have notable careers at the De Meer, albeit in far different ways. Arnold Mühren, brother of Gerrie, was signed from RKSV Volendam for a reported fee of 450,000 guilders.[61] He would play more than 250 games for Ajax. Another signing would have far less playing time, appearing in a single friendly for the club, before being transfer-listed at his own request and moving to Antwerp FC in January 1973. He would have far more success when he returned in a coaching capacity later. His name was Louis van Gaal, and he would coach the next Ajax team to win the European Cup two decades later. As with Michels playing under Reynolds, as with Cruyff under Michels, Van Gaal would absorb the concept of *totaalvoetbal* in his time at the club and Ajax would reap the benefits in the 1990s.

When taking over a club that had won both the European Cup and KNVB Cup in the previous season, the only thing to do is go out and top that by retaining both of those trophies and adding the Eredivisie title as well. No club in any major European league had ever achieved such a feat previously. Even the great Real Madrid teams of the late 1950s had never won both domestic trophies and be heralded as European champions in the same season. If some people had doubts as to whether Kovács was worthy of being Michels' successor – and there were plenty of them – the fact that he did precisely that, losing just a single competitive game in all competitions

---

61 *De Telegraaf*, 15 November 1974.

across the entire season, proved his doubters to be wide of the mark. Before he could do that, however, he also had to prove himself to the squad.

As a former Ajax forward, Michels' playing credentials were already established at the club and among the squad he inherited from Vic Buckingham. Plus, of course, convincing players that you are worthy of taking over a club struggling at the wrong end of the Eredivisie, and still operating on a broadly amateur basis, is not such a big step. When Kovács arrived at the De Meer, things were very different. Ajax were newly crowned champions of Europe and the Romanian had no previous experience with the club, or indeed in Dutch football, to lay out on his CV. His career as a relatively journeyman midfielder had been wholly played out in his native country and he had never reached the heights of playing international football.

Unsurprisingly, when this unknown coach arrived to take over from the legend who had lifted Ajax from the floor to the heights of success, the players who had just been crowned as the best in Europe were initially unconvinced of his worth and would test him out. Steven Scragg is an award-nominated author and member of the senior management team at *These Football Times*. He offered this description of the events: 'Stepping into the unknown, legend has it that in his first training session, Kovács had to field questions over whether he approved of the general length of hair of the squad, while also having to contend with a ball hit to him at knee height, with no quarter given. His responses to both tests were to insist that he had been employed as coach rather than hairdresser and to take the ball down and return it from whence it came, in one fluid movement.'[62] That test had been

---

62 Scragg, Steven, *These Football Times*, 'Ajax' magazine.

passed, but the important one, performances on the pitch and results, still lay ahead.

As was established practice for their pre-season, Ajax played a series of friendly games before the Eredivisie league programme began. It allowed Kovács time to assess the new signings presented to him, plus youngsters promoted from the youth team such as Johnny Rep, who featured in six of the pre-season games and scored three times. The coach could also solidify thoughts on what his first-choice starting line-up would look like when all his options were available.

Unfortunately, that would be far from the case when the serious business got under way on 15 August with an away Eredivisie game against FC Twente. Gerrie Mühren had been injured five minutes into the friendly against Oldenzaal on 20 July. He wouldn't be back in first-team contention until 11 September, and the final Eredivisie match before European competition began. The defence was the main concern though. Krol was still unavailable following his broken leg, although he would return for the next fixture, making a 15-minute cameo appearance from the bench. To compound matters, Wim Suurbier had suffered a serious injury in the final Eredivisie match of the previous season, the 4-1 defeat to Go Ahead Eagles on 6 June. It wasn't until the last day of October that Kovács was able to select both Suurbier and Krol in his starting 11.

Austrian midfielder Heinz Schilcher was one of the other signings, alongside Mühren and Van Gaal who joined Ajax in the summer of 1971, moving to the club from Sturm Graz. He would stay in Amsterdam for three years before leaving for Paris FC in 1973 after being placed on the transfer list at his own request. In those three seasons he would appear in just 35 Eredivisie matches and seven in European competition, but would offer useful cover when other options were unavailable. The fixture in Enschede was just such an occasion.

Schilcher was positioned alongside Hulshoff – the only established member of the back four from the previous season. Swaart was pulled back from the forward line to cover for Suurbier on the right flank and Blankenburg played on the left. Johan Neeskens, Haan and Ruud Suurendonk formed the midfield trio with Dick van Dijk, Piet Keizer and Cruyff in attack. It was a far cry from what the team would look like later in the season, but goals from Suurendonk and Keizer got Kovács's Eredivisie career off to a winning start.

Three minutes into injury time in the following game, at home to FC Den Haag – ADO Den Haag and Holland Sport, who were based in the same city, had merged at the end of the previous season to form FC Den Haag, although the club would revert to the old title in 1996 – it looked like that nascent winning run would end at a single victory. Kovács had named an unchanged side with Krol likely to enter from the bench. The defender made his return to action on 75 minutes, replacing Neeskens and taking over at left-back, with Blankenburg swopping to the right flank and Swart moving into midfield. With time running out, the change brought unintended dividends when Swart, relieved to be in a more familiar role, scored the winner.

It had been a far-from-ideal start to the season, despite garnering successive wins, and the team continued to stutter and splutter over the next few games. Another unchanged team started at Sparta Rotterdam. This time Krol emerged from the bench at the break, with Ajax a goal down to a Klijnjan penalty. He replaced Schilcher as Blankenburg moved inside and the substitute took over on the left flank. On the hour Rep made his Eredivisie debut as Kovács sought a way to get his team back into the game. It took another late Swart goal, eight minutes from time, to take a point.

Krol returned to the starting 11 for the next match at the De Meer against Excelsior but, with Cruyff unwell and absent, Ajax struggled to record a 1-0 win over a team that would only secure four league victories all season, escaping relegation by the finest of margins. There was now just one fixture to play before Ajax began their defence of the European Cup, at FC Groningen.

Cruyff had recovered from illness, but had inadvertently passed it on to Hulshoff who consequently missed the game. Krol started on the left with Blankenburg and Schilcher in the middle. The right of the defence was still an issue though. Unhappy with the outcomes to date as he tried different options to cover for Suurbier's absence, Kovács took advantage of Gerrie Mühren's return to join Haan and Cruyff in midfield and copied Michels' strategy in the European Cup Final, moving Neeskens into right-back. Swart, Van Dijk and Keizer were the attack.

In a game that ended in frustrating goalless draw, however, Swart was injured in the first half and replaced by Suurendonk. Later both Keizer and Groningen's Hovenkamp were dismissed after a fracas. Four days later, Ajax would entertain East German champions Dynamo Dresden at the Olympisch Stadion with injuries, illnesses and a team apparently struggling to either cope with the loss of Michels, the new coach's ways, or both.

They were hardly in an ideal position to begin the defence of their hard-won trophy, and the jury was still out on Kovács, although an early struggle to find form for a new Ajax coach was hardly unusual. Even Michels hadn't achieved instant success. After his initial 9-3 win over MVV in January 1965 he only won two of Ajax's 11 remaining Eredivisie games before the end of the season. That old hackneyed phrase about a week being a long time in politics has often been borrowed to describe changes in football but, sometimes, that temporal measure can be reduced even farther. Against Dresden, a mere 20 minutes was sufficient.

Neeskens stayed in the back four alongside Hulshoff, Blankenburg and Krol. The defence was now settling into a regular pattern, although it wouldn't be complete until Suurbier returned to the right flank late in October. Cruyff remained in his deeper role with Haan and Mühren. Swart, Van Dijk and Keizer led the attack. Dynamo had won the DDR-Oberliga by a six-point margin from FC Carl Zeiss Jena in what was otherwise a very competitive league. Hallescher FC Chemie, who finished in third and qualified for the UEFA Cup, garnered a mere nine points more than FC Rot-Weiss Erfurt, who were relegated. The 45,000 fans at the Olympisch Stadion, however, would see something far less competitive.

Ajax went ahead after just two minutes. A miscued clearing header, following an Ajax corner from the left, fell to Cruyff inside the area. His left-footed volley was also miscued but, fortuitously, the ball bounced to Gerrie Mühren who controlled, turned, and hit a shot on target. In goal, Peter Meyer diverted the ball on to the post, but Sjaak Swart was on hand to bundle the ball over the line.

The second strike was not long in following. A flowing move saw Hulshoff feed Mühren, who sped the ball towards Cruyff on the left, where a turn and darting run took him to the edge of the area and a sharp pass to Van Dijk. The forward killed the pace on the ball and dropped it back into the path of Keizer who sidestepped the first defender before firing home. It was a beautiful piece of football, sorcery on the soccer field, fantasy football played at speed, and far beyond the abilities of the East Germans. Kovács's Ajax were suddenly sparking. The only surprise was that there were no more goals before the break, although an injury to Swart, who was replaced by Rep, did disrupt their rhythm.

That was also the case after the restart, but it didn't mean the end of entertainment and a style of play that was acquiring a *joie de vivre* expressed through *totaalvoetbal*. Cruyff was inevitably leading the show, his deeper role allowing him time and space to collect the ball, turn and run at defenders ill-equipped to cope with his electric movements. One run saw him drive from midfield, swaying past a defender before a neat wall pass with Mühren had him on the flank of the penalty area near the goal line, seemingly boxed in by defender Klaus Sammer's close attentions and with little attacking options. Unperturbed, Cruyff flicked the ball up twice on his foot and then once on his knee before playing it over his own head. The ball headed towards the angle of far post and crossbar as Meyer back-pedalled furiously. Leaping for the ball – it may well have deceived Meyer anyway for the most audacious of goals – but colliding with Keizer as he jumped, flapping at Cruyff's impudent effort, the goalkeeper would have been relieved when the Yugoslav referee Milivoje Gugolović generously awarded a free kick as the ball dropped into the net. Meyer had a reprieve, but football was denied the magical end product that Cruyff had so nearly conjured up. With a dozen minutes to play Rep was also injured and Suurendonk came from the bench to complete the game.

It's questionable as to whether there have been many, if any, more one-sided 2-0 results. Ajax turned in a majestic performance and a comfortable goalless draw in Dresden two weeks later completed the job, sending them into a second-round tie with Olympique de Marseille. It also ignited their season. The first leg against Dynamo was on 15 September, then Ajax would play through to April of the following year, completing 39 fixtures. They would win 36 and draw the other three before losing 3-2 in Deventer, as Go Ahead Eagles reprised their trick of the previous season and enhanced their reputation as Ajax's most tricky opponents.

Ahead of the goalless draw in Dresden, Ajax played two Eredivisie fixtures. The first brought NAC to the De Meer on 19 September and Kovács selected a team largely dictated by suspensions and injuries. Keizer and Neeskens were both serving suspensions following the ill-tempered game against Groningen. Swart's injury sustained in the European Cup tie kept him out, although he would return to claim a place on the bench for the next match and start in the return leg in Dresden. Suurbier was still many weeks away from a return and a slight injury to Gerrie Mühren also ruled him out of the reckoning.

With neither of his previously used options of first Swart and then Neeskens as stand-ins for Suurbier available, Kovács put Schilcher on the right of the defence, alongside Blankenburg, Hulshoff and Krol. The absence of his elder brother allowed Arnold Mühren a place in the midfield three, with Haan and Suurendonk. Cruyff was moved into the forward line with Van Dijk and Rep. The young forward had also been taken off with a slight injury against Dresden but had recovered sufficiently to play. It looked like a make-do-and-mend starting 11 but, with the following wind of the success against Dresden still filling their sails, Ajax certainly didn't play like it. In a five-goal romp, Schilcher opened his scoring account for the club, Van Dijk grabbed a hat-trick and Cruyff added the fifth in the last minute.

The following weekend, a team with the same defence, but Neeskens and Mühren restored to midfield with Haan, and Keizer returning to the forward line, drew 1-1 with PSV at the Philips Stadion in Eindhoven. A goal down at the break, Kovács removed Schilcher, replacing him with Swart in the back line and, four minutes after the restart, Van Dijk equalised.

After completing the job in Dresden, as September turned to October, Ajax had two more league fixtures to complete before travelling to the south of France and the first leg of the second-round tie at the Stade Vélodrome. A home game against NEC saw the Mühren brothers selected to play alongside each other in midfield for the first time and, in a tight encounter, it was Van Dijk who scored the all-important goal in the second half to secure the win. A week later, a team that resembled Kovács's preferred choice from the options available took the short journey across Amsterdam to play DWS. Neeskens was back as Suurbier's stand-in, alongside Blankenburg, Hulshoff and Krol. Haan, Cruyff and Mühren were in midfield, with Swart, Van Dijk and Keizer in attack. A goal from Keizer on 16 minutes and a header by Neeskens from a Van Dijk cross just past the hour garnered another two points, sending Ajax to France in good spirits. Former Ajax star Klaus Nuninga was in the DWS team that day, but the forward was unable to make an impression.

Despite the success of Neeskens as the deputy right-back, Kovács was keen to have the combative midfielder back in his more usual role against Marseille, and Swart dropped back into the defence instead. The move also facilitated Cruyff's move into the forward line next to Van Dijk and Keizer with Neeskens joining Haan and Gerrie Mühren behind them. The French champions had hardly impressed in their first-round encounter against Poland's Górnik Zabrze. They eventually won through 3-2 on aggregate but had fallen behind in both legs before recovering. Any such profligacy against Ajax was likely to be more severely punished. This time, though, it was the French club scoring the early goal.

Inside ten minutes a clumsy challenge on Di Caro offered Marseille an opportunity to put pressure on Heinz Stuy. The free kick was badly scuffed, rolling towards the near post from where it was swept clear. Possession fell to Kula who hit a first-time low shot back towards the Ajax goal. Stuy had it covered but, as the ball flew between the legs of Marseille forward Gress, it struck his ankle and deflected into the opposite corner of the net leaving the goalkeeper watching on in helpless frustration. A charitable analysis would suggest intent on the forward's part. A less charitable view would say the goal had been solely down to good fortune. Whatever the case, Marseille were ahead.

Despite falling behind, Ajax had been the better team up to that point and continued to look the more threatening afterwards. Marseille played with skipper Jules Zvunka as a sweeper, but, deployed as the deepest player, the defender lacked pace to recover if a forward got behind him. That vulnerability nearly cost Marseille elimination in the away leg against Górnik Zabrze, but Włodzimierz Lubański failed to exploit the opening after comfortably outstripping Zvunka.

It was clearly something that Ajax were aware of and twice, ahead of the break, Keizer sought to release Cruyff with long diagonal passes from the left, but each time the delivery lacked the required accuracy to isolate Zvunka against the searing pace of Cruyff. With Ajax dominating and weaving intricate patterns with their play, though, there was always a different route to be exploited, and the equaliser came on 37 minutes. A frustrated challenge on the edge of the box conceded a free kick and, as Keizer stood over the ball, a powerful shot seemed likely. Instead the winger clipped the ball over the defensive wall, precisely inside the post, and left the scampering goalkeeper Carnus floundering.

With the scores now level there seemed likely to be only one winner. On the hour a Marseille attack broke down and Keizer hammered the ball downfield, apparently with nothing but clearing the danger in his mind. Pressing forward, however, Marseille had left Cruyff in the sole care of Zvunka. After the crafted attempts at creating this situation, it had happened on the caprice of chance. Where Lubański had failed to capitalise on his chance in the earlier round, Cruyff would make no mistake. As Keizer's clearance dropped towards him, Cruyff sprinted clear and, with the defender trailing in his wake, he coolly slotted the ball past Canus as he advanced. With the home leg to come, a 2-1 victory was more than acceptable and Ajax played out the remaining time to secure the win.

Kovács retained the same starting 11 for the Eredivisie game at home to Go Ahead Eagles four days later, though the key addition was on the bench where Suurbier, after so many months sidelined with injury, was poised to make his return. Before he took his bow, however, Barry Hulshoff had illustrated just how much of the perfect *totaalvoetbal libero* he had become. On 14 minutes his towering header put Ajax in front, and he added his second goal 20 minutes later, finishing off an assist from Keizer. In between, Ruud Geels, who would join Ajax two years later and score 123 goals in 132 league appearances, had brought the teams level again with a goal sandwiched between Hulshoff's two strikes. It was only a brief reprieve and, five minutes before the break, the game was as good as over as Haan netted Ajax's third after work by Cruyff.

Comfortable with the state of play, Kovács introduced Suurbier at half-time and the returning defender completed what would become the regular Ajax defence for the upcoming seasons. The result was capped off as Neeskens added the fourth goal after more creative work by Cruyff. A week later, other than Swart replacing Van Dijk, the same team that finished against Go Ahead would start for the visit to MVV and goals by Neeskens, Cruyff and Swart delivered a comfortable 3-0 victory.

It was now the end of October and, up this point, Ajax had largely played with a makeshift defence, often denuding the midfield or forward line to find suitable cover for absentees at the back. And yet, in that time, they had remained unbeaten. Suurbier was now back in place and, with no other major injuries to cope with, Kovács could unleash the full flowering of Ajax's *totaalvoetbal*. As Auke Kok mentioned earlier, the Romanian gave the Ajax players more freedom to express themselves, made them more 'Cruyffian' and the release from the discipline of the Michels era lifted the team's performance to a new level. Writing for *The Guardian* in 2006, Jonathan Wilson clearly believed that to be the case. 'Ajax almost certainly produced their most eye-catching football under Kovács,'[63] he asserted. Michels had set the team alight, and the extra freedom offered by Kovács was as petrol poured on to the flames. Marseille were in line to feel the heat when they arrived at the Olympisch Stadion on 3 November for the second leg.

Understandably, with everyone now fit, Kovács selected his first-choice 11 for the game. Stuy was in goal behind Suurbier, Hulshoff, Blankenburg and Krol. Gerrie Mühren, Haan and Neeskens were the midfield trio with Cruyff up front, flanked by Swart and Keizer. It was the team that

---

63 'The man who took Ajax to new heights and the brink of destruction',
The Guardian, 8 January 2008.

would compete in the European Cup Final the following year, when the hugely unfortunate Van Dijk would miss out again.

In his book *The Lost Shankly Boy*, author Jeff Goulding relates the story of George Scott, who could never establish himself in the first-choice 11 at Anfield due to the quality of Liverpool's team. Following the club's decision to sell him, Bill Shankly consoled the young player in his inimitable way: 'Always remember, that at this moment in history you are the 12th-best player in the world, George.'[64] For Van Dijk, the feeling must have been similar; the 12th man to the best 11 in Europe. He had scored the goal that set Ajax on the road to European Cup glory at Wembley and in 1971/72 would still score 31 times in 41 appearances. It's a strike rate comparable to the top strikers in Europe. Displacing Cruyff from the central striker position that afforded Ajax's brightest star in the glittering firmament so much scope to deliver on his talents was simply unthinkable. In May 1972, just 11 days before Ajax faced Internazionale in their second consecutive European Cup Final, it was announced that Van Dijk would move to Nice in the summer; the transfer was completed on 1 July. There was a bittersweet moment for Van Dijk in September 1973 after Cruyff had left Ajax to join Michels at Barcelona. Nice were paired with the Catalan club in the UEFA Cup and, against the odds, triumphed 3-2 on aggregate with Van Dijk scoring the opening goal in the home leg.

Cruyff would enjoy his encounter with Marseille far more than his Barcelona team enjoyed their trip to Nice. The 2-1 win in the south of France had been relatively comfortable

---

64 Goulding, Jeff, *The Lost Shankly Boy*, (Worthing, England: Pitch Publishing Ltd, 2020).

but, in the return leg in Amsterdam, Ajax would be shaken out of any sense of complacency before recovering to deliver an impressive performance. Needing to score at least twice to have any hope of progress, Marseille had little to gain by being overly cautious and began on the front foot, seeking an early goal that would put an entirely different complexion on the tie. As early as the sixth minute, Skoblar chanced his arm with a shot from the edge of the box that had Stuy scrambling as it rippled the outside of the side-netting, but Ajax were quick to respond.

Two minutes later, a crunching tackle by Hulshoff set Cruyff free on the left. He drove into the box before cutting the ball back to Keizer, appearing in the centre, who cannoned his effort against the foot of the post. Another five minutes had passed when Ajax struck the square woodwork of the Olympisch Stadion goals for the second time. This time Keizer was the creator; dribbling in from his left flank, he weaved past three defenders in just a few metres before crossing for Mühren to head against the bar.

At this stage Ajax were dominating with Suurbier a constant threat down the right, cutting infield and even finding himself in the central striking position as the Ajax players rotated roles, pulling the Marseille defenders this way and that. As is so often the way though, the first goal came at the other end, after Haan had clattered into Couécou 20 metres or so from goal. It was a clear free kick, quickly confirmed by Scottish referee Alistair MacKenzie. Skoblar's shot was accurate but lacked pace and should have been easily collected by Stuy. Perhaps unsighted or deceived by the bounce of the ball, instead the Ajax goalkeeper fumbled the shot out to his left. Following in, Bonnel gathered and, from a tight angle, rolled the ball along the goal line for Couécou to tap it over the line.

The goal clearly ruffled Ajax's feathers and, for the next dozen minutes they pressed forward in determined fashion to correct matters. Suurbier pressed down the right, Swart switched into the middle of attack and Cruyff prompted and probed from all over. A fearsome shot by Hulshoff narrowly cleared Carnus's crossbar. Marseille were hanging on and looking for opportunities to counter-attack, but they were few and far between. An Ajax goal felt inevitable and came on 32 minutes. Collecting the ball from deep once more, Cruyff galloped forward as the Marseille defence dropped deeper to protect their penalty area. From 20 metres out, and without any meaningful challenge being registered against him, Cruyff fired a right-footed shot across Carnus and into the far corner of the net to bring the scores on the night level and restore Ajax's aggregate advantage. They wouldn't surrender it again. As the players celebrated, on the bench Kovács drew deeply on his cigarette in contentment.

Marseille were now under almost constant pressure as Ajax sought more goals. Last-ditch defending and a mounting tally of conceded free kicks told the story of a game that was rapidly running away from the visitors, and the second goal arrived six minutes after the first. Keizer drove in a powerful shot that fell to Swart. The erstwhile flank player had now almost wholly left that role to the rampant Suurbier as he moved into the space vacated by Cruyff indulging his wanderlust. Adroitly controlling the ball, he turned and drove it past Carnus. The writing was now clearly on the wall for all to see and, just ahead of the break Haan should have added a third goal, but drove directly at Carnus from a criminally unmarked position in the Marseille penalty area. At the break, the French team were on the ropes and Ajax were primed for more goals in the second period.

During half-time a marching military band entertained the crowd led by a goat mascot. When the players reappeared, Ajax were led out by an entirely different type of GOAT, and Cruyff would offer far more enticing entertainment than the martial music now relegated back to the sidelines, albeit somewhat reluctantly apparently. The players had been waiting on the pitch for almost ten minutes by the time the last bandsman left the field of play. The cheer from the crowd as the second half started was as much for relief as for excited anticipation – well, almost.

Any hopes the French players may have had that perhaps Ajax would now sit back to defend their lead, allowing Marseille back into the game, were quickly dispelled as Suurbier resumed his marauding runs down the right, twice crossing dangerously into the box. Then Hulshoff thundered forward from the back after intercepting, laid the ball off and continued his run into the box, only to be thwarted by Carnus as he jumped for the delivery. All this occurred within 60 seconds of the restart, and before Marseille had escaped their own half. The pattern for the remainder of the game had been set. Marseille had little option but to try and attack, but any forward forays carried the threat of being caught on the counter. It was an impossible balance to achieve.

Eight minutes into the half, Hulshoff suffered a jarring challenge as he retained possession. Socks rolled around his ankles as was his wont, the defender had forsaken the protection of shin guards, but he shook off the effects of the challenge and continued. Injuries, especially to his knee, would eventually tumble this giant of a player, but that wouldn't happen until two years later. In contrast, the next goal would cause terminal damage to the aspirations of Marseille. As the play became increasingly concentrated in their half, both legs and minds began to tire with the unequal challenge of keeping Ajax at bay. Inevitably gaps began to appear and on 64 minutes Swart arrowed a cross in from the right to perfectly meet up with Cruyff's dart between two tiring French defenders to score. Marseille now needed to score three times to progress. Requiring two had given them a mountain to climb but three was entering the realms of fantasy. Unusually, without a cigarette to hand this time, Kovács merely nodded in satisfaction at a job now undeniably completed.

Cruyff was now in his element. Disheartened defenders were easy prey for his coruscating runs from deep, deceiving opponents with sways of the hip and disguised passes. More chances inevitably came and Carnus was asked numerous questions as his defence wilted in front of him. With a dozen minutes to play Kovács withdrew Hulshoff, whose hobbling gait suggested he was still feeling the effects of that earlier challenge. Suurendonk was sent on in his place. It was a swansong appearance for the versatile Suurendonk and he wouldn't appear for the club again. A move to AS Monaco was announced on 24 November, and completed on 15 December. As was the case with Van Dijk, Suurendonk had contributed greatly to Ajax's success without ever becoming an established first-choice selection. The fee was estimated to be 150,000 guilders by one Dutch newspaper.[65]

Two minutes after the change, Cruyff and Keizer played out a short corner on the left. The skipper then evaded a half-hearted challenge and advanced into the area along the goal line before clipping a cross towards the far post. The ball evaded everyone in the area but, closing in from the right, Haan fired the ball straight back and it deceived Carnus to find the back of the net. It rounded out what, by now, had

---

65 *Het Vrije Volk*, 23 November 1971.

become a hugely convincing victory and took Ajax into the quarter-finals and a tie with Arsenal. The only concern was a caution for Neeskens, meaning he would be suspended for the next match in European competition.

Two seasons earlier Ajax had been eliminated from the Inter-Cities Fairs Cup by the north London club, who in 1971 had completed an impressive domestic double, beating Leeds United into second place in the league and defeating Liverpool in the FA Cup Final. Of all the eight clubs remaining in the competition, facing Arsenal was one of the toughest assignments, and a significant step up in quality from Marseille. Ajax were joined by Feyenoord, who had been paired with Benfica in another difficult task. Could there be an all-Dutch final? It was certainly possible. Ernst Happel's team had efficiently disposed of Olympiakos Nicosia and Dinamo București in the first two rounds, amassing 22 goals without reply.

Such musings would need to wait until the new year as European competition went into winter hibernation until March, and domestic concerns moved front and centre. Ironically for both clubs, their first game after confirming their places in the quarter-finals would be against each other in a key Eredivisie fixture in Amsterdam on 7 November.

By this stage of the season, Ajax had won eight of their 11 games to date, drawing the other three. It was highly impressive form but Feyenoord were leading the table by two points from Kovács's men after winning ten and drawing just one of their 11 fixtures. The only result blotting their perfect record was a goalless draw in Utrecht. If Happel's team could win in Amsterdam it would double their lead, whereas conversely a victory for Ajax would wipe it out.

With the distractions of European competition now in cold storage, Kovács could select his best team for the clash with their rivals, and did so, retaining the 11 that overwhelmed Marseille as Hulshoff had shaken off the injury that forced his early exit four days earlier. The first half was as tight and competitive as would be expected when the two top clubs in any league, and indeed the last two European champions, faced each other. At the break neither team had managed a breakthrough. The nearest to a goal came when Swart drifted in from the right and clipped a shot that struck the crossbar and bounced clear. With their two-point advantage, a draw would favour the visitors more than Ajax.

Defender Theo van Duivenbode had enjoyed the previous season's *Klassieker* encounters, scoring vital goals for Feyenoord to deny his old club, but events wouldn't favour him or his team on this occasion. On 67 minutes Gerrie Mühren played a free kick forward and Swart was on hand to convert. Nine minutes later, when Israël inadvertently put through his own goal to double the lead, the victory and points were safe for Ajax. A minor redemption for the Feyenoord skipper with a consolation goal two minutes from time was too little and too late.

It was an important result in the race for the title and Feyenoord compounded their fate by surprisingly losing their next fixture 1-0 at home to Twente. After their almost perfect start to the season, Feyenoord would drop points in three of the next 13 games before Ajax visited Rotterdam for the return fixture on 15 April. As well as the home defeat to Twente, Feyenoord also saw points slip away in a 2-0 defeat to PSV in Eindhoven, and another goalless draw with Utrecht, this time at the De Kuip. Former Ajax player Ton Pronk was instrumental in frustrating the Feyenoord forwards in both games against Utrecht. The dropped points opened the door for Ajax to establish a lead in the league.

Kovács's team responded with 14 wins, plus the single defeat that they endured all season, losing to 3-2 to Go Ahead

Eagles on the first day of April. Once again the Deventer club made 'fools' of Ajax in timely fashion as Ruud Geels netted two second-half goals to turnaround a first-half deficit and win the game. It meant that when Ajax visited the De Kuip in the middle of April 1972, they would lead the table by a single point, and the game would be the first of a trio of fixtures pivotal to defining their season. All would provide victories, and all would be played at Feyenoord's De Kuip stadium. The intervening months, though, would be full of action, both domestically and in continental competition.

There were half a dozen Eredivisie fixtures to complete before the end of the year, and Ajax won them all. For the first three, Kovács stayed with his first-choice 11 as Utrecht were defeated 3-2, Telstar 5-2 – the game in which Cruyff scored his 150th goal for the club – and RKSV Volendam 1-0. At home to FC Den Bosch on 5 December, Kovács dropped Haan to the bench, moved Cruyff back into midfield and gave Van Dijk a rare start. Two goals up at the break, Neeskens was removed with Haan taking over his midfield position. At the end of the game Ajax had added three more goals. Van Dijk wasn't among the scorers and, for the following week, he was out of the team for the visit to his former club.

It was back to the usual starters for a 1-0 victory over Twente, and there were no changes for the visit to Vitesse Arnhem and a 3-1 win, although Rep got a late outing from the substitutes' bench to replace Swart. The victory ended 1971 on a positive note. Despite having a new coach, losing the likes Vasović and Rijnders and suffering injuries to key players, Ajax topped the Eredivisie, were into the quarter-finals of the European Cup, undefeated across the season and their *totaalvoetbal* was sweeping all before them. Things couldn't get better, or could they?

219

The new year started in familiar fashion. A 2-1 victory away to FC Den Haag was secured by the first-choice starting 11. Roodnat had given the home team a surprise lead five minutes before half-time but, within eight minutes of playing time, goals from Keizer and Cruyff had turned things around. It was becoming increasingly significant that when a forward was removed, in this case Swart, Kovács tended to replace him with Rep rather than Van Dijk. The writing on the wall was becoming increasingly clear for all to see.

The following week saw the first round of the KNVB Cup. Ajax entertained lower-league FC Zwolle at the De Meer and Kovács placed Arnold Mühren alongside his brother Gerrie and Haan in midfield, leaving Neeskens on the bench until half-time when he replaced Krol. The Ajax players indulged themselves, scoring eight times with Cruyff and Swart both bagging braces. The others were added by Gerrie Mühren, Keizer, Neeskens and an own goal by Schubert. The younger Mühren was back on the bench for the next game, an Eredivisie fixture at home to Sparta, although he would join the action on 66 minutes, replacing Haan as Ajax recorded a 2-1 win.

There was a three-week break before their next official fixture, and with an eye to potentially lucrative friendlies that could keep the club's coffers topped up and maintain the players' level of match fitness, matches were arranged against HFC Haarlem and Marseille. The games were particularly significant for Van Dijk, who returned to the starting 11 and scored twice in the 4-3 win in Haarlem, and again netted in a 2-2 draw in France that gave the hosts some consolation for their elimination from the European Cup.

The goals must have impressed Kovács, at least temporarily, as, when the Eredivisie swung into action again on 6 February and Ajax travelled to Breda to face NAC, Van

Dijk had usurped Swart in the starting 11. He responded with two goals in a 5-2 victory. There was just over a month to go until the first leg against Arsenal in the last eight of the European Cup and, as the man in possession of the starting position and scoring in consecutive games, Van Dijk would have been happily pondering his chances of a long run in the team but, with Ajax drawing 0-0 against Go Ahead Eagles in their next Eredivisie fixture, Kovács removed the forward at half-time and sent Swart on instead. Three second-half strikes, including one from the substitute, suggested that Van Dijk's run of starting games was about to hit the buffers.

The visit to Excelsior for the next match brought a reprieve. Neeskens was taken ill with a bout of flu and Cruyff dropped back into midfield, allowing Van Dijk to remain in the forward line. Two goals by Cruyff and a couple of own goals brought Ajax a comfortable win. As it had been for the season's first European encounter, the final Eredivisie fixture before the new year's first European Cup game was against Groningen. Back in September, Ajax had laboured to a goalless draw before facing Dynamo Dresden four days later. Now, as spring was trying to elbow aside an Amsterdam winter, Groningen's visit to the De Meer, five days before Arsenal followed in their footsteps, would be very different. Neeskens was still unavailable so Kovács selected the same 11 starters who had triumphed over Excelsior in Rotterdam. Five goals clear at the break, Ajax coasted to a 7-0 win. Cruyff nabbed a hat-trick, Mühren scored twice, and Keizer and Swart completed the rout.

Neeskens' recovery from flu was rendered irrelevant as far as team selection was concerned. His caution in the home leg against Marseille had made him ineligible for the first meeting with Arsenal. The team that had hammered Groningen started against the English champions in what would be Ajax's 50th game in European Cup competition. Difficult selection issues weren't restricted to Ajax. Despite being able to deploy 10 of the 11 who had won the FA Cup Final the previous season, Bertie Mee was still missing players who he would surely have included had they been available.

New signing Alan Ball was still ineligible for the competition unless, or until, Arsenal reached the last four. Kelly, McNab and Roberts were injured and maverick Scottish talent Peter Marinello was laid low with a virus. Writing in *The Times* ahead of the game, Geoffrey Green advocated a front-foot approach from Arsenal regardless of any missing players. 'No good will come of willingly surrendering midfield control to this talented Dutch side,'[66] he cautioned, suggesting that Celtic's demise in the previous season had been due to such negativity. Although the suggestion that tactical naivety was the sole reason for the Scottish club's elimination was more than a touch simplistic, as the game would illustrate.

Despite it being the first week of March, it was still a chilly evening as Arsenal, in their change kit of yellow and blue, took the pitch, waving to the crowd from the centre before peeling off to their half for the warm-up. It was a full two minutes later when Piet Keizer led out Ajax to join them. Despite Green's promptings, the early seconds saw Arsenal defend deep – whether by design or compulsion – as Ajax dominated the play. A through ball found Gerrie Mühren galloping into space. The canny McLintock feigned innocence as he tumbled him to the ground. Greek referee Leonidas Vamvakopoulos was suitably unimpressed and awarded Ajax a free kick on the edge of the penalty area. It came to nought, but the pattern for the opening minutes had been set.

---

66 'Arsenal to learn from Celtic's mistake', *The Times*, 7 March 1972.

Krol appeared on the right flank – for much of the game he and Suurbier seemed to have swopped positions – feeding Cruyff who cut inside, but his shot flew wide of Bob Wilson's near post. Hulshoff fed a ball into Van Dijk. The forward flicked the ball inside but Swart hadn't read his intentions. Enjoying the freedom of his deeper role, Cruyff was popping up here, there and at times seemingly everywhere. Mee had deployed Storey in a midfield role, potentially to pick up Cruyff. It would have been like trying grab hold of mist. Ajax's number 14 was now on the left flank, curling in a cross with the outside of his right foot that deceived Wilson, but just failed to reach Swart on the far post before drifting out of play. Swart connected with a half-cleared header on the edge of the penalty area, but sliced his shot wide.

Hulshoff then collected the ball from another Arsenal long clearance, skipped inside the first challenge, and brushed aside the second, before feeding Cruyff. A feint and turn were too quick for Simpson, who clumsily bundled the elusive Cruyff to the floor, but again the free kick came to nothing. Swart fed Cruyff who drifted out to the right edge of the penalty area, marked by Simpson. Reprising his trick of months earlier against Dynamo Dresden, Cruyff flicked the ball up, and then over his head. Only an acrobatic dive and punch clear by Wilson prevented him scoring.

The selection of Radford, Kennedy and Charlie George promised plenty of attacking threat but, often with only one of them isolated up front as the other two funnelled back to help bail out an overworked midfield, that threat looked extremely blunt. Approaching the 15-minute mark, Stuy had only been required to catch the occasional hopeful, if largely aimless, cross and maintain concentration. In football's typically perverse way, however, as in both games against Marseille, Ajax conceded the first goal.

An overzealous challenge by Hulshoff on Radford conceded a free kick around the halfway line and McLintock hoisted the ball into the Ajax box. Krol headed partially clear and then Keizer sought to nod the ball back into the hands of Stuy. Kennedy had read his intentions though, and, darting forward, stretched out a foot to guide the ball past the goalkeeper and into the net. As robberies go, this one was entered into the column labelled 'Daylight'.

The goal hardly changed the pattern of the game, except for perhaps Arsenal sinking deeper now they had that precious lead to protect. Ajax pressed but, with a penalty area often containing eight or nine yellow shirts, plus Wilson. Getting back into the game was not going to be easily achieved, particularly with the Arsenal goalkeeper in such form.

A minute or so after the goal, a flying save touched a shot from Keizer around the far post. Following the corner, a period of head tennis ended with Wilson collecting and calming his defenders. Krol fed Swart and his dangerous cross was caught by Wilson as Van Dijk challenged. Even Wilson couldn't be everywhere though. A cross from Swart on the right deceived everyone, and left the goalkeeper outside of his far post as Cruyff stretched to flick the ball back towards goal. His effort struck the bar and dropped towards the line. With Wilson struggling to regain his position, it was left to Simpson to clear, with the defender's desperate hack at the ball sending it up and against the bar again before bouncing clear.

Hulshoff drove forward in typical barnstorming style, before Storey's agricultural challenge eventually brought the run to a halt. The free kick led to a corner on the left, but it flew directly into the side-netting of Wilson's goal. The equaliser was not far away though. On 25 minutes, a cross from the right by Haan was headed on by Keizer, then out by Simpson. The ball fell to Mühren who fired a first-time

Rinus Michels in his playing days with Ajax. A duel with goalkeeper Van der Lee of HFC.

The appointment of Michels as coach had a huge effect on Ajax – and Johan Cruyff.

Ajax and Panathinaikos take to the field at Wembley ahead of the 1971 European Cup Final.

Dick van Dijk's glancing header deceives Panathinaikos goalkeeper Takis Ikonomopoulos to give Ajax an early lead.

Substitute Arie Haan is buried under celebrating team-mates as his late goal confirms Ajax's first European Cup triumph, overcoming Panathinaikos 2-0.

Michels is carried on fans' shoulders after beating Panathinaikos.

Michels moved to Barcelona following Ajax's first European Cup triumph. Cruyff would join after the 1973 victory, followed by Neeskens whose move was strangely announced in the middle of the 1974 World Cup finals.

When Michels left for Catalonia, Ajax turned to little-known Romanian coach Ștefan Kovács.

Sjaak Swart's goal was enough to beat Benfica 1-0 on aggregate and take Ajax to the 1972 European Cup Final after a 0-0 draw in Lisbon. That efficient second leg result, however, nearly saw Kovács removed as coach of the club.

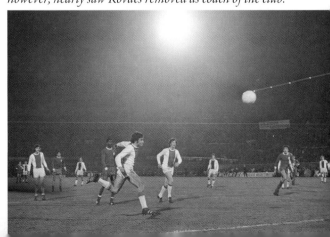

A blunder by Inter Milan goalkeeper Ivano Bordon leaves Cruyff with an easy tap-in to put Ajax ahead in the 1972 European Cup Final

Cruyff's second goal against the Italians ensures Ajax's second successive European Cup triumph.

Kovács is carried from the field after Ajax's victory over Inter Milan.

Mühren fires high past Sepp Maier to score the second of Ajax's four goals as they thrashed Bayern Munich 4-0 in the first leg of the 1973 European Cup quarter-final. Just over a year later, the Bavarian club would inherit Ajax's European crown.

Cruyff and Real Madrid's Ignacio Zoco exchange pennants before the first leg of the 1973 European Cup semi-final.

Barry Hulshoff powers Ajax ahead against Real Madrid in the first leg of the 1973 European Cup semi-final.

Gerrie Mühren is buried among clubmates after scoring the winning goal against Real Madrid in the Estadio Santiago Bernabeu. Earlier his keepy-uppy skills had illustrated the Dutch club's domination over the old aristocrats of European football. This goal sent Ajax to their third successive final.

Johnny Rep (16) celebrates with Haan after scoring the winning goal against Juventus in the 1973 European Cup Final.

Wearing an exchanged Juventus shirt, Cruyff raises the trophy after the 1973 European Cup Final with Barry Hulshoff.

Piet Keizer played in all three of Ajax's European Cup triumphs, captaining the team in 1972, before Cruyff took over as skipper in the following season. Cruyff claimed that losing the captaincy to Keizer once more, after a squad election, led to him leaving for Barcelona.

End of an era. CSKA Sofia's goalkeeper plunges low to his right to save Rep's penalty in the first leg of the 1974 European Cup second round tie in Amsterdam. The miss would cost Ajax dearly. A 1-0 win was wiped out in Bulgaria, and an extra-time goal by Stefan Mihaylov eliminated Ajax from the European Cup for the first time in three years.

low shot on goal. Wilson may have had it covered, but a slight deflection from a defender's foot was sufficient to deceive him and guide the ball into the net. Being level was the least that Ajax's domination of the game deserved, and they now set off in search of a winning goal, with Arsenal throwing up as many barriers as they could.

A drive by Swart fell towards Van Dijk in the area, but his control was less than perfect and Wilson pounced to collect. Cruyff danced and swayed hypnotically on the edge of the area before setting up Mühren for a shot that was blocked. Cruyff and Haan combined to find space on the right for Swart, who cleverly feigned to cross before threading a low ball into the box towards Haan. The midfielder spun and shot but the ball struck the outside of the post. A mistake by Rice, who let a long ball pass under his foot, allowed Mühren space on the side of the area, but his low cross was smothered by Wilson. The same fate followed for a Cruyff header from a deep Swart cross. A step-over and powerful shot by Keizer was blocked by Simpson. The game was all flowing in one direction.

Hulshoff was almost playing as an auxiliary striker as the dying minutes of the first period ebbed away, but Ajax couldn't find a way through Arsenal's packed defence, and then to beat Wilson when that first task had been achieved. At the half-time whistle Arsenal would have been delighted to be level with just 45 minutes of the away leg to play. For Ajax, it was difficult to see how they could have played much better and, on another day, they could have been three or four goals clear. But they weren't, and unless they could add to Mühren's deflected shot, their reign as European champions would be in peril.

For the early minutes after the restart Arsenal showed some attacking ambition, pushing forward and having a couple of, albeit tame, attempts on Stuy's goal. The question as to whether this was a change of tactics from the first period, or merely an attempt to keep the ball as far away from their own goal as possible, was quickly resolved. Their early ambition dwindled and the game assumed the established pattern of the first half as the Dutch crowd tried to do their part, raising a boisterous chant for their team.

Once more Wilson was presenting himself as a formidable barrier to Dutch aspirations, calm under pressure and instinctive in reaction. A low shot by Keizer looked to be heading unerringly inside the near post but Wilson appeared just in time to guide it wide. Sinking deeper to find space away from the suffocating yellow blanket of the Arsenal players massed around their own area, Cruyff probed with beguiling runs and inspired passes, but each attack foundered.

Around 15 minutes in, another Cruyff run took him to the edge of the Arsenal area as he weaved his way inside and outside of defenders' lunges. An exchange of passes with Mühren sent him scampering on into the area but an uncompromising block by Storey ended the venture. The referee disdainfully waved aside Dutch appeals for a penalty but ten minutes later a different decision would sway the tie in Ajax's favour.

The game was now being concentrated into the Arsenal half but with the English club only leaving Kennedy upfield as they defended, hoping the forward could hold up play and allow support to join him when the chance presented itself. Ajax had plenty of possession but the yellow shirts in deep defence did little to concede space inside their area. Shots from distance were allowed, with confidence in Wilson being rewarded with impressive handling. Patience would be just as important as technique if Ajax were to prevail. With 25 minutes to play, Kovács sent Rep out to warm up. He would enter the field but, by the time he did, Ajax had scored.

From just inside the Ajax half, Blankenburg hoisted a free kick forward. It was headed clear but only to Mühren who hooked it forwards once more, and then headed on into the area where first Cruyff was felled, before Van Dijk – pursuing the ball while surrounded by three defenders – tumbled to the ground. Which offence the referee considered worthy of a spot-kick wasn't clear, and neither seemed as clear-cut as Storey's earlier block on Cruyff, but the attention of the players and camera on Van Dijk suggested he was the victim. The forward had battled to make a mark on the game as he struggled to lead the line with any effectiveness against a packed defence. In this moment, however, his willingness to persevere when outnumbered had offered his team a breakthrough.

Arsenal's protests were loud and prolonged, but in vain as Mühren coolly sent Wilson sprawling to his right as he rolled the ball effortlessly into the opposite corner. With 20 minutes to play, Ajax were ahead and, for once, Wilson had been unable to save his team.

At this stage Hulshoff was everywhere, except in defence. With only one Arsenal forward to defend against, Blankenburg was left to mind the back door and Hulshoff shuffled between midfield and the forward line, offering overloads on the flanks or in deeper areas, with Haan dropping back as cover if required. Ajax had largely looked far less likely to score since the break and Kovács sought a way to change that, despite his team now being ahead. For the final dozen minutes or so, Rep replaced the tiring Van Dijk.

Seconds later, Cruyff pounced on a back-pass that left Wilson exposed. The Scottish goalkeeper dashed from his line though, and blocked Cruyff's attempt to clip the ball over him. Rep's introduction added some verve and dash to Ajax's attack, but with time slipping away Kovács sat immobile on the bench drawing repeatedly on his cigarette, betraying concerns that, despite his team's pronounced superiority in the game, a single-goal lead would leave them vulnerable for the away leg to come.

With minutes left, first Swart, then Rep nearly doubled the advantage. A hoisted ball into the Arsenal box caused confusion as it bounced. Swart was able to hook it clear of Wilson towards the far post, with Rep closing in, but Rice threw himself in front of the young forward's shot and blocked it away for a corner. In the last minute a long ball from Krol found Cruyff free around the penalty spot but once more Wilson was on hand, plunging at the forward's feet to clear. When the final whistle sounded, the headline of Geoffrey Green's match report in *The Times* of the following day summed up the situation perfectly. 'Wilson and goal give Arsenal hope',[67] it read, while in the text, Green explained, 'Arsenal may well have sunk like a stone but for a brave rearguard action and a heroic performance in goal by Wilson.' The tie was far from over.

There were two Eredivisie games to play before Kovács took his team to north London to try and confirm their place in the semi-finals. Four days after the first leg, PSV visited the De Meer and left with a 4-1 defeat. Kovács had drafted Neeskens back into midfield and moved Cruyff into the forward line, relegating Van Dijk to the bench. There was brief concern when Hoekema put the visitors ahead after quarter of an hour, but a brace from Keizer and another Gerrie Mühren penalty plus a late own goal by Pleun saw Ajax to a comfortable win. The second match took Ajax to the De

---

67 ' 'Wilson and goal give Arsenal hope', *The Times*, 9 March 1972.

Goffert in Nijmegen to face NEC. Kovács retained the team that had defeated PSV and, in a much closer contest, a single goal by Neeskens just ahead of the break secured the points.

With Neeskens back, Kovács's selection for the away leg against Arsenal was straightforward and he delivered no surprises, retaining the same starting 11 for the third successive fixture. Bertie Mee would have been wishing for similar freedom. Radford was unavailable due to suspension and, to complicate matters further with Ball still not qualified for selection, Kelly was now added to the injury list.

Highbury was packed with more than 56,000 fans for the second leg of a tie that was enticingly balanced. Should Arsenal score first, their away goal secured in Amsterdam would put them ahead on aggregate. If the breakthrough went to Ajax, however, their lead would be doubled and Arsenal would be in dire trouble. The logic suggested that the first goal would be decisive – and it was. With Arsenal in their traditional colours, Ajax played in white shirts and blue shorts, but a muddy surface suggested those shirts would not stay white for long.

The first goal so nearly came in the opening seconds. Peter Marinello, replacing Radford, pounced on poor control by Blankenburg and closed in with just Stuy to beat. The advancing goalkeeper blocked the Scottish forward's shot with his foot, but the ball ran out to Kennedy who blazed the rebound wastefully high and wide. It was a glorious chance squandered, but served to set an already boisterous home support alight. For much of the first leg, Arsenal had been compelled to defend. In the opening minutes of this match it was the Dutch team being pushed back. A break by Keizer and a typically mazy run from Cruyff as Ajax snaffled possession illustrated that the visitors still had plenty of attacking ambition, but Wilson's diving save thwarted Cruyff.

On five minutes, George Graham headed narrowly wide as Arsenal continued to press. Then a brief melee saw the ball drop to Kennedy on the edge of the Ajax box but a swift challenge by Hulshoff averted the danger. Ajax were conceding too many free kicks and, although their back line was dealing with most of the crosses into the box, the offences opened up a very English avenue of attack for Arsenal. The shape of the game was suiting the home team far more than Ajax, although only for a while.

Arsenal's approach was hustle and bustle, disturbing the more cerebral approach of Ajax, but slowly the visitors played their way into the game and the Gunners' crosses into the box became largely ineffective with Hulshoff dominating. At the other end Wilson became more involved as Ajax began to weave some patterns of play together. And yet when the first goal came it was from an error. Krol lifted a ball towards the Arsenal box and, with no Ajax player near to threaten, Wilson scampered from his goal ready to collect. Unaware of his goalkeeper's movement, however, Graham stretched to intercept the cross but diverted the ball towards the empty net. With Wilson helpless, it bounced into the net and Ajax were ahead.

It was the key moment of both the leg and the tie. As *The Times* reported the following day, 'Having been given that early gift [Ajax] merely sat on their eggs and knowing the limitations of their enemy let Arsenal come at them minute after minute with the ball slung hopelessly into the air.'[68] It was a vintage performance by Ajax, but it didn't need to be. Once ahead they played with control and patience, offering up a similar performance to that which overcame

---

68 'Arsenal lose to team who do not have to put their best foot forward', *The Times*, 23 March 1972.

Celtic in Glasgow the previous year. *The Times* continued, 'For Ajax all it needed was a stony patience and a cannily strong defence to see them home.' Arsenal's play was exposed as one-dimensional, and once that was nullified they had little else to threaten with. Ajax were into the last four.

The Netherlands had begun the tournament with the rare luxury of having two clubs competing. At the quarter-final stage, however, Feyenoord fell foul of a rampant Benfica side who overturned a 1-0 defeat in Rotterdam by scoring five times back in Lisbon. With Internazionale and Celtic paired in the other semi-final, Ajax would need to restore Dutch pride and defeat the Portuguese champions to reach their second successive final. Before facing that task there would be two Eredivisie games and a KNVB Cup encounter to deal with. One of the league matches would deliver Ajax's first defeat of the season, and the only one they wouldn't redeem in a second leg.

On the weekend following the elimination of Arsenal, Ajax entertained DWS at the De Meer. Perhaps with an understandable nod towards allowing important players a break, Cruyff was dropped to the substitutes' bench and Van Dijk replaced him in an otherwise unchanged starting 11. The club from across Amsterdam would only survive in the Eredivisie by the slimmest of margins at the end of the season. It was perhaps therefore an indication of growing fatigue, be it mental as much as physical, among the Ajax players that the scoreline was still blank at the break.

There had also been a scare on 33 minutes when Hulshoff, who had done so much to nullify the aerial attacks of Arsenal, was taken off injured and replaced by Schilcher. Past the hour mark the visitors were still level and, on 64 minutes, Kovács felt compelled throw on Cruyff. Any dropped points in such games would allow Feyenoord the opportunity to close the gap in the table. It wasn't until the final eight minutes that the breakthrough came and, even then, it was a fortunate goal. A free kick was deflected past his own goalkeeper by Muller and at last Ajax were ahead. It was a lead they never looked like losing and when Neeskens added a second in the last minute it merely confirmed the outcome.

The performance had been far from satisfactory for Kovács, despite the result eventually going Ajax's way. The conundrum for the coach was whether that was because he had left Cruyff out, or whether he should have rested other players as well. His selection for the next fixture, a KNVB Cup quarter-final against NEC at the De Meer, suggested he was leaning towards the former. Cruyff replaced Van Dijk, reuniting the team that had won at Highbury. Once more, however, it was a below-par performance and only an 88th-minute goal by Keizer edged Ajax into the last four.

There's a legend that the April Fools tradition was invented by the Dutch, going back to the Eighty Years' War when the threat of invasion by the Spanish was at its height. Whether there's any validity in such claims is less than clear. What is clear, however, is that in several Eredivisie games around this period, Go Ahead Eagles proved troublesome for Ajax. Facing a visit to the De Adelaarshorst on the first day of April should therefore have been a herald of caution, especially following two less-than-impressive performances.

The first leg of the European Cup semi-final against Benfica at the Olympisch Stadion was just four days away when Ajax faced Go Ahead, but Kovács selected an unchanged team, perhaps with the hope that they would play themselves back into form. Seven minutes in, that looked like a forlorn hope when Smid put the home side ahead. By the break, however, goals by Neeskens and Cruyff had Ajax in front and, for a while, assuaged the coach's concerns. The second half would tell a different story.

Ruud Geels was hardly a towering presence in the forward line but, across the many clubs he plied his trade with – including later with Ajax – he would score a more-than-decent percentage of his goals with headers. In the second period of this match he added two more to that list and, despite throwing Van Dijk on for Swart with 15 minutes to play, Ajax couldn't find a way back and Go Ahead Eagles had performed their party piece once more. Whether they or their fans hooted 'April Fools!' at Ajax is unknown, but in fairness, also probably unlikely.

For the first time since the early days of the season, Ajax looked vulnerable. The swagger in their game had been compromised by an erosion of confidence and, perhaps, even self-belief. Kovács's selection options were diminished by Rep who, reports suggested, had been excluded for apparent lack of commitment when selected for the B team.[69] The young forward was still six months away from his 21st birthday but, having appeared 16 times for the first team, albeit only twice as a starter, may well have felt that lower-status football was below him.

Much later, reports suggested that Rep felt it was the coach's weakness and deference to Cruyff that diminished his early chances of regular first-team selection. The youngster was apparently convinced that the totemic leader preferred Swart to be in the team, and it wasn't until Cruyff signalled his approval that the coach put Rep in ahead of the veteran. That wouldn't occur until the following season and the club's disciplinary measures put Rep out of first-team reckoning altogether for a month.

---

69 https://www.afc-ajax.info/en/match/1972-4-5-Ajax-Benfica

Benfica's demolition of Feyenoord had marked their card as a team to be treated with utmost respect and, regardless of the recent performances, selecting his regular starting 11 was probably never far from Kovács's mind for the game against the Portuguese champions. Although the talents of José Torres, Mário Coluna and António Simões were now merely remembered legends at the club, *As Águais* still had the goalscoring prowess of Eusébio, and the vastly experienced skipper Jaime Graça in the team that would be travelling to the Olympisch Stadion, supplemented by the likes of Nené and Rui Jordão who, between them, had hit Feyenoord for all five goals in that demolition in Lisbon.

Strangely, perhaps, given that second colours had been required in similar situations during the past, with Ajax playing in their traditional shirts and shorts, Benfica were allowed to keep their all-red strip. The Portuguese club's victory over Feyenoord had been built on a disciplined first-leg performance that restricted Happel's team to a single goal, setting up the second leg to complete the job in the Estádio da Luz. It was no great surprise therefore that in this game Benfica would adopt similar tactics. The first period was tight with the visitors determined to give little away, and deploying whatever methods were required to break up Ajax's play. At one stage a challenge resulted in Keizer's shorts being literally ripped from his legs, requiring him stand on the pitch in just his underpants until replacements were rushed on and dignity restored.

Ajax's recent domestic travails hardly seemed to diminish their aptitude for attack and they kept the Benfica defence busy. On three occasions Cruyff, raiding down the right, caused problems for the visitors' back line. Then, a shot from the other flank saw goalkeeper José Henrique – veteran of the 1968 European Cup Final defeat to

Manchester United – save with his feet, before the ball was cleared. He would do the same minutes later as Cruyff returned to the right and fired in a low cross. At the break, Ajax had enjoyed an overwhelming amount of possession but without asking too many serious questions. Kovács could ask little more of his team in attacking emphasis but the cutting edge appeared to be diminished, blunted by the visitors' determined defence.

In the visiting dressing room, the English coach of Benfica, Jimmy Hagan, would have been full of praise for his team's performance and, with just 45 minutes to play, another excellent away result was well within their grasp. Hagan would lead Benfica to three successive league titles as well as a domestic cup victory during his time in Lisbon. His team were well used to success, and had the scent of another European Cup Final in their nostrils.

When the action resumed, so did the pattern of the first period. Ajax pressed but the visitors hardly seemed overstretched in resisting. A deep and well-drilled defence coped without obvious stress and, when deemed necessary, were content to resort to less acceptable measures to break up attacks. Time drifted away and a goalless drew looked increasingly inevitable. Even when the solid red wall of the Benfica defence was briefly breached, chances were squandered with mishit shots as first Mühren, then Swart, demonstrated. The tension on the pitch was echoed in the Ajax fans among the crowd of 54,261.

Just past the hour mark, a Neeskens clip looking for space behind the Benfica back line, as Mühren bent his wide run, was unashamedly caught by Correia in a passable impression of a goalkeeper leaping for and clutching a high cross. Dropping the ball, he then trotted back to his defensive position, hands aloft in mock apology. There wasn't even a word of caution from Soviet Union referee Karlo Kruasvili, but there was a price to pay. From the free kick Keizer floated the ball towards the far post to meet up perfectly with the run of Swart, whose header flew past Henrique and into the net. Swart may have been nearing his 34th birthday but Johnny Rep would have to wait a while longer yet to usurp the man who had been playing first-team football for Ajax since well before Michels arrived.

While the players celebrated, and the fans roared in relief as much as joy, the visitors merely settled down to see out the remainder of time without conceding again. A 1-0 defeat was far from being the perfect result but, given their goalscoring prowess in home legs so far, it was hardly a disaster either.

Aware of Feyenoord's fate when they travelled to Lisbon with a similarly narrow advantage, Kovács pushed on for a second goal. Van Dijk came on for Haan to bolster the forward line and Hulshoff pushed forward as well. With Benfica offering little in attack, it was hardly a gamble. Late on, a turn by the substitute on the edge of the box created a narrow space but Van Dijk's shot was blocked and, when Keizer fired the rebound narrowly wide, Ajax's best chance of a second goal had gone.

As with Happel's team, Ajax would be faced with the task of defending a single-goal advantage in the Estádio da Luz. To date, in their three home legs, the Portuguese champions had scored 12 goals and conceded just three. If Ajax were to qualify it would require a performance every bit as disciplined as that deployed by Benfica. Ajax would provide it, but with a surprising consequence.

The return leg would take place on 19 April, but Ajax had domestic matters in front of them before that. A KNVB Cup semi-final against RSKV Volendam was sandwiched between Eredivisie games at home to MVV and then, in what was likely to be a hugely influential match in deciding the fate of the league title, away to Feyenoord.

The first task was to secure two points when MVV visited the De Meer on the following weekend. Earlier in the season, Ajax had cruised to a 3-0 win in Maastricht and the visitors weren't expected to offer a sterner test this time. That was certainly the way it panned out. Kovács's regular 11, bar for a rested Cruyff replaced by Van Dijk, started and by half-time Ajax were five goals clear. Understandably, at the break Kovács began to ring the changes. Arnold Mühren came on for Keizer before the second period began and, nine minutes later, Neeskens was withdrawn with Gerrie Kleton sent on to replace him.

Kleton had come through the club's youth structure after joining as an amateur in the 1969/70 season, and this was his Eredivisie debut. Although he would also feature in the KNVB Cup a couple of days later, his career in first-class football for Ajax would only comprise a further three league appearances before he was transferred in September 1974 – ironically to MVV. In this match, however, he contributed to his future employers' downfall by creating a goal for the younger Mühren brother ten minutes after entering the game. By full time, another two goals had been added.

The inevitable consequence of a successful season is that towards the end of it games not only come thick and fast, but each one of them is important. Such was the case for Ajax at this time. There was just a two-day break before the next fixture, the semi-final of the KNVB Cup against RKSV Volendam at the De Meer. Cruyff was again absent from Kovács's matchday selection and the same 11 who had put Ajax five clear at the break against MVV started again. Once more they delivered, Van Dijk and Neeskens scoring in a five-minute spell around the half-hour mark.

Despite reaching the last four of the KNVB Cup, Volendam were enduring a poor season that would eventually see them relegated to the second tier, the Eerste Divisie, having scored just 16 league goals. The chances of a second-half recovery from the visitors were, consequently, somewhere between remote and non-existent. Arnold Mühren was again summoned from the bench at the break, this time replacing Haan, and on 75 minutes Kleton enjoyed his only 15 minutes of KNVB Cup action with Ajax when he replaced Keizer as the team eased into the final. Having successfully negotiated two relatively low hurdles without problems, Ajax were now confronted with two much larger ones.

During the previous season, Ajax had faced Feyenoord in a decisive Eredivisie game just days ahead of the European Cup Final against Panathinaikos and, understandably with the Wembley final very much in mind, they had been beaten by Happel's team who only had the championship to chase and played with a rugged determination that Michels' team were reluctant to match. The defeat cost Ajax the title.

In 1971/72 the scenario was different, if only slightly. It wasn't the final following a few days later, but a massively challenging second leg of the semi-final. Ajax were on 51 points, heading the Rotterdam club who had 48, with each having six games to play. This was the first of three big matches, all to be played at the De Kuip, that would define Ajax's season.

After missing the previous two games, the return of Cruyff for such a vital fixture was inevitable and he slotted into his position as the nominal central striker with Van Dijk once more relegated to the sidelines. Kovács's first-choice 11 took the field on 15 April and delivered a stunning performance. Playing in an all-white kit except for red socks, to avoid a clash with their hosts' traditional red-and-white-halved shirts, the broad red stripe on their shirts was the only thing missing from an otherwise complete Ajax performance in front of more than 60,000 fans.

Despite being reigning champions, and retaining the midfield of Jansen, Hasil and Van Hanegem, plus the defensive solidarity of skipper Rinus Israël and the silky skills of Wery from the team that won the European Cup a couple of seasons earlier, Feyenoord had declined from such exalted heights. Meanwhile, on the other side of the pitch, Ajax were still very much on the upward curve. Inside 20 minutes that difference had been emphasised as first Haan and then Neeskens scored for the visitors. Hans Posthumus halved the deficit midway through the first period but a strike from Cruyff, elegantly completed with a cool finish past Treytel after a pass from Keizer tore a hole in the Feyenoord defence, restored the two-goal advantage.

A dozen minutes after the restart, Cruyff struck again. This time it was Haan with the decisive pass, leaving Cruyff a clear run at goal as Treytel hurtled from his area to meet him. It was a hugely uneven contest. Cruyff skipped clear of the desperate challenge and rolled the ball home from outside of the area as two Feyenoord defenders forlornly chased back. At 4-1 the game was over with Ajax in total control, and the cruellest of endings was delivered inside the final ten minutes. By that stage Feyenoord were a well-beaten team, hoping that the final whistle would sound before they suffered more damage. It wasn't to be.

After a half-hearted Feyenoord attack came to nought, Cruyff sauntered down the right flank with tired defensive legs unable to keep pace. Entering the Feyenoord half he cut inside, faced by a sole home defender. Hearing his skipper's call to the left, he rolled the ball inside the area where it met up with Keizer's supporting run. With time to control, Keizer looked up and passed the ball inside the far post. Watching his shot enter the net, Keizer then stood stationary for a full two seconds, arms by his side, savouring the moment, before turning to meet the embrace of Cruyff.

Had Feyenoord won that game then the gap at the top of the league would have been cut to a single point, but that scenario never looked remotely likely once Haan had put Ajax ahead. The gap was now five points with the same number of games to play, and Ajax were clear favourites to take the title. After the demolition of their closest rivals, few could argue that it wouldn't have been deserved.

The game played in Rotterdam, and the one in Lisbon four days later, would require different performances. The triumph over Feyenoord had been full of a dynamism that had simply overwhelmed their opponents. Conversely, the task at Benfica would be guided by a need for discipline and concentrated defence, but Kovács was confident that the same starting 11 could deliver both times.

Although understandably tight, and requiring Ajax to defend for periods of the game in the Portuguese capital, the only real threat on Stuy's goal was a potential, rather than actual one. As the second half moved on a through ball into the Ajax penalty area forced Blankenburg to turn with a forward in pursuit. Considering a pass back to his goalkeeper too dangerous, the German defender sought to hook the ball over his head and away. Instead it struck his hand as he raised his arm for balance. The referee was Englishman Norman Burtenshaw and had he awarded the spot-kick, few people would have been surprised. Instead, to the enraged chagrin of the Benfica players and fans, Burtenshaw merely waved play to continue and the ball was hacked clear.

In a game of few clear chances, seeing the penalty denied to them caused six, seven and then eight Benfica players to chase the official as he backed away from the baying mob surrounding him. Edging towards the sidelines offered no sanctuary though, and a storm of cushions, bottles and invective rained down on him. Eventually order was restored, but the Benfica players still felt hard done to. At the end of the game the referee's decision had proven to be decisive and Ajax walked away with the goalless draw that would send them to their second successive European Cup Final.

It had been a far from easy passage, and one earned by a performance wherein much of their usual free-flowing football had needed to be sacrificed to maintain a solid defence. Ruud Krol remembered the game well. 'Benfica was a tough opponent in a tough game,' he said. 'But we had a good balance between attacking, pressing football and defence. We knew how to attack, but we knew how to defend as well.' In the other semi-final, Inter and Celtic played out two goalless draws before the *Nerazzurri* won a penalty shoot-out. The Italians would face Ajax at the De Kuip on the last day of May to decide who would be European champions.

It seems perverse to relate following such an organised and disciplined performance but, after the game, club doctor Han Grijzenhout and one of the assistant coaches, John Rollink, sent word to the directors that Michels' work, and the progress that Ajax had made, were being tossed away by Kovács allowing player discipline to be eroded and, that unless things changed, the club was on a slippery slope. A board meeting was hastily convened with the sole topic on the agenda being a resolution to sack the man who had taken the club to a second successive European Cup Final, to the brink of winning the league title and into the final of the KNVB Cup. It seems extraordinary to consider, but Dutch football has a habit of turning over a few tables, especially when things seem to be going so well. It looked like another 'Jan Steen House' moment was on the way.

Instead, contrary to his normally iconoclast nature, it was Cruyff who intervened, rallying the players in support of Kovács and ensuring that all talk of dismissing him was ended. Krol reflected, 'Yes, it was true, that's what happened. It was a strange time as the team was playing so well.' And yet, strangely, the very fact that the players were rebellious enough to stand up to the board and in support of the coach who had eased so much of the discipline that had marked the Michels years almost suggests that there was at least a measure of merit in what Grijzenhout and Rollink had asserted. Even Cruyff would later concede the point somewhat when comparing Kovács to Michels, describing the Romanian as 'a nice guy, but a lot less disciplined'.[70]

With Ajax now five points clear of Feyenoord after their romp in Rotterdam, an opportunity to lock up the title as soon as possible was suddenly tantalisingly close. Back in November, after losing 2-0 to Ajax in Amsterdam, Feyenoord had surprisingly followed up with a home defeat to FC Twente. They would face the same team in their first league fixture after the 5-1 defeat and, sure enough, much as Go Ahead Eagles seemed to have a hold on Ajax, the club from Enschede would assume a similar role with Feyenoord; Ferry Pirard scored a 79th-minute winner.

On the same day, Ajax entertained Utrecht at the De Meer. Retaining the same starting 11 from Lisbon, Ajax initially looked unlikely to take advantage of any Feyenoord slip-up and were drawing 0-0 at half-time. Kovács sent on Van Dijk for Haan at the break, with Cruyff dropping deeper to orchestrate the team. The changes brought quick dividends

---

70 Cruyff, Johan, *My Turn* (London: Macmillan, 2016).

with four goals. Swart, Van Dijk, Mühren and Cruyff all scored in what was, at the end, a comfortable win. Feyenoord's defeat allowed Ajax to stretch the gap to seven points with just eight more up for grabs from the four remaining matches. It meant that if Ajax won their next game, away to Telstar, they would be champions.

Neeskens had suffered a second-half injury against Utrecht and was missing from the starting 11 against Telstar on 23 April in IJmuiden. It looked an eminently winnable encounter for Ajax, despite Neeskens' absence. Van Dijk was in the forward line with Cruyff deeper alongside Haan and Gerrie Mühren, to replace Neeskens.

Midway through the first period it looked like any title celebrations would have to be put on hold for a while when Jonker surprisingly opened the scoring for Telstar. Their lead was short-lived, however, and four minutes later Swart brought the scores level. Even a draw may well have been good enough for Ajax to secure the title as Feyenoord were drawing at home with Excelsior, entering the last 20 minutes of the game. Two minutes later it was Hulshoff up from his defensive position to score the winning goal and make Ajax champions regardless of the result in Rotterdam. Whatever happened from there, Ajax would be playing European Cup football in 1972/73 and the only thing to be decided was whether it would as Dutch champions or as holders of the trophy. Or both.

Wrapping up the Eredivisie title with three games to spare gave Kovács an opportunity to utilise some of the lesser lights in his squad and rest key players for the bigger games to come. For the next league fixture, at home to struggling RKSV Volendam, the coach made a few changes.

Keizer had taken a slight knock against Telstar and was left on the sidelines, although only in a precautionary move.

Neeskens had recovered from his injury but sat alongside the skipper on the bench. Stuy was rested, offering Sies Wever a rare opportunity in goal, and Schilcher came in for the rested Hulshoff. Cruyff was retained in his free midfield role with Mühren and Haan, and a returning Rep entered the forward line with Van Dijk and Swart. Despite the changes, Volendam were never going to offer much of a threat to Ajax and a 2-0 win with an early goal from Cruyff and a late one from Van Dijk were more than enough to take both points. The comfortable victory also allowed Kovács to offer rest for a couple of other players. Haan was removed at the break, with Neeskens sent on to regain match fitness, and just past the hour Arnold Mühren replaced Krol.

Four days later, Kovács returned to his regular first-choice 11 for the second of those three major games at the De Kuip, the KNVB Cup Final against FC Den Haag. It was the chance to lock out the domestic double with the possibility of adding a second European Cup a few weeks later and delivering the club's greatest season.

Back in 1967/68 the double had been denied to Ajax when they lost in the final against the same club, then labelled as ADO Den Haag. It was the day that Ernst Happel first became a thorn in the side of Ajax as he guided the unfashionable *Residentieclub* to their first major trophy since the early years of World War Two, when they had won successive Netherlands Football League Championship (the forerunner of the Eredivisie) titles in 1941/42 and 1942/43. Four of the Ajax players who started that game – Suurbier, Hulshoff, Swart and Keizer – plus Haan, who had entered the fray as a substitute, would have the opportunity to avenge the defeat endured in the early days of Michels' reign. They would do so, but not without a fight.

Cruyff scored the only goal of the first half and, when Gerrie Mühren converted a penalty on the hour, the trophy looked to be heading to the De Meer. Seven minutes later, though, Van Eeden brought Den Haag back into contention when he reduced the arrears to 2-1. The goal injected a little urgency back into Ajax's play and they responded inside five minutes when Cruyff set up Keizer for their third. A late Aad Mansveld penalty just kept Den Haag alive but, at the final whistle, Ajax had got over the line 3-2 to secure that double. For Den Haag, with Ajax already qualified for the following season's European Cup, a place in the Cup Winners' Cup was no small consolation.

The European Cup Final, the last and most important of the three defining De Kuip games, was now a little under three weeks away. Unlike the run up to the 1971 final, and that ferocious game against Feyenoord, this time around Ajax had a couple of league fixtures to fulfil that were of little interest to anyone other than statisticians. A 1-0 win thanks to a late goal by Keizer away to FC Den Bosch took them to their last competitive game before the final, when Vitesse arrived at the De Meer. There were only a little over 6,000 fans present but with places in the starting 11 to confirm for the final, none of the Ajax players were prepared to coast through the game.

By half-time, both Neeskens and Cruyff had scored twice to put Ajax four goals clear. By the time that Veenendaal opened the visitors' account with 15 minutes to play, five more had been added. Cruyff completed his hat-trick, and Van Dijk – making a case for inclusion in the final – had scored twice, with Mühren and Hulshoff adding the others. The total eventually reached 12 with Cruyff scoring his fourth, and both Van Dijk and Neeskens registering hat-tricks.

The final was now just two weeks away and, with no more Eredivisie games to play, Ajax arranged a friendly against Belgian club Beerschot, to be played in Antwerp's Olympic Stadium. Assuming no injury concerns, there was little doubt about the majority of the team to face Inter at the De Kuip. Stuy's place was secure, as was the back four of Suurbier, Hulshoff, Blankenburg and Krol. Further forward, though, there were issues to resolve. Would Cruyff be selected in his central striking role, or deeper as part of the midfield three? Regardless of his starting position, the club's number 14 would inevitably roam across the field as he considered the game required. For Kovács, the issue was whether to leave out a midfield player, probably Haan, and place Cruyff deeper allowing Van Dijk to join Swart and Keizer in the forward line, or retain the usual midfield three with Cruyff in the forward line and Van Dijk missing out.

Despite his hat-trick in the romp against Vitesse, there was a strong clue to Kovács's thinking delivered the following day when Van Dijk's imminent transfer to Nice was announced, although it wouldn't come into effect until the summer, meaning the forward would still be eligible to play in the final if selected. Thirty-two goals in 41 appearances across the season, many of them from the substitutes' bench, was impressive by any standards but, when Kovács announced the team to start against Beerschot, Van Dijk's name was absent. Only Swart was missing from what many considered would be the team to face Inter four days later. With the veteran frontman's absence leaving a vacant place in the forward line, had Kovács selected Van Dijk, it would have been a positive signal that he was, at the very least, in contention for the final. Instead it was Rep moving in to replace Swart.

Understandably, the game was played at a leisurely pace, with neither team overly concerned with the result. At the break Ajax led 2-1 with strikes by Suurbier and Keizer, sandwiching a lone goal for the home team scored by Emmerich. During half-time Schilcher came on for Suurbier; the full-back's place in the final was already guaranteed. Rep was also removed, his already remote chance of playing in the final probably going with it, and Van Dijk was sent on. It gave the forward 45 minutes to persuade the coach that he was indispensable to Ajax's aspirations against the Italians. If goals were required to persuade Kovács, however, Van Dijk would frustratingly fall short. Beerschot's Emmerich was enjoying himself and netted his second goal ten minutes after the restart, drilling a free kick past Stuy to bring the scores level.

In the early months of the 1973/74 season, the possession of the captain's armband would be a key element in the decline of this great Ajax team, with Cruyff's usurping as skipper apparently triggering his determination to leave the club. In this friendly, however, a few minutes after Emmerich's goal, a far more amiable game of 'pass the parcel' with the armband ensued. Keizer was replaced by Kleton on the hour mark, with Cruyff taking over as skipper. Nine minutes later, as Kovács continued to withdraw players, Arnold Mühren replaced Cruyff, and Hulshoff became Ajax's third captain in a nine-minute spell. Neeskens eventually settled the game in Ajax's favour with a late headed goal. By then, however, even the attention of the most dedicated of statisticians had waned, as all thoughts were very much on Internazionale and the European Cup Final.

The contrast between the two clubs and their relationship with the European Cup was striking. Despite being the reigning champions, and competing in their third final in four years, Ajax were still very much on the upswing, and a growing force. Conversely, the last time the Italians had lifted the trophy was in the second of their two successive triumphs, back in 1965. They had also competed in the 1967 final but lost out to Celtic.

Helenio Herrera, maestro of the *Grande Inter* team that had secured those successive European Cups, had left in 1968 and, despite a brief return after the gamble of reinstalling Alfredo Foni – who had won consecutive Serie A titles in the 1950s – had failed to rekindle past glories and he only stayed for two further years. In 1971, former *Nerazzurri* star Giovanni Invernizzi took over in his first managerial role. The midfielder had played under Foni in the glory days of his reign and guided Inter to the league title in his first term, topping Serie A by four points from fellow San Siro occupants AC Milan.

Although Herrera was gone, four of the 11 players who defeated Benfica in his final European Cup triumph seven years earlier – Giacinto Facchetti, Gianfranco Bedin, Brazilian forward Jair and Sandro Mazzola – remained at the club and provided the backbone of Invernizzi's team. With them came the ethos drilled into the squad by their Argentine former coach. *Catenaccio* was still the dominant philosophy and, with the case-hardened experience of Facchetti, Jair, Mazzola and Bedin, plus the added talents of Tarcisio Burgnich and Roberto Boninsegna, who had scored a hugely impressive 24 goals in that season's Serie A programme, the Italian champions represented a major challenge for Ajax.

Not only would the game be a clash of two champion teams, but also a clash of styles. Would the energetic *totaalvoetbal* of Ajax overcome the stifling defensive efficiency of *catenaccio*, or perish in the web of blue-and-black shirts that defended deep, seeking to strike with venom from their lair? The battle lines were drawn for a game that Geoffrey Green poetically described in *The Times* as football being on trial between 'the lighter and darker sides of it – the lighter belonged to Ajax with their fluent smooth attacking play, the darker side belonged to Internazionale with their cunningly constructed deep defence which was tongue and grooved and always so difficult to penetrate'.[71]

Massimiliano Graziani is a journalist with Rai, the Italian radio and television broadcaster, and is coordinator and radio commentator of the long-running broadcast *Tutto il Calcio Minuto per Minuto*. In retrospect, he sees that Inter team in a different perspective, as he commented when discussing this game: 'Inter were a team at the end of the cycle while Ajax were living their top moment.' While there's clear merit in Graziani's assessment of Inter – they wouldn't win the Scudetto again until 1980 – no team that tops Serie A does so without being worthy of the accolade. They were still a formidable team, and arguably the best that the continent had to offer at that time – aside from Ajax. Interviewed in the Greek newspaper *Gazzetta*, Swart certainly concurred with Graziani's assessment: 'We kept the same trunk for five years. We were the same players. I think 1972 is the best year for Ajax. We conquered everything. Bayern and Liverpool have done this, but we come from a small country. Understand the magnitude of our success. We were the best team, we beat everyone. We won the championship, the Dutch Cup, the Champions Cup, but also the Intercontinental Cup.'[72] That Intercontinental Cup triumph would come during the following season, but as Swart commented, 1972 was an almost perfect calendar year for Ajax.

71 'Great triumph for Ajax and Cruyff', *The Times*, 31 May 1972.
72 https://www.gazzetta.gr/football/europe/article/1480798/o-mister-ajax-sto-gazzettagr-megali-omada-o-panathinaikos-mas-dyskolepse-sto-goyemplei-perissotero?amp&fbclid=IwAR0_AfCYsbNOPcQFILn3LWAMGhW8RrK6B7JTtcx_S4AGnba63bilqOXryek (Translated).

With the final being played in the Netherlands, Ajax should have felt more at home than Inter, but there was precious little love for the Amsterdam club among the natives of Rotterdam and any support that Ajax enjoyed would hardly likely to be from local sources. As Geoffrey Green reported in *The Times*, however, fans in their tens of thousands made the short trip to offer boisterous and confident support to Ajax: 'Before the kick-off large group photographs of the Ajax team were in evidence all over [Rotterdam]. The legend above them was this, "Ajax, European Cup winners 1971/72". At the time, that seemed like flying in the face of fate and tempting the gods unnecessarily.'[73] By the end of the game, any charges of Dutch hubris had been emphatically vanquished. David Winner recalled: '[1972] was the definitive performance, and featured the nicest strip [Ajax] ever played in. The thin red line! The crowd looked great too, with the clusters of huge flags. All part of the impression they made on me at an impressionable age.'

The 'thin red line' had the consequence of compacting the white numbers on the back of the Ajax shirts so that they fitted within the band, like some condensed font used to make a long story seem short, or in this case a difficult game appear to be much less so. Cruyff, immortally slim anyway, would adapt and narrow his frame even further, allowing him to slip into gaps that were only fleetingly there and then escape like some supernatural being evading the attention of mere mortals.

When Kovács announced his team, Van Dijk's efforts had been in vain. He had played his last game for Ajax. Stuy was in goal with the regular back four of Suurbier, Hulshoff, Blankenburg and Krol, in front of him. The midfield trio was Haan, Neeskens and Gerrie Mühren as Cruyff took

---

73 'Great triumph for Ajax and Cruyff', *The Times*, 31 May 1972.

his nominal central striking position between Swart and Keizer. The team that had swept all before them during the season were poised to round it off with a thrilling display of attacking football. That certainly seemed to be the case in the first half as Ajax pushed forward almost relentlessly, while Inter sat deep and defended in front of goalkeeper Ivano Bordon who, for most of the opening 45 minutes, was rarely troubled, such was the intensity of blue-and-black wall protecting him.

The first period did offer a prelude to what would, a couple of years later, become one of the most famous moments in international football. A long punt downfield by Hulshoff saw Cruyff jostling for possession with his marker, Gabriele 'Lele' Oriali, by the edge of the Inter box. Wriggling lithely, Cruyff snaffled the ball clear and initially headed away from goal. Was he looking for support from his advancing team-mates? The defender may have thought so as he closed behind him. In an instant, though, Cruyff swivelled and dragged the ball between his own legs, offering the 61,354 people in the stadium and the millions watching on television a sneak preview of what would be christened as the 'Cruyff Turn' when performed in the 1974 World Cup.

A second pivot was like delivering an unnecessary punch to a semi-conscious boxer already on the way to the canvas. Just as Swedish defender Jan Olsson was bamboozled in Dortmund's Westfalenstadion, so was Oriali at the De Kuip. Caught off-balance by the moves, and attempting to turn as adeptly as Cruyff had, the Italian got his feet tangled up and fell to the floor. As with the game in the World Cup, however, the move brought no tangible reward. A rolled pass by Cruyff ran into the path of Mühren but his shot was sliced wide. Nothing to record on the scoreboard but a delight to be treasured in the soul for all fans of the beautiful game.

Being assigned to mark what was probably the best player in the world at the time – Cruyff won the Ballon d'Or in 1971, 1973 and 1974 – would be an onerous task. You can keep the lid on a saucepan of boiling water for so long but the rising heat is relentless. Eventually it gets too hot. Try to hold on and you simply get burnt. Roberto Pennino offered some insight on how Cruyff coped with the attentions of Oriali, after interviewing the Inter man: 'I recently interviewed Lele Oriali and he said something very interesting. Namely: he had studied Cruyff's every movement and during the first quarter of the first half it seems that Cruyff struggled with that. But then Cruyff changed his game, did things that Oriali never saw before, went to different places to create space for his team-mates (and confuse Oriali) and that was that. Remarkable skill, also tactically from number 14.'

Swart did get the ball into the Inter net in the first period but his conversion of a cross from the left was deemed to have been facilitated after a foul, and French referee Robert Héliès brusquely dismissed any half-hearted Dutch attempts to plead mitigation. Ajax also struck the woodwork twice. First a shot from outside the area by Krol clipped the outside of Bordon's far post. Then later, under pressure, Facchetti mishit the ball against the upright of his own goal before it was cleared.

At the break the scores were level and the result was still in the balance. Ajax had done virtually all of the pressing but the *Nerazzurri* had little regard to that. As Geoffrey Green described in *The Times*: 'The Italians had let the Dutchmen run and run and drill and drill and try to ferret their way through, seemingly content that they could absorb everything that was thrown at them.'[74] Inter had secured the Serie A title by scoring just 50 goals in the 30-game league

---

74 'Great triumph for Ajax and Cruyff', *The Times*, 31 May 1972.

programme. In comparison Ajax had more than doubled that total in completing just four more fixtures. The Italians were looking for a clean sheet and a single goal to decide the final. Two minutes into the second period, however, that plan lay in ruins.

Cruyff had already underscored his intentions not to be subdued as the second half got under way. In a typically darting, swerving run, he cascaded like a torrent of water past three defenders before being enveloped on the edge of the area and losing control, but the breakthrough was coming. Out on the right, Swart lofted a high looping cross into the area. It should have been comfortable for either Bordon to catch or Beluggi to head clear. Jumping together, they collided slightly, each falling to the floor as the ball passed over them. It fell to the feet of Cruyff, unmarked on the six-yard line, in front of a gaping net. Where others may have panicked and snatched at the chance, Cruyff was calmness personified as Green reported: 'He turned on the smallest Dutch coin, and coolly steered the ball home into an empty net. He made it look so easy, which of course is always the secret of a master.'[75] While Italian heads sank, Cruyff leapt up in joy, slapping the air in his trademark celebration before being engulfed by his team-mates.

Now behind, Inter were forced to peek out from their carefully constructed *testudo* and, inevitably, the game began to open up a little. For almost all of the first half the action had been concentrated in the Italians' half, but that now had to change. As with a leopard contemplating the abandonment of his spots, however, forsaking the ethos that had served them so well, for so long, was not an easy transformation. At first Inter were nervous and hesitant as they sought a

---

75 Great triumph for Ajax and Cruyff', *The Times*, 31 May 1972.

way back but, as time ticked by, the need to score became increasingly urgent.

Invernizzi sent on Sergio Pellizzaro for a tiring Jair, but Ajax still controlled the game. As Inter edged forwards, Cruyff became even more dangerous. Oriali was now often left in one-on-one situations with Cruyff. It was the most uneven of contests. Aware of their iconic forward's ebullient mood, Ajax sought to feed the ball to him at every opportunity, allowing him to exploit a freedom of space that had been denied in the first period.

Inter were treading a perilous path. They needed to attack but feared conceding a killer second goal. In such circumstances conventional wisdom dictates that Ajax should have sat back and looked to catch their opponents on the break. That was never a possibility for this team. They simply continued playing the game that had dominated their opponents, content and confident that the *totaalvoetbal* that had taken them this far, that had led to them to score the first goal, would also guide them to victory. Roberto Pennino said, 'Ajax was visibly superior to Internazionale, they never stood a chance. In De Kuip, with mostly Ajax fans, it was never a question who would win this final, at least in hindsight.'

The seemingly inevitable second goal came on 76 minutes. An indirect free kick on the left flank was crossed by Keizer and Cruyff rose, amid three defenders at the far post, to nod home. Again the trademark celebration came, but more with smiles than ecstasy on this occasion. Inter were already a well-beaten team. For the last few minutes it was largely a matter of Ajax passing the ball around and playing out time as they weaved intricate patterns with their football. Inter were chasing shadows and not even doing that with much conviction.

As the final whistle sounded Ajax fans poured on to the pitch of their fiercest domestic rivals to exalt their heroes. It had been a majestic performance. 'I think Inter Milan at Rotterdam was the best game. We won the game in Rotterdam – the town of Feyenoord!' Ruud Krol enthused. It's a widely held opinion. Auke Kok is convinced: 'The victory of 1972 was the best, the most "total", real demonstration of what Ajax was capable of in those days.' Menno Pot concurred. 'The best one – no discussion – has to be the 1972 final against Inter, in Rotterdam. Inter were a very tough and somewhat feared opponent. Masters of Catenaccio. That was easily Ajax's best performance in a final (in what was their best year anyway). Also, it was Cruyff's great night as he scored both goals.'

David Winner is very much a contemporary of the author, born just a couple of months after me in 1956. At the time of this victory he was at an age when such performances demanded a permanent place in our affections. He speaks for both of us, 'I was hooked … Ajax played with a gorgeous, hyper-intelligent swagger. They ran and passed the ball in strange, beguiling ways, and flowed in exquisite, intricate, mesmerising patterns around the pitch. They won 2-0 but it could have been five or six. Ajax were like beings from a different, more advanced football civilisation. They were warm and fun to watch. They were clearly wonderful.'[76]

Winner also suggested that, although *totaalvoetbal* had triumphed over *catenaccio*, simply translating that into a victory for the Dutch and defeat for all Italians would be too simplistic. He suggested that the battle lines for the war of styles may not have been crisply drawn down national boundaries, and neither should they have been: 'It confirmed that Ajax's way was better, but *catenaccio* was by no means

---

76 Winner, David, *Brilliant Orange* (London: Bloomsbury, 2000).

banished. Some in Italy actually hoped Ajax would thrash Inter to show it was time to ditch *catenaccio*. But the result wasn't conclusive. Ajax were evidently superior, but it wasn't a crushing defeat. So *catenaccio* and its derivations carried on in Italy (with a brief interruption from Sacchi's Gullit-v Basten-Rijkaard Milan) until a couple of years ago. And the Italians did well with it for decades. I kinda miss it. I liked it when every major football country had a recognisable and different style.'

For all that, as Winner asserted, Ajax were indeed 'wonderful'. They had played almost the perfect season, winning every trophy available to them and losing just a single, unredeemed, game in the almost 60 played across all competitions. Pierre Vermeulen recalled, 'In the Netherlands there was no Dutch team that would or could come near to Ajax, except Feyenoord sometimes with players like Wim Jansen, Willem van Hanegem etc.' Kovács had delivered everything that could have been demanded of a man needing to prove himself worthy of replacing Michels. Not only had his team won trophies, they had done so with the sort of football that still has people eulogising about it half a century later. Ronald Jager readily agreed. 'In my opinion Ajax's best season was 71/72,' he confirmed.

And yet, in *My Turn*, Cruyff recalled his emotions after the victory against Inter and in the midst of the glow of victory strangely asserted that he considered that 'the cracks began to show'. He suggested that the freedom granted by Kovács was now causing problems with the squad as strongly held opinions clashed, and people were not putting 'the collective good of the team first'. He also considered that some had failed to fully appreciate, or even at times understand, their roles within the Ajax system, and that some had even declined to follow instructions with adverse consequences for the team.

It's an analysis that seems to fly in the face of the image that the club was projecting to the outside world, but that link between successful Dutch teams and a 'Jan Steen House' existence appears both eternal and infernal – in every sense of the latter. Many of the charges that Cruyff appeared to be laying against some of his team-mates and coach, others may have felt justified in levelling at him, but perhaps that was just another aspect of the same problem. Ajax had retained the European Cup. The question now was, could they do it again, before what had made them great also became their doom?

Part 5: 1972/73 –
Immortality beckons

THE INAUGURAL European Cup in 1955 saw Real Madrid claim the trophy. The Spanish club then retained it for the next four years, developing the first hegemony of the tournament. From then until Ajax's back-to-back triumphs only two clubs won the European Cup and then successfully defended it. Benfica did it in 1961, lifting the trophy in the first year that *Los Blancos* failed to do so, by beating Barcelona in the final – Barça had eliminated the five-time champions in the opening round. This was also the year that Ajax, under Vic Buckingham, were eliminated in the preliminary round by the little-known Norwegian club, Fredrikstad. Benfica then successfully defended the trophy, defeating Real Madrid in the following year's final.

In 1963 and 1964 the *Grande Inter* team of Helenio Herrera won two successive finals, first beating Benfica and then Real Madrid. Neither Benfica nor Internazionale, however, could follow up and take a third successive title and claim a place in the pantheon of the immortal European teams, alongside Real Madrid. As the 1972/73 season began, that illusive immortality beckoned for Ajax. Now established as the dominant force in European football, and with two European Cup triumphs behind them, could they become the first club since the 1950s to lift the trophy in three successive seasons?

While becoming European champions in 1971 and 1972, Ajax had beaten several top clubs on the way to success. Celtic and Atlético Madrid had provided strong opposition in the earlier competition, then a year later Benfica and Inter had been major obstacles. In pursuit of their third successive crown the path would be the most tortuous of all. First they would need to overcome the club that, 12 months later, would be unveiled as their nemesis. They would then be faced with the West German champions who would not only take the crown that had been relinquished when Ajax were eliminated the following season, but also go on to win three successive European Cups of their own. In the semi-final, they would be paired against the aristocrats of the tournament, Real Madrid, a team committed to eliminating the pretenders to their crown, and seeking access to their unique legendary reputation. Finally, it would be the Italian champions Juventus facing them. Having to beat the champions of West Germany, Spain and Italy to win the European Cup is probably the sternest test for any club. But to reach immortality should be a difficult task. If the 1972 final was the greatest performance, the journey to retaining the trophy the following season was surely the most impressive.

Modern-day football demands that, even when your club is at the very top of the tree, each transfer window offers an opportunity to improve. Fail to take it and other clubs will inevitably close the gap on you. For Ajax in the summer of 1972, six players left for various reasons, although the only one who was consistently in consideration for a first-team place was Dick van Dijk. His move to Nice left a gap in the squad for a forward and among the four who moved to Amsterdam was Anderlecht's Dutch striker Jan Mulder. At the time, several newspapers reported the transfer fee as being 1.2m guilders, although there is no official confirmation of the figure. Despite signing a five-year deal, Mulder's time back in his home country would be blighted by injuries and by January 1975 he was forced to retire after persistent knee problems.[77] He played just 56 Eredivisie games for Ajax, scoring 16 times.

Ajax were also keen to ensure that they secured the services of several of their first-team players. Barry Hulshoff, Ruud Krol, Johan Neeskens and Wim Suurbier all agreed new four-year deals, starting on 1 July 1972, with Horst Blankenburg, Arie Haan and Heinz Stuy signing on for a further three years.[78] Reserve goalkeeper Seis Wever would stay for a further two seasons before moving to MVV Maastricht in a deal that the *Leeuwarder* newspaper reported as being worth 60,000 guilders.[79] Swart was also given a new contract but it was significant that his deal would run for just one year. The winger was just two days short of his 34th birthday when the deal began. This would be his final season wearing Ajax colours.

Losing a player of the pedigree of Sjaak Swart was a loss, but Johnny Rep's demands to be included in the first team were now becoming irresistible. In the new season the as-yet less-than-fully tapped emerging talent of Rep, still in his early 20s, would score 21 goals for Ajax in 35 games in 1972/73, more than doubling the total of ten that Swart netted in 34 appearances. Only Johan Cruyff would outscore the youngster, and then by just a single goal. The 1972/73 season would see the gradual passing of the baton from the veteran to Rep in the role alongside Cruyff and Piet Keizer.

---

77 https://www.afc-ajax.info/en/soccer-player/Jan-Mulder#transfers

78 https://www.afc-ajax.info/en/season/1972-73

79 https://www.afc-ajax.info/en/soccer-player/Sies-Wever#transfers

There would be one other significant change. At the beginning of each season, the Ajax players held an election as to who should be the captain for the new campaign. Two or three players would be nominated and the final decision was decided by a vote among all of the squad. In the previous summer, after Velibor Vasović had left, Keizer was elected. At the start of the season the vote went Cruyff's way. The Ajax version of player democracy would have serious consequences when the next election was held ahead of 1973/74.

Between 18 July and 8 August, Ajax played ten friendly games to tune up for the season ahead and allow Ştefan Kovács to assess his players and decide on his preferred line-up. Some matches were less testing, offering up the chance for players to improve their goals tally. An 11-2 victory over VV Drachten and a 14-2 win at Blauw Geel '38 were just two examples. The final two friendlies, away and then at home on 4 August and 8 August, were hardly fitting into the 'gimme' category though. On the first date 18,000 fans in the Grunwald Stadion watched Ajax defeat Bayern Munich 5-0. Goals from Haan, Swart, Krol and each of the Mühren brothers delivered a comprehensive victory. Four days later the teams met again, this time at the De Meer, and although the score was closer at 2-1 – a couple of late goals by Swart diminished a first-half strike by Gerd Müller – Ajax still came out on top. No one knew it at the time, but seven months later the teams would face each other again in the quarter-final of the European Cup, and although the rewards for the victors would be very different, the outcome across both legs would be similar.

On the weekend following Bayern's visit, Ajax began the defence of their Eredivisie title by beating AFC Haarlem 3-0 at the De Meer. Kovács chose the same team that had so comprehensively seen off Inter in the European Cup Final of the previous season, and was rewarded as Haan headed home in the first half from a Cruyff corner and then added a second created by Swart ten minutes after the break. A penalty from Gerrie Mühren inside the last quarter of an hour completed the comfortable win. The following weekend, the same starting 11 took the field against local rivals FC Amsterdam and came away with a 2-1 win before hosting the club who had become Ajax's *bête noire* of recent times, Go Ahead Eagles.

An Achilles injury kept Keizer out of the team and Arnold Mühren was drafted in to replace him. With the scoreline goalless at the break, it looked as if Go Ahead were weaving their spell over the European champions once more. The curse was broken just after the restart though, when Swart headed Ajax ahead, and he then doubled the advantage with another header, converting from a Gerrie Mühren cross. By the hour Cruyff had added a third after a dazzling solo run. The number 14 was in sparkling form and by the final whistle he had scored three more to hand out a comprehensive second-half beating and take a measure of revenge against the only Eredivisie club to have beaten Ajax in 1971/72.

After winning their first European Cup, Ajax had decided not to compete in the Intercontinental Cup, the games that pitched the Copa Libertadores winners from South America against the European champions on a two-legged basis. In their place, Panathinaikos had played against Nacional of Uruguay, only losing out 3-2 on aggregate, and confirming their worthiness of being European Cup finalists. In the new season, however, Ajax would accept the invitation and face Independiente of Argentina. Before journeying to South America for the first leg, there was one more Eredivisie game to complete as Keizer returned to the usual starting 11 and netted a hat-trick in the 3-0 win over PSV at the Philips Stadion in Eindhoven.

Adding two such demanding fixtures into a busy domestic season always looked like a gamble, especially given the requirement to fly out to South America after playing on 2 September, fulfil the fixture against Independiente four days later, and then be back in the Netherlands for an Eredivisie game on 10 September. Inevitably there would be a price to pay.

By this time, the Intercontinental Cup had garnered a reputation for controversy. There was little interaction between European and South American clubs, and therefore the accepted norms of play were very different, with interpretation of the laws of the game, especially with regard to physical contact, differing widely. Several European clubs, Manchester United in 1968, for example, when they lost out to Argentinians Estudiantes, had seen these games degenerate into little more than running battles. The 1972 edition would have similar undertones.

If Kovács had been tempted to leave some key players back in Amsterdam, he rejected the notion and it was a full-strength starting 11 that took the field at the Independiente Stadium in Avellaneda. The referee, whose ability to maintain control of the game would be sorely tested, was none other than the fabled Tofiq Bahramov, of 1966 World Cup Final linesman duties fame.

The Ajax party arrived in Buenos Aires a couple of days before the game, complete with their own cook and foodstuffs. Ostensibly, the provided reason was that the Dutch simply preferred their own type of food. Any concerns about the sanctity of any locally produced fare may well have been a factor as well. It may well have been a pertinent worry and other things certainly happened, as Argentinian newspaper *El Grafico* suggested years later: 'They [the Ajax group] suffered the classic ritual of South American football: batucadas, pyrotechnics and songs, which did not let them sleep and they had to take pills to fall asleep.'[80]

Five minutes into the game, Ajax were ahead and, at least temporarily, managed to cool the ardour of the 45,000 Independiente fans in the stadium. Wriggling free of a foul by Miguel Angel López, Cruyff drove into the area and fired past Miguel Ángel Santoro. Had the number 14 not been as light on his feet as he was and avoiding the impact, the goalkeeper's two-footed chest-high challenge could have caused Cruyff serious injury. An injury to the iconic captain would occur, but later.

Perhaps it was the goal that sparked the reaction, although it may have been the way that the home team were going to play anyway, but robust tackles very much became the order of the day as the Argentines sought to thwart Ajax's beguiling *totaalvoetbal* with physicality, rather than football. *El Grafico* later described the mood of the game: 'Independiente began to play a "South American" game: friction, strong play, sometimes rough.' It seemed inevitable that someone would be seriously hurt and, with any number of challenges targeting Ajax's goalscorer, Cruyff was always the likeliest victim. It came after half an hour when a ferocious challenge by Dante Mírcoli left Cruyff writhing in pain, requiring him to be replaced by Arnold Mühren.

At half-time there was so much indignation among the Ajax players about the uncompromising and overly aggressive attitude of their hosts that they refused to leave the dressing room for the second half. It took all of Kovács's persuasion to coax them back out on to the field. There were echoes of the game between Ajax and Feyenoord a few days ahead of

---

80 https://www.elgrafico.com.ar/articulo/1057/35907/una-luz-en-el-infierno (Translated)

the 1971 European Cup Final, when the Rotterdam club's abrasive approach had torn victory, and the Eredivisie title, from an Ajax team with an understandably cautious eye on the big day at Wembley. This time there was the whole season, and indeed careers, ahead for the players and many were understandably concerned to get back home without further physical damage. Late on, Independiente skipper Francisco Sá netted to square the game.

After the final whistle, Kovács was furious at the way his players had been treated, complaining, 'This was not football but war. In Amsterdam, Independiente will have serious troubles. One of them, our magnificent pitch so they are not used to play on those surfaces. This pitch is not suitable to play football.'[81] There was plenty of merit in the coach's final charge; video of the game shows the ball bobbling and hopping as it is passed along the ground.

Back in the less frantic environs of Amsterdam, Ajax entertained NEC at the De Meer on 10 September but the cost of the visit to South America was becoming clear. Both Blankenburg and Cruyff were suffering from injuries inflicted in Argentina, with Heinz Schilcher drafted in to replace the German defender and Arnold Mühren continuing to deputise for Cruyff, as he had done for 60 minutes in Avellaneda. A header on 15 minutes by the younger Mühren brother had Ajax ahead at the break, and a further three goals in the second period, the first by Gerrie Mühren and one each by Neeskens and Swart, eased Kovács's team to a 4-0 win. The Nijmegen club hadn't offered much resistance once they fell behind, and were the ideal opponents for a weary and wounded Ajax side returning from the trials of South

---

81 https://www.elgrafico.com.ar/articulo/1057/35907/una-luz-en-el-infierno (Translated)

America. Ajax's next Eredivisie fixture, however, would be a visit to the De Kuip to face Feyenoord.

The hosts had matched Ajax's 100 per cent start in the league, netting 14 goals and conceding just two on the way, and playing a still battle-scarred version of their fiercest rivals was an ideal opportunity to take victory and seize an advantage in the table. Both Blankenburg and Cruyff were ushered back into action, although their levels of fitness were debatable. Any doubts about whether risking less-than-fully fit players for the game were magnified by the condition of the De Kuip playing surface. If the pitch in Argentina had been bone-hard and bumpy, the one in Rotterdam was drenched, with areas of standing water inviting slides and slips, following torrential rain. The concern about going into the encounter without all of his key players won out in Kovács's mind. In a game of many slips, Feyenoord triumphed 2-0 with a goal in each half by Theo de Jong. In the previous season Ajax hadn't lost an Eredivisie fixture until 4 January and their 27th game of the league programme. Now, with just half a dozen played they already trailed Feyenoord by two points.

A first-half injury to Swart at Feyenoord, requiring another Arnold Mühren incursion from the bench, hardly helped matters, and the veteran would be absent for the next league match, as was Cruyff, at home to Groningen. Mühren started in place of Swart and Mulder made his Eredivisie debut for the club in place of the skipper. Twenty-three minutes in the former Anderlecht forward delivered his first significant moment for Ajax, creating the opening for the younger Mühren to score. There were further complications for Kovács, however, when an injury to Suurbier eight minutes before the break took him out of the game with Schilcher covering the right of the Ajax back line.

Mulder had arrived with an injury and, other than the 69 minutes in the friendly against FC Dordrecht in the middle of August, this was his first outing of the season. There was therefore little surprise when Kovács removed him at the break and sent on Johnny Rep. The naggingly persistent injuries to Mulder, alongside the age and declining powers of Swart, would be a key factor in Rep's elevation to regular first-team football. Two second-half goals, first from a direct free kick from Haan and then a penalty by Gerrie Mühren, secured the points.

There were now just four days until the return leg in Amsterdam against Independiente. Surely, logic would suggest, it was an opportunity for Kovács to take stock and ensure that all his players were rested up and ready to go. Instead, a friendly was played against Blauw-Zwart on 26 September. Suurbier recovered to play, and Ajax ran out 7-1 winners, but it seemed such an unnecessary risk just two days before facing the South American champions. Perhaps fortune favoured the brave, and as the fates would have it, no new injuries arose so Kovács was able to field his first-choice 11 at the Olympisch Stadion. If the first leg had been a battle – in more ways than one – as Ajax's *totaalvoetbal* was confronted by the muscular insistence of the Argentinian team, the second would be of an entirely different nature.

Despite the presence of a South American referee – Paraguayan José Romei – who may perhaps have been more empathetic to the type of game Independiente indulged in back in Avellaneda, the Argentinians were much more subdued throughout, as Ajax's *totaalvoetbal* dominated. Perhaps it was the distance from home, or maybe the fact that in this game Ajax's football was simply too hot to handle.

As in the first leg, Ajax struck first, and early. Driving forward from midfield, Neeskens played a pass to Cruyff on the edge of the area. A flick-on from the skipper had Neeskens chasing into the area. Darting between two hesitant defenders, he got to the ball first and, from an increasingly tight angle, guided it past Santoto and into the net. Only 12 minutes had passed. The remainder of the half was played out with Ajax in command but, despite creating chances through their control and elegant football, they had nothing more to show for their efforts at the break. As the hour mark arrived and passed without any further score, Kovács decided to inject a little more youthful endeavour into a team that was coasting to victory without barely getting out of second gear. Swart was removed and Rep entered to deliver an almost instant impact.

Independiente had offered very little threat in the first period, and their languid performance and almost acquiescence to an inevitable defeat continued after the break. The second goal came 20 minutes into the second half after Keizer moved forward with Cruyff alongside him as the Argentinians' defence advanced in a naively straight line, with any covering midfield support absent. It almost invited a pass to be played between the flat line of defenders for Cruyff to run on to. While so much of Ajax's football was imaginative, and capable of seeing options that others missed, on occasions the obvious is the best course. The pass was made and, as defender Eduardo Commisso turned, plaintively appealing for an offside decision that never looked likely to materialise, Cruyff trotted forward into the space and on towards the penalty area. There was still time for the defence to respond had they turned and chased back. Instead they were statuesque in their non-movement as Rep strolled into the penalty area, collected a square pass from Cruyff that eliminated Santoto, and rolled the ball into the back of the net.

The game was now done and the South Americans had clearly accepted their fate. Ten minutes from time the third goal came in an alarmingly similar fashion to the second. Again, a flat back line, bereft of midfield cover, invited a pass between them as Cruyff trotted forward with the ball. Seeing Rep make a darting run from the right, Cruyff rolled the pass into the space behind the defence. Gathering possession around 30 metres from goal, Rep advanced to face Santoto. A wiggle of his hips sat the goalkeeper on his backside and Rep again had an empty net in front of him.

The victory had been comprehensive. There was little doubt that Independiente had given an insipid performance, but perhaps it was the scintillating *totaalvoetbal* of Ajax that had cast them into such despondency. As well as being the champions of the Netherlands and Europe, Ajax were now unofficially champions of the world as well.

Twelve months later, with Independiente again South American champions and Ajax retaining the European Cup, a repeat Intercontinental Cup was on the cards. With the value of experience gained from this encounter, however, Ajax decided not to compete, citing financial issues. Instead Juventus took their place in a single game to decide the winners at Rome's Stadio Olimpico. Independiente took the trophy thanks to a 1-0 victory.

Any Ajax euphoria from the victory over Independiente would be quickly curtailed and on the first day of October they resumed their Eredivisie campaign with a journey to Breda to face NAC. Haan was absent from the starting 11 and Cruyff dropped back into midfield allowing Mulder another start in attack. Perhaps Swart's substitution a few days earlier hadn't merely been a tactical switch, as the veteran wideman also missed the game. Goalscoring hero Rep joined Keizer and Mulder as the front three.

While Ajax had been easing past Groningen, Feyenoord had dropped a point with a goalless draw away to Twente.

The gap was down to one, but it would grow again. In a poor, tired-looking Ajax performance, Brouwers scored in each half to give NAC victory. The disappointment was compounded both by an injury to Cruyff just past the hour, and news that Feyenoord had beaten Den Bosch 4-0. The Rotterdam club were now three points ahead at the top of the table and Ajax's title defence looked to be in trouble.

As holders, Ajax had enjoyed a bye in the first round of the European Cup but would face CSKA Sofia in the second round with the first leg in Bulgaria on 8 November. There had been controversy in the first round as CSKA faced Ajax's old foes, Panathinaikos. The Bulgarians won the first leg 2-1 and then lost the return in Athens by the same score, requiring a penalty shoot-out to decide qualification. The Greeks went first and, after two penalties for each team had been converted successfully, Mimis Domazos had his shot saved. Boris Gaganelov then put CSKA 3-2 up before Severiano Irala was also confounded by the goalkeeper. At this stage the referee then erroneously decided that CSKA had an unassailable lead in the shoot-out and called the game over. With the Greeks trailing by just one penalty, though, the decision had been a monumental error by the official. Panathinaikos appealed and UEFA decided that the entire second leg should be replayed. It took place almost a month later and this time CSKA removed any doubts by winning 2-0 in Athens on 26 October. Thirteen days later, they would entertain European champions Ajax in the first leg of the second round.

Before that date, though, Ajax had another four Eredivisie matches to play and, if they were to apply pressure to Feyenoord then only victories would be good enough. Haan returned at home to Telstar, and Cruyff was fit enough to take his place in the forward line. Rep was left out and Mulder retained his starting spot; by the break Ajax were three goals clear. In a spell of a dozen minutes, Gerrie Mühren converted from the penalty spot, Krol advanced from his defensive position to double the lead and, on 43 minutes, Cruyff created a chance for Mulder to open his Eredivisie goal account. By full time the score was 9-2. Mulder had completed his hat-trick, as had Mühren, Haan scoring the other goal. Successive 1-0 away victories then followed, first at Galgewaard against Utrecht, and then in Enschede against Twente, Cruyff scoring both winning goals. Feyenoord's 3-2 defeat away to Den Haag on the same day had, once more, closed the gap between the clubs to a single point.

The final fixture was at home to Den Bosche, three days before the game in Bulgaria. Swart was back in attack and what had been long established as Kovács's preferred starting 11 began the game. Ninety minutes later, having struck nine goals without reply, Ajax seemed ready to begin the defence of their European crown. Feyenoord's 2-1 win over MVV was marginal in comparison. The gap between the clubs remained at one point but Ajax now needed to turn their attention to continental matters.

CSKA are officially the sporting cub of the Bulgarian army but, in Soviet times, that really meant gathering top players into one club and giving them army commissions so that they were qualified to play. Following their formation in 1948 they had dominated much of Bulgarian domestic football and the league title success in 1971/72, which qualified them for the European Cup the following season, was their sixth in the previous dozen seasons. They were, consequently, regular participants in the continent's premier club competition, although their record once qualified was not all that impressive.

At this stage, their zenith had been in 1966/67 when, surfing a series of fortunate draws, CSKA had reached the last four and faced the Internazionale team of Helenio Herrera. Mirrored 1-1 draws meant a play-off with the Bulgarians losing out 1-0 in Bologna's Stadio Renato Dall'Ara. In future years they would acquire a reputation as being the giant-slayers of the European Cup. In 1980/81 they eliminated Nottingham Forest, who had lifted the trophy in the previous two seasons. In the following campaign they faced, and beat, Liverpool, who had been European champions in three of the previous five seasons. Perhaps their most notable achievement came in the first round of the 1973/74 competition when they became the team to end Ajax's domination of European club football. When the teams met in early November 1972, such events seemed a million miles away.

There was little doubt, if any, that Kovács would select his strongest team and, with a dozen minutes played Ajax were ahead after a catastrophic blunder in the home defence. Out on the left flank Keizer floated a fairly innocuous-looking cross into the box. Despite Cruyff making a hopeful run towards the near post, there seemed little danger as goalkeeper Filipov and defender Gaganelov converged on the ball. In a moment of hesitation, however, both players left the ball for the other to deal with. It passed on unhampered. Standing on the far post, Swart saw the ball arriving with him too late to react with any real control, but it struck him on the knee and bounced into the empty net. Defenders stood with hands on hips in both disgust and frustration as the Ajax players cavorted in celebration at their good fortune.

Although not at the standard of Ajax – which club in Europe was? – the Bulgarians were a more than decent team, especially in their own stadium and, 15 minutes after conceding that comical goal, they drew level through Zhekov, and enjoyed a period of almost parity in the game. A dozen minutes ahead of the break, however, Ajax restored their advantage and took control of both the game, and the tie overall, when Keizer scored their second goal. It was a killer strike and when, on 52 minutes a delightful lofted pass from Cruyff met up with Haan's perceptive run from deep to fire past Filipov, it was merely the cherry on the cake that was already lustrously coated in icing. With 25 minutes to play, and the match won, Kovács withdrew Cruyff and sent on Rep after the captain had taken a knock.

Although the injury to Cruyff was hardly serious, he was absent for the following weekend's Eredivisie game away to Den Haag. Rep continued in his absence and set up the only goal for Swart with just four minutes played. Ajax left the Zuiderpark with their third successive away 1-0 Eredivisie victory. The other league fixture before the home leg against CSKA saw Excelsior visit the De Meer. Cruyff returned with Rep back on the bench, and Arnold Mühren entered the midfield to replace Neeskens. By the break Ajax were five goals clear. Cruyff and Haan had them 2-0 up inside ten minutes, before an own goal by De Mos just beyond quarter of an hour eliminated any chance of an unlikely recovery by the visitors. Arnold Mühren added the fourth on 26 minutes before being injured and replaced by Rep ten minutes later. Cruyff dropped into midfield, allowing the newcomer to partner Swart and Keizer further forward, although that didn't prevent the skipper adding the fifth goal two minutes later. Cruyff completed his hat-trick after the break, with Rep adding two more. On this sort of form few clubs could live with Ajax, and Excelsior were not one of them. The game finished 8-0 to Kovács's team.

Although the European tie was surely won already, Kovács was not minded to take any chances and, with Neeskens returning to his usual midfield role, the same 11 who started in Sofia began the second leg in the Olympisch

Stadion. With the Bulgarian champions wearing green shirts and white shorts, Ajax forsook the red stripe on their shirts for shorts of the same hue. Their performance was anything but off-colour.

The lead acquired in Sofia may well have quelled the coach's disquiet a little when Gerrie Mühren passed up the chance to open the scoring on nine minutes, failing to convert from 12 yards. Around 12 months later the miss would be considered to have serious consequences, but in this game it was the briefest of respites for CSKA and four minutes later Ajax were ahead. A cross from the left was only half cleared and, as CSKA attempted to run the ball away from their area, Neeskens pounced to snatch possession and play a perceptive pass through a crowd of green shirts to find Cruyff with just the goalkeeper to beat. Dropping his shoulder right, before drifting left, he rolled the ball home with Filipov helpless after being deceived by the feint.

Three minutes later, Filipov was beaten again. The visitors had little answer to Ajax's hypnotic play as they rotated both ball and position with practiced ease. Keizer, having dropped back, played the ball to an advancing Blankenburg around the halfway line. With Keizer deeper, Neeskens had drifted to the left flank opening up space in the middle of the field. Receiving and controlling with comfort, the German defender slipped the ball wide to Neeskens, before continuing his run into the space created by the midfielder's drift wide. Neeskens clipped the ball forward first time. Blankenburg sprinted to meet up with it on the edge of the area and volleyed home right-footed. It was a trademark *totaalvoetbal* goal.

With the two-goal advantage from this game on top of the lead earned in the away leg, Ajax were home and hosed, and they eased down into a comfortable second gear, allowing the Bulgarians a rare foothold, but without ever forsaking control, and still carrying a threat. The third goal came with 15 minutes to play. A semi-serious foray forward by the visitors broke down and the ball fell to Swart. The winger advanced with the ball, and then looked up to see Cruyff peeling away from his marker, Stankov, and racing into the CSKA half. The pass was expertly delivered to Cruyff's left-hand side and away from the defender, precluding him from having any hope of an interception. Cruyff drifted left, then cut inside, and outside again on the edge of the area, unbalancing the bewildered and disheartened Stankov, before clipping the ball inside the far post as Filipov dived to cover the near one. As opening games in defence of a title go, this had been a blazingly insistent statement of intent.

After that triumph, however, Ajax's next two games were very much in the manner of being 'after the Lord Mayor's Show'. CSKA had been dismissed with the arrogant swagger of a team full of confidence, but an Eredivisie fixture away to Sparta Rotterdam and the first round in defence of their KNVB Cup at home to NAC would bring Ajax back down to earth with a resounding bump.

The visit to Sparta's Kasteel came on 3 December and Kovács would once again send his first-choice 11 on to the pitch. If there had been concerns of fatigue among his players, the coach would have been reassured when Keizer crashed home a free kick on 21 minutes to open the scoring. Where, back at the Olympisch Stadion a few days earlier, Ajax had been ebullient and exhilarating, this time the display was flat and largely forgettable. It was therefore of small surprise when Sparta equalised on the stroke of half-time as Venneker reprised Keizer's earlier success, also firing in a free kick. Eight minutes after the restart, things got worse as a Kreuz header put the home team into the lead.

With a little more than 20 minutes to play, Kovács sought to fire his team back into the game by replacing Swart with Rep. A goal did come eight minutes later, but it made the score 3-1 rather than 2-2 as Bosveld took Sparta clear, and Ajax were beaten. Sparta had done their city neighbours a big favour by beating their main rivals for the title and Ernst Happel's team took full advantage, winning 3-1 away to FC Amsterdam. The game also saw both Cruyff and Keizer cautioned by referee Charles Corver, meaning the latter would be suspended for the next two domestic fixtures. The first would come the following weekend, and see Ajax's grip on the KNVB Cup relinquished. Cruyff would be absent for much longer, but for a different reason.

Undoubtedly, the cup competition was the least important of Ajax's targets for the season, but it was still one of only two possible major domestic trophies and one they were keen to retain. The draw for the first round seemed to offer a gentle introduction to their defence, pitting Ajax against NAC. The club from Breda were having a mediocre season and would finish third from bottom of the Eredivisie at the end of the season. As such, they hardly looked likely to offer a major obstacle to the double European champions, Eredivisie champions and cup holders. Sometimes, though, the fortunes of football can be very perverse.

As well as Keizer's suspension ruling him out of the trip to Breda on 9 December, Cruyff was also absent due to an ankle injury and wouldn't return to the team until mid-January of the following year. Kovács also decided that this was an opportunity to rest Stuy and offer Sies Wever some game time in goal. Perhaps on another day he would have left Stuy in and selected a different match for Wever to gain more first-team experience. There was, however, the complete first-choice back four in front of him and, even with Schilcher selected in midfield alongside Neeskens and Gerrie Mühren, as Haan moved into the forward line with Rep and Arnold Mühren, Ajax still looked to have a team strong enough to prevail. Indeed, it was the younger Mühren brother who put them ahead approaching the 15-minute mark but, as had been the case against Sparta the previous weekend, they conceded once again minutes ahead of half-time, as a Bouwmeester free kick beat Wever to bring the scores level.

There were no more goals in the regulation 90 minutes and, with no provision for replays, the tie went into extra time with the prospect of penalties to decide the issue if the scoreline remain deadlocked. After the first period of 15 extra minutes brought no goals, Kovács withdrew Arnold Mühren and introduced Swart to try and swing the game in Ajax's favour. Two minutes later they were ahead, but Swart wasn't involved; a cross from Blankenburg was met by Haan who nodded home. With time then ticking away it looked like Ajax had chiselled out the victory, albeit in a less-than-convincing manner. With seconds to play, however, defender Danny Bakker, thrown forward in a late attempt to rescue the game, netted the equaliser for NAC.

Now facing a shoot-out, Kovács may have been lamenting his decision to leave out Stuy but the issue was decided more by the failure of Ajax players to convert penalties than by their goalkeeper's ability to save them. Van Gorp, Vermeulen and Bakker all converted from the spot and as Haan, Hulshoff and Swart all failed, the shoot-out was decided after just three spot-kicks each and Ajax were out of the KNVB Cup. From the heights of defeating CSKA so comprehensively, Ajax had been beaten in their next two matches, albeit the second after a shoot-out. Their next game had now become 'must win' as MVV visited the De Meer. With Cruyff injured and Keizer still suspended, however, it would inevitably be a reshuffled Ajax team facing the visitors from Maastricht.

Inevitably, Stuy was back in goal behind the regular back four. Neeskens returned in midfield and, despite his brief goalscoring sojourn further forward, Haan was also back alongside Gerrie Mühren. Swart, Rep and Arnold Mühren were the front three. Ajax were in need of a quick start to get things back on track. They got it after just five minutes as Arnold Mühren put them ahead. The early goal ignited the team and, five minutes later, the lead was doubled as Haan capitalised on the creative work of Swart. Fifteen minutes later Rep headed home from a Haan cross to put the result beyond dispute. A fourth Ajax goal, Arnold Mühren's second, just past the hour mark was really mere icing on the cake, and a missed spot-kick by Jo Bonfrere for the visitors was an insignificant footnote. If Ajax had been enduring a brief slump, had they now ended it? Unfortunately the victory was the last competitive match before the turn of the year and Kovács would need to wait until January to see if his team had really returned to form.

The Eredivisie resumed on 7 January with Ajax visiting the Alkmaarder Hout in Alkmaar to face AZ '67. Cruyff was still one game away from returning to the starting 11 and Kovács shuffled his midfield and forwards again, seeking a way to compensate for the loss of the team's star player. The Mühren brothers were paired with Neeskens in the midfield as Haan was, once more, shuffled into the forward line next to Rep and the now suspension-free Keizer. Over the recent matches, Arnold Mühren had become a regular contributor of goals and despite him being deployed in midfield for this fixture, he still notched the first strike, scoring on 19 minutes. It was the only goal of the first half but, with Ajax looking far more like their old selves, the second period brought more successes. On 65 minutes a Neeskens header from Keizer's cross doubled the lead and two minutes later Rep profited from an opening created by Krol to score the third. Completing three goals in a ten-minute spell, Neeskens scored again on 75 minutes and Rep delivered a solo run to add the fifth goal with just two minutes to play.

With Cruyff's return now imminent, Ajax had six Eredivisie fixtures to play before the European Cup returned in early March with a quarter-final against Bayern Munich. It was an opportunity to make up ground on Feyenoord, but that was only likely to be achieved if they could avoid dropping any points in that period. There was also the matter of what was to be the unofficial inauguration of the UEFA Super Cup, to be played over home and away legs against Glasgow Rangers.

The idea of the European Cup winners playing a two-legged fixture against the winners of the Cup Winners' Cup to decide the best team in Europe was first devised by the *De Telegraaf* journalist Anton Witkamp. He approached Jaap van Praag, still in place as Ajax president, who seemed enthusiastic about the prospect. When the concept reached the offices of the UEFA president Artemio Franchi, however, it ran into the buffers. Rangers had won the previous season's Cup Winners' Cup, overcoming Dynamo Moscow in the final staged at Barcelona's Camp Nou, and were the prospective opponents for Ajax, but there was a problem.

Due to misbehaviour by some of their fans, the Scottish club were serving a one-season European ban and therefore could not compete in any UEFA-sanctioned match. Undeterred, after discussions between the clubs, it was decided to stage the games anyway and label them as celebrating Rangers' centenary, which had conveniently fallen in 1972. The idea had taken hold with UEFA, however, and in January 1974 Ajax would compete in the first official version of the fixture when they met AC Milan. After all of the glory of the previous seasons under first Rinus Michels and then Kovács, it would represent the only trophy Ajax won in the 1973/74 season. That was for the future, though, and Ajax would meet Rangers with the first leg, away in Scotland, coming after the next Eredivisie fixture.

On 14 January, Ajax made the short trip to Haarlem with a fit-again Cruyff primed for his return. The skipper took his place, in what had now increasingly become Kovács's amended preferred starting 11, with Rep in ahead of Swart in the forward line. A first-half brace from Keizer and second-half goals from Neeskens and Rep were more than enough to secure the points and allowed Ajax to visit Ibrox on an upswing of form. Between those two latter goals, Neeskens had suffered an injury and had to be replaced by Arnold Mühren. The midfielder would be absent for the journey to Scotland, with the younger Mühren continuing to deputise in what was, otherwise, a first-choice starting 11 at Ibrox.

Despite their success in Europe, domestically Rangers were very much playing second fiddle to their cross-city rivals Celtic at the time. They hadn't won the league title since 1963/64 and wouldn't do so again until 1974/75. Although in the previous season they had only fallen short by a single point and, despite the match officially being defined as a friendly, some 57,000 fans turned up to roar their team on.

Kovács had still been working in Romania when Ajax had last confronted Scottish opposition, as Michels guided his team past Celtic on the way to their first European Cup triumph. In that hard-fought encounter, Ajax had set out to deny Jock Stein's team any opportunity to bully them out of the game, giving as good as they got. This match would be different in atmosphere, but Ajax would still prevail.

Any fixture in mid-January Glasgow is likely to be played on a less-than-perfect surface. Not only had the Ibrox pitch been used on multiple occasions, but the inevitable rain and snow had made its most-populated sections areas of mud as much as grass. The conditions would be a key factor in Rangers' equalising goal just before half-time. Ahead of that, though, the irrepressible Rep had put Ajax ahead. Running from the halfway line towards the Rangers penalty area with the ball at his feet, Cruyff attracted defenders towards him like moths to a beguiling flame. Aware of the space created by their concern, Rep spun in behind and a perfect pass by Cruyff allowed the forward to skip clear and clip the ball past Peter McCloy in the Rangers goal with a stab of his right boot. Ajax had controlled the game from the start, despite the energetic play of the home team, and this largely continued towards the break.

Three minutes ahead of half-time, Rangers captain John Greig took a throw-in on the left flank, halfway inside the Ajax half. Seeing Alfie Conn spin away from his marker, Greig's long throw found the forward running towards the Ajax back line. Closed down by Suurbier, Conn clipped the ball into the penalty area to meet up with a right-to-left scything run by Alex McDonald. The forward collected the ball but the angle of his run had forced him wide of Stuy's goal. With little other option he shot towards the far post, as Blankenburg's desperate lunging block came just too late. Stuy should surely have made a comfortable save but, as he plunged towards the ball, the muddy surface of the goalmouth deceived him. The ball slipped between his fingers, struck the far post and rolled into the net. Rising to his feet, Stuy looked down at the mud in front of his goal in obvious disgust. Ajax had conceded late in the first half again. It was becoming a worrying trend. Was fatigue playing a part? If it was, they quickly re-energised.

Rangers were only level for two minutes and this time the roles of Cruyff and Rep were reversed. The latter fed a ball to Cruyff as he ran into the right side of the Rangers box, closely shadowed by Derek Johnstone. Feigning to shoot, Cruyff forced the defender to commit before checking back on to his left foot. As McCloy tried to advance and cut down the angle, Cruyff drove the ball past him and inside the far post to restore Ajax's advantage.

At the break, Rangers manager Jock Wallace sent Tommy McLean on to replace Conn, looking to strengthen his midfield and establish a firmer foothold in the game. It had a measure of success and 20 minutes later Kovács, in a bid to lock down his team's advantage, sent the versatile Schilcher on to replace Keizer. Within ten minutes the game was decided. Pushing into midfield as Cruyff dropped into his own half to gain possession, Hulshoff received a pass from his skipper. Turning and driving towards the Rangers area, the *libero* chose the perfect moment to thread a pass inside of Haan's run into the area, and the midfielder controlled before firing home. A few minutes later, Swart replaced Cruyff as Ajax eased to victory. The match had been testing for many reasons. Travelling in the middle of a season for what was, essentially, a friendly fixture hadn't been helpful and the playing conditions, plus Rangers' energetic play, had all conspired to make it a wearying experience.

There was little time for self-congratulation, or recovery either for that matter, and just four days later FC Amsterdam would make the short trip across the city to face Ajax at the De Meer. Despite the recent journey to Scotland and the newly promoted club having already been beaten in the reverse match in the second Eredivisie fixture of the season, Kovács was not minded to take any chances by resting players and his first-choice 11 won 2-1 after a less-than-fully convincing performance. Haan had scored after just two minutes to give Ajax the perfect start, but an equaliser by Couperus from the penalty spot on half an hour squared things up. Swart took over from Rep at half-time, but it was a second goal for Haan that secured the win on 76 minutes.

On 24 January Rangers arrived to play the return leg of their 'centenary' game at the Olympisch Stadion. With their improved performance in the second half of the first leg, it was logical that Wallace would start with McLean replacing Conn in the only change to the visitors' team. Kovács made a similar move, starting with Swart, who had replaced Rep late in Glasgow. The young forward dropped to the bench but, with how the night panned out, Rep would be needed.

Rangers had been largely outplayed in the first leg on their own ground. Had there been a rare measure of inferiority complex among the Scots, about taking on the double European Cup winners? If so, such concerns had evaporated in the return leg as Rangers gave Ajax all the problems they could possibly have wanted. Just two minutes had passed when Rangers illustrated that they were far from throwing in the towel, despite trailing from the Ibrox encounter. From inside the centre circle Dave Smith played a ball forward to Quinton Young cutting in from the right. The winger failed to control effectively, though, and the ball ran away from him. It rolled towards Parlane who looked to shoot first time. The ball was blocked at point-blank range by Suurbier and fell back to McDonald who hit a screaming shot past Stuy and the Scots were ahead.

If Ajax had approached the game convinced that the hard work had already been done, they had counted without that Scottish cussedness and refusal to accept defeat without a fight. For the next few minutes Rangers pressed, harrying Ajax in possession and hurrying them into errors. The

European champions needed a quick reply and it came ten minutes after falling behind. Out on the left, Cruyff dipped outside and then inside of Johnstone, leaving the defender in his wake as he cut infield. With the defence pulled out of position, Haan exploited the space created, collecting Cruyff's pass on the edge of the box and firing past McCloy.

Rangers were far from done, though, and ten minutes before the break they scored again. McLean hit in an indirect free kick from wide on the right flank. With both attackers and defenders seemingly magnetically attracted towards the near post, the ball flew over all of them to find Young, one of the smallest players on the field, unmarked. A diving header back across the goalkeeper left Stuy helpless. Rangers were ahead again and just one goal away from squaring the aggregate scoreline. Once more, though, Ajax responded swiftly enough to prevent any further momentum falling to the Scots.

Two minutes later, Cruyff hit a corner in from the Ajax left. Johnstone managed to get a slight contact and divert the ball away from the penalty area but without effectively clearing the danger. Mühren arrived at the dropping ball first and flicked it inside to Neeskens running into the area, and the midfielder was tumbled as Craig jabbed out a leg. Grainy video of the incident makes a judgement difficult, but the Scottish captain was adamant there had been no contact. Regardless, West German referee Hans-Joachim Weyland pointed to the spot and Gerrie Mühren drove the ball low to McCloy's left, beating the goalkeeper's dive.

Level at the break, Rangers had only to lament that they had led twice before being pegged back with quick ripostes. For Ajax, the night had been more difficult than most would have anticipated, although one goal for the home side would probably be enough to finally quell the insistent Scottish ardour. Rep replaced Swart for the second half and the game became much tighter with each side appreciating the importance of the next goal, and the potential danger if they conceded it. The decisive strike arrived with barely ten minutes to play. A long free kick down the Ajax right was headed inside by Mühren towards Cruyff, lurking on the edge of the Rangers penalty area. Deftly controlling, he lifted the ball over Johnstone as the defender sought to close him down. Skipping around him, Cruyff collected and drilled past McCloy to finally break the Scottish resistance. At the full-time whistle it was the Ajax skipper, assisted by Neeskens, who lifted the strange trophy – it looked like a saucepan placed on top of a huge pair of spectacles.

A game that had looked likely to be a gentle confirmation of the ascendancy gained in Glasgow had, for much of the 90 minutes, turned into a genuine contest. Ajax's next match would be no 'gimme' either. Returning to Eredivisie duties the following weekend, they would travel to Deventer's De Adelaarshorst to face the always troublesome Go Ahead Eagles.

A more benevolent fate may have selected less difficult opponents for Kovács's players following the victory over Rangers, but it wasn't to be. Despite, or perhaps because of, the six-goal hammering Ajax inflicted on their opponents when they visited the De Meer in August, *De trots van de IJssel Kowet* were typically resolute and difficult to overcome. Aware of the danger of dropped points, Kovács had selected his first-choice team but it still took a penalty from Gerrie Mühren to secure the victory and points. Ajax would have been relieved to see the back of Go Ahead for another season.

So far, Ajax had been fulfilling the requirement of winning all their Eredivisie games before the European Cup restarted in order to pressurise Feyenoord. There were now just three more league matches to complete ahead of Bayern

Munich visiting Amsterdam on 7 March, and two before the encounter with Feyenoord. On 10 February, PSV visited the De Meer. The gradual transition from Kovács's first-choice starting 11 including Swart, to being one that featured Rep instead, was almost complete and the young forward again started alongside the ten other regulars.

Justification for the shift in the coach's preferences were illustrated when Rep scored twice inside the opening 25 minutes, the first coming after Cruyff created the chance with just five minutes played. Swart was still a valuable member of the squad, though, and when, five minutes after going two goals ahead, Ajax needed a replacement for the injured Keizer, Kovács turned to the veteran winger. Twenty minutes into the second period Ajax effectively closed out the win when Cruyff added the third goal following a free kick by Blankenburg. With the points secured, Kovács sent Arnold Mühren on to replace Cruyff for the final 20 minutes. A late goal by PSV's Danish winger Bent Schmidt-Hansen was of little consolation to the team from Eindhoven, who were well beaten by that time.

Ajax's surprise elimination from the KNVB Cup meant that, unusually for such a successful club, they had no fixture the following weekend, with the day being allocated for cup ties. In the absence of domestic opposition, instead of allowing the players a break the club opted for a brief journey to Greece, playing twice in three days. First they faced PAOK Thessaloniki, where 45,000 fans watched the European champions play out a 1-1 draw against the hosts on Valentine's Day. Ajax then travelled to play Olympiakos Piraeus, winning 2-1 in front of another bumper crowd, this time totalling a little more than 40,000. The friendlies allowed Kovács to keep his squad match fit as he rotated his players, and the Ajax finances ticked over nicely as Greek fans flocked to see them in action. With no injuries incurred on the odyssey, coach and club hierarchy were both satisfied.

Back in Eredivisie action the following weekend, Ajax travelled to Nijmegen's De Goffert to face NEC. Back in September Ajax had scored four goals without reply when their hosts had visited the De Meer, and they would repeat that scoreline in the return fixture. The only change to the regular starting 11 was Schilcher starting on the right of Ajax's back line, as Suurbier was struck down with flu. By half-time Ajax were three goals ahead as first Keizer, then Cruyff, and Keizer once more breached the home defence. The only concern for Kovács came just after Cruyff's goal, as an injury saw him substituted and Arnold Mühren came on in his place. It may have been a precautionary move though, with the following weekend's fixture in mind to ensure that the club's star players would be fully fit to face Feyenoord, and there was little danger in weakening the team against this level of opposition. The match was rounded out on 87 minutes when Krol scored the fourth goal after a solo run through the NEC defence. All eyes were now on the meeting with Feyenoord.

Since the turn of the year, Ajax had won all six of their league games, but Feyenoord had matched them win for win and were two points ahead of them at the top of the table. There would still be a further 11 Eredivisie fixtures to be completed after the big one, but the result at the Olympisch Stadion on the third day of March would be decisive in determining who would be the champions at the end of the season.

There were good and ill tidings for Kovács ahead of kick-off Suurbier had shrugged off his bout of ill health and was fit to return, but this was counterbalanced by the unavailability of Hulshoff through injury. The big defender would also miss the European Cup quarter-final first leg against Bayern Munich and the following Eredivisie match away to Groningen. Schilcher slid across from right-back into the middle of defence to partner Blankenburg. The Austrian was no Hulshoff – there were very few defenders in the world who could have stepped into his boots without being a downgrade – but Schilcher was competent and adaptable. He would hardly put a foot wrong, but the same could not be said for a player who Ernst Happel had been compelled to select.

On 21 January, Feyenoord hosted FC Utrecht at the De Kuip and secured a 2-1 win to keep them at the top of the Eredivisie table. There had been a cost, however. Regular goalkeeper Eddy Treytel would miss the next three league matches, with reserve Ger Reitsma taking over. The Rotterdam-born stopper had been capped once for the *Oranje* under-21 team, but his career with Feyenoord hardly suggested that he had fulfilled any early promise. He would play just five Eredivisie games for the club, with four of them coming in this season. In his first couple of appearances after taking the gloves from the absent Treytel, Feyenoord enjoyed comfortable wins, defeating Groningen 5-1 at home and then travelling to Breda for another five-goal haul, this time without reply against NAC. The next match would be against Ajax, and the absence of Treytel would prove to be very expensive.

Understandably for such a key fixture, almost 53,000 fans crammed into the Olympisch Stadion, and those supporting Ajax were raising the roof inside the first 60 seconds. Keizer had the ball on the left flank and fired in a low cross that caused panic in the Feyenoord defence as it passed through the narrow gap between retreating defenders, each fearing that any contact would result in an own goal, and a goalkeeper hesitant to commit himself to a cross that looked beyond his reach. Neeskens' slide to try and convert the delivery fell short and the danger looked to have largely passed as the ball ran on to Rep beyond the far post. With little other option given the acute angle, the young forward shot with any chance of scoring unlikely in the extreme. Reitsma had shuffled across his goal to limit Rep's target and the ball thudded into his chest. Unable to collect cleanly, however, he stumbled backwards with the ball before getting to his feet. Immediately, both Neeskens and Rep claimed it had crossed the line and a quick glance towards the linesman by referee Charles Corver confirmed the case. Frustrated and embarrassed, probably in equal measure, Reitsma decided to punish the ball for his own error and smashed it downfield in obvious anger. There was, however, more embarrassment to come for the unfortunate replacement.

A dozen minutes later, an almost carbon copy of the first goal doubled Ajax's lead. Standing over a free kick to the left of the Feyenoord area, Keizer lofted the ball into the box. It flew over the heads of Rinus Israël and Wim van Hanegem, once again reaching Rep beyond the far post, this time in the air. Throwing himself forward into a dive to reach the ball, Rep flicked a header back towards the far post as Van Hanegem jabbed out a foot in a forlorn attempt to block. Perhaps deceived by the midfielder's movement, the bounce of the ball rising up before him seemed to unsettle Reitsma, but he should still surely have done better. With Rep's effort hardly having much pace on it, Reitsma had both hands on the ball but it slipped from his grasp like a bar of soap and bobbled towards the far post. A desperate attempt to hook clear by Israël came to nought and, as the ball nestled in the back of the net, Reitsma bowed his head, hands on his knees. This time it was Israël punishing the ball for its perceived misdemeanours as the Ajax players celebrated another slice of good fortune, and Rep claimed his tenth Eredivisie strike of the season. It's questionable as to whether any of the previous eight, or the remaining seven that he would add before the end of the campaign, would benefit from as much good fortune.

Inside the final couple of minutes, substitute Lex Schoenmaker, who had replaced Joop van Daele on the hour, forced a shot past Stuy after a header by Van Hanegem had created an opening. It was too late to make any impression on the result, though, and the win took Ajax level on points at the top of the table, with their superior goal difference holding sway. The following weekend's fixtures would see them go two points clear as they continued their winning ways, and Feyenoord stumbled again, despite having Treytel back in goal. Before then, however, Ajax had the little matter of a European Cup quarter-final first leg against West German champions Bayern Munich to contend with.

The Bavarian club were at the beginning of the era when they would come to dominate German football and, indeed, in the following season they would embark upon their very own hat-trick of successive European Cup triumphs. The Bundesliga success that qualified them for Europe's premier club competition – finishing three points clear of Schalke 04 – had only been their second since World War Two, the first coming three years earlier. In the first round of the European Cup, after a 1-1 draw in Istanbul's Mithat Paşa Stadyumu against Galatasaray, they eased into the next round with a 6-0 thumping of the Turkish champions in the home leg. The second round was a canter against the Cypriots of Omonia as Bayern rattled up 13 goals on aggregate without conceding in reply. It was therefore a confident team that arrived in Amsterdam for the opening leg of the quarter-final, despite only winning three of their last five domestic games.

Ajax's *totaalvoetbal* had elevated them to being champions of Europe, and widely regarded as the best team on the planet. Success, however, also invites accompanying problems. Ajax's triumphs had opened the eyes of the footballing world. The secret was now out. It's said that imitation is the sincerest form of flattery and, across the border, German football had been watching and taking notes, as author, journalist, broadcaster and presenter Rafa Honigstein confirmed: 'In the 1973 game between Bayern and Ajax, you see a lot of the German players doing things that would have been seen as intrinsically Dutch at the time … Defenders going forwards, people moving around. So, a lot of the Dutch football had already been adopted by the better German teams. You had to go where your marker didn't want to be. So, it was less a big philosophical construct, but more the consequence of having skilled players. Breitner playing left-back and midfield. Beckenbauer, a midfield player, playing in defence. These things were happening at Bayern and in Germany at the time, but they just never had the same kind of philosophical underpinnings.'

Bayern were coached by Udo Lattek, who had joined in March 1970 having never worked at a senior club side previously. However, with the strong recommendation of the influential Franz Beckenbauer, who had played under Lattek in the former Bayer Leverkusen player's time as assistant coach of *Die Mannschaft*, they gambled on the 35-year-old. As with Ajax's gamble on appointing the virtually unknown Kovács, it was a decision that would bring rich dividends. Alongside Beckenbauer, Bayern already had the outstanding goalkeeping talents of Sepp Maier and the outrageous goalscoring of Gerd Müller in their squad. Lattek would add Paul Breitner and Uli Hoeneß and all would feature in the game at the Olympisch Stadion on 7 March 1973 when a reported 53,230 were privileged to watch one of the most exhilarating performances in the history of the European Cup.

With no new injuries from the Feyenoord game to complicate matters, Kovács was able to select the same starting 11. The absence of Hulshoff for such an important match was a big concern, but there was no chance of rushing the big defender back into the team. His injury would keep him out of action for another ten days. To avoid a colour clash between the kits, Bayern opted to play in a Barcelona-esque outfit of red-and-blue-striped shirts and blue shorts, with Ajax in their traditional colours. From the kick-off, Ajax quickly established their pattern of play, keeping possession of the ball, switching it between players as they probed for an opening. Bayern harried and chased, sometimes too enthusiastically. A hasty challenge from behind by Roth on Cruyff in just the second minute was sufficient for Swiss referee Rudi Scheurer to issue the game's first caution. Fortunately it was also the only one of the game, and Ajax were quickly back into their stride, buzzing inventively around the Bayern box.

Matches of this era between Dutch and German teams, be it at club or international level, carried an extra edge for those from the Netherlands. The still-sore wounds of wartime memories, less than three decades old, made it inevitable, and each Ajax attack brought passionate responses from the crowd. With just four minutes played the biggest roar of the evening so far erupted as Rep ripped a volley towards the Bayern goal, but it was deflected wide of Maier's far post and away for a corner.

As Rafa Honigstein suggested was the case, Bayern were also playing a fluid game with Breitner consistently drifting away from his nominal full-back role to support the midfield, as others dropped in to cover. At other times, it was Beckenbauer advancing with the ball at his feet, and even the rugged defender Hans-Georg Schwarzenbeck occasionally took a turn to prompt attacks, seduced to ignore the insistent demands of years of experience by the seemingly wanton freedoms now available to him. The centre-back even had the visitors' first shot at goal. After receiving a short free kick from Breitner, he galloped forward to the edge of the box before striking, but the effort was instantly charged down. Twelve minutes later their second effort came from Beckenbauer. *Totaalvoetbal* was Ajax's game, however, and if the Bavarians had become enthusiastic converts to the new pattern of play, Ajax were the masters of it and, in any like-for-like contest, the Dutch would surely hold the upper hand and, for most of the first half, that was how things panned out.

By the midway point of the first 45 minutes, Ajax had established control. Although the Bayern players still looked to attack using rotation of positions when in possession, the defensive element of *totaalvoetbal*, pressing to force errors when out of possession, had been largely abandoned. Each time an attack broke down the Germans would funnel back into their own half, only looking to challenge as the ball came into their defensive third with their deep block designed to negate Ajax's fluid football by staying compact and denying space and freedom in the danger areas.

With 15 minutes of the half remaining Bayern were now only moving forward with infrequent breaks. Ajax were dominating possession and position on the field. With most of the Bayern players dropping deep to defend, there was little chance of any coherent build-up from the back and through midfield. Despite this, Maier had yet to be tested to any great extent. Very much the same was true of Stuy at the other end, with the Ajax goalkeeper being far less involved in the game; collecting back passes and taking goal kicks were his main contributions. Conversely, Maier would see much more of the game as it progressed and became increasingly employed as the pressure grew on his defence with each passing minute, tipping shots wide or over the bar, then plunging at the feet of the Ajax forwards.

On the Ajax bench, the trilby-hatted Kovács fidgeted nervously, drawing anxiously on another cigarette, and complaining to Bobby Haarms alongside him that their team should be ahead. On the other bench, Lattek, in a flat cap, was almost motionless, leaning forward as he stared intently at the game, only breaking his concentration to occasionally glance towards his watch.

With seven minutes to the break the first goal nearly came from a Maier error. A low cross into the box from the right seemed to carry little danger. Unaccountably, though, as the goalkeeper plunged to collect, he allowed the ball to slip under him and travel, almost unimpeded, towards the net. It took a last-gasp recovery from Roth to slide in and hook clear.

Roth may then have been fearing the worst just minutes later when a late challenge on Cruyff as he slalomed and shimmied his way to the edge of the penalty area brought the admonishing whistle from referee Scheurer. Having received that early caution, there was the nagging fear of another serious offence being deemed sufficient for a dismissal. Rising to his feet, the anxious glance towards the official betrayed Roth's concern, but nothing followed and he quickly disappeared into the mass of Bayern defenders preparing to defend the free kick. Scheurer contented himself with the task of ensuring a ten-yard gap between ball and wall – or as near to as he could establish. Gerrie Mühren's clipped effort floated over the line of defenders, but dropped gently into Maier's welcoming arms.

The pressure continued to mount, though, and nearing the break an advancing Suurbier played a neat wall pass and fired a shot from the edge of the box. Maier stretched out an arm as he threw himself to the left. The merest of touches on those over-size gloves was just sufficient to divert the ball on to the post and away, and at the break the game remained goalless. What had begun as a cerebral tactical battle had developed into Dutch domination, and edged towards a siege as it moved towards the second half. Another 45 minutes without an Ajax goal looked unthinkable – and it was.

Lattek may have been of a similar opinion as, starting the second period, Bayern threw themselves forward in a frenzied opening. Such moves carry dangers though, and, as Ajax played themselves clear, Rep was suddenly in space inside the Bayern area. Only an unaccustomed failure to control the ball rescued Lattek's team, as it ran away from the young forward and Maier scrambled it behind for a corner.

Bayern immediately swung back with another attack and a less-than-elegant challenge by Neeskens, as Hoeneß sought to turn and enter the box, brought a free kick. Roth's attempt to find Hoffman's darting run down the side of the Ajax wall was too strongly hit and ran out of play. Bayern's next foray saw a deep cross from the right headed back across goal by Müller. It fell to Hoffman around five metres from goal but, in the anxiety of the moment, composure deserted him as he leant back when striking for goal and the ball flew high over Stuy's crossbar. Watching the opportunity squandered, Müller turned and slapped both his hands to his sides in frustration. If Bayern's newfound attacking intentions were going to bear fruit, such profligacy could not be afforded. A couple of minutes later the rationale for such an assertion would become clear.

A ball into the box was half cleared and fell to Keizer around ten metres outside of the penalty area. Advancing, he struck in a powerful shot with his supposedly weaker right foot that bounced just in front of Maier. Parrying, but unable to collect the ball, Maier merely spooned it out towards Haan following up. Haan drove it over Maier and into the net to put Ajax ahead. As the crowd erupted in celebration, the Ajax players ran to congratulate both players involved in the goal. Nine minutes had been played since the restart. Despite Ajax not being able to break down the Bayern defence across the whole 45 minutes of the first half, just a quarter of an hour after opening the scoring, they would be three goals clear.

For the following dozen minutes or so, the pattern of the first half was reprised. Ajax pressed insistently with Bayern forays forwards infrequent and mainly ineffective. Each time they lost possession there was a rush to funnel back into defensive positions and prepare for another wave of attacks. A single-goal defeat with the home leg to come wouldn't have been disastrous, but to fall two behind to the double European champions would give them a mountain to climb back in Munich. There was a rare breakout when a long ball found Hoffman galloping clear down the left with Müller racing to support through the middle. His attempt to find the little striker was poor though. The ball ran harmlessly into Stuy's arms and Müller's frustration rose again. It had been the briefest of respites as Ajax assumed dominance once more in search of the second goal, which came with 68 minutes showing on the clock.

A throw-in deep in the Bayern half, taken by Rep, was hooked into the box by Schilcher. A header clear dropped to Gerrie Mühren and a right-footed volley exploded from the midfielder's foot, arrowing into the roof of Maier's net. It left the goalkeeper forlornly clawing at thin air. Bayern were now in trouble, but worse was to follow – and quickly. Dutch celebrations exalting Mühren's spectacular strike had hardly quelled when Ajax attacked again. Another weak header opened up a chance for Cruyff to follow his team-mate's template, but his effort was blocked behind for a corner. Bayern were like a boxer on the ropes, shipping punishment, with little to offer in return, and the partisan crowd roared Ajax on. Cruyff's corner was floated in and Haan rose at the near post to guide the ball over Maier and into the net. Knockout! Ajax arms were raised in triumph. Bayern hands were on hips in despair. With two goals conceded in barely a minute, Bayern needed to clear their heads or face a humiliation against the now-ebullient Dutch.

Rep stole possession from Zobel inside his own half and cut infield, weaving clear of Bayern lunges. Running into the Bavarians' half between Beckenbauer and Schwarzenbeck, ball at his feet, it was a race. Beckenbauer fell behind first and with Rep a metre into the area, Schwarzenbeck launched into a desperate challenge, playing the ball with his right foot and simultaneously felling Rep with his left. The crowd roared for a penalty. Another goal now and the score could have run into anything that Ajax wanted, but Scheurer had been left trailing far behind by the speed of Rep's break. He was in no kind of position to make a decision but he did so, opting for caution and deciding that the offence had taken place a metre outside of the penalty area. It clearly hadn't. The linesman should surely have pointed out the folly of such a decision but failed to do so. Mühren's free kick flew high and wide and Bayern escaped.

Bayern needed a reply but their first attempt to do so only led to a crashing foul by Beckenbauer. As the attack broke down, Ajax launched a rapid counter-attack down their left flank. Krol burst clear of the first challenge but was felled by the second. Underestimating the Dutch defender's pace, Beckenbauer launched himself into a challenge as Krol played the ball forward again. Krol got to it first, and the German's

297

lunge only found Krol's ankles. It was almost a microcosm of the game to that point. Ajax had simply been too good and too quick. Bayern were consistently second best, and often second to the ball.

Dutch voices filled the air in celebration as the crowd watched their team dismantling the visitors from Germany. Decades of festering enmities were given voice in joyous release. Lattek glanced at his watch again. Was he hoping that time would slow down so that his team could get back into the game, or wishing it to fly, so that they could escape further damage? Whatever the case, neither scenario would happen. Kovács merely smoked his cigarette, looking far less agitated now.

Entering the last few minutes, Ajax seemed satisfied by their three goals but the crowd, ignited by the experience of seeing a disdainful Netherlands triumph over Germany, wanted to feast on more. It was a hunger fuelled by years of painful memories. They urged Ajax to score once more to drill home the lesson. Half-chances came and went. Haan, Cruyff and Mühren took shots but with the seconds ebbing away it looked like the celebrating crowd would have to be satisfied with three.

Then, entering the final minute, Krol crossed from deep on the left flank. Cruyff leapt salmon-like above the Bayern defenders, flicking the ball past Maier and inside the far post – 4-0. At the final whistle the roar was deafening; hats and cushions were hurled into the air. Ajax had taken Bayern Munich apart and a four-goal win in no way flattered their performance. It was perhaps their best to date. As Rafa Honigstein remarked, the Germans were on the way with their own version of *totaalvoetbal*. On this evening though, the masters of the art had demonstrated how long a journey was still to be travelled. On that March evening in 1973, as

Amsterdam celebrated, no one knew, and surely no one could have guessed, that the team so comprehensively beaten would, the following season, take over the crown of being European champions and reprise Ajax's successes.

Four days later it was back to the more mundane matters of the Eredivisie for Ajax, and a journey to Groningen's Oosterparkstadion. Games against the *Trots van het Noorden* (Pride of the North) were a relatively new experience for Ajax, and all other Dutch clubs in the Eredivisie as well. The club had only been formed in June 1971 as the successor to GVAV, gathering up all the available talent from the various clubs in the municipality, and playing their first season in the top tier. They would finish 13th at the end of the campaign before a combination of financial difficulties and political infighting led to their relegation the following year.

Despite the continuing absence of Hulshoff, taking the points for an away victory looked a fairly straightforward matter for Ajax. Given they were now level on points with Feyenoord at the top of the league, and the Rotterdam club had a comfortable-looking home fixture against Twente, there looked to be little room for errors. A first-half goal by Neeskens and one after the break by Rep efficiently got the job done with the minimum of fuss. The only concern for Kovács was an injury to Keizer just before the hour. Swart was sent on to replace him, but the problem had eased sufficiently for the winger to play in the following weekend's fixture. At full time Ajax also received the unexpected bonus that Feyenoord had been beaten by Twente at the De Kuip.

At the break, and already trailing to a first-half goal by René van de Kerkhof, Happel had problems. An injury to Wim van Hanegem, the influential Feyenoord playmaker, meant that he would be unavailable for the second period and was replaced by Franz Hasil. Five minutes after the restart a second Van de Kerkhof strike gave Feyenoord a mountain to climb and, when Jan Jeuring added the third just before the hour, the result was set. A late consolation goal by Hasil with ten minutes to play hardly changed anything. Feyenoord had now lost consecutive games and their two-point advantage over Ajax had been reversed. Top spot in the Eredivisie now belonged to Kovács's team. Even if Feyenoord won all of their ten remaining games running to the end of the season, their pursuit would be forlorn unless Ajax slipped up. They wouldn't.

Next up for Ajax was a visit from NAC, who had eliminated them from the KNVB Cup back in December on penalties. It would be the strangest of seasons for the club from the southern Netherlands. They would make good on their success against Kovács's European champions by going on to lift the KNVB Cup for the only time in their history, defeating NEC Nijmegen 2-0 in the final on the last day of May, and yet they would only avoid relegation by three points. The triumph qualified them for the Cup Winners' Cup the following season, where they would be eliminated in the first round by East German club 1. FC Magdeburg, who would go on to lift the trophy after beating AC Milan in the final.

Ajax would avenge the defeat and loss of the KNVB Cup to the visitors, but the victory would come with a price and cause consternation in the camp with the return leg in Munich just four days away. Perhaps considering that the young forward would benefit from a break, Kovács dropped Rep to the bench, selecting Swart to play in the forward line alongside Cruyff and Keizer, and was happy to have Hulshoff back in place alongside Blankenburg. Things began well for Ajax; on 13 minutes, Haan headed home from a Gerrie Mühren corner and the returning Swart doubled the lead ten minutes later. The points were secured but Cruyff had taken

a knock and had to be removed at the break, with Arnold
Mühren replacing him.

Swart underscored his claims for a place in the upcoming
European Cup second leg by scoring again ten minutes after
the restart. On the bench, Rep must have been thinking that
the veteran was making a strong pitch for his place in the
attack, but was granted a chance to stake his own claim on
70 minutes when he replaced Keizer. His last-minute goal,
created by the attacking play of Suurbier, may just have been
enough to swing things in his favour. The big headache for
Kovács was the injury to Cruyff. Not only would he miss
the game in Munich, he would also be compelled to sit out
the next two Eredivisie matches as well. Those four goals
netted in the Olympisch Stadion were now looking even more
important.

Kovács had been impressed enough by Rep to have the
young forward start in attack, with Swart back on the bench.
Perhaps due to Cruyff's absence, the lack of any requirement
to attack with four goals already safely pocketed, or a
combination of both and other factors, there were changes in
both the Ajax team and attitude when compared to the first
leg. Eschewing the opportunity to slide Rep into the middle
and put Swart on the right, the coach opted for another
playmaker rather than forward to replace the absent Cruyff.
Haan was moved forward from midfield nominally into the
centre of the attacking trio, although for much of the game
he would adopt a deeper position, leaving just Keizer and
Rep up front.

With Haan absent from midfield, there was a gap
alongside Neeskens and Gerrie Mühren. Going for a like-
for-like replacement, the latter's younger brother would have
been the obvious answer but, like Swart, Arnold Mühren
was sitting on the bench. Instead, with Hulshoff in the back

line, Kovács opted for the versatile but more defence-minded Schilcher, who had performed well when covering for the *libero*. The captain's armband needed a new home as well due to Cruyff's absence. Keizer had skippered the side in 1971/72, and Hulshoff had done the honours in the past as well. Instead it was given to Krol, who would later have the job on a permanent basis, captaining the team from 1974 until he left in 1980. It looked like a line-up designed to defend, deny and hit on the break. Given they had four-goal cushion it was an entirely sensible approach, and yet inside the first seven minutes Ajax had increased their aggregate lead and dropped the wettest of blankets over any fanciful Bavarian dreams of a dramatic recovery.

Comfortably collecting a long, hopeful ball into the box, Stuy immediately looked upfield. With Bayern pressing anxiously for an early goal that may offer hope of an unlikely comeback, the defence had been left dangerously exposed. Stuy hit the ball long towards the Ajax left flank, where the white-shirted Keizer, and Breitner, now wearing the narrow red and white stripes of Bayern, were positioned. The defender got to the ball first, but Keizer was only half a step behind him. Maier had advanced a little from his goal but when Breitner tried to head the ball back to him from just outside the area, it was woefully short. Keizer dipped inside and, when Maier closed on him, the winger neatly lifted the bouncing ball over him and over the line.

Breitner chased the ball forlornly but could only fish it out of the net, head bowed with his club's slender hopes now surely cast to the four winds. Reprising his non-celebration-celebration after the goal when Ajax had mercilessly set the cap on their rout of Feyenoord, Keizer stood motionless, arms by his side awaiting his team-mates. Rep arrived first, then Haan, then Neeskens. There was none of the exuberant joy that had greeted the goals in Amsterdam two weeks earlier, just contented smiles, accepting that the job was now all but done.

It was. Bayern attacked dutifully but scoring six times against the double European champions was the stuff of fantasy that even *Boys' Own* writers wouldn't consider. From this point forward the only realistic target was to win the game and salvage a measure of pride. There were further injury concerns for Ajax 20 minutes after going ahead, with Blankenburg having to leave the field. Kovács dropped Schilcher into the middle of the defence, with his midfield berth now giving Arnold Mühren a place alongside his elder brother and Neeskens. The German defender would miss the next two Eredivisie games and only return to the starting 11 at home to Twente on 7 April, just four days before Ajax faced the Spanish giants of Real Madrid in the first leg of the European Cup semi-final.

The first step on the home team's road to restoring some pride came three minutes later. A corner from the Bayern left was flicked on inside the six-yard area by Müller. The ball struck Krol and rebounded past a startled Stuy for an equaliser on the night. Hardly ecstatic, the Bayern players' celebrations were probably muted by the state of the tie, and the inevitability of its final outcome, but the cheers from the home supporters suggested that they, at least, still believed in miracles. Eight minutes later that defiance was leant a little support as Bayern went ahead. A through ball from the right sliced between Hulshoff and Schilcher to find Müller running clear, with Dutch appeals for offside carrying little conviction. Reaching the edge of the area, Müller arrowed his shot across Stuy and inside the far post, with deadly accuracy. Bayern now led but still needed another four goals. At least there was a glimmer of hope though, albeit faint.

For the remaining eight minutes of the half, Bayern pressed with renewed vigour and, had they breached the Ajax defence again before the break, perhaps mission impossible would merely have become mission improbable. It wasn't to be. Even with Schilcher replacing Blankenburg, the Ajax back line and Stuy were an accomplished unit and, with the tigerish Neeskens and the Mühren brothers, plus the deep-lying Haan denying Bayern time and space on the ball to build attacks, the momentum of the second goal gradually dissipated as the second half went on.

It seemed like a minor inconvenience at the time, and hardly sufficient to dent Kovács's satisfaction at his team's progress, but a caution issued to Keizer by English referee Ken Burns on 57 minutes would have repercussions later in the competition. Aside from the injury to Blankenburg, and the as yet unknown consequences of Keizer's indiscretion, the game had carried little to concern the coach, but that would change with just two minutes left when an injury to Gerrie Mühren took him out of the action. It would have little effect on this match but carried greater significance in the longer term with the midfielder being unavailable for a month.

At full time, Ajax had eased into the last four of the competition. Bayern had the satisfaction of securing a win in the home leg, but for much of the tie they had been well beaten and largely kept at arm's length. With Blankenburg and Mühren now joining Cruyff on the injury list, the price of progress to the last four was becoming potentially expensive. When Telstar visited the De Meer on 8 October, Ajax had feasted on goals, recording a 9-2 victory. The return fixture was the first Eredivisie game after the visit to West Germany and, largely due to Ajax's worrying injury list, it would be a far closer affair.

All clubs have to endure periods when injuries hit, with the more successful ones who inevitably play more games at higher levels of competition often seen to be increasingly prone to such problems. Over their time as the dominant force in Europe, however, Ajax had been more fortunate than most, allowing first Michels and then to a greater extent Kovács to rely on a core of a dozen or so players with significant changes in the team often a case of steady evolution rather than make-do-and-mend maintenance. The less-than-fully competitive Eredivisie would have helped their cause, as perhaps would the early elimination from the KNVB Cup in the 1972/73 season, although it would hardly have felt like that at the time. Perhaps the major exception to this would have been the ill-fated Jan Mulder, whose time in Amsterdam was blighted with knee injuries. For the trip to Velsen-Zuid in North Holland, however, there were plenty of holes in the Ajax team to plug.

With Schilcher standing in for Blankenburg as the only change from the regular defence the back line was less of an issue, but in midfield things were less straightforward. To add to Kovács's woes, on top of Gerrie Mühren's injury, Neeskens was also unavailable. It meant that if Haan had been retained in the forward line, as had been the case against Bayern, none of the regular midfield trio would have been in place. Sensibly, Kovács decided not to take that risk and Arnold Mühren started alongside Haan who was dropped back. That still left one further place to fill and, with Schilcher required to play in defence, the options were limited.

Barend Kist had joined Ajax from junior Amsterdam club Ovvo in the summer of 1972 and was contracted to the B team for the 1972/73 season. In his time with the club, the away game at Telstar would be his sole appearance in the starting 11 as he slotted into the vacant midfield berth. The following season, then contracted to the C team, he would make a single appearance from the bench, before moving on to DWV in the summer of 1974. When there are a compact group of regular players favoured by the coach, the fate of players such as Kist is not unusual. With the option of maintaining Haan in the forward line compromised by the requirement to be the senior figure in midfield, Kovács recalled Swart to the right flank, slid Rep into the centre and had Keizer in his usual position on the left of the three.

With so many changes to the team there was little surprise that Ajax struggled to develop a cohesive pattern of play and offer any kind of concerted attack on the home goal. At half-time, with the breakthrough still eluding his team, Kovács removed Kist and sent on Gerrie Kleton to replace him. Faring better than Kist, although only marginally so, Kleton would make four Eredivisie appearances before moving to MVV in the summer of 1974. The substitution was hardly much of an upgrade though, and Ajax continued to labour in search of a goal. It would eventually arrive with just four minutes to play as the veteran Swart found the back of the net and kept Ajax's lead at the top of the table intact.

It was an unusual, and unwelcome, situation for a club used to taking the majority of domestic fixtures in their stride to now be struggling to overcome supposedly inferior opposition. Across the last couple of Eredivisie seasons, aside from games against Feyenoord – and Go Ahead Eagles of course – there were only odd occasions when Ajax found the domestic going difficult, but as 1972/73 moved towards its climax, both at home and in the European Cup, the smooth passage to victory that they had become accustomed to was being imperilled by injuries to key players.

The following weekend saw Utrecht visit the De Meer. The same defence was in place, but Kovács was delighted to have Neeskens available again to assume his position alongside Haan, and Arnold Mühren was chosen to complete a much more recognisable trio. Once more, Swart, Rep and Keizer comprised the forward line. The opening phase was tight, but when Hulshoff rampaged forward to open the scoring after creative work by Rep a lot of the tension began to lift. Seven minutes later it was Rep profiting from Haan's bravery to score the second goal, and likely securing the points. In creating the goal, though, Haan had been injured and had to leave the pitch. Just as Neeskens had returned to the midfield, Kovács now had to contemplate losing Haan. Fortunately the damage was less serious and, after sitting out a midweek friendly against Anderlecht, he was fit for the following weekend's Eredivisie game away to Twente. Kovács had dispensed with the idea of selecting Kist, and sitting alongside Kleton on the bench for this game was Bram Braam. The 21-year-old midfielder would in fact have an even shorter Eredivisie career than Kist. The 55 minutes he was on the pitch for against Utrecht, as he was sent on to replace Haan, would comprise his total playing time in league fixtures for Ajax, before moving to MVV in the summer.

There was a brief period of concern for Ajax a dozen minutes after the break when Karel Bonsink halved the arrears, but a goal by the returning Neeskens eight minutes later calmed things down. It allowed Kovács to remove Swart and send on the more pragmatic Kleton to see out the game, and Ajax eased over the line for another win. The win completed a – fortunately brief – difficult period. A couple of domestic fixtures that would normally have been regarded as offering relatively comfortable victories had been negotiated successfully, if not with totally convincing performances. The wins had been important, as while Ajax struggled Feyenoord had enjoyed two comfortable victories. Having defeated Den

Haag 2-0 at the De Kuip, they then thumped Excelsior 6-1 away. Ajax's lead at the top of the table remained at two points. Now Kovács could look forward to having more of his regular players available for selection with key games on the horizon.

Despite the injuries sustained, and players easing themselves back into contention for selection, Ajax chose to travel to Belgium two days after the Utrecht win to play a friendly against Anderlecht. A team featuring a blend of regular, and some very irregular, starters with four substitutions played out a 2-2. The contest was fairly low key and played at an understandably gentle pace. It was, however, significant for the debut, and only appearance for Ajax, of a little-known and lesser-spotted forward who would later achieve great fame with the club. His name was Louis van Gaal.

On 7 April, four days before the first leg of the European Cup semi-final, Kovács was able to select something approaching his first-choice starting 11 in the Eredivisie against FC Twente. Blankenburg was back to partner Hulshoff in the centre of defence. Haan's injury had proven to be nothing to seriously jeopardise his inclusion and, back in the forward line, was the mercurial Cruyff. Only the unavailability of Gerrie Mühren compromised the coach's options, with Schilcher covering in midfield.

Whether it was a matter of the returning players easing themselves back into match fitness or perhaps the lingering effects of injury, there was still a measure of coherence lacking from the team as Haan's first half strike was the only goal of the game. Cruyff had been removed at the break to be replaced by Arnold Mühren. At the time it merely looked cautious, but events four days later would focus a different light in the decision. Swart replaced Rep with ten minutes to play as the game petered out and Ajax eased over the line. At the same time, over in Rotterdam, Feyenoord had coasted into a 3-0 lead at half-time in the local derby against Sparta. By the end, however, that advantage had been wiped out as the visitors earned a draw to share the points. Happel's team fell further behind in the title chase, now trailing Ajax by three points with just six matches to play.

Four days later, Real Madrid would visit the Olympisch Stadion. It would be a clash between the *Ancien Régime* and the upstarts from a backwater league in northern Europe, between the six-time winners of the European Cup and the club that had won it for the last two seasons, between the orthodoxy of Spanish football and the new paradigm of *totaalvoetbal*.

Despite dominating in Spain, Real Madrid hadn't won the European Cup since 1966 when they beat Partizan Belgrade – and Velibor Vasović – in the final. *Los Blancos* wanted what they considered to be almost their property back in their trophy cabinet in the Spanish capital. Ajax wanted to usurp the old order and establish themselves in its stead. More than 300 years previously, the nascent Dutch Republic had been formed after defeating Phillip II of Spain on the Eighty Years' War, establishing themselves as the new dominant power in Europe. Across 180 minutes of football, Ajax would seek the same goal.

Coached by the legendary Miguel Muñoz, who had won three European Cups as a player with the club in the competition's first years and then returned as a coach to add two more, the Spanish champions had eased through the first round against the minnows of Iceland's Keflavík. The second round was a more difficult assignment against Argeş Piteşti of Romania, and a 2-1 defeat in Piteşti's Stadionul 1 Mai had left plenty of work to do. In the return leg the score was mirrored at 2-1 to the home side before Santillana scored his second goal of the night, with just three minutes to play, and sent Real into the quarter-finals. The draw paired them with Dynamo Kyiv and a 0-0 stalemate in the away leg set them up for a comfortable 3-0 win back in the Estadio Santiago Bernabéu. The four teams left at the semi-final stage were Ajax, Real Madrid, Juventus and Derby County. They represented the cream of European football; the reigning champions, together with the champions of Spain, Italy and England. Only the winners of the Bundesliga were missing from Europe's top league, but Ajax had already eliminated them.

Kovács would surely have dearly wanted to have Gerrie Mühren available for the first match, but that option would be delayed until the return leg two weeks later, so Schilcher would continue to deputise alongside Neeskens and Haan. More than 53,000 fans were in the stadium, overwhelmingly Dutch, and the teams entered the field to a raucous welcome walking out slowly, with Kovács trailing behind the Ajax players, ever-present cigarette at the ready. In the crowd, several Ajax supporters waved banners depicting Real Madrid as a bull, with the matador wearing their club's colours, and entrancing the bull with his cape, adorned with an image of the European Cup. The stage was set.

Even before the game started, the difference in appearance of the two sets of players heralded how they would approach it. Almost all of the Ajax players sported copious amounts of hair on heads, chins and cheeks, rebellious iconoclasts to the core, with the bearded Hulshoff looking the epitome of Bohemian counterculture; Ajax's own Che Guevara. In comparison, the Spaniards were tidy and clean-shaven, disciplined and organised, heirs to an empire overthrown, but still lamented. The Spanish players were numbered one to 11, but not the Dutch. Blankenburg carried 12, Hulshoff 13, Haan 15 and Rep 16. Cruyff had 14, as always. The home team's numbering was reflective of their free-thinking ethos, compared to Real Madrid's adherence to tradition.

Straight from the kick-off Ajax made their intentions clear. The ball was rolled back to Krol who paused, looking for options upfield, before squaring to Blankenburg. Sensing an opening, the German defender quickly arrowed a ball to Cruyff, who turned and unleashed a shot, but it was deflected wide. Inside the first 20 seconds Ajax had their first corner, as the unusually blue-shirted players of Real Madrid dropped back to defend. The pattern for much of the game had been quickly established. The set piece came to nothing as Neeskens, with his long sideburns, couldn't direct his far-post header on target, again deflected behind. Another corner accrued, and then a third. Finally, under intense pressure from Rep, García Remón, Real Madrid's goalkeeper, fumbled the ball over the line, but few disputed East German referee Rudolf Glockner's decision that he had been fouled.

For much of the half it would be Ajax pressing, but Real Madrid still carried a threat and, from their first corner, on six minutes, Santillana so nearly opened the scoring. Amancio's deep cross from the right drifted beyond the far post and Santillana punched the ball back high across goal with a well-directed header. The ball flew over Stuy guarding his near post and dropped towards the net. Fortunately, Blankenburg was on the line to head clear, and Ajax sprang forward again.

The visitors' attacking ambition was largely restrained, with forward play limited by insistent defensive imperatives. It was hardly the play of Di Stéfano, Gento and Puskás, but this Real Madrid team was but a pale shadow of the one that had dominated the early years of the European Cup and, sitting on the bench, Muñoz was as aware of that as anyone else. Possession was very much the property of Ajax, and with

Hulshoff pounding forward regularly, the reassuring presence of Schilcher to cover as required facilitated such freedom.

There was, however, an absence of the sharp-witted, darting, cutting edge that Cruyff's play so often inspired. Time and again, Ajax's attacks broke down on the edge of the area as Muñoz's blue barrier protected Remón efficiently. Was Cruyff fully fit? Had the decision to remove him at the break against Twente been far more significant than many realised at the time? Following his substitution against Twente, Cruyff had insisted he would be playing against Real Madrid despite rumours of an injury swirling around in the press. He was, but should he have been? Ajax's four-goal advantage earned in Amsterdam had insulated them against the loss of Cruyff for the away leg against Bayern Munich. In this game they were looking for something similar to take to Spain but, if the mainspring of their forward play was compromised, could that be achieved?

On 20 minutes Neeskens found space in the area to head towards goal, but the effort was blocked. It was an increasingly rare opportunity to strike from that sort of position. Most of the efforts on Remón's goal had come from long-distance shooting by Haan, Neeskens and Keizer. None had significantly troubled the goalkeeper. As Ajax built once more at the midway period of the first half, a ball to Cruyff saw him instantly turn and advance before being felled by Grande's uncompromising two-footed lunge. Wincing, Cruyff hauled himself to his feet, to receive the sort of consoling apologetic pat from the offender that was surely more for the official's attention than that of the injured Dutchman. Cruyff limped away from the incident slowly. Had he been carrying an injury, the challenge would hardly have hastened any recovery.

On the Ajax bench, Kovács had now graduated from cigarettes to a Sherlock Holmes style of pipe. Finding a way past the Real Madrid defence was, however, proving to be anything but elementary. By contrast, in the visitors' dugout, Muñoz sat observing impassively, wrapped in a mackintosh, arms folded as tight as his defence was on the field.

In the final 15 minutes of the first period, Hulshoff was a more permanent figure in the Dutch midfield and often further forward as Cruyff dropped deeper. The captain was now often betraying a slight limp in his gait, waving his arms in frustration at his team's inability to strike with any effectiveness, and perhaps also his own depleted mobility. Even Schilcher was joining forward thrusts, leaving just Suurbier, Blankenburg and Krol as insurance against the rare Spanish forays from defence.

As their team laboured without success, the massed ranks of Ajax fans became increasingly tense – their frustration matching that of Cruyff – but were bereft of the means to do much to address the issue. The Real Madrid defence looked secure and were growing in confidence. A shot from a tight angle by Keizer was parried away by Remón eight minutes ahead of half-time. It drew a roar from the crowd but was never likely to bring a breakthrough. At the break, after banging their head against the blue wall of the Real Madrid defence, all Ajax had accomplished was to gain a headache.

The Spanish champions left the field satisfied by their work, and knowing that, if they could repeat that performance for another 45 minutes and with the home leg to come, a place in the final would be well within their reach. That banner brandished by the home fans ahead of kick-off, depicting Ajax as a matador and their opponents as a bewildered bull, had effectively been reversed by the action of the first half. Were Real Madrid about to complete the job by plunging the *estoque* into Dutch dreams of a hat-trick of European Cups?

The following day, writing in *The Times*, Brian James was less than impressed by Ajax's inability to break down the Spanish defence, and Cruyff's performance in particular. He was playing, James remarked, 'Clearly without full fitness, and even more clearly without full commitment.'[82] The scribe went on to suggest, 'For the first half, indeed, [Cruyff's] greatest contribution was as chairman of the instant inquests on every under-developed chance. [His] gesturing impatience with team-mates will scarcely have improved his popularity already waning fast within the squad.'

It was undeniable that the performance of both the team, and Cruyff, had been below the very high standards set across the last couple of seasons, especially during the demolition of Bayern Munich, but they had still dominated against the Spanish champions despite having failed to find the back of the net. Cruyff was clearly less than fully fit, but even a half-fit Cruyff was probably superior to the alternative options available to Kovács.

The comments about Cruyff's relationship with his team-mates may well have had merit, but disagreements with a squad of strong personalities was hardly anything particularly unusual, even though the one centred around Cruyff would grow and fester across the coming months.

Ajax's brisk start to the first period had promised much but delivered little of any tangible value. Kovács was clearly less than satisfied and, although he had done little wrong in the first period, replacing Schilcher with Arnold Mühren suggested a more progressive approach to the second period. It soon materialised.

---

82 'Ajax struggle through at end of unconvincing match', *The Times*, 11 April 1973.

The opening seconds of the second half suggested that *Los Blancos* had lost little of their steadfast concentration, so effectively demonstrated ahead of the break. Standing over a free kick just outside of the Spaniards' penalty area, Cruyff waited for a late Suurbier run outside of him, hoping to catch the defence with their minds still dawdling in the dressing room. The instant reaction of no fewer than three defenders as they crowded out Suurbier's advance suggested that such hopes were forlorn. Thrusts forward by the defender would become a feature of the second period though. If the Spanish approach hadn't differed, there was a new urgency in the Ajax players, eager to contest possession further forward and, with Suurbier becoming an increasingly troublesome factor on the flank, keener to strike forward with zealous speed. A header forward found Rep scampering ahead of his defender. A jerk on his arm by Touriño halted the progress, and the resulting free kick came to nought, but Ajax's increased pace in the game and speed of movement, as well as thought, would cause more problems as the half wore on.

Krol drilled a low cross into the box from the left, but the Spanish defenders watched it run harmlessly by with no Ajax players able to take advantage. Haan robbed Touriño as he turned casually after receiving the ball from a throw-in. The ball was quickly moved on to Neeskens on the edge of the box. His shot was scuffed, and easily gathered by Remón, but Ajax's pressing game was beginning to force errors and find gaps in the visitors' defence, as it became increasingly difficult for Real Madrid to maintain any kind of studied possession. The press became suffocating.

Another press and choking of hurried possession brought Ajax a free kick on the left as Krol was fouled. Keizer crossed deep and Rep climbed to head back across goal. Among a crowd of blue shirts, Cruyff darted forward to prod the ball

315

home, but he had done so with the aid of a foul and the goal was ruled out with little protest. There was still nothing on the scoreboard, but the crowd were encouraged by Ajax's improvement and the sharpened threat they were posing. They roared in approval, urging their team on to greater efforts. A couple of minutes later, Remón was forced into a diving catch to cut out a cross from the left with Neeskens and Rep poised and waiting. The goalkeeper's wasteful clearance only found Suurbier and Ajax pressed again. The pressure was building and Real Madrid's composure of the first 45 minutes was being replaced by something far less reassuring, as Ajax established clear domination.

With Suurbier pressing forward on the right, and Krol mirroring his play on the left, Ajax overloaded in wide positions, but it left potential gaps at the back – especially given Hulshoff's repeated incursions into midfield and beyond. Assisted by a rotating cast of supporting players, though, Blankenburg was calm and effective, providing tackles and interceptions and marshalling the offside trap with calm confidence. So much of the play was concentrated in the Real Madrid half and, increasingly, in the final third of it. Runs forward by Haan and Neeskens from midfield not only added to Ajax's attacking threat, but also offered Hulshoff space to move forward as the play was compressed.

Just past the hour, blocking a full-blooded shot by Neeskens in the most sensitive of places, Pirri fell to the floor clutching his groin in pain. Play continued for a while as the agonised midfielder rolled around on the floor. Eventually the referee blew his whistle and, after treatment and some less than totally sympathetic encouragement from his colleagues – especially skipper Zoco, who seemed to be trying to slap his team-mate into health – Pirri climbed to his feet, ready to continue. More discomfort was to follow for Real Madrid.

From Ajax's next attack, Hulshoff advanced to crash a fierce shot against Remón's bar. Two minutes later the goalkeeper was plunging low to his left to stop a Neeskens shot. It was becoming a question of how long Real could resist before their creaking defence capitulated under the pressure.

The answer came on 67 minutes. Out on the left, another free kick offered Keizer a chance to cross into the box. His effort struck a defender standing barely eight yards from the ball, and ballooned into the air. Dropping short of goal, it was headed on by Krol. The box was crowded but Haan's leap took him clear as he nodded the ball down towards Hulshoff, striding forwards and clear of marking defenders. There was no doubting the bearded *libero*'s intentions; driving low with his right foot, he hammered the ball into the corner of the net. Remón was clearly unsighted by the crowd scene in front of him, but it's doubtful if it made any meaningful difference. From just a few yards out the ball was past him in a flash, and Ajax had the lead. The wild celebrations both on the pitch and among the Dutch supporters were fed by both joy at the goal and the release from frustration. A 1-0 defeat was hardly disastrous with the home leg to come, but both teams now seemed to sense that the remaining 25 minutes or so would be key in deciding who would reach the final.

Ever since the break, Ajax's determined front-foot approach had pressurised the overworked Real Madrid back line into conceding a series of free kicks. The opening goal came from one of them, and the next threat would arrive from a similar source. Cruyff was blocked and bundled to the ground on the edge of the penalty area. Keizer seemed the likely taker, but Hulshoff rumbled past him and, with the adrenaline of the opening goal still coursing through his veins, he smashed another shot on target. It drove deep into the wall of defenders and bounced clear, but the visitors would not be as fortunate from the next such opportunity.

Ajax players were buzzing in and around the Real Madrid penalty area like troublesome wasps, looking to deliver a sting while defenders turned this way and that trying to block out dangers. A neat passage of play ended with Arnold Mühren playing a wall pass with Cruyff before clipping in a curling shot that left Remón clawing at fresh air, but glanced off the top of the bar and over.

Haan had seen his instant low shot from the edge of the penalty area blocked and then gathered by Remón seconds earlier, when Cruyff was baulked by Benito after jockeying with the goalkeeper as he tried to clear upfield. Racing forward in determined fashion, Glockner awarded a free kick to Ajax, his arm ramrod straight in the air, to indicate it was indirect. Benito argued without success and then had to endure the wrath of Zoco, furious that his team-mate's lack of discipline had led to another Ajax opportunity. He was right to be worried. Nine minutes after a free kick had led to the opening goal, Benito's foul would bring the second.

Glockner eased the Spanish defensive wall back as Keizer stood over the ball. Would it be a clip into the air, or perhaps a tap to one side for another Hulshoff thunderbolt as the defender stood menacingly, ten yards behind the ball? As Keizer nudged the ball to his right, the plan was clearly the latter, or at least a variation. Instead of Hulshoff it was Krol striding on to it and hitting a low drive past the wall and beyond Remón. In the defensive wall, now rendered irrelevant by the shot, the words passed between Zoco and Benito aren't available, but the general flow of the brief conversation can probably be imagined. On the Ajax bench, Kovács puffed on his pipe with an inscrutable Sherlock Holmes expression. Two goals ahead now, the case had been cracked. Well, not quite.

Two minutes later, Hulshoff slid into a tackle on Amancio around the halfway line as Real Madrid laboured to create some forward momentum. The ball became stuck under the defender's feet as he lay on the ground, inevitably causing problems as the Spanish forward tried to kick it clear. With team-mates on both sides rushing to support their player, a pushing and pulling melee ensued. Increasingly loud and repeated sounds of the referee's whistle provided background music but little in the way of restoring order. As tempers calmed, cautions to each side were inevitable. Glockner identified Amancio as one of culprits and then added the name of Keizer to his notebook to square things up. In the context of the game it mattered little but, with Keizer's caution in Munich now brought into the equation, the vastly experienced winger would be missing for the return leg in Madrid.

Two goals down, and with Ajax looking increasingly satisfied with their lead, Real Madrid began to threaten with as much conviction as they had at any stage throughout the game. Score before full time and there would be an entirely different look to the tie. Aguilar threatened down the left but Hulshoff, back in his defensive role, shepherded the danger away. From the clearance, the Spanish came again. Grande threaded the ball through to Santillana and Krol felled the forward on the edge of the box. The defender protested that he had won the ball, but to no avail, and this time it was a Spanish free kick in a dangerous position. Stuy placed seven players in his defensive wall but the number was insufficient. Amancio tapped the ball sideways for Pirri to run on to and fire inside Stuy's far post; Real Madrid had snaffled an invaluable away goal. The balance of the tie may now have swung back slightly in their favour. Spanish celebrations suggested they believed that to be the case.

Ajax were now compelled to attack again. Keizer volleyed in a shot from a tight angle that Remón blocked, and Rep had a header tipped over the bar by the goalkeeper. There would be few other openings as the minutes slipped away and the Real Madrid defence had something worthwhile to bite on to again. A final chance fell to Neeskens, matching up his run with a clipped pass from Haan, but contact on the ball was weak and Remón happily fell on it.

Seconds later, with Ajax fans already streaming from the stadium, the full-time whistle brought the game to a close. Downcast Dutch players and Spanish ones with arms raised in the air suggested how each of the teams viewed the result, and how it affected their prospects for progression to the final. Brian James summed up how that late goal had changed the complexion of the tie, describing it as being 'perilously balanced'.[83] It was, and if Ajax were to maintain their aspirations for a third European Cup, an outstanding performance in the Spanish capital would be required.

Before that assignment, Ajax had two Eredivisie games to play. Win both and there would be just four more league fixtures to follow and the three-point advantage over Feyenoord would feel increasingly invulnerable. On 15 April, Ajax travelled to play FC Den Bosch at the De Vliert. The home team were enduring a torrid season; they would finish at the foot of the table and be relegated to the second tier. Ahead of kick-off, the game was considered to be a comfortable fixture for Ajax and, following the physically and emotionally draining encounter against Real Madrid, Kovács tweaked his starting line-up. Despite being substituted at the break in the semi-final, Schilcher was back in a midfield berth.

---

83 'Ajax struggle through at end of unconvincing match', *The Times*, 11 April 1973.

Alongside him and Neeskens in the centre of the pitch was Arnold Mühren, who had replaced Schilcher in the week. Haan was left out. The same applied to Rep, as Swart was drafted back into the team.

Schilcher had been a valuable asset for Kovács across the season, with the versatile Austrian able to step in and efficiently block holes across the back line or in midfield when one of the regular starters were absent. His two goals in this game, the only brace in his time with Ajax, secured the points, despite a late consolation for the home team. Schilcher would feature in four of the last six Eredivisie games but would miss out in the remaining European Cup fixtures, only returning to continental competition in 1973/74 as a 78th-minute substitute for Neeskens in Ajax's ill-fated first round away leg against CSKA Sofia. It would be his final appearance before moving to Paris FC the following month, after being granted a transfer at his own request in pursuit of regular first-team action. His time in in the French capital would be brief and disappointing and after just 17 league appearances he moved on to Nîmes and then later to Strasbourg, before returning to Sturm Graz in 1978 for the final four years of his playing career. In 2007 he would return to Ajax's employment, working as a scout, until his death in 2018, aged 71.

For a time, the victory over Den Bosch appeared likely to have effectively closed out the title race. Feyenoord were trailing 1-0 away to MVV with just a dozen minutes to play, but late goals by Wim Jansen and Rinus Israël secured the points and kept them just about in the hunt. The following Saturday, Ajax were back at the De Meer as Den Haag visited. Kovács was delighted to welcome a recovered Gerrie Mühren back into the starting 11. With Haan and Rep also returning, the starting 11 looked very much like the team that would line up against Real Madrid four days later – save for Keizer who would miss out in Spain due to suspension. The game against the relegation-haunted Den Bosch had been an unexpected struggle. Conversely, Evert Teunissen's Den Haag would finish in fifth position, but Ajax would canter to a comfortable victory against them.

It took until five minutes before half-time for the breakthrough to come as Haan headed home the opening goal but, once the visiting defence had been breached, Ajax rattled in another four in the second half. First, Cruyff profited from work by Keizer to add the second on 61 minutes. Four minutes later, Schilcher replaced Hulshoff as Kovács exercised understandable caution with his team now two goals clear and in control. With 20 minutes to play Keizer would have the coach lamenting his enforced absence in the Spanish capital as he scored the third goal with a solo run before despatching past Ton Thie in the visitors' goal to make victory certain. One minute later the winger turned provider again, creating an opening for Rep, who also notched the fifth goal three minutes later. With 15 minutes to play Kovács withdrew Keizer, replacing him with Arnold Mühren, as would be the case from the start in Madrid. Another late Feyenoord goal, this time by Van Hanegem, edged Happel's team home against AZ '67 at the De Kuip. But, with the gap still three points and now just four games to play, unless Ajax fell away badly the Eredivisie title was surely staying in Amsterdam.

On their way to European Cup success, Ajax had faced several difficult away legs with visits to Celtic and Atlético Madrid in 1970/71, plus Arsenal and Benfica the following year. The visit to the Spanish capital looked every bit as challenging as those games and, with the Bernabéu packed to the rafters with 110,000 *Madridistas* bellowing out 'Hala Madrid' and roaring *Los Blancos* on, it certainly was.

There may have been a measure of contemplation in Kovács's mind as to whether Arnold Mühren or Swart was the best option to replace the suspended Keizer, and selecting the midfielder Mühren rather than the veteran forward was an early indication of how the coach was looking to approach the game. With the slenderest of leads to defend, caution was prudent for the visitors and with Real Madrid only needing a 1-0 win to progress to their ninth final, and their first since 1966, Muñoz was hardly likely to send his team out in an attacking frenzy. The Spanish coach also had issues, missing a key player, with Santillana being unavailable. With *Los Blancos*, as the home side, wearing colours that fitted that description, Ajax were wearing all-red as Cruyff kicked off. Unsurprisingly, the attitude of the coaches led to a tense and largely negative opening 45 minutes. The following day, *The Times* described it as 'a display of basically defensive football by both sides'.[84] Few other observers would have disputed the assessment.

The result in Amsterdam had clearly encouraged Real fans that the second leg was the chance to restore the established order of things and see their club ascend back to their rightful position at the top of the European footballing tree. Muñoz may have preached caution and patience to his players, but the packed terraces of the stadium had little mind for such matters, turning the Bernabéu into a seething cauldron of passion with a heat as hot and white as the shirts of their team. Across the opening period of the game, each time Real Madrid gained possession, a ferocious roar arose from the packed tiers of stands, demanding a goal. Inevitably Ajax were pressed to defend, but they did so with a calm and experienced efficiency, shielding Stuy and

---

84 'The Old Masters Make Way', *The Times*, 26 April 1973.

offering threats on the break. The first attempt on their goal came from a Grande header as he supported the attack, but it was tame and bounced accommodatingly into Stuy's welcoming arms.

With five minutes played, Ajax could easily have been down to ten men. Stretching to gather a long cross from the left, Remón's momentum carried him into a glancing blow on Rep as he tumbled to the ground. It was clearly accidental and hardly significant. Considering that to not be the case, however, Rep instinctively flicked out a foot at the prone goalkeeper. It carried far more gesture than malign intent, but Remón's dramatic reaction was designed to suggest otherwise, inviting Belgian referee Vital Loreaux to deliver a sanction. Several white-shirted players surrounded the official demanding retribution, and the fans hollowed in angry echo. Fortunately for the young forward, the referee was only a matter of yards away, found the goalkeeper's unwarranted theatrics hugely unimpressive, and merely cautioned Rep.

With the first 15 minutes safely negotiated, Ajax began to play their way into the game and a jinking run into the box by Haan held out promise of the opening goal, but his shot was deflected wide. Then a Cruyff break and low pass across the edge of the area just eluded the stretching Neeskens. Rep closed in from the right flank but his shot was wide. The home team had the majority of possession but without causing undue concern for Stuy and, although Ajax's attacks were rarer, they carried as much menace. A Krol run and pass to the returning Gerrie Mühren opened up another opportunity requiring Remón's attention. Then Cruyff fired wide from the edge of the area.

By the midway point of the first half, the home fans had settled into an acceptance that patience, rather than frenzied attacking may well have been the best policy, and the game settled into a pattern with both teams looking to hit on the break. There was a brief flurry of excitement across the stadium when a shot on the turn by Aguilar cannoned into Blankenburg as he threw himself into a block. Had the ball struck his arm? If it had, from the range of a mere couple of metres such intervention was surely unintentional. Appeals on the pitch were briefer than those from the fans, but neither brought any reward as the ball was scrambled away for a corner. A goalmouth melee followed the restart, with both efforts on goal, and attempted clearances, blocked, but Stuy eventually calmed Dutch nerves by diving on the ball. With the match drifting towards half-time, an incisive pass found Cruyff in space inside the area with time to control the ball. Jockeying his marker, he opted to pass rather than shoot, but Gerrie Mühren's run on to the ball was thwarted by a challenge. The ball ran wide and away from danger.

By the break it was still goalless. Fleetingly brief glimpses of goal and half-chances had been the order of the day so far, with neither goalkeeper over-extended. Both coaches would have felt a measure of satisfaction. Ajax's lead remained intact and Real Madrid still needed just a single goal to go ahead on away goals. The perilous balance identified by Brian James remained in place but, just half a dozen minutes after the restart, that balance would tilt strongly in favour of Ajax.

The early minutes of the second period had suggested little in the way of change as the teams took up their respective defensive positions again, and probed diligently. Then, injecting pace into a game that seemed to be played in second gear, Krol powered down the left flank, evading two challenges as he drove into the penalty area. His cross was cut back looking for a red shirt but only found Benito, who deflected the ball away. It ran out of the area towards Gerrie Mühren, charging forward from midfield. Striking first time, he hit a low shot that looked to be covered by Remón as the goalkeeper shuffled to his left. Having cleared the danger once, however, the presence of Benito would again come into play. Standing around the goal area line, the defender was transfixed as the ball struck his leg, diverting it wide of Remón and into the net.

Indisputably there had been a measure of fortune to the goal but, as the first half had progressed, Ajax had looked increasingly dangerous and, if any team was going to score, the Dutch champions had looked the more likely. Muñoz reacted quickly. From needing one goal to take the box seat, his team now needed three. Patience and measured concentration were suddenly less appropriate; a measure of urgency was required. González was replaced by Marañon as Real Madrid's approach to the game changed. Approaching the hour mark, a corner from the left found the head of skipper Zoco, but Stuy scrambled across to parry and then collect the header. It was the closest the home team had come to breaching Ajax's defence, but near misses were of no value to *Los Blancos*. The best opportunity to force their way back into the game was to follow just moments later.

A key element of Ajax's *totaalvoetbal*, one that was embraced by the *Oranje* under Michels at the 1974 World Cup, was the offside trap when facing a free kick, with defenders rushing out in unison to catch unwary attackers stranded in an offside position. It's a tactic that requires hair-trigger timing. Delivered correctly, it both nullifies and frustrates opponents in equal measure. If the officials consider that timing to be awry, however, it can lead to disaster. In this game that was so nearly the case.

A lofted free kick into the Ajax box was the signal for the red tide to charge forward and claim offside. The linesman failed to comply with the ploy and the ball travelled unhindered to Grande inside the penalty area with no defender close enough to challenge, and just Stuy to beat. Controlling the ball with his chest as it bounced up, Grande shaped to lob over the advancing goalkeeper and into the unguarded net as defenders raced back to cover. The effort lacked sufficient height, though, and Stuy managed to get his fingertips to the ball sufficiently to deflect it wide of goal and, following up, Aguilar failed to connect as he tried to hook the ball home from a tight angle while the towering figure of Hulshoff closed him down. Real Madrid's best chance had come and gone. Ajax defenders pointed to each other accusingly. It had been Suurbier dallying for a fatal moment before joining the charge, but they had escaped.

Real Madrid's plight was now double-edged. They needed to press forward, but one more break for Ajax and a second goal would surely end any meaningful resistance. It nearly occurred on two occasions, both from chances created by Cruyff. Drifting in from the left, he drew two defenders towards him before slipping a pass across the box for the advancing Rep. The young forward took a shot but Remón managed to block it. Conventional wisdom would have had Ajax in solid banks ahead of Stuy, but *totaalvoetbal* had different requirements. Hulshoff charged into midfield as Haan dropped in to cover. Firing the ball towards Cruyff, the defender continued his advanced run as the captain laid the ball back into his path. A last despairing challenge managed to choke the shot, and Cruyff couldn't benefit from the loose ball.

On 67 minutes Muñoz played his last card, removing Amancio in favour of González Pérez. It would make little difference. Although the majority of possession lay with the Spanish club, the greater threat on goal was coming from Ajax breaks. Crosses into the box were either headed clear by Hulshoff or dealt with by Stuy catching or punching clear and, with Dutch forwards available to drop back and cover any breaking defenders engaged in counter-attacks, attacking openings were few and far between for the home team. Following that one earlier aberration, Ajax's offside trap was now functioning with sublime efficiency.

With 15 minutes to play and hope draining away from the home team, Cruyff played Rep in for another breakaway but he was blocked off the ball as he advanced towards goal. The referee adjudged that the challenge amounted to obstruction and Ajax had an indirect free kick deep inside the Real Madrid penalty area, albeit at a tight angle. A clipped cross was cleared and Hulshoff fired wide from outside the area as the ball fell towards him.

The Spanish champions were now looking mortally wounded, resigned to their fate as their aspirations leaked away with each passing minute, teased and tormented like a bull at the hands of a matador, as Ajax eased their way confidently into a parity of possession. A killer finish was required. Ironically it came, not from a goal, but with an extravagant piece of self-confident skill. The game was being played out at almost walking pace as Ajax jealously hoarded possession, stroking the ball around with confident assurance, when a crossfield pass from Suurbier arrowed towards Gerrie Mühren in space on the left. Instantly coaxing the ball under his spell, he flicked it up in the air from right foot to left and back again, once, twice, three times, back and forth, before cradling it on his left foot and rolling a pass towards an overlapping Krol. Goals win games, and Mühren's deflected strike had effectively settled this one. For the player, however, there was greater symbolism in that brief passage of exuberant play. 'It was the moment when Ajax and Real Madrid changed positions,' Mühren recalled much later. 'Before then it was always the big Real Madrid and the little Ajax. When they saw me doing that, the balance changed.'[85]

Ruud Krol also remembered the tie against the club who had become synonymous with the European Cup: 'I think we had two good games against Real Madrid. At home, it was very difficult, but we won 2-1. But we had a very disciplined defence that could play if we need to keep the scores against us to zero, and that was our force.'

Ajax would play their third successive European Cup Final, and their fourth in five years. That showpiece occasion would take place on 30 May in Belgrade, the capital of the now-defunct Yugoslavia, and Ajax would, for the third time in those four finals, face the champions of Serie A. In 1972/73 the Scudetto was adorning the shirts of Juventus.

Under Czechoslovakian coach Čestmír Vycpálek, the Old Lady of Turin had secured the title by a single point from AC Milan after the Rossoneri's late run of six wins and a draw in their final seven Serie A fixtures fell just short of eliminating the gap to Juventus. It was their first championship for five years, but they would go on to confirm their status as one of Italy's top clubs by winning a further eight Scudetti across the next couple of decades. In the 1972/73 European Cup, a team boasting a forward line of José Altafini, Franco Causio, Pietro Anastasi – who had become the world's most expensive footballer when he moved to Turin from Varese for £440,000 five years previously – Fabio Capello and the Old Lady's favourite son, Robert Bettega, looked well equipped to travel deep into the latter stages of the competition in pursuit of their first continental trophy.

A 3-1 aggregate triumph over Marseille in the first round had come courtesy of a 3-0 home win comfortably wiping

---

85 Wilson, Jonathan, *Inverting the Pyramid* (London: Orion, 2014).

out a 1-0 defeat in France. A brace from Bettega, plus a goal from German forward Helmut Haller, eased the Italian club through to the second round. They were then paired with East German champions Magdeburg, and two single-goal triumphs took them into what would be a nervous quarter-final against Újpesti Dózsa. With 15 minutes of the second leg played, Juventus's dreams of European glory looked to be in tatters. A goalless draw at the Stadio Comunale had left Vycpálek's team with it all to do when they visited Hungary for the return leg. Things quickly deteriorated from there as a first-minute goal from Ferenc Bene, and another 12 minutes later by András Tóth, had the Italians heading towards the exit door. Juventus fought back, though, with goals from Altafini after half an hour and Anastasi ten minutes after the restart.

Away goals carried the day and Juventus progressed to the last four, where they would face Brian Clough's Derby County in a controversial encounter that would leave the outspoken Clough raging about Juventus's approach. Regardless, a 3-1 home win and goalless draw at the Baseball Ground meant elimination for the English champions and a first European Cup Final for Juventus. It would be a novel experience for the players representing the Old Lady, compared to an Ajax team with so much experience of such matters and, as will later be discussed, there is a theory that this disparity was a major issue in deciding who would lift the trophy in Belgrade.

Before the Ajax players could contemplate such lofty matters, there was still an Eredivisie title to be secured. They held a three-point lead and a healthy goal difference advantage over Feyenoord. It was surely sufficient to carry them over the line. On the following weekend, they would travel to Rotterdam to begin their quest to close out the league, not to face Feyenoord – they had already fulfilled the De Kuip fixture – but instead to play Excelsior. Keizer slotted back into the starting 11 and Arnold Mühren returned to the bench in an otherwise unchanged side from the one that had triumphed in Madrid.

Excelsior had endured a difficult season, not least from the 8-0 mauling they had been subjected to by Ajax at the De Meer back in November 1972, and they were tumbling towards relegation. Nevertheless, as referee Charles Corver blew for half-time in this encounter, the scoreline stubbornly remained goalless. Maybe it was an emotional hangover from the victory in Madrid, a fatigue induced by that game and the travelling incurred, perhaps just a lack of form, or a combination of several factors, but Ajax had laboured to create much of anything against a team who, come the end of the season, would have lost 21 of their 34 league fixtures, scoring just 24 goals and conceding 70. What had looked like a comfortable game to ease his players back into the bread-and-butter of Eredivisie competition, after the exquisite fare of Madrid, was now presenting Kovács with football's equivalent of a case of indigestion.

Before the restart he swapped the Mühren brothers, sending Arnold into action and Gerrie to the bench, but was rewarded with little tangible improvement. Perhaps fresh legs, unimpeded by the exertions in the Spanish capital, was the answer. On 63 minutes Swart replaced Rep as Kovács emptied his hands of cards, and entering the final 15 minutes it was beginning to look as if Excelsior could do their fellow Rotterdammers an unexpected favour and restrict Ajax to a single point. Just as the game appeared to be up, though, Neeskens prised open a chance and Cruyff converted to deliver a hard-fought victory. At the same time, Feyenoord were playing away to HFC Haarlem and, whereas Ajax had managed to scrape a victory, Happel's team failed to break down the home defence and could only draw. After a match that suggested for so long that their three-point lead was looking vulnerable, by the end of the day it had grown to four. The only disappointment for Kovács was a caution for Cruyff that meant a suspension and his absence from the next game, seven days later, when Sparta Rotterdam came to the De Meer.

With the captain unavailable, the obvious options for Kovács were to either bring Swart into the starting 11 or reinstate Arnold Mühren to the forward line. Instead he opted to place Schilcher into midfield with Neeskens and Gerrie Mühren, and push Haan forward to play between Keizer and Rep in the sort of deeper-lying role often required of the absent Cruyff. Sparta, coached by Leo Steegman, had already caused Ajax problems in the league, when they got the better of Kovács's team during their 3-1 home win in early December having fallen behind to a Keizer free kick. Sparta threatened to take the points once again.

With just seven minutes played Stef Walbeek gave the visitors a lead, but fortunately for Ajax there was little time to dwell on the goal conceded. Five minutes after Walbeek's strike, Rep capitalised on work by Keizer to equalise and, by half-time, the creator had turned goalscorer and Ajax led 2-1. Once more, Kovács traded Mühren for Mühren at the break, together with Swart replacing Blankenburg, who had sustained an injury. Arnold replaced Gerrie in midfield, Schilcher dropped back to partner Hulshoff, and Haan resumed his normal midfield role as Swart joined the front line. Despite now playing further back, Haan doubled the advantage ten minutes after the restart, with Rep adding a fourth as the game passed the hour. A late Sparta goal by Nol Heijerman was scant consolation.

Feyenoord rattled in seven goals at home to FC Amsterdam, but it did nothing to reduce the four-point lead that Ajax held with just two fixtures each to play although it nibbled away at the goal difference deficit. It would now take two substantial victories for Happel's team and correspondingly heavy defeats for Ajax if it were to be overturned. The following weekend, Ajax would head to Maastricht's Stadion De Geusselt to play a mid-table MVV team with little to play for, needing just a point to send such outlandish speculation into the realms of irrelevancy. It would take a major shock to lose the title now but, in football, things are seldom certain.

Following a fairly unspectacular career as a player, George Knobel took up coaching at Breda-based amateur club VV Baronie in 1966. Three years later he was appointed coach of MVV, after they had finished 13th in the Eredivisie. Across the next few years there seemed to be little in the way of any sustained improvement as MVV hovered around the middle of the table. In fact, since the start of the 1969/70 season, in the seven games where MVV had faced Ajax they had lost six and drawn the other, scoring just once, while the Amsterdam club had racked up 21 goals. As against Excelsior, though, taking things for granted in football is always dangerous. Knobel's charges would deal Ajax a blow and, extraordinarily, across the next two seasons, the MVV coach would first be given charge of Ajax, and then the *Oranje*. In both roles, the man described to the author by Dutch football journalist, commentator and former owner and chief editor of the football magazine *ELF Voetbal*, Jan-Herman de Bruijn, as a 'small-town coach' would prove himself to have been woefully over-promoted for his abilities.

As the teams took to the field in Maastricht on 13 May 1973, however, no one could have foreseen Knobel's future taking such a spectacularly unexpected turn. Blankenburg was still struggling with the injury that saw him substituted at half-time against Sparta, and Schilcher continued to partner Hulshoff at the heart of the back line in a team that was otherwise very much the first-choice starting 11, although by the break, with the scoreline still goalless, an injury to Keizer had seen the winger replaced by Arnold Mühren.

Much as had been the case against Excelsior, Ajax appeared sluggish as they struggled to create openings against a team they had scored eight past earlier in the season. Their situation was hardly helped by Keizer's withdrawal; the injury would keep him out of the final Eredivisie fixture the following weekend. After half-time the game ticked on without either defence being breached and it became increasingly clear that a single goal would probably decide the destiny of the points. It came with 15 minutes to play.

Unlike in Rotterdam when Cruyff had struck to secure the win against Excelsior, it was MVV celebrating as Jo Bonfrere put Knobel's side ahead. Suddenly Ajax's seemingly firm grip on the Eredivisie title looked a little less secure. News coming through from Deventer that Feyenoord were leading Go Ahead Eagles 4-2 hardly helped. Seeking a repeat of events after he had played the same card a couple of weeks earlier, Kovács removed Rep and sent the veteran Swart on to try and salvage the game. The gambit failed to achieve the desired result, as did Ajax, and the four-point lead was down to two as Feyenoord maintained their advantage until full time. The safety net of the goal difference advantage now assumed increased importance.

Definitively locking out the title almost three weeks ahead of the European Cup Final would have been ideal for Kovács and Ajax. Had they been able to take just a point from the Maastricht visit, coupled with their early exit from the KNVB Cup, it would have allowed the coach and players plenty of preparation time without the pressure of competitive matches to play. The loss to Knobel's team had denied them that luxury – at least in cold, hard statistical terms – but the massive advantage in goal difference was surely sufficient security. Nevertheless, when AZ '67 visited the De Meer the following week, it felt very much like there was still work to be done.

Blankenburg returned to reclaim his place in defence for the game, allowing Kovács the opportunity to field a full-strength team apart from Keizer, who was replaced by Swart. Notably, other than in friendly games at the end of this season and the preamble to the following one, it would be the veteran's last start for Ajax. Once more, however, Ajax failed to score in the opening 45 minutes as the first half remained goalless. Kovács's team appeared to be experiencing a collective drop in form with the biggest game of the season now just 11 days away. Thanks to an early brace by Leo Shoemaker, Feyenoord were leading 2-0 at the break in their home game against PSV but, even if Ajax had fallen to an unlikely defeat, the Rotterdam club would require a swing in their favour of greater than 20 goals to overcome the goal difference deficit. Any danger of squandering the title was only contemplated by the most obtuse of pedants. Of greater concern to Kovács was that, even taking into account the 4-2 win over Sparta, there had been worrying patches across each of his Ajax's last four games. A lift in his team's performance was required.

The hour mark came and went, and still Ajax failed to break down the visitors as tension and frustration grew in tandem, and Arnold Mühren replaced Rep. There were just 15 minutes to play when Hulshoff delivered the breakthrough, heading home from a Suurbier cross. With the dam breached,

Ajax scored twice more in the remaining minutes. First Cruyff created an opening for Swart to score what would be his last Eredivisie goal for the club, and Gerrie Mühren completed the scoring. It had been a revival of sorts, albeit a late one, but the three goals eased concerns at the De Meer, with the league programme now successfully completed. A 60-point haul placed them two clear of Feyenoord in the final reckoning. They had scored 102 goals, the highest in the league, and conceded just 18, again the best record. There was little doubt that Ajax remained the top club in the Netherlands. The question now was whether they could claim the same status across the continent in what would be the 1,000th European Cup encounter.

That issue would be decided on 30 May, after Ajax played two friendlies. With a break of 11 days between the AZ '67 fixture and the final in Belgrade, it gave Kovács the opportunity to both keep his players active and play out any questions he may have had about selection. One player certain to be in the starting line-up against Juventus was Cruyff and, due to a reported ankle injury, the captain was kept wrapped in cotton wool to ensure his fitness. In the first of the two friendlies, Ajax played in a charity game against a team formed from the construction workers who had built the Centrum '45 centre in Oegstgeest, near Leiden in South Holland. The centre, still operational at the time of publication, offers care for people suffering the effects of chronic trauma. Unsurprisingly, Ajax were 3-0 up inside the first 15 minutes with Mühren, Swart and Rep scoring, before easing off and politically allowing the opposition to score three second-half goals and end the game as a draw. All proceeds were donated to the centre.

Two days later, Ajax returned to the De Meer and played a team from the Dutch military. Across the years, with conscription in place in the Netherlands until 1995, the military team had seen many young players come through its ranks before moving on to successful careers with clubs and the national team. At one time it had also been coached by Jan Zwartkruis, then a captain in the Dutch Air Force, who would later take over from George Knobel after the 1976 European Championship and guide the *Oranje* to the 1978 World Cup in Argentina. Players who featured in the teams of Zwartkruis included Rob Rensenbrink, Jan van Beveren, Henk Houwaart and Willy van der Kuylen, plus Barry Hulshoff and Jan Mulder. The 1973 vintage was hardly a bumper crop, though, and Ajax eased to a 7-1 win.

Neither game was played with a full-on commitment, but it would still have been a relief for Kovács to be able to select his first-choice 11 for the final. By this time it had become clear that the coach would be leaving Ajax when his contract expired at the end of the season. Following an interview in Belgrade ahead of the final, *The Times* reported how relaxed the Romanian appeared, describing how countering Juventus's defensive style was not something he had specially planned for. 'We will cope with each situation as it arises,' he confirmed. 'You cannot plan these things in advance.'[86] Coping with situations as they arise was something that Ajax would need to do when Kovács departed to take over the French national team that summer.

Given his outstanding success in Amsterdam, to many it seemed somewhat negligent of the club to allow him to leave. Conversely, it may well have been a case of that very success convincing Ajax that it was safe to do so. Having selected a virtually unknown and largely unheralded candidate to take over from the seemingly irreplaceable Rinus Michels, and

---

86 'England despondent and without excuses', *The Times*, 28 May 1973.

seen the club continue to prosper, why not try the same thing again? Such serendipity is rarely repeatable though, and would clearly not be in this case, but such considerations and later laments were for another day. If Ajax were to ascend to the pantheon of the truly great club sides in history, overcoming Juventus needed to be achieved first.

Writing in the *The Times* on the eve of the final, Geoffrey Green suggested that, despite Ajax being applauded for their success and lauded for their expansive *totaalvoetbal*, 'Not since the mighty Real Madrid held the trophy for five successive seasons has one club dominated the European football season as Ajax have done in recent seasons ... their flowing football and irresistible skills have achieved and earned the admiration of fans in every country in which soccer is played.'[87] Although they were widely favoured to win against a relatively novice Italian club, Green had 'a funny feeling' that it could be Juventus's day. Yet, almost arguing against that idea, he added that while 'Ajax had ten full internationals in their squad and [would] be at full strength' that wasn't the case for Juventus and 'Cuccureddu and Altafini might still be omitted at the last minute in favour of Haller and Bettega'. When the starting line-ups were announced, Green had at least been partly correct about the team. Cuccureddu was on the bench but Altafini started. Haller was on the bench, but Bettega started. Green's 'funny feeling', however, was shown to have been well wide of the mark.

In marked contrast to their previous finals, with Juventus winning the toss to wear their first-choice colours of black and white stripes, Ajax would play in all red. It wouldn't be the only thing that looked strangely unrecognisable about the

---

87 'Juventus could wield the stick and keep the carrot', *The Times*, 29 May 1973.

reigning European champions. Whereas their two previous victories had been filled with fast-flowing, exhilarating football, the pace of this game would differ sharply, as Menno Pot explains: 'The 1973 final in Belgrade, against Juventus, was a very boring affair: a very early goal (by Rep) and then, well, nothing.' It may be a slight oversimplification, but there remains plenty of merit in the description.

The final began with Juventus dropping deep, allowing Ajax to dominate both possession and position. They did so at walking pace, passing the ball around with hardly a challenge arising. There was an understandable element of caution in Juventus's tactics, but it also played into Ajax's hands, as Ruud Krol recalled: 'It was very hot in Belgrade. We were not prepared for that, because we were coming from Holland. I think we were playing in 30 or 32 degrees in the evening. So, it was not so easy for us in that game. We were not only playing against Juventus, but the climate was also not in our favour.'

It wasn't, as Geoffrey Green's report of the game the following day attested to: 'After a hot, sultry day, came this hot, steaming night.'[88] Those early minutes, with Juventus set on defence and Ajax seeking to preserve their energies, set the pattern for much of the remainder of the game and, when Rep opened the scoring with just five minutes played, as Pot asserted, it was the key moment of the game.

Neeskens had possession deep in the Juventus half, walking forward, looking to draw a defender forward and create space. The black-and-white-shirted players ignored the invitation, staying resolutely deep in their defensive formation. He slipped the ball left towards Blankenburg moving forward.

---

88 'Dutch strolling layers add touch of sovereignty to their third cup', *The Times*, 31 May 1973.

The centre-back was largely freed from defensive duties with the opposition rarely inclined to press forward. He returned the pass to Neeskens and then received the ball again. This time, the German checked left and then right, still unchallenged, before crossing towards the far post. Closing in from the right flank, Rep rose above Gianpietro Marchetti and looped a header over Dino Zoff into the far corner of the net. The Italian plan to sit deep and defend, looking for a break that one of their talented strikers could exploit in pursuit of a single-goal win, was in tatters. In contrast, Rep's emotions were entirely different. Understandably, despite the way the game played out, the young Dutch forward has very fond memories of that Belgrade evening. 'Juventus was a top match for me,' he explained. 'I scored the only goal to win the game.'

Early goals can often serve as the fuse that ignites a game, as the team conceding is compelled to attack. That wouldn't be the case this time though. Juventus continued to sit back and allow Ajax to stroke the ball around unhurried and unhindered. Later Rep would express surprise at the Italian club's reaction to falling behind, suggesting that it felt like they were more afraid about conceding another goal than encouraged to press for an equaliser. 'Juventus were so frightened,' he recalled. 'We were surprised. A good team but they did nothing. They seemed satisfied to lose 1-0. We were waiting for them. Come! But nothing. For the public, I'm afraid, it was a very bad game.'[89] As Rep suggested, Ajax patiently awaited the change in tactics that would open up the game – like some prize-fighter standing in the centre of the ring while his adversary remains seated on his stool – but it never came.

---

89 https://www.theguardian.com/football/2001/apr/10/sport.comment1

Were the Juventus tactics governed by a fear of Ajax's goal threat as Rep suggested? Massimiliano Graziani considered that any fear, and desire for caution, felt by the Juventus players may well have had a different driver: 'Juventus was paying for the fact of playing the first great European final in its history. The celebrated Ajax had nothing to prove while Juve, I imagine, lived in a diametrically opposite state of mind.

'I have no doubts in believing that Juventus were scared, but I think it has nothing to do with defensiveness. For Juventus it was the first European Cup Final and faced with an opponent who was preceded by his fame. Ajax was the "wonder", talked about all over the world (and still talked about today!). They were the reigning champion team, winning two years in a row. I think there was a personality gap: the overflowing one of the Dutch, and the one still to be affirmed at the international level of the Italian team.'

As a comparison, and to illustrate the point, Graziani recalled the situation that the Ajax players had found themselves in when they lost their first European Cup Final to AC Milan, back in 1969. 'After all,' he added, 'speaking of personality – even the Ajax of the young Cruyff, four years earlier, had conceded four goals in the final against the Milan team of Ballon d'Or winner Gianni Rivera.' It's an entirely valid point of view.

Whatever the cause, however, the result was unaltered. Ajax dominated possession and Juventus largely allowed them to do so, providing they didn't threaten to add to the lead. It meant that, for large parts of the game, there was almost a non-aggression pact in place, albeit unspoken and unconfirmed. Ajax still created chances. A Cruyff shimmy and shuffle penetrated the first line of the Juventus defence before playing the ball wide to an overlapping Suurbier.

The full-back's powerful cross shot was on target but Zoff smothered comfortably.

For all their caution, Juventus did enjoy rare moments of opportunity. An error by Keizer in midfield gave the ball to Anastasi, who quickly fed it on to Altafini sprinting towards the Ajax box with the ball at his feet. Fortunately for Ajax, the pace of Haan allowed him to catch the forward just as he was about to unleash his shot, and slide in to tackle. The ball ran tamely through for Stuy to collect.

It was a rare moment of hope for the Italians and, minutes later, Haan was in the other half of the pitch, probing for another opening. Striding forward, he rolled the ball right towards Suurbier, once again supporting the attack. Moving forward unchallenged until he reached the edge of the penalty area, the defender clipped a delicate ball towards the penalty spot. Rising above Francesco Morini, Gerrie Mühren first headed it into the air then, as it dropped, acrobatically flicked a left-footed shot towards goal, but it cleared the crossbar with Zoff in close attendance.

Still inside the first 45 minutes, Cruyff advanced from the left into the middle of the Juventus half, walking, then almost stopping, as he surveyed the options before him. No opposition player sought to close down the danger. Cruyff carried the ball deeper, towards Morini, then swerved past him before hitting in a shot that flew wide of the far post. The time and space allowed to the skipper looked to be bordering on the negligent. In their anxiety to maintain a disciplined deep defensive line, Juventus were inviting such thrusts.

Next it was Krol walking forward with the ball towards the Juventus area. The pace of the play had slowed even further by this time. Maybe it was the unaccustomed heat of the late-May Belgrade evening as described by Krol and confirmed by Green; perhaps it was Juventus's reluctance to engage in the game with any real measure of aggression; perhaps a combination of both, but at times players, even when in possession, were often standing still. Eventually Krol played the ball inside to Haan, deep in the Juventus half but in copious amounts of space. The midfielder advanced for a few yards before any hint of a challenge suggested it was time to chance his arm. His drive flew over the bar.

Heading towards the break, Hulshoff lofted a free kick forward from the halfway line. On the edge of the penalty area, the unforgivably unmarked Mühren jumped but, fortunately for the Italians, the ball cleared his head. On it went, bouncing in the penalty area as first Morini with his head, then Marchetti with his foot, ineffectively attempted to clear, but only hoisted the ball into the air. As it dropped, Cruyff wriggled clear of Marchetti just metres from goal but at an angle. Feigning to shoot, he drew Zoff towards the near post before firing across goal instead. Closing in, Mühren met up with the ball on the six-yard line as skipper Sandro Salvadore failed to intercept. A goal looked inevitable but the ball was too low to head and too high to connect with his foot. Caught between two incompatible stools, Mühren tried to almost chest it home but was unable to control the contact effectively due to the pace on the ball, and it bounced wide.

By half-time it hardly been a game of high excitement. In *The Times* of the following day, Geoffrey Green reported that Ajax had played in a 'whirl, a kind of magic roundabout'.[90] Perhaps so, but it takes two to tango, and for so long in the first half Juventus had declined their invitation to respond to Ajax's mood music, mostly sitting back and merely observing, akin to wallflowers at the village hall dance. They wanted

---

90 'Dutch strolling-layers add touch of sovereignty to their third cup', *The Times*, 31 May 1973.

to join the game but caution got the better of them, stifling their ambition. In the headline to Green's article, Ajax were described as 'strolling players'. It was apposite to both the pace of the action and Ajax's comfortable domination of their opponents.

The second period began with a Mühren effort on goal that flew over Zoff's crossbar. In the minutes that followed Juventus would attack more; they had little other option but to do so. Assured of their superiority, however, Ajax largely played within themselves and, as Green's report poetically suggested, they 'began to strike attitudes that were more or less gracefully passive'. Perhaps less than 'graceful', there was a strange moment just as Zoff sought to restart the game following Mühren's errant shot. As was very much his wont, Hulshoff's socks were round his ankles, and home referee Milivoje Gugulović insisted that he resolve the situation. Shrugging resignedly, the towering defender did so. It may have been better for the game and the entertainment of fans watching in the stadium or on television had the advice to 'pull your socks up' been delivered to the Juventus players instead. An upgrade in their first-half performance level was clearly required.

It may have been caused by an injection of urgency by Vycpálek during the half-time break, but there was a discernible change in the Italian attitude in the early minutes after the restart. If Vycpálek was seeking to brew up a storm of more attacking play from his team, however, there would be clouds of activity, but precious little resultant precipitation to rain on Ajax's serenely confident parade. They continued to control the game with a comfortable ease, while not overextending themselves, and with Stuy rarely troubled. Just past the hour mark Vycpálek looked to sharpen the cutting edge of his team, removing the largely ineffective Bettega and replacing him with the German forward Helmut Haller. Time was now drifting away from *I Bianconeri* and they had still hardly registered any kind of meaningful threat on the Ajax goal. The same was largely true at the other end as well but, with Ajax in full control and comfortably containing Juventus's attacks, that was of little concern to them.

Approaching the final 20 minutes, Italian frustration began to show as the realisation that they were being comprehensively outplayed nagged persistently at their composure. Giuseppe Furino was booked for a thigh-high lunge at Cruyff as he skipped past his opponent for the umpteenth time. There had been no attempt to disguise the offence as anything other than merely halting the captain's progress with little regard for the location of the ball. Cruyff climbed to his feet, shaking his head in condemnation, but it was easy to understand the frustration driving Furino's assault. It was becoming increasingly clear that Juventus's labours were fated to be in vain.

Frustration led to physical and emotional fatigue and, in turn, to lapses of concentration as gaps began to appear in the Juventus defence. An incisive pass had Rep behind the Italian back line but his cross just eluded the diving Mühren. As Juventus tried to clear, the same player's challenge diverted the ball to Haan. Exploiting the space created by the turnover, he galloped forward from midfield to the edge of the area before driving in a shot that Zoff parried but failed to collect. Following in, Rep was closely shadowed by a recovering Silvio Longobucco. The Italian should have got to the ball first but Rep's resolve was stronger. Jabbing out a foot, he lifted the ball over Zoff as the goalkeeper recovered his position and flung up an arm in a desperate attempt to block the shot. The ball evaded him but slipped wide of the far post as well. Rep slapped his hands together in disappointment but, with

Juventus being kept at arm's length from Stuy's goal by the domination Ajax enjoyed, it mattered little.

With a dozen minutes remaining, Vycpálek played his final card with Cuccureddu replacing Franco Causio, and a minute later a corner from Haller was headed over by Altafini. Stuy watched with untroubled disinterest as the ball sailed metres high over his head. Tellingly, it was probably the closest Juventus had come to any meaningful effort on his goal since the break. Two minutes later, a shot from distance by Marchetti was closer, but still off-target.

Although the Italian need was far greater as the game headed towards full time, it was Ajax looking more likely to score. Despite their *totaalvoetbal* often being played at half pace, interchanging of positions and confident control of the ball throughout the team was still evident. Inside the final ten minutes Suurbier advanced and played a wall pass with Hulshoff on the edge of the Juventus box before having his shot blocked. Then, after exchanging passes with Cruyff from a corner on the left, Keizer lofted the ball into the penalty area to meet up with a charging run by the *libero*. Towering over Zoff's attempt to punch clear, Hulshoff's header looked destined for the net but bounced on top of the crossbar and then behind for a goal kick. Minutes later, referee Gugulović called for the ball to be rolled to him as Juventus prepared to take a free kick. He picked it up, cradled it under his arm and blew the whistle to end the uneven contest. Ajax had their third successive European Cup.

The game itself has been dissected on numerous occasions since, provoking a wide range of opinions. In many ways it lacked the dash and daring of their previous two final triumphs, and yet was probably the most comprehensive victory of them all. Writing in *The Times* three days later, Geoffrey Green reflected on the events of that Belgrade evening, opening with, 'Seldom have I experienced such a wide gulf of varied opinion about a match as Wednesday's European Cup Final.'[91] The venerable scribe was bang on the money. Later, he concluded in the article that there was far more to football than the fare served by the physical thud and blunder of English game at the time, explaining that Ajax had 'learnt to play with their brains as well as their feet' and that even when giving the impression of playing at a walking pace, 'the ball itself is nearly always moving at speed and they could have scored another three of four goals with greater urgency on that night'. It's interesting to ponder for a moment as to how differently the final would have been perceived if Ajax had played no differently, but won by the three or four goals that Green suggested was well within their compass.

Twelve months or so later, another Dutch team, in another major final, also scored an early goal but, instead of adapting their play to the conditions, opponents and requirement of victory, they opted for unabashed arrogant flair and self-indulgence. The watching world was enthralled and so many fell in love that team, but the result went against them. The game ended in defeat as West Germany recovered from being a goal down to lift the World Cup and doomed the *Oranje* to being probably the best team never to have won the World Cup; certainly the most admired.

In their final Ajax had 'got the job done'. They adapted their tactics to combat both the way that their opponents played and the unfamiliar and uncomfortable heat of the evening. The game was managed so well that, despite the energy-sapping conditions, the same 11 players who started in red also finished it. It may have tempered the entertainment

---

91 'European champions play with brains as well as feet', *The Times*, 1 June 1973.

value of the final, but the superiority of Kovács's team is surely not something that should be placed in Ajax's demerit column. How superior were they? Ronald Jager recalled a quote from Bobby Haarms in 1996: 'Haan asked me during the final against Juventus how many more minutes there was to play. I thought three minutes so I was putting three fingers in the air, including my little finger. Haan then said, "Two and a half minutes?" It was 1-0, the final, and they were making jokes.'

Green wrote in his article, 'The Dutch, in particular, were most critical of Ajax's performance in victory.' It's an assertion supported by the reaction of Sonny Silooy when asked by the author for his take on the game. He pulled no punches: 'The final in Belgrade was the "shit game". Perhaps Juventus were scared because, at that time, no other team could beat Ajax, perhaps only Feyenoord.' It's pertinent to note that, given the exuberance of the other two finals, and the lofty standards that Ajax had set across the previous seasons, even a comfortable win in the European Cup Final can be perceived as worthy of such a comment. It is therefore an understandable comparison, but there's always room for mitigation. In June 2020, Sjaak Swart was speaking to the Greek gazzetta.gr website when he explained how Ajax had needed to compromise their gameplan for the final. He hadn't played, but remembered the complexities of the match: 'In 1973 with Juventus it was more difficult because they were playing *catenaccio*.'

Whatever the individual view of the final, however, the result not only meant Ajax had become the first club since Real Madrid to win, and then twice successfully defend, the European Cup, they had also beaten the champions of Serie A, the home of *catenaccio*, in successive finals.

Author David Winner doubted whether, despite these consecutive wins, and even the ease of the victory in 1973, it would be valid to argue that *totaalvoetbal* had destroyed *catenaccio*. Again, it's an issue with any number of opinions and, of course, no definitive answer. Ruud Krol, for example, perhaps understandably, would disagree with Winner. When canvassed by the author for his thoughts, his reply suggests that Ajax had been set on a pilgrimage of sorts, inspired by Michels: 'When Michels started, he wanted to knock down the *catenaccio* of Italy. That was our strength and we believed in that. So much training, so many hours to arrive at what was our goal to do that, and that was, of course, fantastic. I think it's true that *totaalvoetbal* destroyed *catenaccio*. It was very difficult to play against Italy and Italian teams in that time. But it is true that we destroyed that. We put another system on the field, another way to play and enjoy football on the field and everybody was talking about Ajax in the years of the '70s. We had fantastic players, of course, and coaching in our team, including, of course, Johan. We reached our goal.'

It's perhaps grist to Krol's mill that Italian clubs had won four of the previous seven European Cups before Feyenoord lifted the trophy in 1970, including when Milan beat Ajax in 1969, before Ajax went on to their three titles. Following 1973, no Italian club won it again until Juventus in 1985. Just like a coin, however, there are two sides to most issues, and Massimiliano Graziani has a different take: 'I believe that *totaalvoetbal* in those years got the better of all European football, not just Italian football. And the main merit, in my opinion, is the great players that Ajax could field regardless of the way they played. The fact remains that Dutch football was a sort of "68 of football", a way of playing that went beyond the codified roles, expression of a revolutionary philosophy with respect to everything that existed before, but also to what will come after. The great Bayern, who [would] take the place of Ajax in Europe, for example, [would] play attack but often defending [with] a man with very specific roles and tasks, thus combining innovation and tradition. And also, the new figure of the *libero*, who instead of covering behind the defenders, as in the best tradition of the *catenaccio*, leaves the penalty area ball and chain to become a deep playmaker is an idea that was born and is modelled on universal and unrepeatable qualities of Franz Beckenbauer.

'I am convinced that at the highest level players are more important than coaches and that tactical ideas, whatever they may be, need talented interpreters to become successful. Even the defensiveness of Herrera's great Inter (the maximum expression of the so-called *catenaccio*) was exalted on the counter-attack thanks to the technical qualities of the various Corso, Mazzola, Jair and Suárez. And on the absence of Italian teams at the top of Europe, which lasted until the mid-1980s, I think the football autarchy decided by the [Italian] federation also influenced [things], which for 14 years (from 1966 to 1980) closed the borders preventing the big clubs from registering the best foreign players.'

Graziani makes several valid points about how the decline in European Cup fortunes of Italian clubs after 1973 can be explained. All are valid to a greater or lesser extent. His comments about how Ajax developed a way of playing are perhaps the key point. Whether *totaalvoetbal* destroyed *catenaccio* or not isn't the point. Ajax's *totaalvoetbal* overcame all systems played in Europe and beyond, not just the one favoured in Serie A, no matter how attractive a simple 'white hat v black hat' argument may appear. Celebrating *totaalvoetbal* is far more important than considering its ability to have seen off *catenaccio*.

There's one point where both Krol and Graziani are locked in step. As, or perhaps, even more important than the development of the *totaalvoetbal* philosophy was the availability of an outstandingly talented group of players who could appreciate its requirements and deliver on them. At the forefront was Cruyff himself, the conductor of the orchestra, but there are others worthy of mention. Canvassed by the author, Menno Pot offered his thoughts: 'If you'd do a nationwide (or international) survey on the streets I would expect most people to name Cruyff first and Neeskens second. The two Johans, who played for Barcelona together. But if you'd do your survey in Amsterdam alone the most fondly remembered player would be Piet Keizer, for sure. As a matter of fact, many older Amsterdammers will say Johan was the best, but Piet was even better. Keizer was a few years older than Cruyff. He was like an older brother to Johan. Later on, they became best mates – and then "enemies". Piet Keizer [was] an intellectual type, too. He had a certain darkness in his eyes. He didn't say much, almost never spoke to the press, but he is also known as the only one who could tell Johan to shut up, or to tell him he was wrong. They were not on speaking terms for decades, but they loved each other in the end.

'Another very popular guy: Sjaak Swart, "Mister Ajax", who played more games for Ajax than anyone else. Sjaak was an old hand, almost ten years older than the Cruyff generation, but he's still alive and kicking (literally: he still plays football for the Lucky Ajax veterans' team) and looking sharp. Another one I always loved (perhaps the nicest man of the lot) was Barry Hulshoff, if only because of his taste in music. Everyone else in the team liked slick middle-of-the-road music, particularly a Dutch vocal group called The Cats. Barry was a rocker. He was into Led Zeppelin, Deep Purple and Golden Earring of course, Dutch rock legends of the era.'

The image of the bearded Hulshoff, the 'Viking', once described to the author by Jan-Herman de Bruijn as a 'rocker', is an easy one to appreciate, especially with his rebellious reputation, and yet he and the others in the team produced delightfully harmonious music. Pot's mention of Keizer as perhaps the second most important player after Cruyff is not unusual. Auke Kok also flagged up the winger's importance, among others, advocating, 'The genius of Keizer, the quickness and toughness of Krol and Suurbier, the dynamics of Neeskens, Mühren and Haan.'

That 'genius' was also lauded as an inspiration to his own style of playing by Pierre Vermeulen: 'Where a lot of my friends had Cruyff as their idol, I was more of a Piet Keizer guy. He played [in] the position I played in the youth of Roda JC so I always watched him closely whenever Ajax played. His scissor movement (we call it in Dutch *de schaarbeweging*) was something I imitated every day at training sessions until I mastered it and could use it in the matches I played. Keizer's way of playing was a great inspiration for me. Although my version of this movement would be eventually slightly different. Keizer played [standing] straight up, and [my stance was] lower in the movement, not standing up straight, in order to get a bit more pace in the movement to get by the defender. But Keizer was my idol, a phenomenon.'

To mention some but ignore others may be perceived by some as almost a criticism by exemption. That would be folly, however, as Pot, Kok and Vermeulen would surely agree. Stuy and Blankenburg were of course key elements in Ajax's success, and many would sing their praises – much as Pot did about the goalkeeper in previous pages. Vasović especially should also be acknowledged. The likes of Rijnders and Van Dijk were major players in the success of the side, plus others such Schilcher are worthy of mention, who often deputised, but seldom diminished the whole.

The European Cup Final had rounded out the long list of Ajax's official fixtures, but there was still one more game to play, and on 3 June, Kovács led his team for the final time in a friendly away to Willem II. The club that had finished a lowly 14th in the second-tier Eerste Divisie would entertain the three-times European champions on their compact Gemeentelijk Sportpark in Tilburg. Apart from Neeskens and Keizer, both of whom had received knocks against Juventus, as was his wont on so many occasions when others would have counselled against it, Kovács sent out his first team and Ajax cantered to a 7-2 win. Cruyff scored two of them. No one knew it at the time, of course, but he would play just two more Eredivisie games in Ajax's colours.

In an interesting aside, guesting for Willem II on that day was MVV player Willy Brokamp, who would score one of the home team's consolation goals in the final ten minutes. In August 1974 Ajax would bring the forward to the De Meer on a three-year contract. Reports suggested a huge fee was involved: 'Various newspapers, including *De Telegraaf* of 31 August 1974, report an amount of around 1m guilders. Later in *De Telegraaf* of 14 September 1976, an amount of 1.2m guilders is mentioned.'[92] Brokamp would return to the Maastricht club just two years later. His value had now substantially diminished if newspaper reports of the day were accurate. The same article explained, 'In that same *De Telefgraaf* of 14 September 1976, a sale amount of about 300,000 guilders is mentioned.'

Ajax's season ended with the Eredivisie title secured, their third successive European Cup confirmed and their status as one of the greatest clubs in European football history assured. *Totaalvoetbal* had taken them to the very summit of the world game. Now, however, for the second time in just a couple

---

92 https://www.afc-ajax.info/en/soccer-player/Willy-Brokamp#game_
    details (Translated)

of years, they would lose the coach who had taken them to European glory. Many would argue that so much of the success had been down Michels and what he had created before his departure to Barcelona. As Menno Pot suggests, such a stance cruelly diminishes the role of Kovács to almost that of a mere caretaker. 'People generally regard Ajax's Golden Years as Rinus Michels' accomplishment,' he told the author. 'And almost completely omit Kovács from the story, as if he just took over and picked up a couple of European Cups that Michels deserved the credit for. It can't be that simple, of course.'

Kovács was different to Michels in so many ways, not least his less authoritarian manner. Whereas the former coach was a strict disciplinarian with his players, valuing their respect above their affection, the Romanian took a softer approach, gifting greater freedom both on and off the pitch. In the case of the latter, to some it was like removing the brakes from a car, and delighting in its ability to thrill as it careered along, mowing down all of the opposition in its path before eventually, and inevitably, crashing and burning.

The full extent of Kovács's contribution to Dutch football wasn't lost in that resulting conflagration. Steven Scragg suggested, 'There is an argument to be made that the [*totaalvoetbal*] that was displayed by the Netherlands at the 1974 World Cup might not have been what it was had Kovács not let the Ajax contingent loose between 1971 and 1973.'[93] If there's merit in Scragg's suggestion, and there's an inescapable logic to it, it offers up the irony that not only did Kovács profit from the bequest of Michels when the latter moved to Barcelona in 1971, but the favour was paid back three years later, when Michels inherited the Kovács-modified Ajax contingent for his World Cup campaign.

---

93 Scragg, Steven, *These Football Times*, 'Ajax' magazine.

In a retrospective of Kovács in *The Guardian* during early January 2008, Jonathan Wilson posited an astute quote: "'Kovács was a good coach," the midfielder Gerrie Mühren told David Winner in *Brilliant Orange*, "but he was too nice. Michels was more professional. He was very strict, with everyone on the same level. In the first year with Kovács we played even better because we were good players who had been given freedom. But after that the discipline went and it was all over. We didn't have the same spirit.'"

Being a player who came through under Michels, Mühren's view is understandable. Conversely, so too is the opinion offered by Rep, whose best times in the Ajax team coincided with the Romanian's tenure as coach. As he commented to the author, 'Kovács was a nice coach, I had fun with him.' The same was not probably true of players' relationships with Michels.

Taking his lead from Mühren's view and others that he references, Wilson concludes that, in the final analysis, Kovács's easier manner with his players may have ultimately doomed the club, despite the success he had; a price to pay for the grace bestowed by the gods of football: 'He was not, though, tough enough. Where a ruthlessness lay beneath [Bob] Paisley's shabby cardigan [as Liverpool manager], it seems probable that Kovács was too nice, lacking the steel to rein in Cruyff as he took on an increasing prominence in that second season … By giving that squad the freedom to reach its peak … Kovács also paved the way for its destruction.'[94]

Was Kovács really the ideal man to take up the baton left by Michels when he left, the man to allow the full flowering of the seeds planted by Michels, and worthy of praise for his

---

94 https://www.theguardian.com/football/2008/jan/08/europeanfootball.
ajax

success and that of Ajax as they continued their domination of European club football, as suggested by Menno Pot? Or was he merely someone who did little more than stand back with a watching brief as his charges ran free, eventually to their doom? Fifty years later the answer is still less than clear, but as with most such conundrums, reality may well lie mainly in the middle, distant from both extremes.

Whatever enlightened perspective half a century of reflection can offer now, at the time Ajax's reign as the kings of European football appeared safe. The coach had left and the new man selected to replace him, MVV's George Knobel, was relatively unknown. That had been the case with both Michels and Kovács, however. Most players in the squad were still at their peak, or as yet to reach it. Of the players who had triumphed in Belgrade, Stuy was 28, and of his back line Suurbier was the senior figure, but still only 28 too. Hulshoff was 26, Blankenburg 25, and Krol the youngster at 24. In midfield only Mühren was past his mid-20s, having celebrated his 27th birthday on 2 February 1973, while Haan was 24, and Neeskens only 22. In the forward line, Keizer was the most experienced of the trio, and the 'old man' of the team, but wouldn't be reaching 30 until 14 June 1973. Rep was very much the young tyro, still only 21. Cruyff, most importantly of all, was just 26 on 25 April 1973.

Ajax possessed a young team, full of stars who were case-hardened in winning the continent's – and indeed the world's – most prestigious prizes, expertly committed to playing to a system that had proved itself superior to all around it. The future looked to be dazzlingly bright. What could possibly go wrong? As things transpired, the answer was almost everything. From high atop the mountain, the only way is down.

Part 6: Departures, decisions and laments

BEFORE THE new season got under way, there would be several departures and arrivals. Among the leavers alongside Sjaak Swart, who announced his retirement at the end of the 1972/73 season, was Louis van Gaal. His contribution to the Ajax cause had been that sole appearance in the friendly away to Anderlecht. Almost two decades later, his appointment as head coach would be far more noteworthy than his time spent on the pitch. Bran Braam also left, joining MVV, as the Maastricht club's manager moved in the opposite direction.

George Knobel took over the seat previously occupied by Rinus Michels and Ștefan Kovács on 1 July 1973. Given the success of his predecessors, Knobel had big shoes to fill. The upcoming season would suggest that his feet were far too small. At 50 years of age, he was of a similar vintage to Kovács when Ajax plucked him from the relative obscurity of eastern European football to assume control after Michels had decamped to Barcelona. Whereas the Romanian had won the Divizia A title and two national cups in his home country, Knobel's personal trophy cabinet was occupied mainly by undisturbed dust.

His MVV team had, of course, secured that 1-0 win over Ajax as Kovács's team eased towards the Eredivisie title in the latter days of the previous season, but his time with the Maastricht club could probably be described as mediocre at best. During 160 games in charge he had won 54 times, drawn 49 and lost 57. While his team had averaged 1.26 goals across that period, they had conceded 1.27 at the other end. It hardly looked like a compelling CV. Describing Knobel to the author, Jan-Herman de Bruijn was hardly gushing with praise: 'He was fairly OK as a coach, but not as a "big-city" coach. He was a failure with Ajax, for the same reasons he was a failure later on for the national team … He never had the personality to put his mark on the events.' Ruud Krol would concur: 'Knobel was not really an Ajax trainer. In the beginning it was OK, but after it was not good. He was not a man with our mentality. He was from the south and we were mostly from Amsterdam. Amsterdam people are different to those from the south. He was not a big success. No.' That perceived inability to handle players with large abilities, personalities and even larger egos, quickly revealed itself.

At the end of the first day of pre-season work at the De Lutte training camp, Knobel opened his mouth and planted his foot squarely into it. Across the last three seasons Ajax had played under three different captains as they dominated Europe. For 1970/71 season, under Michels it had been Velibor Vasović. Then Piet Keizer assumed the captaincy for the following season. Finally, it was Johan Cruyff in Kovács's last term in charge. It had become traditional for the players to hold a ballot to decide between nominated candidates at the beginning of each season to elect the captain for the coming term. After being apparently informed by Bobby Haarms of the custom, Knobel decided to raise the issue on the very first day of his tenure.

In one respect, what he did was hardly wrong, and yet, given the nature of the incumbent skipper, it may well have been naive in the extreme, offering himself up as a hostage to fortune should Cruyff not be re-elected. The move may have been in keeping with custom, but Cruyff was hardly accustomed to being treated the same as anyone else, very much the first among equals. Knobel was surely not ignorant of that fact and, if he was, he shouldn't have been. The potential consequences if things didn't play out well for the club's iconic star were obvious. A more cautious approach may well have been to canvass opinions first and judge how best to deal with the issue without leaving himself open to perceptions of ill-judged actions.

Unsurprisingly, Cruyff had merely assumed that he would have been granted an extension to his role without recourse to the sorts of trivial matters that mere mortals are compelled to subject themselves to, and had even suggested to some players that he merely continue in the role. Knobel's declaration of the election, however, scuppered that. Even then, Cruyff may well have felt his position was secure. No one would surely stand against him – and yet they did. Cruyff was both angry and disappointed that some of his team-mates had nominated Keizer for the election. He felt slighted and unappreciated.

A forensic investigation into the original sources that led to Ajax's decline from their mastery of European football may well lead to this very moment in their history. Ronald Jager believes that the election may have been just a cover for something that was already decided, but it offered both a convenient justification for his actions, and perhaps also revealed how the club's hierarchy were ill at ease with the player's influence. Jager explains, 'I think Cruyff would have left, even if he was … the captain again, but he was furious about the decision.' In a *Voetbal International Special* in January 1989 called 'De Veertigers, een Gouden Generatie Topcoaches' ('The Forties, a Golden Generation of Top

Coaches'), Arie Haan said the board of directors at Ajax were asking the young players to vote for Keizer, because Cruyff and his father-in-law Cor Coster became difficult. 'As a young player I listened to that advice. It was very stupid of me to do so.'

If true, it's open to conjecture as to what the directors were trying to achieve by encouraging players to vote for Keizer. If they had merely been seeking to give Cruyff a 'bloody nose', take the captaincy from him, and put him in his place, they had massively overplayed their hand. If, on the other side of the coin, it was a genuine attempt to drive him out of the club, such crass folly would achieve its aim. The influence of the directors may not have been the sole reason that some of the players voted for Keizer though. Johnny Rep considered that Cruyff's dominance at the club had caused bitterness with some team-mates, especially among the younger ones, and he often blamed anyone but himself when things went wrong. Even a misplaced Cruyff pass was always the receiving player's fault for not anticipating it and being in the correct position. The thin line between insistently pushing for perfection and adopting a dictatorial attitude can often blur into obscurity. For Rep, Cruyff's rejection as captain may well have been a symptom of that line being invisible.

After the votes were tallied, Keizer had won, and would assume the captaincy once more. For Cruyff it delivered a crippling blow to his relationship with Ajax in general and his team-mates in particular. He perceived the result as a betrayal, and said he 'suffered the kind of injury you can't see with the naked eye. The blow was particularly severe because we weren't just fellow players but also close friends.'[95] Cruyff also felt that players who thought as Rep

---

95 Cruyff, Johan, *My Turn* (London: Macmillan, 2016).

did had misjudged him, suggesting that Kovács's *laissez-faire* approach required him to be the man to tell the hard truths when it was needed.

When asked for his opinion, Sonny Silooy had great sympathy for Cruyff: 'Cruyff was playing chess on the field, and not everyone can play chess. He thinks two steps ahead and if you're not thinking two steps ahead also it is not good. And not everyone can think two steps ahead. It is not easy. Some players understand him very quickly, with others it takes time. When you have Cruyff in your team you're never going to lose. Sometimes, he may have a bad day, but usually, if you have Cruyff, you're never going to lose. When he came back to Ajax, we won the league, then Ajax said goodbye to him. He goes to Feyenoord. We beat Feyenoord 8-2 early in the season in Amsterdam. But they have Cruyff, and they win the league.'

Clearly, in such matters, the more worthy argument is often defined by which side of the fence you're sitting on. What wasn't up for debate, however, was that there was a fence, and it was too high to climb over, or at least it deterred some from trying. Cruyff later related that, upon hearing the result of the ballot, he went straight to his room and called Cor Coster, his father-in-law and agent. His time with Ajax was done. Coster needed to find him another club.

Cruyff wasn't the only player to feel less than pleased with the new coach. Perhaps it was to try and establish some kind of authority, or maybe even to prepare the ground should his tenure not go well, but Knobel also suggested that there were serious problems at the club in terms of discipline off the field. In an interview, he criticised the players' behaviour with regard to drinking and womanising, suggesting that relegation may well be on the cards if things didn't improve. It was hardly likely to be the soothing balm needed, and caused resentment with some players, Haan in particular.

The young midfielder openly expressed his anger to the coach regarding the accusation, and some reports suggest that he was influential in Knobel eventually being sacked the following year. The coach clearly thought it to be true. At the end of the season, Haan played every minute of every game in the 1974 World Cup under Michels. When Knobel was extraordinarily later appointed to take over as coach of the *Oranje*, he excluded Haan from every squad he selected. Such discord hardly suggested a positive outcome for the season.

After a run of their usual pre-season friendlies, Ajax's Eredivisie title defence began on 12 August with a visit to FC Groningen. The team selected by Knobel was the same 11 that had defeated Juventus back in May, with one notable exception. On 4 August, Spartak Trnava visited the De Meer for a friendly. Knobel had selected the same starting 11 from the game in Belgrade, with the clear intention of this being his preferred line-up for when the more serious games came along,

Things looked to be going well for Ajax up until the hour. Rep, Barry Hulshoff and Johan Neeskens had each scored to put Ajax comfortably ahead, but an injury to Heinz Stuy seriously incapacitated the goalkeeper. Without the option of a back-up on the bench, Stuy soldiered on but was clearly severely hampered and the Czechoslovakians scored five times in the final 25 minutes to steal the game. It would be the final time that the team who had won the European Cup would ever play together. Stuy's injury would keep him out of action until mid-September, with Seis Wever deputising. By the time he returned, Cruyff was in Catalonia.

Even without their regular custodian behind the defence, their opening Eredivisie fixture appeared to offer Ajax a comfortable way to ease themselves into the domestic programme. FC Groningen would end the season relegated after winning just seven league games. It was the three-time champions of Europe against the team that would finish at the foot of the table. At the break, however, the scoreline remained goalless. It was an omen of ill tidings that would follow across the season.

Knobel removed Horst Blankenburg ahead of the restart, and sent on Heinz Schilcher to replace the German defender, but with little immediate improvement. A full 65 minutes had been played before Ajax achieved the breakthrough. Ironically, it was two of the players who would long harbour ill feelings towards Knobel who combined to open the scoring, as Cruyff created the chance for Haan to strike. Three minutes later the lead was doubled, and the points were secured, when Cruyff added his name to the scoresheet. With the game surely won, Knobel then withdrew Neeskens to send on Arnold Mühren. Cruyff and Wim Suurbier added late goals to turn what had looked like a difficult problem at half-time into a comfortable win. It was far from a happy time for the club's fans though. With the deal to take Cruyff to Barcelona now in place, supporters at the De Meer would have one final chance to watch their star player perform for them. It would happen the following weekend when FC Amsterdam made the short journey across the city.

FC Amsterdam had only existed for 15 months or so, having been formed on 20 June 1972 when the junior Amsterdam clubs of Blauw Wit and DWS merged, taking up residence at the Olympisch Stadion, home to some of Ajax's most celebrated victories of recent years. They would enjoy brief success, finishing a creditable fifth in the Eredivisie in 1973/74 and reaching the quarter-finals of the UEFA Cup the following term after progressing past Internazionale. Their days in the sun were soon to be curtailed, though, as the clouds of decline and relegation to the Eerste Divisie followed in 1977/78. With diminished crowds and declining fortunes on the pitch, the club were unable to justify tenancy at their 64,000-capacity home and left the Olympisch Stadion in 1980. Two years later, they were disbanded.

As with so many things that would happen to clubs based in the Dutch capital across the next few years, that future was unforeseen, and FC Amsterdam arrived at the De Meer in a confident mood having defeated PSV in their opening Eredivisie fixture. With Ajax set for what was, at various times, either a wake for Cruyff's departure or a celebration of his genius in the white shirt with the broad red stripe, the visitors would be bit-part players in a theatre where the Catalonia-bound superstar demanded centre stage for his swansong.

Just a minute after half-time, the show was proceeding in line with Cruyff's script as Ajax led 4-1. He had created goals for Mühren, Krol and Neeskens, and a penalty from Mühren completed the quadruple. A spot-kick from former Ajax youth player Theo Husers for the visitors was akin to annoying heckling from those who should only have been there to quietly watch and admire. It was, however, but a brief diversion from the plot that Cruyff had written. That storyline demanded a goal from the man himself but, when the fifth strike came along it was Suurbier delivering.

At the end of all epic tales, though, the hero is destined to perish in the flames of his own glory, and Cruyff knew how to deliver a line. With 20 minutes to play he received a pass and galloped clear into the FC Amsterdam half, towards goal. Opposing him was Jan Jongbloed who, 12 months later, against all expectations, and some would argue logic, was plucked from the obscurity of a single cap, earned a dozen years previously when he conceded a goal in a five-minute cameo appearance for the *Oranje*, to be the first-choice goalkeeper as the Dutch came oh so close to winning the 1974 World Cup. Having already fished the ball out of the back of the net on five occasions earlier in the game, Jongbloed was hardly the perfect candidate to forget his preordained role in Cruyff's theatre. As he advanced to close down the forward, Cruyff calmly rolled the ball between his legs and into the net. He was no fat lady but his song had now been sung. The party was over. Before the game restarted, both Cruyff and Hulshoff trotted from the pitch to be replaced by Arnold Mühren and Schilcher. To the standing acclamation of the De Meer, Johan Cruyff exited stage left.

As the old theatre maxim goes, you should always leave the audience thirsting for more. That thirst would last for seven long years before Cruyff would wear the Ajax shirt again. The future of the team that had looked so bright just a few short months earlier was now cast even further into doubt by his departure. Reports suggested that Ajax would receive a world-record fee of some 6m guilders – equivalent to approximately £1.34m at today's rates) in exchange for Cruyff. To many Ajax fans, the feeling was akin to having your house burgled, your prize possessions stolen away, and having to claim on an insurance policy that never truly replaces what has been lost, never mind the emotional pain. Despite the deal being agreed in August, the transfer window in Spain had already closed. It meant Cruyff couldn't play any official games for his new club until 1 December. As with the fee received, that was of little compensation to those at the De Meer who now had to contemplate the future of their club without their talismanic leader.

From this point, many pundits considered the decline of Ajax to be inevitable. Auke Kok dislikes the word: 'I don't believe in "inevitable". As I wrote in my biography [of Cruyff], way before the summer of 1973 the relations between Cruyff and the other players got worse. [He] was too big a star in other players' eyes, and the egos of the others became too large as well. They thought they could do it also without their leader. Which obviously wasn't the case.' It's significant that Kok's words have an echo with the thoughts of Cruyff after the European Cup Final when he spoke of 'cracks appearing' despite the triumph.

Ruud Krol was on the pitch, looking on, as Cruyff walked away and out of Ajax. Did he feel that he was also watching the end of an era for the club? 'The team of course was not any more on that level [after he left]. Johan had left and that was something of course that we missed. But we were of course also unlucky that Jan Mulder had his knee problems and that meant we were missing our central point [of attack]. But no one replaced Johan. He was not a typical number nine. He was everywhere, so we had no replacement for him. I think the board made a big mistake. They sold Johan for a lot of money, but they don't want to make an investment to get another good player. For example, we could have bought Heynckes maybe for one and a half million. It would not be the same, because Heynckes is not on the same level as Johan, but [we could] have stayed on high quality.'

While neither Kok nor Krol saw the departure of Cruyff as pre-defining the decline of Ajax, both believed that it left the club deeply damaged, especially because, as Krol suggests, despite the swelling of the bank balance no even vaguely suitable replacement was signed. Like an oversized tower built of Jenga pieces, with a key element wantonly removed, the Ajax edifice tottered and swayed as Cruyff left for Barcelona. Few fans were convinced that Knobel was the steadying hand required to keep things balanced, as the next few Eredivisie games illustrated. While Ajax avoided defeat, their performances looked as shaky as that tower.

The first Eredivisie game without Cruyff was away to NEC on 12 September. Ajax had scored ten goals in their first two league matches, conceding just one in reply. That form would quickly evaporate. Pointing up Krol's comment about the error of not signing a replacement for Cruyff, Knobel placed Gerrie Kleton in the forward line between Rep and Keizer. As curious decisions go, this seemed right up there. Kleton was no Cruyff, of course, but no one expected him to be. And yet the player Knobel selected in place of the totemic forward was making his first, and only, start in an Eredivisie game for Ajax. All his previous league appearances had been from the bench and he had never yet entered the scoresheet. Even stranger perhaps was the fact that, less than two weeks later, he would be transferred to MVV.

Unsurprisingly, Kleton's time on the pitch lasted for just over 60 minutes before he was replaced by Arnold Mühren. That hour had seen Ajax struggle and splutter as they battled to overcome the loss of Cruyff, despite being gifted the lead following an own goal by Kornelis with 28 minutes played. The first game without Cruyff was always going to be difficult but, entering the closing minutes, Ajax and Knobel, at least had the satisfaction of claiming that a hard-fought victory confirmed that the team's fighting spirit and morale was still intact. Even that was denied them when referee Charles Corver awarded the home team a penalty with time ticking away. Ad Mellaard beat Wever from 12 yards to equalise and gain NEC their first point of the season following defeats in their opening couple of matches. The draw dropped Ajax from top spot in the league as both Feyenoord and Utrecht recorded their third successive victories, but worse was to follow.

The following weekend brought FC Twente to the De Meer, with 26,000 fans needing to be convinced that losing Cruyff wasn't going to be the disaster they all feared it would be. Kleton was dispensed with, and Knobel took a leaf out of the books of Michels and Kovács, advancing Haan to the forward line, hoping that the versatile midfielder could provide some of the much-needed creativity that had been largely absent in Nijmegen six days earlier. Moving Haan up left a gap in the midfield but, instead of promoting Arnold Mühren from the bench to a starting berth, Knobel opted for the more cautious approach in selecting Schilcher instead. If, after conceding that late goal against NEC, Knobel was looking for more solidity and an increased ability to defend a lead, he would be disappointed.

Late in the game, Ajax again led by a single goal, this time scored by Rep on 33 minutes, but Knobel's plan to strengthen his team's ability to hold on to an advantage would unravel with 15 minutes to play when Theo Pahlplatz scored. Trying to pull a rabbit from the hat, Knobel chose to replace Neeskens with 19-year-old Pim van Dord, but to no avail. At the final whistle the full impact of Cruyff's departure and the sad realisation that, despite still being a team with outstanding players, Ajax were now a much-diminished force without him, settled like a dark cloud over supporters as they trooped slowly out of the stadium. The dream years of league titles, domestic cup triumphs and three seasons of being European champions suddenly felt a long way in the past.

Things had changed in Rotterdam too. Ernst Happel had left the De Kuip in the summer, moving to the south of Spain to take charge of Sevilla, with Feyenoord appointing the NEC coach Wiel Coerver in his place. Whereas Knobel had struggled in his new post in Amsterdam, albeit with the loss of Cruyff as a key factor, Coerver had Feyenoord purring along like a well-maintained engine. While Ajax were dropping points, Coerver's team were far less careless. Four successive wins had them top of the league and their latest victory, a 4-0 thumping of the previously unbeaten Utrecht, had actually allowed Ajax to rise into second place, but they still trailed by two points.

There was reason to hope for a quick improvement in Ajax's fortunes as their next league fixture would take them to Breda to face NAC. The early games of the season had been difficult for fans at the NAC Stadium. Three defeats and a draw had left them marooned at the foot of the table and, while Ajax were labouring to a point against FC Twente, PSV had plundered seven goals against Breda. It was a chance to get Ajax's season back on track. Knobel had been astute enough to leave well alone where possible in his team selection, with most of the players established as automatic choices under Kovács also starting under the new regime. That policy was enhanced against Breda with a now-fit Stuy returning to the team. Ahead of him were Suurbier, Hulshoff, Blankenburg and Krol. Schilcher was retained in his midfield role alongside Gerrie Mühren and Neeskens with Haan in the forward line alongside Rep and Keizer.

Both teams needed a win for widely varying reasons and, after an inconclusive first half an hour, fate smiled on Ajax when, for the second time in three games they were gifted the lead through an own goal. This one was conceded by Felix Muller, who was substituted moments later by home coach Henk Wullems in favour of Frans Bouwmeester. The change hardly helped matters for Breda, and two minutes later a Mühren header put Ajax two clear and surely on the road to a comfortable win. At the break, Knobel exchanged the Mühren brothers and Arnold took his older sibling's place in midfield as Ajax looked to lock out the game.

Despite the return of Stuy, however, there were still frailties in defence and, when Bertus Quaars pulled a goal back just past the hour, a victory that had looked so secure was suddenly cast into serious doubt. That doubt was given life just seven minutes later as Ajax conceded again, when Piet van Dijk netted the equaliser. Once more Knobel had watched his team take the lead only to see the opposition draw level, and this time they had done so after leading by two goals against the team rooted at the foot of the Eredivisie.

It's inviting to ponder the consequences had another win slipped through Ajax's fingers but, fortunately for Knobel, such thoughts were packed away for another day when Suurbier restored Ajax's lead with a dozen minutes to play. Two minutes later Van Dord was again sent on from the bench, replacing Rep. It was a win but it hardly felt that way. After two draws, the reigning European champions had struggled to victory by the odd goal in five against a team without a victory in the season to date, and that with a late goal, and sending on a defender to replace a forward to see out the result. To many, as Krol mentioned earlier, Knobel seemed to be a poor choice to replace Kovács, and the way the season was going only added fuel to that fire.

Ajax's next fixture was at the De Meer against table-topping Feyenoord. During this era, *Klassieker* games between Ajax and Feyenoord were often season-defining and, almost without exception, the very definition of 'four-point' games as swings between the two clubs were regularly measured by the finest of margins at the end of seasons. It wouldn't be the case this time, but it would serve to give much-needed breathing space to Knobel. Ajax's beleaguered coach decided on two changes as he sought to reignite the season. Blankenburg was absent after an injury, with Schilcher partnering Hulshoff at the heart of the defence. Haan dropped back into midfield and Arnold Mühren started alongside Rep and Keizer.

In most of the games where things had gone awry for Ajax so far in 1973/74, they had taken the lead, often in the early stages. This time it was Feyenoord who opened the scoring when Wery beat Stuy on 32 minutes. Coerver's team looked the more accomplished and for 20 minutes or so either side of the break they were fairly comfortable but, when Gerrie Mühren connected with a pass from Keizer, Ajax had the chance of a revival. For the first time Knobel eschewed making changes and was rewarded with just three minutes to play when, capitalising on work by Haan, Arnold Mühren completed the family double to snatch the winning goal. Suddenly the world looked a brighter place for Ajax fans as their team swept to the top of the table on goal difference. With victory over their main rivals secured, and sitting atop the Eredivisie, perhaps Knobel wasn't so bad after all. Optimism can be a fickle mistress though. On the last day of September, Ajax travelled to Alkmaar to play AZ '67, where another win would add weight to the theory that a corner had been turned. As it turned out, if a corner had indeed been turned, it only led to a dead end.

Retaining the same starting 11 that had beaten Feyenoord, Knobel was forced into a change with less than half an hour played when an injury to Schilcher brought Blankenburg – who had recovered sufficiently for a place on the bench – back into the defence. By this time though, Ajax were already trailing. An 11th-minute penalty by Kirsten Nygaard had put the home team ahead and punctured Ajax's balloon of confidence that had been inflated by the win over Feyenoord. Ajax would grab a second-half equaliser from Rep but, with seven games now played, the pattern of the season was set. A team that had consistently beaten the best that European football had to offer, playing out a complete league campaign with just a single defeat and picking up plenty of silverware in the process, were now dogged by inconsistency. Failing to win games against lesser opposition and then rallying to overcome feared rivals hardly suggested a successful domestic season, and so it transpired. Ajax were, however, European champions and retaining their title could still deliver an outstanding year. Piet Wildschut recalled thinking that this was the stage where Ajax were best measured, as he considered the condition of the team after Cruyff left: 'Of course, that had to do with the decline, but I still think Ajax [was] a powerhouse competing against teams from other countries.'

Including a high-profile friendly against Manchester United, Ajax now had four games to play before Wildschut's theory would be put to the test. In the first round of the 1973/74 European Cup they were drawn to face CSKA Sofia. Given they had comfortably triumphed against the Bulgarians in the previous season's competition, winning 3-1 in Sofia and 3-0 at home, it looked like a gentle reintroduction to continental competition. In this season, though, an ability to win in games that looked comfortable on paper had proved to be – with apologies to students of Greek mythology – Ajax's Achilles heel.

Rather than sending the reigning champions in pursuit of defending their crown against CSKA brimming with confidence, the three Eredivisie games played before entertaining the Bulgarians would merely underscore the inconsistency of their performances. A single-goal defeat to Manchester United at Old Trafford on 3 October was hardly calamitous and, when they returned to domestic action four days later, a 5-0 win over FC Haarlem at the De Meer was encouraging, as was the fit-again Jan Mulder who scored the second goal 44 minutes into his return to the starting 11, after Neeskens had netted earlier. Mulder's comeback saw Arnold Mühren take a place on the bench, but the roles were reversed after 63 minutes when the understandably tiring striker was given an early rest. Five minutes later, the newly arrived substitute capitalised on Krol's creativity to score the fourth goal. Gerrie Mühren kept the family honours in balance when he closed out the scoring with the fifth goal just a couple of minutes later.

The following week, Ajax visited Utrecht. After a strong start to the season the *Domstedelingen* had slipped down the league towards the sort of mid-table position they would end the term in, and had suffered a 5-0 beating at the hands of PSV the previous weekend. After scoring five times themselves in their previous game, Ajax would travel with confidence. Aside from Arnold Mühren replacing his elder brother who had been injured in training that week, Knobel retained the same starting 11 and would have been looking forward to another comfortable win when Haan profited from work by Mulder to open the scoring after just seven minutes. It would prove to be something of a false dawn. Six minutes later, Leo van Veen equalised and, although Suurbier would restore Ajax's lead within three minutes, Van Veen would again bring the teams level before the break. It would need a Rep penalty – with regular taker Gerrie Mühren absent, Rep had assumed spot-kick duties – three minutes from time to get Ajax over the line. It was another unconvincing win in a game where that should hardly have been the case.

In the final match before European competition started, Ajax entertained PSV at the Olympisch Stadion, where they would face the Bulgarian champions four days later. Gerrie Mühren's return to fitness relegated his brother to the bench in an otherwise unchanged side that saw Mulder extend his rare run of consecutive games and lead the attack. The Eindhoven club were enjoying a rich vein of goalscoring form. Following the five scored against Utrecht, they had remarkably doubled that number against Go Ahead Eagles. It was therefore hardly a surprise when Sweden striker Ralf

Edström took out his frustration for failing to find the back of the net in the previous week's ten-goal romp and netted the first goal on half an hour. A second-half Rep penalty, retaining the job despite Gerrie Mühren's return, brought the scores level but the game ended in a draw.

After ten Eredivisie matches, Ajax were surprisingly topping the table by a single point from Feyenoord despite winning only six and drawing the other four, after the Rotterdam club were surprisingly beaten 3-2 by Telstar. No one knew it at the time, but as Ajax's league form continued to worryingly swing this way and that for the remainder of the season, Coerver's team would lose just one more match on the way to winning the title and lifting the UEFA Cup, beating Tottenham Hotspur in the final. In Ajax's next fixture they would also pursue continental glory as they began the defence of their European crown.

CSKA, nominally, the army team of the then communist Bulgaria, had become serial winners of their domestic league. The triumph that qualified them for the 1973/74 European Cup was their third in succession as they finished a comfortable eight points clear of runners-up Lokomotiv Plovdiv, scoring an impressive 80 goals in 34 matches. Numbered among their ranks was Petar Zhekov, who ended the 1972/73 season as Bulgaria's top marksman with 29 goals, and had found the net against Ajax in CSKA's 3-1 defeat in Sofia the previous season. But this was a team with plenty of firepower. Apart from the goalkeepers, of all the players used by coach Manol Manolov across the league season, only defenders Boris Gaganelov, who appeared in all 34 games, and Dimitar Yakimov, who played in just one, failed to register a goal. The surely unintended 'collectivism' suggested by such statistics was very much in tune with the country's dominant political philosophy.

Although they had reached the semi-final of the 1966/67 European Cup before losing to Internazionale by the narrowest of aggregate margins, CSKA would earn continental acclaim in the decade from 1973 for eliminating the reigning European champions on three separate occasions, later knocking out Nottingham Forest then Liverpool in successive seasons in the early 1980s. CSKA's reputation as European club football's ultimate giantkillers would, however, begin in 1973/74, and Ajax were in the firing line. As phrases go, 'firing line' would later appear to be an apt description for the events that would unfold at the Olympisch Stadion on 24 October 1973.

While Ajax had enjoyed a first-round bye, courtesy of their status as reigning champions, CSKA had reached the second round by overcoming Austria's Wacker Innsbruck 4-0 on aggregate, with the potent Zhekov scoring two of the goals to underscore his threat. The overall victory was comprehensive enough, but there seemed little evidence that this version of CSKA would be any more of a problem than when they were beaten home and away as Ajax progressed serenely to their third European crown.

Although many of the names on the Ajax team sheet selected by Knobel were similar to those who had faced the Bulgarians 12 months earlier – Mulder for Cruyff being the main difference – the first leg, and the tie as a whole, would take an entirely different tack. Whether Ajax's preparation had involved a focus on not being physically intimidated by their visitors, or it was merely a reaction to events on the field, Knobel's players were giving as good as they got as muscular play dominated at the cost of skill and creativity. By doing so, Ajax wantonly sacrificed their trump card, casting aside *totaalvoetbal* in pursuit of a rugged denial to be physically dominated. Both teams contributed to what was a fierce encounter, with Ajax sacrificing most to be a part of the conflict. CSKA goalkeeper Jordan Filipov ended the game with a broken arm, but the result inflicted more terminal damage to Ajax's European ambitions.

Mulder opened the scoring after just 12 minutes, and all seemed as it should be as Ajax controlled the play, but the game quickly deteriorated into a scrappy sequence with numerous fouls breaking up the play. Four minutes ahead of the break came what would prove to the key moment in the tie. Welsh referee William Gow pointed to the spot and Ajax had an outstanding chance to double their lead. In the game against CSKA 12 months earlier, Ajax had also been awarded a penalty. At the time, Gerrie Mühren had gone into the game with a 28-2 record from 12 yards but Filipov had saved his shot. It made little difference to the overall outcome but the memory may still have been festering at the back of Mühren's mind when Gow made his decision, and the prospect of facing the same goalkeeper from the spot loomed. Additionally, the midfielder was less than fully fit having missed the game against Utrecht and played at below 100 per cent against PSV. In both of those games Ajax had been awarded penalties, Rep taking and scoring both. The question now was how, given his recent injuries and record from the spot against CSKA, was Mühren feeling about taking the penalty? There had evidently been doubt in Knobel's mind should the situation occur and it had been decided to leave the matter for Keizer to decide as captain.

At such times, confidence is often the deciding factor and, as Rep seized the ball, it was clear he was prepared to take responsibility. Mühren offered little in the way of argument and, effectively, the decision was taken out of Keizer's hands. Score and, with the half-time break imminent, Ajax would have been well on course for a win and, potentially, to build a bigger lead to take to Sofia.

Rep stepped back, advanced and struck the ball firmly but the fates had turned their smiles away from Ajax. Filipov had guessed correctly. Diving, his outstretched hand pushed the ball against the post and away, reprising his feat of 12 months earlier. The chance had been squandered and, despite increased pressure in the second half, Ajax would travel to Bulgaria with just the slenderest of advantages. Afterwards Rep declared that he was done with penalties and would always leave them to Mühren in the future.

Things were made worse for Knobel when Keizer was forced from the field with an injury. Arnold Mühren replaced him for the final 15 minutes and would do so in the starting line-up for the two upcoming league matches, although Keizer would play the second half against MVV and confirm his availability for the trip to Sofia. The second leg would take place on 7 November, two days after Bonfire Night, but there would still be plenty of fireworks to go round.

Before the journey to eastern Europe, Ajax faced two Eredivisie fixtures, first entertaining Go Ahead Eagles at the De Meer and then travelling to Maastricht to play Knobel's old club, MVV. If the result against CSKA had been a shock to the Ajax system, they would rebound with encouraging vigour in these two matches. Four days after the game at the Olympisch Stadion, with the exception of Arnold Mühren starting instead of Keizer, Knobel sent out the same starting 11 against Go Ahead. Over recent seasons, Go Ahead, now coached by Jan Notermans, had often been an irritating stone in the shoe of Ajax on their journey to league titles. That wouldn't be the case this time.

By the half-hour mark Ajax were already two goals clear; a Neeskens strike on 23 minutes was quickly followed by a header from Mulder seven minutes later. Twelve minutes after the break it was a case of 'what could have been' as Mühren scored from the penalty spot, and then repeated the feat 60 seconds later. Blankenburg added the fifth on 70 minutes, heralding a brief flurry of activity as Neeskens was cautioned by referee Ben Hoppenbrouwer, before being substituted for Van Dord. Jan Veenstra scored a late consolation for the visitors as time drifted away.

After the result against CSKA, the win was precisely what the doctor had ordered to restore confidence. It also kept Ajax two points clear at the head of the Eredivisie. Seven days later, the game in Maastricht would build on that. With no reason, other than the return to fitness of Keizer to change a team that had performed so well in the previous game, Knobel opted to leave the recovering captain on the bench and retain the same starting 11 for the visit to his old stamping ground.

At half-time Ajax led by a single goal, created by Rep and converted by Haan just three minutes before the break. Knobel decided it was time to return Keizer to the action and Arnold Mühren was removed for the second period. Still just one ahead at the hour, Ajax accelerated clear in the final period. First, Mulder profited from Gerrie Mühren's work to notch the second and, heading towards the final ten minutes, Rep did the same after Hulshoff had rampaged forward to create the chance. With the game now won, Knobel removed Rep on 83 minutes, sending Van Dord on to see out time, but received an added bonus as the young substitute scored his first Eredivisie goal to bring Ajax's goal tally to nine across the two league games. It was the sort of form and results that had largely been missing since the opening two matches of the season, when Ajax had rattled in a total of ten goals in games against Groningen and FC Amsterdam, with Cruyff in the team. Ajax were scoring plenty and conceding few. Mulder was fit, playing and scoring, and Keizer was back. Even Knobel's substitutions seemed to be blessed with a little magic. Everything pointed towards a good result in Bulgaria, and then on to retaining the Eredivisie title.

More than 51,000 fans were crammed into the Levski Stadium on that early November evening to see if their team could achieve something that the most celebrated of the continent's biggest and best clubs had failed to do over the preceding three years – eliminate Ajax from the European Cup. The single-goal deficit gave them hope and history preached caution. The first half proved to be tightly contested without either team threatening with any real menace. Ajax were the better team and largely controlled the game, but the Bulgarians were both resolute in defence and boisterous in attack when the chance to go forward presented itself.

Midway through the second half, just as Ajax were beginning to sense that a goalless draw, and progress, was there for the taking, they conceded. Collecting the ball deep in his own half and to the right of the penalty area, Keizer was hustled out of possession by a quick challenge. A Cruyff-like cross with the outside of the right foot caught the Ajax defence out of position, allowing Dimitar Marashliev to rise efficiently and head past Stuy, The aggregate scores were now level. The celebrations of the Bulgarian players were in sharp contrast to the attitude of the Ajax players, who recognised that their grip on European club football's greatest prize was now in peril. The spectre of Rep's missed penalty in Amsterdam suddenly loomed large.

Sensing the danger, Knobel removed Neeskens for the added defensive nous of Schilcher soon after the goal and Arnold Mühren replaced Mulder as full time was reached without any further goals. Manolov had declined to use his bench before the 90 minutes were up, but did so as the first period of extra time ticked by, with Plamen Iankov replacing the goalscorer. Neither of the coaches' changes made much difference to the game's pattern and there were just five minutes remaining before a play-off would become necessary when Manolov played his final card. Stefan Mihaylov was a 24-year-old forward who had joined CSKA from Velbazhd Kyustendil on a free transfer – as all Bulgarian transfers at the time were – two years earlier. Across 97 games for the club he would score 35 goals. Only one would be in European competition – it would come in this match.

Sent on to replace midfielder Tsvetan Atanasov as Manolov sought a winning goal, around 60 seconds had passed since the substitution when Mihaylov would write his name as the answer to many a football-based quiz question as to who scored the goal that ended Ajax's European Cup domination. Running on to a cross from the right, Mihaylov drilled the ball past Stuy to win the game as the goalkeeper appealed hopefully, but forlornly, for an offside decision that never looked likely. Peeling away in jubilation, Mihaylov's fresh legs had carried him all the way back into the CSKA half before his celebrating team-mates could catch him. Fame was instant but also relatively short-lived. A few short years after that goal, Mihaylov would retire from football in order to return to his hometown and take up a career as a miner.

The remaining minutes drained away with Ajax failing in vain pursuit of an unlikely equaliser. The man destined to quit football for a career underground had cast Ajax's crown from their heads. At the end of the season the European Cup, which had sat in Ajax's trophy cabinet for three years, would depart the De Meer. It would not return for more than two decades. As Norman Fox suggested in the following day's edition of *The Times*, it was 'the end of an era'.[96]

---

96 'End of an era as Ajax fall to the soldiers of Sofia', *The Times*, 8 November 1973.

In Europe that was so, but in domestic matters, Ajax were still a team to be feared as a young Piet Wildschut making his way at the time Groningen remembered: 'They always were a dominant force. Playing against Ajax was always THE game of the year.' After losing their European crown, they rallied for a while, winning eight of their next ten Eredivisie games, including a 9-0 demolition of Wildschut's Groningen team on 6 January 1974. The player who would go on to star for Twente and PSV, and also feature for the *Oranje* in the 1978 World Cup, was only 17 at the time, and still six months away from making his debut for the club, but such results clearly fed into his assessment of games against Ajax.

Typical of Ajax's league form, however, that nine-goal romp was followed by a stuttering performance and surprise 1-0 defeat to city neighbours FC Amsterdam. The inconsistency was frustrating but the fallout was more of a stumble than a catastrophe as top spot in the league was still retained and, three days later, a thumping 6-0 win over AC Milan in the home leg of the UEFA Super Cup in Amsterdam after a single-goal defeat in Italy took that trophy to the De Meer. Score nine times, then lose, then go on to put six goals past the *Rossoneri*! Ajax's form was reaching peaks and troughs with alarming regularity, and fate had a much more damaging blow in store for them across a three-week period in February.

On reflection, the warning signs were probably there for anyone alert enough to recognise them during the previous week's fixture, when Ajax only managed to overcome NEC at the De Meer thanks to two late Hulshoff goals. On 3 February they travelled to Enschede to face FC Twente who were then in third, just two points behind them. Rep had been injured, and substituted, ten minutes into the second period against NEC and would start this game on the bench, as Knobel kept faith with German forward Arno Steffenhagen who had joined a couple of months earlier from South African club Hellenic Cape Town and was making only his fourth start. Rep would return to the action, replacing Steffenhagen midway through the second period, but would fail to break the deadlock as the game ended in a goalless draw. Failing to pick up both points was hardly ideal, especially as Feyenoord's 2-1 win over Utrecht closed the gap between the two to just a single point, with a visit to the De Kuip just a couple of weeks away.

Before that match, Ajax would entertain NAC at the De Meer. A 2-1 victory was welcome enough but a serious knee injury to Hulshoff midway through the first period would have long-term consequences, both for the club and player. Despite an abortive return lasting just 35 minutes, two months later Hulshoff's season was done; in an attempt to return early, further damage was sustained. Not only would the commanding presence of the defender be denied to Ajax for the rest of the season, any hopes of Hulshoff making it to West Germany for that summer's World Cup were also dashed. It would later become clear that a player who had scored six goals in 14 appearances for the *Oranje*, playing as a defender, would never appear for the national team again. Hulshoff wouldn't return to the Ajax side for any sustained period until October 1974, and then for fewer than ten games before being struck down again. It meant a further a period of absence that lasted until August of 1975. In reality, he would never be the same player he had been before that fateful February afternoon in 1974.

Of more immediate concern to Knobel was how to fill the giant gap left by Hulshoff with probably the season's pivotal game, away to Feyenoord, due the following weekend. Coerver's team had kept pace with Ajax, winning 2-0 at PSV as Ajax were collecting the points against NAC and, after this game, there would be just nine more Eredivisie fixtures to decide the fate of the title. Pim van Dord was the obvious choice and he would continue to be so for much of the remainder of the season and beyond. Ironically, Van Dord would also see his career cut short by injury when he was forced to retire in 1980, aged just 26.

The game began worryingly for Knobel as Ajax's reshuffled defence conceded the opening goal to Theo de Jong on 14 minutes. It was tight, as so many of the meetings between the clubs across recent times had been, with few chances created or offered, and at the half-time whistle the score remained 1-0. Two minutes after the restart, though, that changed as Keizer equalised following work by Mulder and, 12 minutes later, Ajax looked to be heading to victory when Gerrie Mühren fired a penalty past Eddy Treijtel. Even though the focus of Ajax's *totaalvoetbal* had invariably been on their exhilarating forward play, defence was never neglected as attackers dropped deeper to cover when defenders took on the role of forwards. Across the years of their three successive European Cup triumphs, this commitment had not only resulted in Ajax having the best scoring record in the Eredivisie but also the meanest defence. In 1970/71, under Michels, they conceded 20 goals across the 34 league games, with the same total the following year when Kovács took over.

In 1972/73 that number fell to just 18. Under Knobel, however, with *totaalvoetbal* diminished after the Romanian departed, security at the back was compromised, as Ruud Krol explained: 'In 1973/74 we had lost the highest level. As well as Johan, some players left. Neeskens was leaving. Arie Haan was leaving. The system was not good. Rep was leaving. The *totaalvoetbal* was not there anymore. It was completely different, and the atmosphere in the club was also completely different.' In previous seasons Ajax's defence could inspire confidence to see out leads, but in 1973/74 they would concede 30 goals, an increase of 50 per cent on the worst of their returns under Michels or Kovács. Both Feyenoord and FC Twente would concede fewer, and that vulnerability would cost Ajax in this game. With less than five minutes remaining Lex Schoenmaker scored and the final whistle signified a draw.

As against Twente, a draw, away to a club just below you in the league looks like a good result but, just as Feyenoord had profited from Ajax dropping a point in Enschede, so too this time did Twente, coasting to a 7-0 win at home to De Graafschap. Ajax now had two clubs sitting just a point behind them, with their inconsistent form, loss of Hulshoff, and defensive vulnerability threatening to see their campaign fall apart. It was of little surprise when it happened.

Ajax were eliminated in the semi-final of the KNVB Cup and, at the tail-end of the Eredivisie season, a series of poor results saw them lose the top spot. A 3-1 loss to PSV on 23 March followed, unsurprisingly given recent history, by a 2-2 draw away to Go Ahead Eagles on the last day of the month proved to be the key turning points as Feyenoord and Twente both climbed above Ajax. Knobel's team would not return to the summit in the remaining weeks of the season. From there, unexpected defeats to De Graafschap – who would finish in a lowly 14th position – and Telstar, plus draws with Sparta and Roda JC, who ended a place below De Graafschap, doomed Ajax to finishing third. As they faltered, the consistency of Coerver's Feyenoord and Ron Jans's Twente was sufficient to secure the top two spots.

Knobel departed Ajax on 12 April, pointed towards the exit door surely to no one's great surprise, and to the relief of several Ajax players. The long-serving and popular Bobby Haarms was given temporary control of the team until the end of the season, but by then the damage to Ajax's domestic campaign was beyond redemption. Hans Kraay, coach of Ajax's *bête noire*, Go Ahead, was given the job for the following season, but left after a short and unsuccessful tenure. After a brief caretaker role by Jan van Daal, Rinus Michels returned to his spiritual home in 1975 but, by then, much of the magic had dissipated.

Extraordinarily, given his record with Ajax, following the 1974 World Cup as Michels went back to Barcelona, the job of heading up the hugely talented *Oranje* team comprising many of the players who had become a lesser team under George Knobel at Ajax was given to none other than Knobel himself. The target was to win the 1976 European Championship. He failed to do so and ended up with a squad riven with divisions, disagreements and dissatisfaction. After trying and failing to resign on several occasions, only to be vilified by his employers who eventually brazenly briefed the press against him, he was finally granted his wish after the Dutch had been eliminated by Czechoslovakia. Knobel's time both with Ajax and the *Oranje* suggests that he was man promoted above his level. As Jan-Herman described him, he was a 'small town coach' and he got lost in the big city.

Some have argued that Knobel was always destined to fail at the highest level with Ajax, not because of any lack of coaching ability, but because he had been handed the poisoned chalice of an Ajax bereft of Cruyff, and an aging team. The absence of Cruyff would have been a heavy cross for any coach to bear, but the argument of Ajax being old and with many star players in decline hardly stands up to logic. The average age of the team that lost out to CSKA across the two legs of the tie was slightly under 26.50, and not a single player had reached their 30th birthday. The loss of Hulshoff was a serious blow but, by then, the European Cup had already been lost. As Auke Kok suggested, there was little reason to consider such a drastic decline as being 'inevitable'.

And yet it seemed to be so. David Winner suggests that Cruyff leaving was the key factor, and, once he had moved to Barcelona, others were bound to follow: 'It's all down to Cruyff leaving, and then most of the others follow.' Winner also suggested how Krol was the notable exception. He stayed with Ajax until 1980, but may have come to regret that loyalty: 'Krol hung around a long time but later said he wished he'd left earlier.' What though of Knobel, the author enquired of Winner. What was his role in the decline? 'Don't know much about Knobel,' he replied. 'People in Amsterdam rarely mention him.'

Considering his sole season in charge failed to deliver a single domestic honour for only the second time since Michels' first full season at the De Meer, and that he also oversaw the three-times European champions eliminated at the first hurdle of their defence, that may well be for the best.

Part 7: Legacy

SO PERHAPS it's time that the likes of Cruyff, Neeskens Hulshoff, Krol and Haan were considered alongside Rembrandt, Vermeer, Steen and Hals. The canvas they adorned with majestic brushstrokes may have been green, rather than white, but the captivating beauty and mesmerising magnificence of their own type of artistry truly makes them also Dutch Masters.

Those artists of 300 years ago bequeathed to the future a legacy of genius that is even more precious now than it was in their time. Very much the same can be argued for the legacy of the Ajax teams that entertained, enthralled and enchanted a mere five decades ago. Before declaring my own thoughts on this legacy, I canvassed the opinions of others. Some are already quoted in the book, whole others may offer a particular insight given their history and experiences. In alphabetical order, here are their thoughts:

Jan-Willem Bult is a former professional and KNVB-qualified coach. He's now an international film and TV maker, football expert, and initiator of the Twitter account @Netherlands1974.

'My football roots are in the '70s. In 1970 at the age of eight I joined my first football club, S.C. Leeuwarden. But as a young boy I already grew up playing football small spaces on the streets, on lawns, at the playground, and I was privileged that the older boys asked me to play with them. I remember scoring a goal in one of such occasions, at the playground of the village where I learned kicking a ball.

'Whether playing on the streets or at the football club, attacking football was obvious. The teams were picked by the best players, usually the strikers. The last players that were picked had to defend. And one of them was doomed to be the goalkeeper.

'Though football at the club was more organised and we played in formation, the execution of it was always adventurous. We ran all over the pitch but from my first street football match on I knew that you had to take over each other's position.

'Attacking football in formation with freedom of movement, the roots of Dutch football. We always wanted to play as close as possible to the opponents' goal in order to have more chance to score a goal. That's why we, the strikers, always demanded the defenders to move forward and back us.

'When I got a bit older (12+) we also started to talk about football among each other. Not only about the best and worst moments in the game but also about how to use the space. And how to create it when there was no space. When to make an individual action and when to move with the whole team. Exactly the basics of what was later named [*totaalvoetbal*] by analysts. And *Zeister Visie* by policy makers.

'World Cup '74 still had to happen, but the Ajax style was already our major source of inspiration. We learned the tricks of Cruyff and Keizer, copied the rushes of Swart and Rep and played long passes like Krol. Probably kids closer to Rotterdam did the same with Moulijn, Van Hanegem and Israël. At the clubs we all learned to play in 4-3-3 formation, in reality 3-4-3 with the *libero* moving to the midfield. I have played in the first teams of ten clubs all over the country and only by exception we played 4-4-2. For me being a typical nine that would be one of the reasons to move to another club.

'After 1974 when we were suddenly calling our football [*'totaalvoetbal'*], we started to understand in our subconscious. Everything that made our football attractive by nature now became a holy grail. Coaches and players started to shout it during the trainings and the matches. "All together forward"; "Use that space"; 'Take over"; "Now offside trap".

For me, having played it all my life, [*totaalvoetbal*] brings opposites in balance: freedom (no other word could be mentioned as the first) and responsibility; creating space and using small spaces; team performance and individuality; formation and organised chaos; attack and defence (only in that order).'

* * *

Massimiliano Graziani is a journalist with Rai, the Italian radio and television broadcaster, and is coordinator and radio commentator of the long-running broadcast Tutto il Calcio Minuto per Minuto.

'[The Ajax team of the 1970s] is perceived as something unique and unrepeatable, just as the Dutch national team was unique and unrepeatable in all respects: from the colour of the jersey to the wonders it offered on the pitch. Ajax and

Dutch football in the 1970s are perceived in the collective imagination as a revolutionary football phenomenon that borders on legend: teams that attack in 11, defenders who turn into strikers and "flying goalkeepers". The "flying goalkeepers" were those who, in improvised matches in the courtyard below the house, could leave their goal (made with jackets placed on the ground instead of poles) to rush towards the opponent's goal. Usually the flying goalkeeper, in popular culture, was the one on the team that had one less man and who could also play with his feet to help his team-mates. And when I think of my childhood flying goalkeeper, total Dutch football comes to mind. Breaking the mould. The utopia achieved.'

* * *

Auke Kok is a Dutch author and journalist, and two-time winner of the prestigious Nico Scheepmaker Award for sports books. As well as his work appearing in newspapers and magazines, and featuring on television and radio, he wrote the famous 1974. Wij waren de besten *book, a reflection on the 1974 World Cup, among 13 other titles, including his latest work, a biography of Cruyff published in 2019.*

'In general, the style of Ajax and *Oranje* ('70s) was propaganda for attacking and tactical skills as a way to be successful in times when the emphasis was more and more on defence … running and hard labour.

'Probably Brian Granville was right in stating that the real [*totaalvoetbal*] was played by Ajax and West Germany (1972), and would add *Oranje* 1974. Feyenoord also had some aspects of total football, but not as outspoken and consequent as Ajax.

'I'm still happy to see teams play [*totaalvoetbal*]. Like Italy did last summer [in the 2020 European Championships].

Wonderful to watch, intelligent, cheerful, full of variations. *Calcio Totale!'*

* * *

Ruud Krol played more than 500 games for Ajax across a 12-year career, winning two European Cups, two European Super Cups, an Intercontinental Cup, six Eredivisie titles and four KNVB Cups. He also captained the side from 1974 until he left in 1980.

'When I am travelling in the world, still now, the people are talking about the Ajax team of the '70s, and still the *Oranje* team of '74. When you talk about Ajax and winning three times in a row, that is easy but we lost in '74 and still people talk about that team, the kind of football they play, not the team who won. The laws were different, the ball was heavier, but *totaalvoetbal* was a revolution in football.'

* * *

Rob McDonald is a former professional player and coach with a number of Eredivisie clubs after moving to Dutch football from Hull City in 1979. He is now a professional mediator searching for clubs for investors and investors for clubs in Europe, and living still in Holland

'Everybody in Holland would love to play the way Ajax did but you need the players. The philosophy is still to play football with a build-up play from the back and some high pressure when necessary. The number of teams who have played a kick and rush game in Holland can be counted on one hand.

'The extreme high-pressure game that Ajax and the Dutch national team played calmed down [by the end of the decade] but again the philosophy to play football on the ground was embedded in many teams. The Dutch coaching courses (in which I took part to receive my UEFA Pro Licence) also coached specifically the Dutch [*totaalvoetbal*] philosophy.

'I am proud to say I have met many of the players from that era such as Cruyff, Van Hanegem, Krol, Rijsbergen, Suurbier. Rep and I played together with Neeskens at FC Groningen in Holland. They were not only gifted with special tactical and technical skills but mentally they were winners and hated losing. I played against [Cruyff] when he had just returned to Ajax. I only played once against him and that was the famous 5-5 game in Amsterdam. He came back to a great team with the likes of Rijkaard, Lerby, Van Basten, Silooy, and many others and he was the general, keeping everybody alert and coaching where they should stand, etc. When the final whistle went, I ran over to him to shake his hand simply because I had followed him as a teenager and admired and respected the way he played.'

* * *

Roberto Pennino is a Dutch lawyer of Italian descent living in the Netherlands. He's also an author and freelance journalist focusing on Dutch football.

'Dutch football has been shaped by the magnificent Ajax-era of 1971–1973, although Feyenoord shouldn't be forgotten in the process. That excellent Ajax team with all those long-haired geniuses, played football of a different planet. It was sometimes referred to as "football of the next century" and that qualification proved right. The pressing of that team is still the schoolbook example of how to impress, fatigue and disturb the opponent, and is copied both nationally and internationally over decades until today.'

* * *

*Menno Pot is an Amsterdam-based music journalist and football
writer, an Ajax columnist in* Het Parool *and hosts a weekly Ajax
podcast for the newspaper, called* Branie *('Swagger'). He has also
written six books about the club.*

'Ajax 1971–1973 is the measure of things in Dutch football.
Even people who hate Ajax (and there are many of them) will
admit that that team was the best football team Holland ever
produced.

'PSV won the European Cup in 1988, which was a
fantastic achievement and great for them, but not one taxi
driver in Rio de Janeiro or Taiwan remembers that team.
Why not? Simple. They didn't win a game after the winter
break: it was all 0-0 and 1-1. The final against Benfica was
a 0-0. PSV won on penalties. The football was not very
entertaining. And guess what? No one outside of Holland
really remembers them.

'But wherever you go, taxi drivers know Cruyff, Rep and
Neeskens, even though the PSV win was 15 years later. That
proves that the football "does" matter. Holland 1974 is a more
famous, more legendary team than many teams that did win
the World Cup.

'There's a long list of great clubs that won European
trophies at some point, but the "Golden Ajax" surely were
one of those rare teams that really changed football. The
name Ajax stands for a certain philosophy, an approach to
the game. That legacy was created in 1971–1973, the club's
defining years. And they were so cool. The long hair, the
swagger, the self-confidence. They were rock stars.

'Ajax put Dutch football on the map, basically – and
younger generations of Dutch football fans are still very aware
of that (and will generally give them the credit for it).

'At the same time, more and more people realise that the Ajax team of the early 1970s wasn't just about beauty. They could be absolutely merciless as well. People like Neeskens, Suurbier and Hulshoff were troopers, hard as nails. They must have been quite intimidating in their day. So, the "beautiful Ajax" was a bit of a street gang. I can totally feel how irresistible that must have been.

'The style of play known as *totaalvoetbal* remains the most important part of [Ajax's] legacy, of course: a style of play that gave the Netherlands its football identity and is still seen as quintessentially "Dutch" (whatever that means): freedom within a framework of very strict rules.

'When you say Belgium, Sweden, Austria or Romania, most people think nothing in particular. But when you say "Holland" people think of a style, a certain aesthetic in football. That's the enduring legacy of Rinus Michels and Johan Cruyff – and it's quite something.

'The funny thing is: the term "*totaalvoetbal*" was almost never applied to the great Ajax of 1971–1973. It became common football lingo in 1974, referring to the *Oranje* team – and then applied to Ajax 1971–1973 retrospectively.

'Dutch football fans of all ages know the term. Even youngsters will say, "Yeah, *totaalvoetbal*, Michels and Cruyff and all that, the '70s" – although some argue that Feyenoord were the first team to play *totaalvoetbal*, in 1969 and 1970.

'But the term is no longer in use. It's a term from the past. The 4-3-3 system and football played "the Cruyff way" are now generally referred to as "de Hollandse School" ("the Dutch School") and it's the subject of a never-ending discussion about playing football "the Dutch way" in modern times: it made us great, but is it also the reason why we never win? Can it still work in modern football? To which extent are the ideas still valid?

'*Totaalvoetbal* was the first incarnation of the "Dutch School", you could say. It's still very much the measure of all things in Dutch football.'

* * *

Steven Scragg is an award-nominated author and member of the senior management team at These Football Times.

'There are many teams that define an era, but there are very few that define an ethos; Ajax very much fall into the latter category. The totality of their football was no enigma, and there was no riddle to unwrap, as so much of what Rinus Michels and Ștefan Kovács peddled on a football pitch was bound in simplicity. All the best football is.

'Ajax played to simple principles of football within a bubble of common sense, yet shrouded in the most hypnotic confidence in themselves, and an imperious mastery of the ball.

'Innovators, they took the simple teachings of the likes of Jack Reynolds and Vic Buckingham and expanded upon them. Possession of the ball was sacrosanct, and flexibility was key. At Ajax's peak, they were so fluid that positions were interchangeable, any player was free to roam, so long as a team-mate had dropped in to cover. So much of what we see from the contemporary game's best teams is grounded in the examples set by Johan Cruyff, Johnny Rep, Johan Neeskens, Barry Hulshoff, Gerrie Mühren and Piet Keizer *et al*. High defensive lines, compressed play, the pressing game, none of it is new, it is simply reinventing the wheel and putting a different coloured kit on it. Ajax were doing it half a century ago, and Pep Guardiola's coaching mantra is a descendant of the Amsterdam movement via the tutoring of Cruyff himself.

'From the vision and control freakery of Michels, to the freedom bestowed upon the team by Kovács, there was great intelligence in all departments at Ajax, but within that came increased ego and power struggles. Ultimately, the only team that was capable of toppling Ajax, was Ajax themselves.'

* * *

Sonny Silooy played almost 300 games for Ajax in two spells totalling 14 years. He is a former assistant coach to the Dutch national team and former coach of the under-18 and under-19 teams. He's a senior consultant and ambassador at the Ajax Coaching Academy, currently attached to Sharjah FC.

'I'm currently working on a three-year deal at Sharjah FC in UAE to implant the philosophy of Ajax. The way of playing, the way of training and the way of communicating with each other. The Cruyff legacy is being taught in Ajax academies across the world.

'The legacy of those teams is the Ajax academy and the philosophy that is used by Ajax across the world. It's the Cruyff quality, controlling the ball in one-on-one situations. It's the playing style that we teach. When you have the ball, when you don't have the ball. It's also about player development, concentrating on their strengths and making them even stronger.

'Here at Sharjah, we still teach the same Ajax philosophy, the Cruyff philosophy, the Michels philosophy, one v one, two v one, three v two, four v three, all small games. Only at the end of the week do we play a big game. It is still happening now. What was happening at Ajax in the '70s and '80s we still do at the moment. Get in space to receive the ball, pass the ball well, control the ball, pass the ball, play simple.

'I have worked with the three best coaches in the world, Michels, Cruyff and Van Gaal, and basically, they all tell you the same.

'Ajax was different in the '60s and '70s, and they are different now. They have different setups, different training sessions to other cubs – and they need to win every game. That's the mentality of Ajax.'

* * *

David Winner is the author of Brilliant Orange, *widely acknowledged to be the definitive book on Dutch football.*

'There are several [clubs] in the image [of the Ajax team of the early 1970s], who all look like slight advances on the original because players get ever-quicker and ever-stronger. But there's nothing as radically new. Pep's golden Barça would probably beat that Ajax, but they're a successor team. Ajax '95 would give them a game. Ditto AC Milan of '89. There are quite a few successor teams. Peak Wenger Arsenal. The best modern Bayerns. Klopp's great Liverpool were fantastic (and may be again). Pep's City. But that's the point. They all follow in the boot steps. They don't create something completely new.'

* * *

Having considered the comments of others, it now falls to me to offer my thoughts on Ajax's legacy. Of all the sections in this book, all of the research, interviews and YouTube videos consumed, the writing, the rewrites, amends, additions and exclusions, preparation for this section has been the most difficult.

There are many wise words in the above comments, but it's interesting to note that, although there's a fairly common thread suggesting that the *totaalvoetbal* of the early 1970s Ajax teams has influenced contemporary football and attitudes to it, there's less consistency about how and why this may have happened. Very much as with the origins of the *totaalvoetbal* philosophy and its key tenets, its legacy, though widely acknowledged as important, is just as difficult to pin down. It's an interesting point to ponder.

As with the delight taken from the great art of Rembrandt and Vermeer, of Steen and Hals, any appreciation of beauty is so often decided by the perception of the beholder. Experts and aficionados can point to the finer points of the most celebrated works of art, to craft and creativity, technique and talent, elegance and exquisiteness, but there is no true quantitative measure by which to calibrate such things. There is no universally accepted scale for offering marks ranging from one to ten. To my mind, the very same is true when trying to establish which element of the vast and varied legacy left by this Ajax team is most worthy. Is it enough to say that the legacy is that they were merely beautiful?

Before Rinus Michels arrived at the De Meer, and won the Eredivisie title in the 1965/66 season, his first full season in charge, Ajax had only been Dutch champions on three occasions since the end of World War Two. After his arrival and up to the time that Ștefan Kovács left to take over the France national team at the end of the 1972/73 season, they would win it on no less than six occasions in eight years, and finish as runners-up in the other two. In the same period, Ajax lifted the KNVB Cup just once in pre-Michels time, before adding four more triumphs after he arrived and before Kovács's French leave. This of course is to say nothing of four European Cup finals, and three successive victories. Is it enough to say that their legacy is one of outstanding success?

Going back to Sonny Silooy's comments above about the Ajax philosophy and legacy, the adherence to that philosophy still benefits both Ajax and the *Oranje* as players who have worn the famous white shirt with the broad red stripe have gone on to successful coaching careers, carrying those ideals with them.

Since Michels' brief return in 1975 there have been 30 coach appointments at Ajax, several of which have been repeated. Of them, more than half were coaches who had previously played for Ajax, including Cruyff, Hulshoff, Van Gaal and Krol all who played under both Michels and Kovács, plus Bobby Haarms who played alongside Michels and then served as an assistant to both him and Kovács during the glory years of the early 1970s. Louis van Gaal was also was a player under both coaches and, in 1995 as coach, returned the European Cup – then rechristened as the Champions League – to Ajax.

There's a similar tale to tell with the Dutch national team. Since the turn of the century, nine of the appointments to become coach of the *Oranje* have been to former Ajax players, but this carrying of the torch for the Ajax way of playing hasn't been restricted merely to coaching in the Netherlands.

Michels played under Reynolds. Cruyff played under Buckingham, Michels and Kovács. When Cruyff left Ajax in 1973 his suitcase was packed with the accumulated knowledge of playing at the club. He had the understanding of playing at an Ajax with a structure laid out by Reynolds, and of having his talent nurtured and developed by Buckingham, Michels and Kovács. When he became coach of Barcelona, he unpacked all of those experiences and delivered them to the benefit of the Catalan club. The influence of Ajax spread beneficially around Barcelona and forms part of the club's system even to this day. Pep Guardiola played under Cruyff. Ronald Koeman and Xavi Hernandez played under Guardiola, and so the baton was passed on. Is it enough to say that the Ajax legacy has continued and does still continue to shape football philosophy at the highest level?

Pushed to come up with a definitive answer to each of those questions, the only appropriate response is to say that while none of them are sufficient in isolation, combined they may come within touching distance of being so. For me, the legacy of the Ajax teams who won three successive European Cups in 1971, 1972 and 1973 is that they not only proved that beautiful football can triumph, but their *totaalvoetbal* also planted a precious seed in the soul of football. It's a seed that has grown and flourished wonderfully, and continues to do so.

Football has so much to be grateful to the Ajax team of the early 1970s for. They were indeed, very much, 'the envy of some, the fear of others and the wonder of all their neighbours'. They are unarguably worthy of being lauded as the 'Dutch Masters'.